Planning for Tourism, Leisure and Sustainability

International Case Studies

Planning for Tourism, Leisure and Sustainability

International Case Studies

Anthony S. Travis

International Tourism Consultant

www.cabi.org

CABI is a trading name of CAB International

CABI Head Office	CABI North American Office
Nosworthy Way	38 Chauncy St
Wallingford	Suite 1002
Oxfordshire OX10 8DE	Boston, MA 02111
UK	USA
Tel: +44 (0)1491 832111	Tel: +1 617 395 4056
Fax: +44 (0)1491 833508	Fax: +1 617 354 6875
Email: cabi@cabi.org	Email: cabi-nao@cabi.org
Web site: www.cabi.org	

A catalogue record for this book is available from the British Library, London, UK.

Library of Congress Cataloging-in-Publication Data
Travis, Anthony S.
Planning for tourism, leisure and sustainability : international case studies / Anthony S. Travis

    p. cm.
 Includes bibliographical references and index.
 ISBN 978-1-84593-742-3 (alk. paper)
 1. Sustainable tourism – Case studies. I. Title.
G156.5.S87T73 2011
910.68′4-dc22

2011011312

ISBN-13: 978-1-84593-742-3 (HB)
ISBN-13: 978-1-78064-681-7 (PB)

First published (HB) 2011
First paperback edition 2015

Commissioning editor: Sarah Hulbert
Editorial assistants: Alexandra Lainsbury, Gwenan Spearing, Katherine Dalton
Production editor: Fiona Chippendale

Typeset by SPi, Pondicherry, India.
Printed and bound in the UK by Marston Book Services Ltd, Oxfordshire

Contents

Dedication

This book has to have a twin dedication.

First, to my wife Philippa and to my three children, Abby, Theo and Sandy, without whose support and understanding nothing would ever have been achieved.

Secondly, to my rich global village of work friends, made in over 50 years of work and travel in Poland, Slovakia, the Netherlands, Wales, New Zealand, Scotland, the USA, Canada, Slovenia, Croatia, Serbia, England, Norway, Ireland, Hungary, China, Australia, Albania, Austria, Estonia, the Maldives, Algeria, Israel, Jordan, Turkey, Italy, France, Switzerland, Denmark, Sweden, Germany, Romania, Greece, Cyprus, Spain, Belgium and Bulgaria. The shared learning has grown thanks to them.

Aims

In looking back over a span of 50 years' worldwide experience as a tourism planner, my aims in this book are not only to remind readers of how this new field has developed in its own right, and of the creative planning responses to identified problems as opportunities, but also to do it in a comparative way. I will do this by comparing:

- the integrated planning response to water threat and needs for leisure and tourism in a crowded capitalist country like the Netherlands, with economic- and tourist-development responses in a water-short immigrant nation with a mixed economy like Israel;
- the socialist planning for sport and social tourism of a post-war Poland, in dire economic circumstances, with capitalist regional development in the 2000s in a huge, hot, dry, remote region of North West Australia (which is twice the size of Poland!); and
- tourism planning and development of an island archipelago state in the Indian Ocean that is barely above sea level (the Maldives), with hi-tech planning for global warming and sea rise in a below sea-level state such as the Netherlands.

Whether the issues have been maritime and coastal tourism that are compared, or the changing urban or resort condition, or looking at scales of planning (ranging from the national and regional, down to the local and site scales of application), the book fully employs this comparative approach, for the benefit of the reader.

Tourism planning may be linked to or integrated in urban and regional planning, or tackled as a separate system of planning. On the national scale, tourism may be planned via National Master Plans, Comprehensive Development Plans, as Facet Plans or Indicative Plans. On the regional scale Tourism Strategies or Indicative Plans may be done, while below this level subregional proposals may be for Tourist Destination Areas, or local plans, resort plans, down to project and site development plans.

A primary purpose here is thus a comparative and evaluative one, approaching both current and retrospective case studies, contrasting them so as to get important long-term lessons out of specific and time-related situations. The book is targeted both at planners and at tourism planners, whether in training or in practice, as well as those who hold key interests in planning as decision makers, advocates and stakeholders.

Contributors

Dr Ton van Egmond, Senior Tourism Lecturer and Tourism Consultant, NHTV University of Applied Sciences, Breda, The Netherlands. E-mail: egmond.a.@nhtv.nl

Jan Vidar Haukeland, Senior Research Sociologist in Tourism, Institute of Transport Economics, Oslo, Norway. E-mail: jvh@toi.no

Arwel Jones, Regional Development Consultant. E-mail: arwel@celtic.co.uk

Jim Kaucz, Australian Regional Planner, Pilbara Region, Western Australia. E-mail: jim.kaucz@planning.wa.gov.au

Wanda Kaucz, Australian Regional Planner, Pilbara Region, Western Australia. E-mail: wanda.kaucz@planning.wa.gov.au

Dr Marko Koscak, Heritage Tourism Consultant, Slovenia. E-mail: Marko.koscak@siol.net

Emeritus Professor Anthony S. Travis, Urban and Regional Studies, The University of Birmingham, and International Tourism Planning Consultant. E-mail: tony.travis@btinternet.com

Ivica Trumbic, Project Manager, United Nations Environment Programme (UNEP)/Mediterranean Action Plan (MAP), Global Environent Facility (GEF) Strategic Partnership for the Mediterranean Large Marine Ecosystem (Med Partnership). E-mail: Ivica.trumbic@unepmap.gr

Tourism Foreword

For too long, particularly in the 1950s, 1960s and early 1970s, tourism was seen by many countries as a cash cow, and apparently little more than that. Examples abounded of unplanned or barely planned resorts, their sole objective seeming to be to separate visitors from the contents of their wallets, with little or no thought given to the environment.

Concrete monstrosities built on many parts of the Mediterranean coast, for example, perhaps offered people from colder, northern climes the opportunity to bask in sunshine at an affordable price. However, the newly constructed resort towns had little of the character of the host country and, as a result, did equally little to help that country in the long term.

It wasn't all bad; there were examples of sensitive and well thought-out development. None the less, by the early 1970s, there was considerable mistrust about the negative influences tourism would bring to places bold enough to consider its potential for economic gain.

There couldn't have been a better time for the emergence of a number of notable thinkers and planners, of which Tony Travis was one of the most prominent, and the most gifted. He held the view that tourism could be a force for economic and environmental good at the same time. He was a leader in the belief that, if tourism could be absorbed by the host environment, rather than dominate it, there could be a bright and sustainable future for it.

His research, guidance and teaching, helped to nurture a number of people from a wide range of backgrounds, who became first generation experts in the field. Slowly at first, but with gathering pace, the development of sustainable tourism and the effective marketing of the industry reached new and impressive levels of sophistication. People began to think of heritage, conservation and tourism in the same breath, as it became clear that, with careful planning, they could and should be interdependent for the combined greater good of the environment and the economy.

I was fortunate enough to have the opportunity to join the industry in the early 1970s and to benefit from the guidance of Tony Travis. My grounding in the principles of planned growth, which would generate economic well-being without destroying the very fabric of what the visitor came to see, formed the bedrock upon which my career and the careers of many of my colleagues was built.

This book offers a plethora of examples of how countries, regions and local areas have tackled the tourism and environmental challenges they have faced. There are excellent case studies, many learning points and numerous issues are investigated and commented upon.

Thanks in no small part to works of this depth, I feel that the future of the tourism industry can be a very bright one. I firmly believe that it can be a force for economic good, it can help to arrest rural depopulation, it can help to foster international understanding and it can bring people together.

The challenges in the future will be many. But if we can learn from our failures, as well as from our successes, the needs of the environment can be addressed and, at the same time, the economic well-being of that environment can be enhanced. An analysis of the case studies, contained within the chapters that follow, can only help towards achieving those goals.

Jeff Hamblin
Former Chief Executive
The British Tourist Authority

Heritage Foreword

Tourism corrupts. Absolute tourism corrupts absolutely. But it doesn't have to be like that. In this book Tony Travis brings a lifetime's experience to bear in demonstrating, through an eclectic mix of case studies, that tourism can be a creative and responsible force for good and the key to the revival, survival and continuing prosperity of communities all over the world. Further, his observations on national planning studies demonstrate the essential nature of the relationship between the conservation of landscapes, exemplified in a wide variety of environments, from deserts to coastlines, and the uses to which they are put. His illustrations show that there are no easy answers but what they do to great effect is to offer exemplars of approaches that can shape and inform the way in which people interact with places and how tourism can be sustained as a component of that relationship.

Since 1887, when Lord Acton famously declared that power tends to corrupt, he has been proved right in a tragic number of cases. Look around the world today and there are tyrants still roaming wild whose crimes, because they don't matter enough to enough people, are allowed to continue unfettered. The tyrannical power of tourism in its unmanaged state is not dissimilar but at least there are grounds for optimism. There are unlimited examples of good practice; the challenge is to use them to influence the rest.

Give mankind the opportunity to move about the world and he will take it. Give him the net disposable income and he will chose to spend a surprisingly – and increasingly – high proportion of it in someone else's back garden, whether invited or not. For Lord Acton and his generation it was the few who could afford such luxuries. But even then it was a rapidly expanding few, made prosperous by the fruits of industrialisation and given the means to travel by the spread of the railway. There was another factor too, as pertinent then as it is now; that the newly prosperous lived increasingly in towns and cities and their delight was to spill out for a few days or weeks each year and spend some time in a different place. For some that meant a resort, designed and built for their pleasure, where there were plenty of people like themselves; fellow workers from the cotton mill all on the beach together in Blackpool, the world's first working-class resort. In one sense these resorts represent the most benign form of tourism, not least because the resource is designed from scratch for people and their enjoyment.

But for others, the aspirational cognoscenti, their pleasure was in visiting places that nobody else had yet found. Their effects can be more insidious, at worst like a plague of locusts sweeping through innocent landscapes and communities, moving on when – as inevitably happens – others follow them and the taste of discovery and revelation starts to pall.

For the host communities affected by these tidal movements there is no turning back, visitors and their spending become a crucial part of the local economy and the only way to sustain a way forward is to encourage more of them. Meanwhile, the adventurous have fled in search of new delights untainted by people like themselves.

To this catalogue of apparent gloom we can now add the tricky concept of sustainability. In the age of ever-cheaper air travel more people can travel to more places than ever before. And more of them will go as far as they physically can before they pause. No longer is money a restricting factor and, in the absence of a flat earth, there is no edge for them to fall off when they get there. And, paradoxically, as awareness of climate change and carbon issues grows, so too does our ability to say to ourselves, this is not something that directly affects me. My flight to a beach 5000 miles away is acceptable because it is me. Tourists, after all, are always other people.

So, today, everywhere is accessible to everyone. For the first time in human history there is nowhere left on earth to hide. And it is that factor – and perhaps that factor alone – that gives us both pause for thought and the means of taking stock. Just as we can start to see the limits of the world's resources so too we can see the boundaries of our capacity and need to travel for the sake of it.

This book is about taking stock, about understanding the limits, creatively shaping the opportunities, moulding the relationship between people and the places that, by visiting, they increasingly see as their own. It is not a textbook of what to do and not to do, more a series of pertinent and perceptive object lessons drawn from Tony Travis's exceptional and unique experience of planning and responsible tourism over some 40 years. The historical perspective is crucial, for here we can see and begin to understand the roots of current thinking and practice.

Tony Travis was one of the first in this field, pioneering through his research and teaching the concept that only through an integrated approach, bringing conservation, planning and management together as parts of a single debate are we likely to see truly sustainable outcomes. Some of the studies in this book are from 30 and more years ago. Seen through the lens of our current concerns they are perhaps more relevant today than when they were written. This book is a gold mine of such examples, and you don't even have to visit a gold mine to taste the benefits.

Sir Neil Cossons
Past Chairman
English Heritage

Introduction

Man's primary urge in development for the last 2000 years at least, has been to exploit the natural and human resources of the planet, for his material benefit and advancement. Mid-20th-century Man's resource management failures led to the move from remedial towards sustainable management ideas in that period. The roots of sustainable development and of sustainable tourism development long pre-date the Brundtland Commission Report (1987), which was a critical kick-starting phase of political action on the world scale, in planning for sustainability, but one can point to roots in some five earlier streams in human history:

1. The ecological wisdom of indigenous peoples living within the tight parameters of harsh ecosystems, achieving long-term survival, and that of their host habitat. Thus the Aborigines of Australia, living within the tight constraints of its desert ecosystem, or the Bushmen of the African Kalahari Desert, and the indigenous tribes of the tropical rainforests of South American Amazonia, all exemplified sustainable management philosophies and practices.

2. The nature conservation movements, rooted in romantic literature and art, with the writings of Henry David Thoreau and John Muir, and leading to the mid-19th-century creation of Yosemite National Park, and the start of a worldwide movement in creating National Parks, and later nature reserves and other categories of protected habitats and ecosystems.

3. Man's learning to deal with critical natural resource problems – such as too much or too little water – in his host environment. For example, the long history of the Dutch people in claiming a land from the marshes, riversides and sea. They started 'impoldering' as early as the 14th century! The Nabbatean civilization in the Middle East about 2000 years ago created an urban society in a desert environment, based on skilful water extraction, conservation and survival in a harsh habitat. Nearly 2000 years later, Israelis, in the same desert, have to try out archaeological restoration work to relearn such desert survival skills.

4. Man's suffering from failure to intelligently manage rich, natural-resource habitats, for example the ploughing up of US prairie grasslands for mono-agriculture, and creating the 'Dust Bowl' in the interwar 20th century. It took ruin, rural migration and major economic recession collapse to get the resultant 'New Deal' and the creation of a Tennessee Valley Authority (TVA) to control the waters of a huge river basin, create dams, water management, and develop responsible agriculture and farming using new hydro-electric power to regenerate an economy. This and other water-economy lessons in the USA pre-dated the national water-economy plans for nations like Poland and Israel.

5. Land-planning lessons from late 19th-century and early 20th-century thinkers and practitioners, laid foundations for town and country planning systems and statutory planning in many European countries after the end of the Second World War, in the 1940s. Land-use planning later took on other management tasks such as air quality management, environmental impact assessment and other elements of the later sustainable environmental management.

Resource Conservation

Modern ecology literature first introduced ideas of sustainability, while the public face of environmental sustainability, in world terms, had to await the Brundtland Report in 1987. This was well after the push for responsible global environmental management which surfaced in the 1960s and 1970s, with work such as that of the Club of Rome and E.F. Schumacher's *Small is Beautiful* in 1973, where he writes:

> This…is…due to our inability to recognize that the modern industrial system, with all its intellectual sophistication, consumes the very basis on which it has been erected. To use the language of the economist, it lives on irreplaceable capital which it…treats as income…three categories of such capital: fossil fuels, the tolerance margins of nature, and the human substance.

From 1987 to 2002 a sequence of over 20 world conferences after Brundtland, has taken Man from sustainability to sustainable development and on to sustainable tourism planning. Now, in the early 21st century, the perceived global management problems have accelerated both in urgency and in scale, as scientific evidence points to Man's causal role in 'global warming' due to his excess production of carbon dioxide, his damage to global oxygen production (by destruction of tropical rainforests), all associated with the dangerous 'hole in the ozone layer'. National governments, such as that of the Netherlands, are forced to do reports such as the 2008 Delta Commission Report on raising sea and river defences to cope with expected sea rise, and the UK Government to commission the Stern Report on the environment. Sustainability of life and habitat has become a practical concern. The role of tourism, both as one of Man's fundamental freedoms and as giving rise to the world's largest industry, has key new roles to play. Short-term horizons are inadequate to protect the vital interests of successive generations of life in future, on this exceptional planet.

Effective resource conservation of our built and cultural heritage is an even younger notion than that of natural resource and landscape conservation and management. The 19th-century concept of National Parks pre-dates the protection and listing of historic buildings and monuments, let alone cultures, which has generally been more of a 20th-century idea. Yet, in relation to tourism, it is the mix of the diversity of climates, heat and snows, diversity of habitats, of landscapes, of architecture, of cultures, languages, monuments and cuisines that give rise to much of tourism and leisure travel. Modern Man is as guilty as his predecessors not only of deforestation, environmental damage and pollution, but is still guilty of destroying the habitat of native peoples in the tropical rainforests (see Hanbury-Tenison, 1984). Though we deplore the past fate of the North American Indian, the Australian Aboriginal and the New Zealand Maori at the hands of 'white settlers', the land-grab and forest resource destruction today in places like Amazonia continues this vile process.

Responsible Development versus Exploitation

The notion of 'development', so vital to modern, industrial and urban society, is synonymous with large-scale exploitation of key natural resources such as land, minerals and water. Large-scale agricultural and pastoral outputs are vital to feed the growing huge urban populations. Conservation is a concomitant of development, but the political and economic power of conservation agencies is marginal. Internationally, the International Union for Conservation of Nature (IUCN) and the World Wide Fund for Nature (WWF) are the prime advocates for environmental and natural resource management, biodiversity and species protection. At the global level the United Nations Educational, Scientific and Cultural Organization (UNESCO) is the primary agency for identification, listing and protection of the world's built and cultural heritage, and to a lesser extent, the world's natural monuments. In effect they have largely to rely on effective actions by national governments and agencies. UNESCO cannot enforce protection. When in 2008 the nations of the world had such difficulty in dealing politically and economically with the so-called 'credit crunch' that made world capitalism creak, one fears for the global will and ability to deal effectively with alternative energy production, and resource conservation and management issues.

Linking Conservation and Development

Developed nations today are self-congratulatory if they achieve 5% or 10% of their territory being allocated for National Parks and National Nature Reserves. These are the areas of strict resource, habitat and landscape protection. Yet today much scientific evidence points to the need for greatly increased national forest cover, at a time when deforestation is at an unprecedented scale in world terms. Wetlands need extension, but we destroy them – estuaries, with their rich biotic production, are locations for intensive economic development. Sustainable energy sources which are carbon neutral are needed, as are actions which will reduce deserts and not aid desertification. Further, wise management of alpine zones under pressure, and of polar zones, are key issues which are only partially addressed. While the post-'87 rush of conferences and writing about sustainability is notable, we must be careful about sustainable tourism and apply critical evaluation. This book is part of the move towards sustainable tourism, but it is early days, and while many examples to date are good in terms of direction, all are only partial in terms of achievement of sustainability, for the sorts of reasons which I have already given in this sobering introduction. Worldwide examples are taken in this book, from initiatives in the last 50 years that have demonstrated partial answers to providing sustainability; none have achieved totally sustainable tourism, but move part of the way towards sustainability. The author very much agrees with van Egmond's statement on p. 188 of *The Tourism Phenomenon* (2008), where he writes:

> U.N.E.P.'s Agenda for Sustainable Tourism clearly demonstrates that focusing on both economy, social and cultural aspects, and environmental issues, as well as visitor fulfilment, is extremely complex. Tourism that is sustainable in every respect will be difficult to achieve. That is why we refer to sustainable tourism development – trying to achieve sustainability – rather than sustainable tourism.

Some sustainable tourism products, such as cycling in the Netherlands, rail-based international holidays and 'deep ecology' ski or foot-based holidays in Norway, are among the positive elements already found.

Determinants

To put this into context, one needs to take an historical perspective, and co-relate four streams of change (Fig. I.1), which writers such as Sigaux (1966) and Towner (1984) have emphasized:

- wealth, power and access to travel;
- technologies of travel;
- development of a tourist industry; and
- from laissez faire to planning, and the limits of change.

Alternatively, one can co-relate critical changes in scale, over time, of population growth, human mobility, and related energy and resource consumption (see Fig. I.2). For the interdependence of tourism, and heritage resources see Fig. I.3.

Four streams of change			
Wealth, power and access to travel	Technologies of travel	Tourist industry development	Laissez-faire, planning impacts and limits of change
1660: The 'Grand Tour' of Classical Europe	Horse, carriage, road, sail, start of steam	Travel for courts and the rich	Laissez-faire provisions
1840: Start of the railway age	Rail, coal, steam, steel transport technologies European, American and African rail	1851: Test case for Great Exhibition; Thomas Cook; domestic tourism; world packages	Laissez-faire development of cities, ports and systems, risks and failure, paternalistic philanthropy, public health action
1880: Mass sea travel	Steamship liners	Commercial rail and sea offers	Start of planning in Europe and North America
1914–1918	Dirigibles and military aircraft	War	Industrial pollution, health hazard
1920	Commercial air travel and sea-cruising	Middle-class international holidays	Suburbia
1939	Airwar		War
1945	Peace		Reconstruction
1950	Sea travel, car	Holiday camps	Post-warplanning, Clean Air Act 1956
1960: Mass air travel	Jumbo jet, charters	Universal travel for North West Europeans	1960s' Club of Rome; Roots of sustainable tourism
1990	Economy airlines		Start of sustainable tourism
2000: Global warming, energy crisis,terrorism, natural disasters			
2005: Nowhere is remote, carbon-neutral initiative, responses to global warming			

Fig. I.1. An historical perspective: four streams of change.

The Impacts of Economic Globalization on Tourism

In the 19th and 20th centuries the developed world was associated with urbanization, industrialization and rural de-population, but by the beginning of the 21st century, not only the developed world but much of the so-called 'Third World' or 'developing world' is associated with the growth of vast urban agglomerations or so-called 'megalopolises' with 10, 20 or more million inhabitants in each of them. By 2000 there were already 20 cities each with a population of over 10 million. In order to function, these world cities, which are found on all continents, demand and generate world flows of raw materials, energy, foods and goods. Such urban magnets are found as much in China, India and the Americas, as in Europe. The flows of materials, goods and ideas generated by them, is equalled by the change in scale of world tourism flows, but the populations of these world cities have unequal access to these travel opportunities.

Exploding Numbers of Tourist Destinations

The tourism or travel explosion of the last 50 years – from 1955 to 2005 and beyond – has seen shifts in the location of new tourist destinations, as fashions, surplus disposable income, types of tourism and mass access to

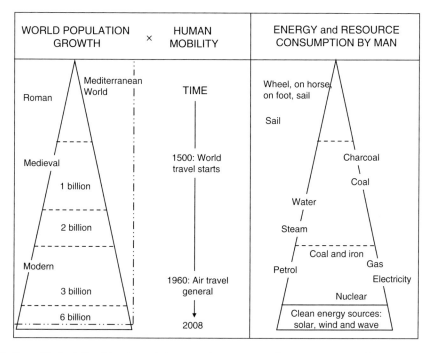

Fig. I.2. The critical relationship of population growth to energy and resource consumption.

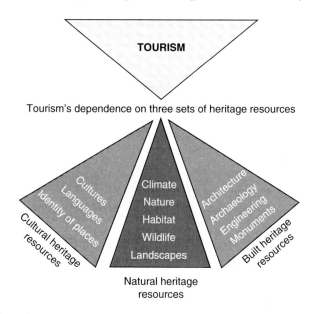

Fig. I.3. Tourism's dependence upon three sets of heritage resources.

cheap international travel, has changed the map of tourist destinations. Taking the example of European-generated tourism movements, the shifts in destination development have been from traditional North European resorts on the coasts of the UK, the Baltic, North Sea and resorts of the French and Italian Rivieras, first to Spanish (and Portuguese)

Costas, then to Majorca and west Mediterranean islands, then on to the Adriatic development of the Yugoslav coast, and to Greece, Turkey and Cyprus. The desire for guaranteed winter sun led on to development of the Canaries and Madeira to satisfy North West Europeans, to Florida and the Caribbean, supplementing North American movements there, and to the sun belt of the Red Sea – to Egyptian Sinai resorts and to Gulf of Aqaba resorts in Israel and Jordan. European initiatives have also led to the exploitation of 'dream-islands' in the Indian and Pacific Oceans, so that places like the Maldives and Seychelles, Mauritius and Fiji have developed, while exotic cultures and low prices drew them on to places like Bali, Goa and to Thailand.

The expansion of cruising in the last decade has extended visits to the Baltic, Norway's fiords, the Caribbean, the Mediterranean, to the edge of Alaska, and sea-based visits to the Polar regions. The growth of outward Japanese and Korean world tourism, and of North Americans touring their own continent, have been significant, but we have yet to see the impact of massive change when large-scale outward Indian- and Chinese-generated tourism 'hits' the globe. The design

of resorts in the last 50 years has been largely placeless; the new tourism lacks cultural understanding and respect for host cultures – as can now be evidenced in resultant law cases in places such as Dubai and the Maldives. Only pilgrimage tourism shows respect: when the visitors, for example Islamic tourists on the Hajj visit a traditional Islamic society – Saudi Arabia. Then cultural norms of hosts and guests are shared.

Figure I.4 outlines the tourist system.

What is sustainable tourism? Sustainable tourism is redefined by Travis (the author) as:

> Man's responsible long-term use and re-use, for tourism purposes, of human resources, and of three sets of heritage resources – natural, cultural and built –to meet effective consumer demand within the limits of the capacities of those resources, for the benefit of both the tourists and of the permanent resident communities at the tourist destinations.

And what is sustainable tourism planning? Sustainable tourism planning is redefined by the author as:

> Defining and developing practical action programmes comprising a bundle of

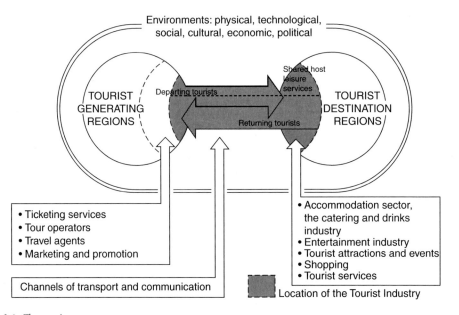

Fig. I.4. The tourist system.

WORK-RELATED	Business tourism Meeting tourism Conference tourism Exhibition and trade fair tourism
LEARNING-RELATED	Educational tourism Language and skill acquisition Holidays Gap year tourism Cultural tourism Literary festival
HEALTH-RELATED	Spa treatment tourism 'Wellness' tourism Hospital treatment abroad: medical tourism
PLAY and LEISURE-RELATED	Pop festival tourism Gap year tourism City break tourism Sports tourism: winter sports, water sports, air sports Ecotourism and nature tourism Nature trek holidays Birdwatching holidays Walking and cycling holidays Climbing holidays Cruising holidays Beach resort holidays Cultural tourism Festival and event tourism Hen and stag parties abroad
SPIRITUAL and BELIEF-RELATED	Pilgrimage tourism Beachcomber tourism Backpacking tourism Treks to meet gurus

Fig. I.5. An indicative spectrum of types of tourism.

development and conservation policies, and achieving their realization through fiscal and agency means, to deliver sustainable tourism products.

There are many 'tourisms', and an indicative range is given in Fig. I.5. These are crude indicative 'tourisms'. However, much past so-called theory of tourism was drawn from leisure theory literature, shaped by writers such as Veblen, Maslow, Kelly and Dumazedier. Latterly, within the tourism field itself, the contributions of writers such as Plog, Schmoll, Iso Ahola, Erik Cohen, Weber, Krippendorf and McCannell are notable. Recently newer writers such as Wang, van Egmond and Jenkins are deepening our understanding of the tourist himself.

Four types of model are explored in case studies in this book:

- Model A: multiple stakeholder model, with maximum destination community benefit (MSM-CB). This includes the North Pennines Growth Point, Mid-Wales Festival of the Environment, the Slovene Heritage Trail, and others.
- Model B: tourism carrying capacity assessment models (TCCA). This includes a range of case studies given in Part III.
- Model C: sustainable tourism planning models (STP) examples. These extend from early experimental models of the 1970s

A protected area is an area of land and/or sea especially dedicated to the protection and maintenance of biological diversity, and of natural and associated cultural resources, and managed through legal or other effective means.

Although all protected areas meet the general purposes contained in this definition, in practice the precise purposes for which protected areas are managed differ greatly.

Protected Area Management Categories

IUCN has defined a series of six protected area management categories, based on primary management objective. In summary, these are:

CATEGORY Ia: Strict Nature Reserve: protected area managed mainly for science

Definition   Area of land and/or sea possessing some outstanding or representative ecosystems, geological or physiological features and/or species, available primarily for scientific research and/or environmental monitoring.

CATEGORY Ib   Wilderness Area: protected area managed mainly for wilderness protection

Definition   Large area of unmodified or slightly modified land, and/or sea, retaining its natural character and influence, without permanent or significant habitation, which is protected and managed so as to preserve its natural condition.

CATEGORY II   National Park: protected area managed mainly for ecosystem protection and recreation

Definition   Natural area of land and/or sea, designated to: (a) protect the ecological integrity of one or more ecosystems for present and future generations; (b) exclude exploitation or occupation inimical to the purposes of designation of the area; and (c) provide a foundation for spiritual, scientific, educational, recreational and visitor opportunities, all of which must be environmentally and culturally compatible.

CATEGORY III   Natural Monument: protected area managed mainly for conservation of specific natural features

Definition   Area containing one, or more, specific natural or natural/cultural feature which is of outstanding or unique value because of its inherent rarity, representative or aesthetic qualities or cultural significance.

CATEGORY IV   Habitat/Species Management Area: protected area managed mainly for conservation through management intervention

Definition   Area of land and/or sea subject to active intervention for management purposes so as to ensure the maintenance of habitats and/or to meet the requirements of specific species.

CATEGORY V   Protected Landscape/Seascape: protected area managed mainly for landscape/seascape conservation and recreation

Definition   Area of land, with coast and sea as appropriate, where the interaction of people and nature over time has produced an area of distinct character with significant aesthetic, ecological and/or cultural value, and often with high biological diversity. Safeguarding the integrity of this traditional interaction is vital to the protection, maintenance and evolution of such an area.

CATEGORY VI   Managed Resource Protected Area: protected area managed mainly for the sustainable use of natural ecosystems

Definition   Area containing predominantly unmodified natural systems, managed to ensure long-term protection and maintenance of biological diversity, while providing at the same time a sustainable flow of natural products and services to meet community needs.

Fig. I.6. The IUCN definitions of protected areas (Source: IUCN, 1978).

and 1980s, to UK Task Force 1988–1990, World Tourism Organization (WTO), Local Agenda 21 models, onward.
- Model D: resource management and planning models (RMP) which extend from the national and regional planning

case studies in Parts I and II, IUCN and WWF work, to sophisticated emergent models of the 2000s.

Fig. I.6 lists the IUCN definitions of protected areas.

Part I

International and National Scales of Tourism and Leisure Planning

1 World and National Systems of Heritage Resource Classification (RMP)

At a national scale of action, there are examples across the world of national government action and that of federal governments, going back as far as the middle of the 19th century, to conserve and protect precious natural environments and built heritage monuments. However, while the idea of heritage conservation globally was mooted after the First World War, it was the scale of world losses in the Second World War that led to the effective start of world action in the realm of conservation in the post-war period. Conferences and meetings from the late 1940s to the late 1960s, led to the key actions of UNESCO in the early 1970s, and the IUCN in the late 1970s, to change things radically. The IUCN was founded in 1948, and UNESCO, as part of the United Nations (UN) organization, was similarly founded in the post-war period.

UNESCO World Heritage Convention

The mechanism for heritage protection at the world level was created by the General Council of UNESCO adopting the World Heritage Convention concerning the protection of world cultural and natural heritage in 1972 and 1975, and setting up a committee of 21 states as parties to that Convention. By 2008 over 145 states were party to the Convention protecting the natural and cultural heritage treasures of the world. Some 185 states have now ratified the World Heritage Convention. UNESCO was to be curator, in partnership with nation states as joint conservators and funding bodies.

The World Heritage List now contains some 878 properties worldwide. This comprises 679 built/cultural heritage sites, 174 natural sites and 25 that are mixed in character. It ranges from cultural monuments such as the Taj Mahal in India, the Athens Acropolis in Greece, Paris' Notre Dame Cathedral in France, to the Great Wall of China and Auschwitz Concentration Camp in Poland. In terms of natural monuments, it ranges from National Parks such as Kokadu in Australia, Plitvice Lakes in Croatia, to Kilimanjaro in Tanzania and Yosemite in the USA.

IUCN Protected Areas

The IUCN is the oldest and largest global environmental network, having some 1000 governmental and non-governmental organizations (NGOs), 11,000 volunteer scientists in over 160 countries, and its own professional staff of 1000 in some 60 offices. Its world headquarters is at Gland in Switzerland. Its mission is 'to influence, encourage, and assist societies throughout the world to conserve the integrity and diversity of nature and to ensure that any use of natural resources is equitable and ecologically sustainable'.

The IUCN is responsible for the World Conservation Strategy. In 1978 the IUCN published a report entitled *Categories, Objectives, and Criteria for Protected Areas*, and this gave a classical system of definitions and categories for natural area protection. This classification is shown in Fig. I.6 in the Introduction. Many countries later adopted this system for application to their national territories. In 1980, IUCN also produced a World Conservation Strategy in cooperation with United Nations Environment Programme (UNEP) and the WWF. This aimed to create a global system of protected areas of various categories, covering the full range of bio-geographic types represented on the planet.

Significance of World Heritage to Tourism

Conservation of the world's natural, spiritual and cultural heritage is vital for Man's civilized survival and biotic survival, and is also critical to world tourism. The cultural and natural monuments provide the icons of world tourism, as seen in the Grand Tour in 19th-century Baedecker tourism, as well as in 20th-century so-called mass tourism. The challenge is how to conserve these monuments, as well as interpreting them, managing the visitors and the sites, so as to make them sustainable, and yet available to future generations of visitors.

The current explosion of international cruise tourism to formerly restricted world cities, such as St Petersburg, gives rise to the enormous expansion in visitor numbers to attractions in these World Heritage Cities, such as the Hermitage Museum, leading to debased visits, frustration, wear and tear, due to the absence of adequate visitor management systems and services. Capacities have to be set for such sites, otherwise debasement of the visitor experience, and excessive wear to the heritage site can result.

The negative experience of the Lascaux Caves in France, with their pre-historic cave paintings, resulted from absence of adequate management, and lack of environmental controls, with cigarette smoke damaging the priceless paintings. Now visitors can only visit a facsimile site, in a concrete cave, to get an ersatz experience of photocopies of the paintings on the walls.

Tourism Contribution to Heritage Conservation

In the light of such failures, it is critical that tourism (which depends upon heritage) should contribute to conservation, via a range of alternative means. These can include entry charges to heritage sites, tourist taxes via hotels and catering services, and government subsidies.

National Systems of Heritage Classification and Conservation

At the national scale, many young nations have used UNESCO and IUCN criteria as bases for establishing systems of classification and protection for their natural and cultural heritage resources. Countries such as the USA and the UK have complex national conservation systems which pre-dated the world systems. Many countries have Antiquities Ministries and Environment Ministries, with very different systems of heritage classification and conservation. The role of voluntary sector agencies in this field is also a notable variable among nations. Bodies like the National Trust in England and Wales, the Royal Society for the Protection of Birds (RSPB) in the UK, or Den Norske Turist Forening in Norway have valuable roles in bridging the heritage conservation and tourism management fields. Millions of volunteers and members of trusts in the developed world are critical in their work in conserving and restoring nature and cultural monuments.

One of the most interesting innovations in heritage classification was the wider policy-oriented Outdoor Recreation Resources Review Commission's (ORRRC) classification which was published by the Rockefeller Commission in the 18 volume 1962 report,

Fig. 1.1. The Taj Mahal, a UNESCO protected monument (photograph courtesy of India Tourism).

called *Outdoor Recreation for America*. In 1970, a report entitled *Recreation Planning for the Clyde, Firth of Clyde, Scotland, Phase 2*, was published by the Scottish Tourist Board (Travis and Consulting Team, 1970). This report attempted to adapt the ORRRC approach to European conditions. In Chapter 13 this is examined in more detail.

What is important at the national and regional scales is to have robust systems of classification and protection that range from prime national heritage down to vernacular architecture, local habitat reserves, cultural and natural monuments, and these should be linked to regular and adequate conservation management budgets, plus staff with adequate technical skills and means to do the conservation work.

Many of the 'icons' of tourism are UNESCO- or IUCN-protected monuments (such as the Taj Mahal; Fig. 1.1), which are examined in the text later in the book.

2   Planning for Tourism in a Post-industrial Society – a National Case Study from the UK (RMP)

Introduction

In the period from 1950 to 1980, the UK became a test case not only for planning generally, but also latterly in the planning for tourism. At the 1950 start date of the period, the UK in its phase of utopian post-war planning, had set up, or was to establish some seven systems: (i) for obligatory town and country planning; (ii) for the development of 'new towns' in their regional contexts; (iii) for National Parks, conservation, and access to the countryside, in England and Wales; (iv) a National Health Service; (v) nationalization of coal, electricity, gas and the railways; (vi) conservation of the built heritage – split between public and voluntary sectors; and later (vii) a national motorways network, from the 1960s onwards.

In 1968/69, for similar logical reasons, national legislation created a clear and logical system for the development, management and marketing of tourism in the UK. National Tourist Boards were set up for Scotland, England, Wales and Northern Ireland, and a British Tourist Authority (BTA) created as the primary overseas marketing agency for all UK inward tourism. The scale and significance of London, and of London to British tourism, led to the setting up of a London Tourist Board.

The UK system worked well, and covered not only marketing, research and intelligence, but also tourism development functions. Like many things in UK history, the system was changed before it was fully evaluated, and since then not only has the English Tourist Board (ETB) disappeared, but the vital development function, with its associated financial instruments, has gone.

In this chapter London tourism is looked at in two time periods:

- in the 1970s and 1980s when the official tourist system was being shaped, and problems and needs defined; and
- in 2008, at a stage of development and change when sustainable tourism ideas had been introduced, and planning for the London 2012 Olympics was under way.

By contrast, a case study is also given of a rural tourist growth point experiment in the North of England, from the 1970s, to reflect innovative tourism ideas of that era, with the first multiple stakeholder model (MSM).

Elsewhere in the book are other examples from UK tourism planning which give a fuller picture of its dimensions. These examples include:

- English National Park and rural planning case studies in Chapter 16;

- Scottish regional tourism planning in Chapter 13;
- Welsh post-industrial coalfield tourism development in Chapter 20;
- Scottish historic city conservation and tourism planning in Chapter 29;
- English and Welsh coastal planning in Chapter 24; and
- English post-industrial city centre planning in Chapter 34.

Now let us first turn to the London case study.

Tourism and a Metropolitan Pressure Point: a Case Study of London Tourism in the Late 1970s (RMP)

As indicated by Sir Henry Marking, then Chairman of the BTA, in a speech given at a 1978 Conference on 'Tourism Growth and London Accommodation': 'the success of London determines the level of failure or success of British Tourism'. In terms of national balance of payments, this was borne out, as 67.5% of expenditure by 1977 overseas tourists in England, was in London. However, very different patterns emerge when the significance of London to British domestic tourists is analysed compared with that for international tourists. In 1977, under 10% of all trips made by UK tourists were to London (i.e. 11 million out of 121 million), while 67% of all overseas originating tourist movements to the UK were to London (7.8 million out of 11.5 million). The comparison, in terms of spending, and of economic impact is even more dramatic. Eleven million UK tourist visits to London generated an expenditure of £200 million in 1977 compared with the £1350 million spend by a much smaller number of overseas visitors to the city, who were staying longer. Thus, international tourism was economically important to London, and dominated visits to the UK. Domestic tourism was a minor contributor to the London economy. The gross impact of international and domestic tourism upon London was impressive: 18.8 million tourists per annum (p.a.) were spending £1550 million! The attraction of

London was assumed to be sustainable, and there was little competitive pull to other UK cities, in the 1970s.

London as a pressure point in UK tourism

London was the locus for 32% of all tourist spending in the UK, and the destination for 67% of all inward international tourist movements to the UK in the 1970s. London and Edinburgh (to a far lesser extent) were the two main UK tourist destinations for foreign visitors. The rapid build up in visitor numbers, length-of-stay pressures and amount of money being spent meant that for peak periods demand outstripped accommodation supply, and there were localized problems of congestion, crowding and competition for access to travel and services, all occurring at points in Central London, which was the focus of international and domestic tourism. The 1970s' problems generated many reports, studies and conferences. The resultant evidence suggested that London gained enormous net benefits from tourism, but there were planning and management problems to be tackled.

Though there was a slight decline in London's pull as a holiday destination for UK visitors, its draw for business and conference tourism was undiminished. The holiday or leisure motive was the dominant one for foreign visitors (55% gave this as their primary motive), because of its manifold attractions – built heritage and commercial, educational, cultural and leisure-related attractions.

The benefits of tourism to a world city

Statistical evidence given in 1970s *Regional Fact Sheets*, the *English Heritage Monitor* and the *Tourism Discussion Paper* showed the economic value of tourism as an industry to London. In 1977 it generated some 250,000 full-time jobs, of which about 140,000 were in the hotel and catering sector (ETB, 1978). The average foreign visitor in 1977 was spending £235 per head on London visits. Sales of tourist services, employment generation, tax and rate returns from tourist industry premises were of great economic importance. Some 25% of shopping expenditure in Central London was estimated to be from overseas tourist spending. Selected shops attributed up to 50% of their sales to tourists. Overseas tourists in London were spending 35% of their budget on shopping, and 36% of them were staying in hotels. In the 1970s, sales of tourist services of all types were worth £450 million p.a. to Inner London!

The growth of business and conference tourism was increasingly important. It was estimated that of £250 million of value added tax (VAT) returns in the UK due to overseas visitors, 66% of it was generated in London. Rate returns, income and corporation tax returns, excise duties and VAT returns attributable to tourist industry activities were all already major contributors to the London economy.

In the context of conservation and tourism, it was notable how great the pull was of built and cultural heritage for visitors to London. In 1977, no less than three million visitors paid to enter the Tower of London, which was the most popular site for which an entry charge was made. Some £2.75 million was the total tourist spend at this one site! However, London's four most popular indoor tourist attractions did not charge entry: (i) four million p.a. visiting the British Museum; (ii) 3.3 million p.a. visiting the Science Museum; (iii) three million p.a. visiting the Natural History Museum; and (iv) Westminster Abbey was also drawing some three million visitors p.a. From 1976 to 1977 there was a 17% increase in visitors to London heritage sites. Conflict between resident and tourist access to tourist sites was already evident. Nevertheless, 76% of a sample of London residents interviewed by the ETB in 1978 felt that the benefits of tourism outweighed its costs or disbenefits!

London's tourism problems

By the 1970s the scale and growth of London tourism already generated many problems including:

- The loss of housing stock due to creeping property conversion processes.

- The world role of London in terms of its built and cultural heritage resources, shopping, entertainment, business, education, financial and administrative concentrations all led to over concentration of tourist demand for accommodation and services upon central locations.

- Over concentration of tourist visits to selected locations created excess pressures on travel infrastructure, and upon some heritage sites. Some 75% of tourists visited Trafalgar Square, 72% went to Piccadilly Circus, 70% to Buckingham Palace, 66% to Westminster Abbey and 50% to St Paul's Cathedral.

- Crowding and congestion of specific roads with cars, coaches and taxis, crowding of some underground stations and pavements of some shopping streets and their shops (e.g. those in Oxford Street, Piccadilly Circus, Carnaby Street and Kings Road), plus congestion in some popular street markets.

- How could local de-concentration from Central London to Outer London, and the fringes of London be achieved? Could visitors be persuaded to visit lesser known forests, heaths, commons and attractions which were getting fewer than 50,000–100,000 visitors p.a.? Must tourists go simply to see the 'icons of world tourism'?

- How could visits be encouraged to other regions of the UK, lessening pressure on London, and boosting under-visited regions and cities?

- Seasonality affected London to some extent, but not as much as it did other regions.

- How could the low spend of UK tourists in London be increased?

- How could direct financial contributions from tourism be channelled to aid conservation? The fabric of heritage sites maintenance is costly but visitors do not generally pay to visit them.

- How could future tourism growth be dealt with? Estimates in the 1970s put 12–20 million as the London 1990 visitor level.

- How could the shortage of hotel beds, which was notable in the 1970s, be dealt with.

The scale and array of tourist problems was large, but viewing the economic benefits accruing to London from tourism, justified the strong subsequent public policy action thrusts, and private capital responses which were to transform London tourism by early in the new Millennium.

Problems at tourist pressure points in London

To illustrate residents' responses to London tourism in this period, the 1978 Greater London Council (GLC) paper *Tourism: a Paper for Discussion* stated that:

> Most Londoners recognize how important the money tourists spend has become to London, and to the nation. This was confirmed by a survey of London residents' opinions on tourism recently undertaken for the ETB. The survey not only sampled the general opinions of Londoners but particularly those of residents and workers in three areas specially frequented by tourists (Soho, South Kensington and Greenwich). Few felt that they personally had benefited from tourism, but only a small percentage of those interviewed felt that they had been inconvenienced by the tourists.

The only important disadvantages mentioned were to do with overcrowding, congestion and over-pricing. Only in South Kensington was there a significant number of residents who appeared to be unhappy about the number of tourists visiting London.

From all the evidence then, tourism pressure points or problem localities were the South Kensington museums' area, the Tower of London Precinct, five key shopping areas already listed, plus Westminster Abbey, St Paul's Cathedral, and the streets where large-scale on-street parking of tourist coaches and cars occurred.

The London boroughs which suffered from tourism's impacts were: (i) the City of Westminster; (ii) Kensington and Chelsea; and (iii) Camden. Here, local authorities and the public were resistant to further hotel development, and wanted decentralization of hotel provision and of visitors (Fig. 2.1 shows the concentration of hotels in Central London in 1974). Loss of housing stock, problems of parking by coaches and cars, disturbed nights

from arrivals and departures at unsocial hours, as well as competition for public transport and commercial retail services, were indicative of the problems. These issues led to policies for tourist de-concentration within London, and changes in traffic management.

Mechanisms for planning and managing London tourism

The GLC then existed as the upper tier authority responsible for strategic planning, transport, historic buildings, arts and entertainment, as well as for regional parks, and took a special role in tourism planning as it came into being. As early as 1971, it issued a policy paper entitled *Tourism and Hotels in London* (GLC, 1971), and during the decade took the initiative in joint planning ventures about tourism, with regional and national tourist boards, and with the London boroughs. The mechanism of the statutory planning system via its 'Development Plans' and 'Structure Plans' partially absorbed tourism planning within them, as a type of facet-planning. Thus the Greater London Development Plan, the Development Plans, Structure Plans and some Local Plans for London boroughs, all contained tourism policy sections.

The complexity of London tourism-planning roles in the 1970s needs emphasizing, not because of lack of machinery, but because of the range and conflicting interests between all the private and public sector actors involved.

At the simplest level, within the public sector there were two tiers of local government involved, and varying attitudes of lower authorities depending upon their location in Inner or Outer London. Inner boroughs were against more tourism, some Outer ones were also against it, while others were undecided in attitude. This all made it even more confusing to the three levels of Tourist Boards involved.

National tourism planning and London's role

By the 1970s a strategic approach to national tourism planning in the UK needed to optimize

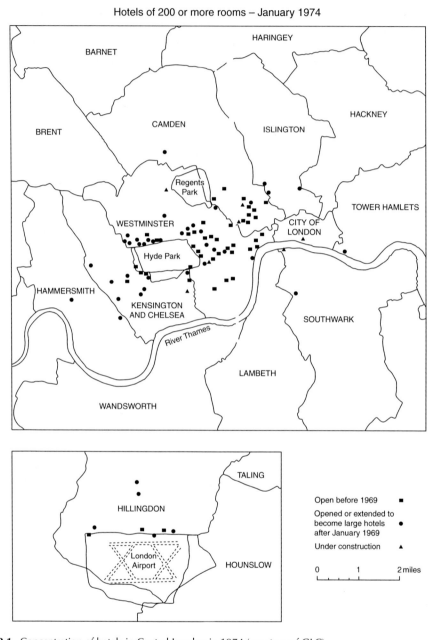

Fig. 2.1. Concentration of hotels in Central London in 1974 (courtesy of GLC).

on London's assets, while undertaking strongly promotional policies for under-developed tourist regions. Thus decongestion policies within London, as well as decentrali-zation from London to its wider region, and the rest of the country was important. The Secretary of State for Trade had responsibility for tourism, for the Tourist Boards and for tourism planning. The Secretary of State for the Environment was responsible for physi-cal planning, environmental quality control, recreation planning and built heritage conser-vation. Other related powers were within the Department of Education and Science and the

Department of Industry. This jurisdictional jungle made it difficult to get a national overview, or of achieving integration in the many forms of regional planning, conservation and development. The wording of the critical Development of Tourism Act partly overcame this structural problem.

However, with equally complex public sector systems and bureaucracies, countries like France, Poland and Israel were all able to achieve some coordination in the interests of tourism planning. Therefore, there was reason to be hopeful about the next phase of national and inter-regional tourism planning in the UK, where London's tourism roles would be effectively resolved and reconciled.

Decongestion, de-concentration and managing London tourism

In the 1968 GLC Development Plan, the question of tourism was raised twice: (i) where tourism was treated as an economic activity; and (ii) where the potential and future planning of the Thames for recreation and amenity was considered. The document under-estimated the importance economically of tourism, referred to pending tourism legislation, and was inadequate for the needs of the time.

By 1971 with the new Tourism Act in force, a hotel-building phase started, international tourism expanded and the GLC changed its attitude to tourism. The 1971 GLC discussion paper *Tourism and Hotels in London* reviewed tourist accommodation demand and supply, conflicts relating to tourism and the need for a strategy for London tourism! It stated that: 'Tourism is a major growth industry in London, which planning can do much to assist, and which should have the serious consideration that is given to other forms of economic activity.'

Policy options, and the means of locating and implementing desirable changes were all factors addressed, and even the question of a tourist 'hotel tax' was raised. The discussion paper concluded with the need for urgent action.

This started a period of cooperation and public consultation, which resulted in a 1974

advisory plan called: Tourism in London – a Plan for Management. It set out an approach to plan making, roles and justifications for planning as an activity, with its services, and made suggestions about realization and monitoring.

Three objectives were set out, namely to:

- ease congestion for the benefit of tourists and of Londoners;
- ensure that accommodation matches the needs of tourists in all respects; and
- provide guidelines for tourist infrastructure provision and maintenance.

A consultation and advisory phase in 1973–1974 preceded a period of even larger-scale tourism growth, especially from 1976 to 1978. With UK tourism expenditure reaching £4804 million by 1977, and London experiencing an unprecedented tourist boom, further review became essential in the 1977–1978 period. The response came in the GLC's *Tourism: a Paper for Discussion* (1978) and the holding of a major conference on London tourism.

The 1978 paper set out to:

- Decongest tourism activity both in London and beyond by creating development thrusts along the Thames to London Docklands and to other edge locations.
- Spread the seasonal peaking of tourism by promoting off-peak holidays and out-of-town day trips, changing conference timing and creating a midwinter arts festival.
- Get a better fit between tourist accommodation demand and supply.
- Get tourism to specialize more, and define target markets.
- Boost the use of the Thames for transport, pleasure, activities and a spread of functions.
- Improve services ranging from cleaning of buildings and streets, to conservation, pedestrianization, major road programmes, and recycle heritage building stock such as Covent Garden Market and the disused St Katharine's Docks.
- Provide an inner city focus to use tourism as an economic trigger mechanism in the inner urban economy.
- Raise the question of a tourist tax in a UK context.

Evaluation of the 1970s' approach

The foregoing text illustrates a history which will help many world cities now entering this process of big city tourism planning. The emergence of effective tourism planning in 1970s' London laid the foundations for radically improved tourism products in the transformed London of the 2000s. Responsive planning for tourist accommodation and services is now a highly developed sector of urban economies. However, the key linkage between tourism development and transport planning for all modes in big cities is still often inadequately handled in planning, while the critical interaction of local planning for and management of urban leisure services generally is left unrelated to tourism planning in most countries. It took a long time for London to wake up to the value of tourism to the urban economy, let alone plan for key strategic locational needs, as well as recognize the interdependence of tourism, conservation of heritage resources and transportation management.

A 2008 retrospective evaluation of London tourism

Decentralization in London

By 2006 a better spread of tourism activity was being achieved in London, due to the growth of new attractions on the South Bank – including the London Eye, the National Theatre and the Tate Modern Gallery, plus the extensive redevelopment of London Docklands, with major conference, exhibition and entertainment venues there, plus a new financial district at Canary Wharf in Docklands, and the rebuilding of the Wembley Stadium in its suburban setting. Though an estimated 31% of London tourism visitor spend was still taking place in Westminster, other London boroughs were growing in popularity (Table 2.1).

Decongestion/decentralization nationally

By 2006, according to Visit London, there had been a notable growth in tourism to UK provincial cities, which had done much to increase their tourism appeal, so that not only

Table 2.1. Tourism activity by London boroughs in 2006.

Borough	Overnight visits (million)	Day visits (million)
Westminster	5.4	33.3
Kensington and Chelsea	1.7	10.3
Camden	1.2	8.2
Tower Hamlets	0.4	4.3
City of London	0.6	4.1

Edinburgh but also Manchester, Birmingham and Glasgow were competing in the international market. While London retained its dominant share of overseas tourism to the UK (taking some 48% of the total), by 2006 Edinburgh was attracting 4%, Manchester 3%, Birmingham 2% and Glasgow 2% of the total incoming overseas tourists. Over 12% of international tourism was now going to UK cities other than London. Thus their joint appeal was equal to one-quarter of that of London! The Birmingham case study in Chapter 34 demonstrates the ways in which this UK city has increased its tourism competitiveness.

London's sustainability as a tourist destination

London is a 2000-year-old city which started as a minor provincial settlement in the Roman Empire, eventually grew to be a world city and seat of an Empire, and remains a primary world tourist attraction with an incredible diversity of appeals to many markets. Despite modern terrorist incidents on its underground trains and buses, its appeal is not diminished. It is estimated that tourist numbers have dropped since 1978, from 18.8 million to 15.3 million, but London still greatly outstrips New York, Paris and Hong Kong in its visitor numbers! Furthermore, the value of tourism to London has greatly increased: namely from £1550 million total tourism spend in 1978 to £16.6 billion in 2007. London has also changed in its population. By 2006 30% of its population was non-indigenous, and it has become more cosmopolitan, coping with ever more tourisms (or tourist segments) and new niche markets. London is sustainable as a tourist destination as its many urban parts are recycled, giving rise to new 'ethnic' quarters, new shopping activity centres, new forms of health tourism and edu-tourism.

Economic sustainability of London

As a world city, London's tourism was valued at £16.6 billion in 2007. Though it has gone through periods when the pound sterling was an expensive currency in exchange terms, it is now becoming cheaper and its appeal remains very buoyant. Due to the vastly expanded and renewed hotel and accommodation sector, London now offers 245,000 tourist beds, in all forms of accommodation. As a World Banking Centre and theatre centre, it is unparalleled. In 2007, all business tourism was worth £3279 million to London, while also in that year 13.6 million theatre attendances were recorded, with a box office value of £470 million – largely based on tourist support.

Traditional markets for London tourism have been supplemented by growth in Asian and European markets. Shopping tourism, educational tourism and event tourism have all grown. With the recent completion of the new Wembley Stadium and the ongoing construction of the 2012 Olympic venues in London, sports tourism is also due to expand. Development of new out-of-town shopping centres and the new Kings Cross shopping district will take place, with further decentralization being encouraged.

Environmental sustainability

By 2007 some 42% of London tourism was for holiday purposes, 31% for business and conference purposes, 10% visits to friends and relatives (VFRs) and 4% for study. The success of the Congestion Charge in reducing private car traffic in Central London, aided environmental quality, as did a range of environmental improvements in key locations such as Oxford Street, the South Bank, Docklands and Kew Gardens. The formal proposal in 2008 to create a huge new National Park, extending some 30 miles along the Thames Estuary, fundamentally changes the stock of heritage outdoor natural resources in the London Basin, and on London's doorstep!

Cultural sustainability

The growth and broadening of London's high culture and popular culture offers has put it in a prime competitive position among world cities. Five of the world's most popular museums in 2007, were in London. The British Museum, with 5.4 million visitors p.a., was the third most popular world museum. The Tate Modern, with 5.1 million visitors was the fourth most popular, the National Gallery with 4.1 million the sixth, the Natural History Museum with 3.6 million the seventh and the Science Museum, with 2.7 million, the eighth most popular on the world list. By comparison, Paris has only two museums on the top list, and New York only one.

Cultural, business, shopping and theatre attractions led to the value of international holiday tourism and leisure activities in London being worth £3137 million in 2007, nearly three times the value of domestic spend in these sectors in London. As overseas tourists stay an average of 6.2 days for their stay in London, this has enormous economic spin-off effects.

Sustainable transport

Though over-dependence on air transport access to London for international tourism is not sustainable, some other indicators of change in the transport sector are a source of encouragement. The opening of the high speed rail (HSR) route to London from Paris and Brussels, and the creation of the newly renovated St Pancras International Railway Station, plus other rail developments, led to a 10% growth in inward rail movements to London in 2007. A feasibility study was underway in 2008 regarding the HSR development links in the UK to Scotland, Wales and Northern England. If such a system were realized this could help enormously to increase sustainable transport access to London.

Within London, the intensive use of its extensive underground and light rail systems, as well as of bus and coach services, are sustainable. If road traffic to Inner London was (as is claimed) reduced by 15% due to the Congestion Charge, there are hopes yet of growing private car use in London being arrested. The better general spread of attractions, shopping and major sports complexes, will aid better loading of parts of the public transport system and help tourist journeys incidentally. However, the 2012 London Olympics will present the greatest challenge to the functioning of London's transport system.

Event planning for London's 2012 Olympics

London planning for the 2012 mega-event is based upon applying criteria of sustainability. The Olympic Games will have a wide spread of events at a range of sports venues – both across the UK and across Greater London. Central Olympic Park in East London is used as an opportunity both to reclaim poisoned land and to create new parks, a clean river and facilities, which will have long-life, community after-use (Fig. 2.2). The Olympic Park's creation involves cleaning land and water, integrated transport planning for regional rail, local train and underground rail, as well as cycle and foot trail access – to aid all the participating athletes, officials, media, sponsors and spectators. It is an exemplary transport plan.

Transport to the Games is thus based on low carbon use and public transport access. It is rare to find event planning which is low carbon or carbon neutral in intent. Negotiated retiming of residents' holidays, local work hours and many such sensitive adjustments have been made, to aid the workability of travel for all involved in the Games. By 2009 arrangements in transport planning and management seemed to be exemplary.

For the Beijing Games planning in a state capitalist society involved a massive state sector planning system. In the UK's complex mixed economy, it is a challenge to deliver a complex package such as the Olympic Games. The planning agency for staging the London Olympics is the London Organizing Committee of the Olympic Games and Paralympic Games (LOCOG), with a budget of £2 billion (raised from the private sector), while the delivery agency for realizing the transport infrastructure and the building superstructure on the ground, is the Olympic Delivery Authority (ODA), with a £9.3 billion budget. However, as seen in Fig. 2.3 those two

bodies must work in concert with a big range of partners/stakeholders – in the governmental sector, public, commercial and voluntary sectors.

Preliminary evaluation of the Games approach

The sound detailed planning and development of the Games, is complemented by a sustainability governance structure (Fig. 2.3), with reporting to the Commission for a Sustainable London 2012, and principles made into sustainable themes for the Games, and translated into legacy promises, which will change physical realities on the ground. The complex integrated planning being conducted for the 2012 Games provide a test model for potential future attempts to plan change comprehensively in a mega-city like London.

Overall, the London case study shows a remarkable success story. Even though the London Tourist Board has become Visit London, the marketing and research functions remain, but the tourism-planning functions have again been re-allocated, with further changes in the local government structure for London. The 2012 Games planning shows a leap forward in sustainable planning. However, if the expected sea rise occurs as a result of global warming, it is unclear as to whether the Thames barrage has adequate capacity to cope with any eventuality that may affect the River Thames and its lower reaches. New scales of challenges wait to be faced.

The Growth and Development of Tourism in a Remote English Region: the North Pennines – a Growth Point for Tourism (MSM-CB)

Introduction

A newer aspect of UK tourism planning in the 1970s was featured in England's Northumbria region. That region included the counties of Northumberland, Tyne and Wear, Durham and Cleveland, and is situated in the extreme north-east of England, some 200–300 miles

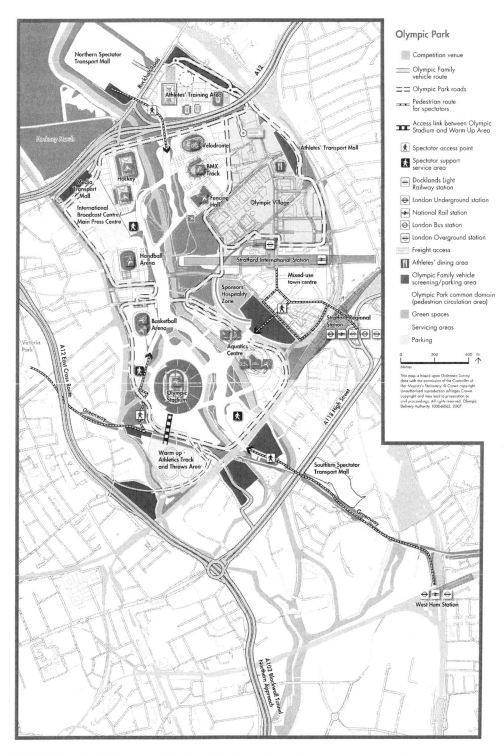

Fig. 2.2. Olympic Park (courtesy of ODA and Ordnance Survey).

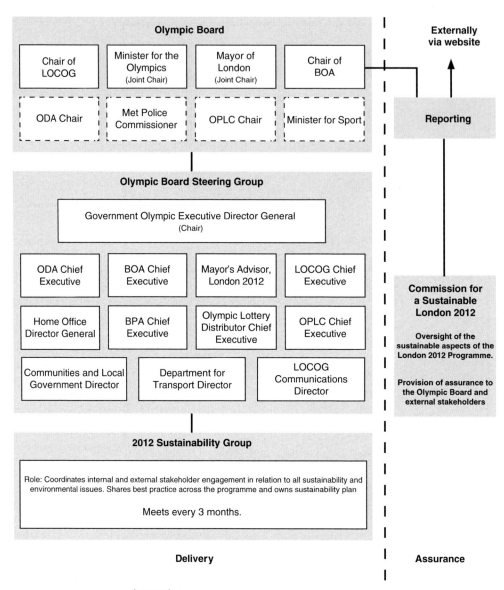

Integration

In February 2009, London 2012 published its Sustainability Guidelines for Corporate and Public Events (such as conferences, cultural events and promotional launches). These have been developed primarily for our internal event organisers and those involved in delivering London 2012 corporate and public events, such as venue managers, suppliers, licensees, commercial partners and media organizations. The guidelines will be kept updated following event experience and feedback.

Fig. 2.3. Sustainability governance structures. BOA, British Olympic Association; BPA, British Paralympic Association; LOCOG, London Organizing Committee of the Olympic Games and Paralympic Games; ODA, Olympic Delivery Authority; OPLC, Olympic Park Legacy Company (Source: LOCOG, 2007).

from London. Commencing in 1977, as a result of a government initiative, this was an experiment in integrated tourism planning and development. It demonstrated tourism planning as a type of regional economic development, aimed at creating a labour-intensive industry, which is sympathetic to its host environment.

The new initiative evolved from an appreciation of the tourist industry's economic significance, because of its importance nationally to the balance of payments, and regionally as a tool to redress uneven development. Increasing numbers of visitors from abroad, the opportunities to spread their activities in time and space, and the emergence of a more mobile domestic population with increased leisure time, were all factors of critical importance in this context.

As a result of the Minister's initiative, 'the growth point scheme' (as it was called) was introduced to evaluate whether more could be done to take advantage of the tourist appeal of remote and less developed British rural regions. Such regions were well away from the more popular tourist centres, such as London, Edinburgh and Stratford-upon-Avon, which were favoured by foreigners. It was thought that there were subregional locations which could absorb large numbers of domestic and foreign tourists, off-season, and benefit the ailing local economy of such places. This could take place in localities which needed to develop their economy and their tourist resources, thereby helping arrest depopulation and rural decline.

Legal basis of action

The vital Development of Tourism Act 1969 contains a Section 4 which reads:

1. A Tourist Board shall have power (a)... to give financial assistance for the carrying out of any project which in the opinion of the Board will provide or improve tourist amenities and facilities in the country for which the Board is responsible. (b) with the approval of the relevant Minister and the Treasury, to carry out any such project as aforesaid.

2. Financial assistance...may be given by way of grant or loan or, if the project is being or is to be carried out by a company incorporated in Great Britain, by subscribing for or otherwise acquiring shares or stock in the company, or by any combination of those methods.

3. In making a grant or loan in accordance with... this section, a Tourist Board may... impose such terms and conditions as it thinks fit, including conditions for the repayment of a grant in specified circumstances; and...shall have effect for securing compliance with conditions subject to which any such grant is made.

National approach to Tourism Growth Points

The ETB, through the Department of Trade, was empowered to offer financial assistance to tourist projects within areas of high unemployment, called 'Development Areas' (shown on Fig. 2.4). As a result of a government initiative in November 1978, the areas eligible for economic assistance were also being extended to 'Intermediate Areas'.

After the Section 4 Scheme of Development Area Tourism Grants were introduced in 1971, more than £8 million of capital was injected (mainly on a basis of response to local initiatives) in a range of tourism development projects, such as improved infrastructure, providing information, creating new activities for tourists, as well as attractions and various forms of accommodation. Tourist Board staff awaited approaches from individuals or companies which were prepared to invest in tourism, and wanted to obtain financial assistance to ensure the vitality of their proposals.

The scheme had already achieved much: £8 million of 'Trigger Investment' by government generated a total investment in excess of £30 million. The large scale of the total investment was for a modest scheme. Action by central government had already created scattered development schemes in Development Areas, where its policy had been a nurturing and responsive one.

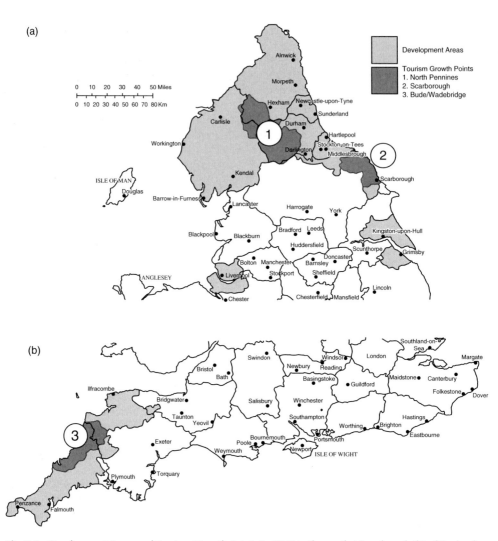

Fig. 2.4. Development Areas and Tourism Growth Points in 1978 in the north (a) and south (b) of England (courtesy of ETB).

After 6 years of operating this largely responsive Section 4 scheme, the Minister then suggested focusing development on the new 'growth points for tourism' – in essence carrying the Section 4 approach a stage further, by shifting on to an active encouragement phase. This would help to create several interactive new tourist attractions and tourist services. Interrelated developments when organized comprehensively, including their effective marketing, could help to attract tourists more effectively to such locations, than would

the provision of random and unrelated developments.

The government therefore set up three experimental areas: (i) around Scarborough, in Yorkshire; (ii) between Bude and Wadebridge in Cornwall; and (iii) in the North Pennines, between Northumbria and Cumbria.

This was an experiment. The three pilot areas were to test a new approach to development and the market, by this new tourism initiative. Each of the three selected areas was regarded by ETB as having the right intended characteristics. Outline proposals were put forward for discussion, with an emphasis on full local consultation taking place about the acceptability of the general development concept, and upon the extent and content of proposals, as well as their environmental implications.

'Consultation' in this instance was not a token process, but meant effective involvement of the local communities and all interested parties. It needed to be a fully-fledged, comprehensive action, so that ultimately national and regional tourist boards, planning authorities and conservation bodies, would all share the general goal of trying to get economic renewal of the three areas. It was the first public attempt at a multiple stakeholder partnership model in the UK.

Introduction to the case study of the North Pennines

Full consultation did take place in the instance of the North Pennines. Public meetings were held in various locations, with all the public sector stakeholders in the tourism, recreation, sport, conservation and environmental fields. A Regional Working Group was set up to monitor reactions to and to help evolve a manageable and realistic plan for new tourist development. It was the first time in this context in the UK that all such organizations were brought together with the shared purpose of developing tourism. The results of their deliberations were successful in planning terms. Similarly, the output of the fully-fledged consultation exercise was a satisfactory one. Potential conflicts were overcome, and agreement was reached on the method of approach towards development and marketing, and to research. This was achieved by a growth of mutual trust and understanding, and the sharing of purpose.

The Regional Working Group was aware from the outset that a development budget of £3 million was envisaged to cover the 3-year development period. Approximately £1 million of this would be from the ETB, via the Department of Trade. It was understood that most of the schemes would be wholly financed by private or local authority funds, as it was believed that the character of the scheme would generate an atmosphere conducive to development. It was equally understood that some development might be financed by a mixture of private and public funds. The Group was told that the Minister would be prepared to inject investment assistance provided that there were sufficient projects for the realization of the scheme, and that it was reasonably clear that the 'right' kind of partnership – both in terms of finance and of experience – would be forthcoming.

Character of the region's resources

First, it is necessary to introduce the North Pennines as an area, for it was the largest of the three English Tourism Growth Points. The North Pennines is a sparsely populated rural area, with a limited number of towns and villages. It covers an area approximately 50 miles north to south, by 15–25 miles from east to west. In general terms, the area is characterized by high moorlands, with valleys deeply penetrating them. The road summits at the valley heads are at a relatively high altitude, in English terms, being at roughly 500 m (1500 feet) above sea level.

The high open moorland contrasts with the valley floors of pastures enclosed by dry stone walls. The valleys contain the best agricultural land, the main settlements and primary lines of communication. The valleys have a distinctive character of large-scale landscapes, which distinguishes them from those in the Yorkshire and Lancashire Pennines.

Most of the proposed Tourism Growth Point's area has a bold and attractive landscape. It was known from the outset of the project, that the area was to be included in the proposed 'North Pennines Area of Outstanding Natural Beauty'. Furthermore, the moorlands and upper reaches of the valleys are of considerable ecological importance. There are two National Nature Reserves (NNRs) in Upper Teesdale, which is one of the area's three main valleys. One of the NNRs includes Widdybank Fell, which with its rare and scientifically important arctic alpine flora had to be conserved. Careful consideration needed to be given to any development, to protect the area's special ecological heritage and high quality landscape.

The magnificent large-scale landscape offered both selective opportunities to develop tourist potential and to conserve scenic heritage. There are good communications on the periphery of the area. Furthermore, the peripheral zones were important because of their robustness and potential ability to absorb visitor facilities without detriment to the more fragile upland landscapes. The northern part of the area incorporates part of the very popular central section of Hadrian's Wall (the Roman Wall) which is a UNESCO World Heritage Site. The Wall sits within the Northumberland National Park. It was realized that any proposals for tourism development would need to pay regard to strategic plans for the Hadrian's Wall area, which were already underway.

Criteria for change

There were two key economic bases for promoting tourism to the Growth Point:

• the need to help arrest rural depopulation, and therefore to generate new local rural jobs; and
• the need to generate additional income to the local community.

There were, however, some serious constraints, which had first to be overcome. These were: (i) a shortage locally of overnight visitor accommodation; (ii) a weak external image; (iii) a lack of focus for tourism; and (iv) the major environmental protection requirements to be satisfied.

In assessing the basic needs, the provision of additional tourist accommodation became an important proposal component, as a means of encouraging tourist stays, rather than day-visiting. This provision was seen as a means of producing an immediate economic impact.

The development opportunities therefore fell into four groups:

• provision of serviced tourist accommodation and catering facilities;
• self-catering tourist accommodation;
• tourist attractions and amenities; and
• infrastructure provision.

Tourism proposals

Within serviced tourist accommodation and catering the creation of 450 new bed spaces was agreed upon by the Working Group, to augment the existing 1300 tourist bed spaces in the region. Additionally, 375 beds were proposed within tourist self-catering accommodation, to augment the existing limited capacity of 230 such beds. An increase of 200 pitches for camping and touring caravans were to be on the area periphery, and not in its core. A 50% overall increase in tourist accommodation (i.e. 800 bed spaces) was agreed as appropriate in terms of the area's tourist economy.

The Working Group also saw the need to encourage more sporting activities such as horse-riding, sailing, canoeing and orienteering. Consequently, it was agreed that discussions on this should involve not only developers, but also the whole spectrum of public and voluntary sector bodies interested, the discussions aimed at economic success, but also to meet local community needs, plus the protection of nature and of the landscape affected. Emphasis was put on recognizing ecological fragility and landscape quality protection, when siting new provisions in the Growth Point.

With regard to attractions, proposals were made to encourage those which would emphasize local identity and reflect the area's history. This would include industrial archaeology, history, interpretation and promotion of craft centres, which sold products of a more regional character.

The potential need for tourism infrastructure and facilities (such as visitor car parking, toilets, tourist information centres and signage) was seen, and also the need for environmental improvement policies in selected locations.

Multiple stakeholder partnership: the Growth Point as a test model

Thus a unique total scheme was created by a wide range of bodies, some of which were the traditional opponents of tourism development. The planning of a total package, approved by the Minister, illustrated well how tourism development and conservation of heritage environmental resources are essentially interdependent.

To emphasize the comprehensiveness of the scheme, additional key elements were included. These covered promotion of the development package and its later marketing, plus monitoring of the project's results. As past interest in the area's tourist potential had been negligible, a concerted effort, and media launch, were all required to achieve 'lift off'. Detailed negotiations took place with key commercial interests like the breweries, regarding catering and building extensions to existing pubs and inns to increase the bed capacity for visitors. Farmers had to be encouraged to see tourism as a potential additional cash crop, and see that redundant farm buildings could be recycled for profitable new uses related to tourism income.

Regarding the farming sector, a planning design scheme to help farmers get planning permission with their building conversions, was initiated. As part of the 'marketing push', the inclusion of the area as part of wider tour packages, plus participation in overseas trade workshops and press and trade familiarization visits were proposed. Coordination of local authorities' roles and actions in the tourism sphere was recognized, as was the need to link to tourism attractions close to the Growth Point, as they were already tourist magnets.

Finally, with reference to research, it was agreed that a comprehensive research programme would monitor changes and performance, as 200 additional jobs in tourism was the target.

Evaluation of the Growth Point

By the 1980s it was possible to evaluate the effectiveness of the scheme, and its series of inter-related projects. The aim had been to show that cooperation can produce a comprehensive and integrated approach to tourism planning in a remote rural upland region. Comprehensive planning was undertaken in a short time period.

This comprehensive multiple stakeholder partnership model was new to rural England, and demonstrated a new approach: one of partnership between all the actors involved in tourism development and in natural heritage resource conservation and management. Many of the parties, who, in the past, had been assumed to be in conflict, were able to work closely together, in partnership. This scheme showed that cooperation and agreement can be achieved in planning terms both for tourism planning and for joint resource management, simultaneously, and anticipated future stakeholder partnerships that have since been seen in many countries, from the 1980s to the present day.

3   Planning for Economic Reconstruction and Change in a Post-war Communist State: Case Study of Poland (RMP)

Introduction

After the Second World War, Poland was so ravaged by the huge scale of destruction, and loss of life, that it took great will power and the concerted means of a communist state, to rebuild a nation, its life and economy, within new national boundaries. It became a test case in planning with limited means, under one political system, and then in the 1990s went through a second revolution, to change back to the capitalist state it had been in the 1930s. Most of this case study relates to the communist period, but a shorter latter part addresses the process and implications of the changeover.

The Challenges of Post-war Poland

Poland in 1945, under the control and influence of the Soviet Union, lost its eastern territories to Russia, and was compensated by being given part of East Prussia and other parts of East Germany. Geographically, the country moved westwards, while politically it was bound to the USSR, to the east. Largely a lowland country, sitting on the Great European Plain, Poland has been a victim of geography – attacked in its history from Russia to the east, from Sweden and Lithuania to the north, or by Germany or Austria and France to the west.

Occupying a land area of over 312,000 km², Poland is a large country, which in 1946 had a residual population of nearly 24 million, having lost six million or 22% of its pre-war residents killed in the war. The scale of destruction was enormous: 40% of all development in Poland was destroyed, 30% of the nation's housing stock was lost, as was 38% of national wealth. The capital city, Warsaw, was virtually wiped out, and an early decision was whether to abandon or to rebuild that major city. Issues of national identity and spirit affected key decisions in that period.

The basic challenges of that era were: (i) national reconstruction of a nation which was basically rural (but for three industrial zones); and (ii) to deal with its industrialization, urbanization, transportation and water supply. Conservation of national heritage was both psychologically important for a changed nation, and practically important for its identity, education and residual leisure. Thus the Catholic Church, National Parks, protected areas and restored built heritage, all had key roles in a state where survival by economic development was the prime concern.

The changes from 1945 to the mid-1960s were dramatic; urban population increased from 31% to 68% of the national total, while the population working in industry grew to 62% of the total, with agriculture down to 38%

and still dropping. Old heavy industry in the Silesian Coalfield, textiles in Lodz, and shipbuilding at Gdynia/Gdansk were supplemented by growth in new manufacturing and processing industries.

The Stage of Development and Motivations for Planning

Poland was thus a nation in transition from a rural to an urban industrial state in the postwar phase, with highly centralized governmental decision making, and radical policies imposed on the nation, as part of a political and bold economic manifesto. The state controlled all means of production, and could compulsorily purchase land. The proposed collectivization of agriculture failed due to individualism, the strength of rural smallholders, and a strong private enterprise tradition, in a nation whose roots were rural, in a land that was 25% wooded, and had 10% of its territory in lakeland, rivers, fallowland and rural settlements.

Industry and commerce were overwhelmingly run by the state and cooperative sectors, with a small residual private sector in housing, and very small enterprises, such as commercial milliners, with a few employees. Strong central government was complemented by 17 voivodships, or provinces, plus five major cities with voivodic or regional status. By 1962, of 746 towns in Poland, only 22 had over 100,000 residents. Elected bodies sat at the national, regional (voivodic) and local (poviat) levels. All of the three levels were given physical and economic planning powers, but the central authority could overrule lower tiers.

The aims of national change were to use public control over production, energy, economy, water and development, to achieve economic growth and wellbeing, with national economic and physical plans allocating roles and resources to specific regions and sectors. Redistribution of population was planned, linked to economic and physical reconstruction, and 'social improvement' via urbanization, industrialization and redevelopment of slum housing.

The Levels and Forms of Planning

From 1946 onwards the great emphasis was upon national and regional planning, with national economic planning dominant, but it having a spatial or physical component. Regional planning was about allocation of economic resources to regions, but their spatial, locational and transport elements were included. Local planning was largely the planning and control of physical development, but within parameters laid down regionally. The system was a top-down decision-making one, until 1955, when a degree of devolution was introduced, and it was not until 1965 that real devolution on selected matters was possible. Effective national planning of the physical environment did not come until 1972, by which time devolution was meaningful.

The structure of physical planning organization by the mid-1960s, according to Dr R. Dylewski (Institute of Physical Planning and Municipal Economy, Warsaw) is shown in Fig. 3.1, and the development of physical planning in Poland from 1945 to 1972, as defined by Dylewski and Travis, is given in Fig. 3.2.

The three levels of planning involved very different types of plan making, from plans made on the national level, via the regional level to the local level. National plan preparation was primarily economic – concerned with economic production in terms of sectors, such as those of manufacturing industry and agriculture, but also of the 'water economy', urban settlement development and infrastructure. The Water Economy Plan was an interesting example of communist resource planning, as it dealt with river navigation, water supply, water quality control, pollution control, flood control, development of reservoirs for urban water supply, water power, and use of lakes, rivers and sea for recreational use by workers. National guidelines were given for agriculture, the pattern of the settlement system, urban growth, industrial expansion and contraction, communications and transportation (especially railways), recreation planning, and the protection of landscapes for nature conservation, wildlife protection and amenity.

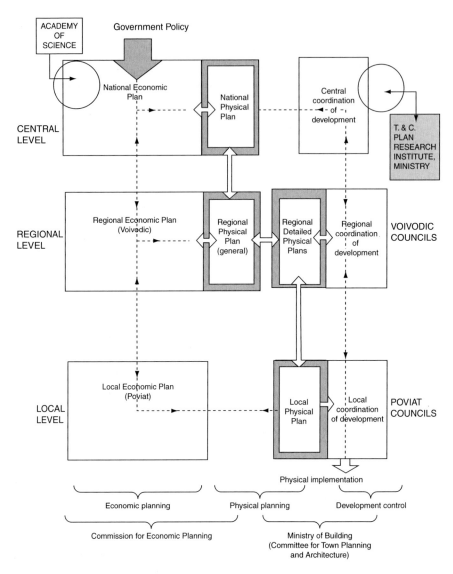

Fig. 3.1. The structure of physical planning organization in Poland in the mid-1960s (courtesy of R. Dylewski).

With regard to regional plan preparation two sorts of plan were prepared: (i) 'General Regional Plans' which were integrated economic and spatial plans for each region, covering all its territory; and (ii) 'Detailed Territorial Plans' which were plans for parts of the region, covered by the General Regional Plan, which were selected as areas of major change and/or of major conservation actions.

Local plan preparation was to be at three levels. First, as 'General Plans' for towns or conurbations, dealing with structure, land use and communications. Secondly, 'Detailed Plans' were to be prepared for parts of towns or conurbations where major changes were proposed (i.e. action-area plans). Finally, 'Executive Plans' were to be the site plans for development either inside or outside of specified action-areas.

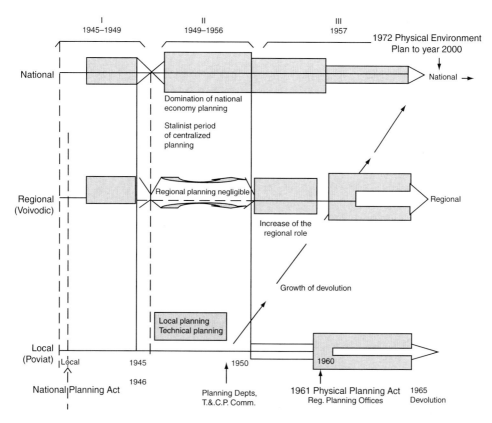

Fig. 3.2. Development of physical planning in Poland from 1945 to 1972 (defined by R. Dylewski and A.S. Travis).

This scale was to be very important in a land where destroyed built heritage of historic urban quarters (such as the Old Town of Warsaw) was to be reconstructed so as to look externally as it was before the war, but with modern internal amenities added. Historic castles, palaces and town halls were all rebuilt as they had looked before their destruction.

Strong state controls developed a nation heavily dependent upon public transport by rail and road, for access to priority leisure provisions for workers' 'remedial leisure time', and their holiday provisions in trade-union provided holiday centres, plus cooperative and voluntary sector provisions in the mountains, in the forests, at inland water centres and upon the coast.

An innovative bridge between the economic and physical planning systems was made by Professor Malisz's development of Threshold Analysis Theory, which became extensively used in Polish planning, and was later used in Yugoslav coastal development planning, and Scottish physical planning!

Planning for Leisure, Sport and Tourism in the 1960s and 1970s

From 1962 onwards, a Polish Government General Commission on Physical Culture and Tourism had central responsibility for overviewing sports provision and achievement, the leisure and refreshment of workers in their non-work time, and for their one annual holiday away from home. Leisure, sport and tourism in Poland, in this period thus had several components:

- provision for the rest and renewal of workers in their non-work hours, in their home regions;

- access to and encouragement to participate in high-achievement sports;
- provision of social tourism opportunities
domestically, for workers, youths and
retirees in their one annual holiday away
from home; and
- commercial tourism opportunities for
foreign visitors, to help the balance of
payments – the majority of tourists came
from the Council for Mutual Economic
Assistance (Comecon) countries.

The nationwide plans for leisure and
tourism were first drawn up in 1966 and 1969,
though an earlier large-scale regional tourism
development plan had been prepared for the
newly acquired long Baltic coastline.

Domestic tourism was provided by
trade unions (e.g. for coal miners and steel-
workers) for their members, by professional
associations (e.g. architects and writers) for
their members, with the Government and the
Party providing prestigious resorts for high
government circles. International tourism
was offered to foreign visitors by Orbis – a
state monopoly provider of hotels, restaurants, holiday packages and associated transfers. By 1974 up to 7.9 million foreign visitors
p.a. were visiting Poland, and 80% of these
were from Comecon (communist) countries.

Polish domestic and international tourism drew on three sets of resources:

- geographic accessibility of destinations
to home and foreign markets;
- the great natural resources of coasts, rivers,
lakes, forests, old woodlands, the mountain
zones, trails and facilities for tourists; and
- built and cultural heritage resources of
historic cities and towns, castles, palaces, monasteries, pilgrimage sites, birthplaces and battlefields and special sites
such as the salt mines of Wielicka and
former Nazi extermination camps like
Auschwitz.

By 1972 a new Environmental Ministry
was tackling large-scale environmental protection. Thus, as shown in Fig. 3.3 a complex system of National Parks, landscape
parks, Areas of Landscape Protection, nature
reserves, rural parks, old and new woodlands, Green Belt forests, tourism areas, and

major urban parks, was all in the process of
being created.

Taken overall, by the 1970s a domestic
tourism and leisure system had emerged
which was relatively sustainable in its
resource elements, in terms of natural heritage environment conservation and access,
and also as far as built heritage was involved,
but the newly built resorts and accommodation facilities had a short economic life in
terms of consumer market response. With
regard to transport, general access by rail
was energy efficient, but the steam trains,
using coal, were polluting and carbon producing, while the public road transport services were equally energy efficient, but based
on fossil fuel use were again carbon producing. Air transport was under-developed, and
the road system was a traditional one, at that
time lacking a network of motorways. Thus
in this post-war phase Poland did achieve
national reconstruction, physically and economically, with systems of leisure and tourism
provision, plus heritage resource conservation realized. Some of the obvious shortcom-
ings were in terms of personal freedoms and
local decision making, but despite gradual
liberalization of the political system, no one
expected the fundamental political and economic system changes that were to come to
Poland by the 1990s.

1990s and the Return of the Mixed Economy to Poland

In the aftermath of the 'Solidarity' phase, and
the collapse of the Berlin Wall, a period of
radical change to the economic and political
systems of Poland took place from 1989/1990
onwards. From 1992 to 1994 a European Union
(EU)-funded PHARE Tourism Development
Programme was realized in response to a
Polish Government request, to aid the systemic changeover process, and deal with four
aspects of tourism change. These four aspects
were:

- institutional strengthening;
- tourist product development;
- tourism promotion (marketing); and

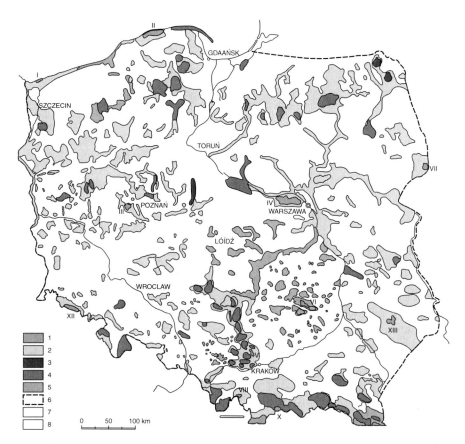

Fig. 3.3. Landscape protection in Poland. 1, National Parks; 2, proposed National Parks; 3, legally approved landscape parks; 4, proposed landscape parks; 5, Areas of Landscape Protection; 6, rural parks; 7, forests and Green Belt forests; 8, tourism areas (courtesy of Z. Karpowicz).

- tourism management and manpower development (i.e. vocational education and training for the tourism industry).

As at that time tourism was still under the aegis of the State Sport and Tourism Administration (SSTA), an intensive national re-tooling exercise was required for Poland to create a new competitive commercial tourist industry in a short time.

The Programme of Change

Initial changeover work included drafting new tourism legislation, and consumer protection legislation, to deal with the sudden appearance (and disappearance of) 'fly-by night' commercial travel agents. National market research on key foreign markets was carried out, trainers were trained in tourism marketing, and the first marketing literature in Polish was produced. There was privatization of state properties together with an enormous scale of foreign investment by multi-nationals in new hotel stock in three key cities. A Programme of National Infrastructure Development, with EU and World Bank help, led to the development of a national system of motorways (with service centres), investment in large new airports in three cities, plus some modernization of bus and railway stations. There was preparation of a National Tourism Strategy together with a re-assessment of national image and priority given to tourism marketing, but the development and improvement of tourist attractions safeguarded marketing integrity. Under-developed rural tourism was also aided.

Factors Against Sustainability

The following acted against the development of sustainable tourism in Poland: (i) the explosive increase in capacity of airline access to and from Poland and the introduction of cheap airlines; (ii) the great increase in private car traffic; and (iii) the growth in carbon emissions. However, by 1993, counteracting these factors, were seven examples of a move towards sustainable tourism in Poland:

1. The work of the Institute for Sustainable Development in Warsaw, aiding integrated major environment and wildlife protection programmes in north-east Poland.
2. The work of the France-Pologne Foundation, feeding back to Poland the French experience of Gîtes de France, and work on spa renovation and modernization.
3. Work by the Polish Ministry of Agriculture on sustainable farm tourism, via its regional colleges.

4. Creation of new eco-trekking opportunities by the voluntary sector in the mountains and in the Lake District of Mazuria.
5. The development of 'PTTK' – a Polish voluntary-sector tourist body aiding eco-sightseeing for members.
6. Clean-up campaigns to deal with poor and dirty air quality in the cities, and cleaning the waters of dirty rivers and the polluted sea coastline.
7. The establishment of new commercial eco-tourist firms developing ecotourism offers in Poland and abroad.

Sustainable Tourism Products

Post-war Polish sustainable tourism products include rural walking tours, lake and river boating holidays, birdwatching and climbing offers – based on access by train or coach. Since the late 1990s expansion of private car ownership and of major road developments, rather than rail modernization and expansion, now put at risk some existing good sustainable products. The introduction of cheap international air transport has enabled the growth of outward and inward international tourism, but with a heavy carbon footprint.

4 The Pilbara: a Sub-national Australian Study in 21st Century Resource Development Planning

Jim and Wanda Kaucz

Introduction

The Pilbara is a vast, diverse region – extending over an area of 507,896 km² – approximately 20% of the area of the state of Western Australia (WA), or equal to one and two-thirds the size of Poland. Located between the 20th and 23rd parallels, the region is defined on the west by the Indian Ocean and on the east by the north–south border of the Northern Territory (Fig. 4.1). The region supports a sparse resident population of about 41,000 people, according to the 2006 Census (Australian Bureau of Statistics, 2006). This compares with a population of over 38 million in Poland. The major settlements of the region are: (i) Port Hedland; (ii) Karratha; (iii) Newman; and (iv) Tom Price.

The Pilbara is one of the largest mineral-producing provinces in the world. In recent decades, the Pilbara has become prominent because of the success of its resource-based industries operating successfully in the global economy. The exploitation of its large reserves of minerals and hydrocarbons has given the region major economic significance, to both WA, and to the Commonwealth of Australia. The salient features of the region are summarized in Table 4.1.

Physical Setting

The Pilbara is a diverse region. It has mountain ranges, deserts, plains and numerous offshore islands. Climatically, the region is defined as semi-arid, having high temperatures, low and inconsistent rainfall, and a high level of moisture evaporation. Rainfall is usually associated with cyclonic activity – a phenomenon that impacts upon the region between November and April each year, to varying degrees. The Pilbara is considered the most cyclone-prone area in Australia.

The region can be divided into three planning subregions (Fig. 4.2), which relate to groupings of bioregions, namely: (i) the coastal plain and offshore islands; (ii) The Pilbara tablelands; and (iii) the Pilbara desert country. Each has its own unique characteristics and natural and cultural heritage values.

Historical Perspective

Culturally and economically, the Pilbara is the product of the cultural legacy of its indigenous Aboriginal people; plus the European settlers' pastoral legacy, and the more recent and ongoing mining legacy. The Pilbara is home to a number of indigenous people, who have a strong traditional connection to the landscapes,

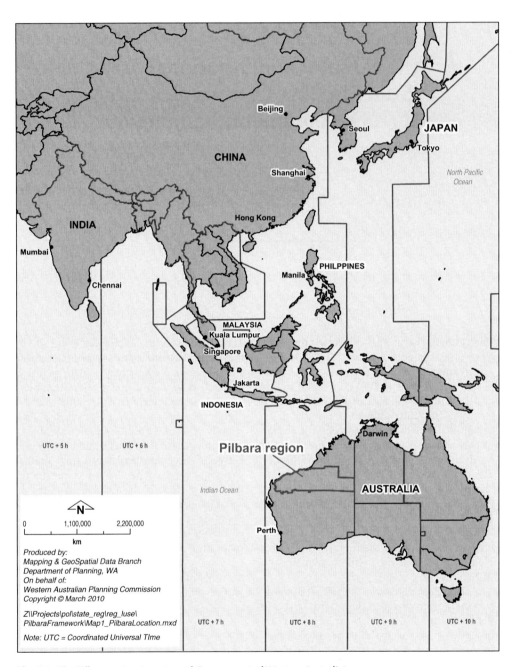

Fig. 4.1. The Pilbara region (courtesy of Government of Western Australia).

which provide the basis for their spirituality, beliefs and social systems. There is archaeological evidence to suggest some 30,000 years of indigenous settlement. Over 30 distinct socio-cultural groups are evident, and indigenous culture and kinship networks remain strong.

Early European settlement occurred at Roebourne and the port of Cossack. Early development was associated with pastoral use and gold mining on the land and pearl fishing offshore. Until the start of iron ore mining in the 1960s, the only towns were Onslow, Roebourne, Point Samson (which

Table 4.1. Salient features of the Pilbara.

Feature	
Semi-arid region	Challenging environment for urban development
	Highly remote location
Displaced Aboriginal heritage	Aboriginal kinship networks and cultural heritage
	Gradual urbanization of Aboriginal population
Pastoral settlement	Cattle grazing was the dominant land use until the 1960s
	Fishing/pearling at Port Hedland, Onslow and Point Samson
Rapid settlement growth since the1960s	Town populations: 5450 (1966) > 38,120 (2006)[a]
Region's economic importance (gross	23% of WA's raw gross state product (2006/07)
regional product: A$7.6 billion)	8% of WA's employment (2005/06)
	45% of WA's export income (2006/07)
	61% of WA's gross resource production (2006/07)
Key settlement issues	Land development constraints
	Housing supply and affordability
	Community facilities and services

[a] These are the summation of census population counts for the region's urban areas (1966 and 2006) rounded to the nearest ten (Australian Bureau of Statistics, 1966, 2006).

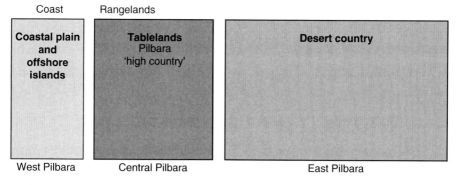

Fig. 4.2. Pilbara planning subregions.

Table 4.2. Settlement establishment (Source: Western Australian Planning Commission, 2009).

Coastal settlement	Date	Inland settlement	Date
Roebourne	1866	Marble Bar	1893
Cossack	1872	Nullagine	1899
Onslow	1883	Wittenoom	1947
Port Hedland	1896	Tom Price	1967
Point Samson	1910	Newman	1968
Dampier	1966	Pannawonica	1970
Karratha	1968	Paraburdoo	1971
Wickham	1970		

replaced Cossack as the port servicing Roebourne), Wittenoom, Marble Bar, Nullagine and Port Hedland. Today's settlement pattern is largely the product of mining development that had its genesis in the 1960s. This

especially applies to the inland settlements of Newman, Pannawonica, Paraburdoo and Tom Price, but also to the coastal settlements of Dampier, Karratha and Wickham (see Table 4.2).

Pilbara's Population

The Pilbara towns experienced significant population growth from the mid-1960s to the early 1980s. However, this has levelled out in more recent years (Fig. 4.3).

The key features of the Pilbara's population structure are:

- relatively low median age: 31;
- relatively high ratio of males to females (55:45);

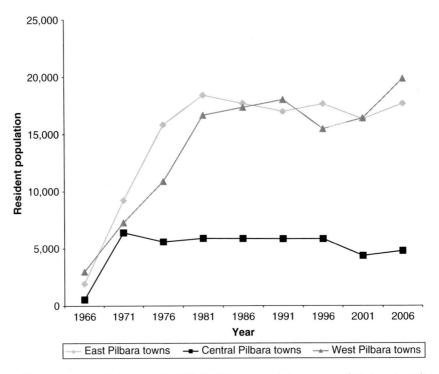

Fig. 4.3. Pilbara towns' population growth: 1966–2006 (courtesy of Government of Western Australia).

- high proportion in the pre-school and prime school age groups (0–14);
- relatively low proportion in the senior high school/tertiary age group (15–24);
- high proportion in the prime working age group (25–54);
- low proportions in the pre-retirement (55–64) and retiree (65+) age groups;
- high median individual, family and household incomes;
- relatively high residential turnover rate (the so-called 'churn factor'); and
- significant transient fly-in fly-out (FIFO) population.

Economic Drivers

With a gross regional product of A$7.6 billion, the Pilbara accounts for:

- 23% of WA's raw or crude gross state product (2006/07);
- 8% of WA's employment (2005/06);

- 45% of WA's export income (2006/07); and
- 61% of WA's gross resource production (2006/07).

The Pilbara's contribution to the total value of WA's mineral and hydrocarbon production in 2006/07 was 61%. Together, BHP Billiton, Rio Tinto and the North West Shelf venture account for just under half of the state's total exports.

A Demand-led Approach to Development

The Pilbara's mining-based economy evolved in the late 1960s. It was developed largely on the basis of overseas (American) capital investment, with the mineral ore being supplied to overseas markets (such as Japan). Initially the commodities being mined were gold, and later asbestos. When the Australian Federal Government relaxed its restrictions on the export of iron ore, which had been imposed at the start of the Second World War, this mineral then became the prime commodity, and its exploitation underpinned the development of the urban infrastructure in the Pilbara region. By 2010, the region's main iron ore market was China, which had become a major investor in the developing mining of the region's magnetite iron ore reserves.

Mining company roles

The region's system of mines, railways and ports underwent a process of rationalization, through the roles of BHP Billiton and Rio Tinto Iron Ore companies. BHP Billiton assumed responsibility for Newman (Fig. 4.4) and to some extent for Port Hedland, while Rio Tinto Iron Ore assumed responsibility for Tom Price, Paraburdoo, Dampier and Wickham. In Rio Tinto's case, being the municipal manager for five townships placed a considerable burden upon the company.

Offshore hydrocarbons

The development of the 'North West Shelf' in the 1980s was to become WA's largest export project, generating almost A$12.75 billion in export revenues (2008), through the resultant sale of liquefied natural gas, oil and condensate. This sector has experienced a degree of value adding with the development of Indian-owned Burrup Fertilisers at Dampier in 2003. It is anticipated that Dampier's fertilizer industry will be further expanded on the basis of Indian investment. Major new initiatives in the hydrocarbons sector are: (i) Woodside's Pluto project (A$11 billion Dampier facility); and (ii) Chevron's Gorgon project (A$43 billion Barrow Island facility).

Supply-led Resource Potentials

There have been a number of government-led initiatives that have assisted the development of the Pilbara's resource sector. The most significant of these were the development of the

Fig. 4.4. Mt Whaleback mining terraces at Newman (photograph courtesy of Gordon Bluk).

town of Karratha and the construction of the Dampier–Bunbury natural gas pipeline – during the times of the Brand and Court Liberal-Country Coalition Governments.

The town of Karratha was gazetted (i.e. formally designated) in 1968 by the West Australian Government, to meet the growing demands of the resource sector on the town of Dampier, which had been originally developed by Pilbara Iron. Karratha was intended to house both Pilbara iron workers and workers on the North West Shelf projects.

The Dampier–Bunbury gas pipeline (1596 km in length) was constructed by the State Energy Commission (SECWA) with the support of Alcoa and it was commissioned in 1985. The pipeline (often referred to as 'the backbone of WA') transports natural gas from the processing facility on the Pilbara's Burrup Peninsula, down to Perth's industrial hub at Kwinana and industries in the Bunbury area, in the state's south-west. The pipeline currently contributes up to 50% of WA's primary energy use and fuels up to 60% of the state's electricity generation capacity. This pipeline is interconnected with all the other major gas transmission pipelines in WA.

Other significant support infrastructure provided by the government include the region's road system and four airports with runways capable of accommodating Boeing 737 aircraft.

Comparisons with Past Resource Development Areas in Australia

The big difference between the development of the Pilbara, and that of the early gold mining centres – such as Ballarat and Bendigo, in the State of Victoria – is that those early goldfields were relatively close to Melbourne, with a temperate climate, a rich hinterland, and offered a wide range of economic and social opportunities. Pilbara's remoteness, its climate and other constraints have made it a much more difficult region to develop, with far higher development-cost thresholds to cross in the process.

Constraints

Infrastructure

When large-scale modern mining started in the 1960s, this remote region had minimal infrastructure. There were no sealed roads, railway lines, airports, water pipelines, nor electricity transmission lines in the region. The only existing urban infrastructure was at Port Hedland, Roebourne, Marble Bar and Nullagine. In order to extract the minerals, the mining companies were thus required to provide, in addition to the mine-site facilities, a rail network, urban and port infrastructure, power, water and waste-water treatment plants.

Railways and ports

The mining companies constructed three mine-to-port standard-gauge railway systems – reputed to be the largest privately-owned rail system in the world. This system has been rationalized as two independent networks, controlled by BHP Billiton and Rio Tinto Iron Ore. A third rail system has been established by Fortescue Metals Group (FMG), which accesses the port of Port Hedland. Two additional rail systems were under consideration by 2010: (i) one linking mining areas to the south of the region with a potential new port at Dixon Island, to the west of Cape Lambert; and (ii) the other linking mining areas to the north of Newman with Port Hedland.

There has been a continuing legal battle by the 'junior' mining companies to gain access to these major established railway networks. Urban infrastructure has had to be provided in six new settlements and port infrastructure has had to be developed in three new ports.

Energy

Energy provision has been an additional constraint. Initial use of diesel has given way to use of offshore gas-fired power stations to provide power to the mine sites, and the growing number of towns in the Pilbara region. Despite the availability of constant sunshine, the use of solar power in the Pilbara tends to be restricted to street lighting and to powering installations such as level crossings, pipeline pumps and telecommunications in remote situations. However, small hybrid diesel/solar power stations were proposed by 2010, for the remote settlements of Marble Bar and Nullagine.

Water

Initially, bore fields were associated with the seasonal river systems and in one instance a dam (that of Harding Dam serving the town of Karratha). The inland mining areas were producing a water surplus by 2010, as the mining activities were excavating below the water table. However, the coastal areas were about to experience a significant water shortage by 2010, as the urban areas at Port Hedland, Karratha, Dampier and Onslow were all set to expand significantly. There is the prospect of moving to greater reliance on seawater desalination as the main source of domestic water supply.

Housing

The availability and cost of housing is a major issue for the region. The resource companies have been and remain the main suppliers of housing. The majority of the region's dwellings were built in the 1970s and are in need of renovation or replacement. Major housing shortages have led to workers and their families resorting to the use of temporary accommodation, such as cabins and caravans. Apart from the lack of stock, a key issue is affordability – particularly for contractors and service sector workers, who are not provided with housing as part of their employment packages. State government agencies such as 'Land Corp' and the Department of Housing are making significant progress in housing provision.

To meet cyclone construction standards, house construction is primarily steel frame on a concrete pad with ribbed steel cladding. To speed up delivery, *in situ* construction is being supplemented by the use of pre-assembled modules, transported in the main from Perth and Queensland. BHP Billiton has been proactive in designing more environmentally sustainable dwellings – good examples being the new ecovillages in Newman.

Community facilities

After provision of work and housing, the quality of community facilities, such as health and education are major factors, influencing the length of time a family will stay in the region.

Health and education

Although there have been significant improvements, the standard of the region's hospitals and schools continues to be a cause of concern. Most expectant mothers travel to Perth for giving birth, and many senior secondary school children finish their education at a Perth private school.

Childcare

In the Pilbara a childcare place is as valuable as gold! These are highly valued by industry. Childcare allows the primary care giver the opportunity to re-join the workforce, thus increasing the size of the local labour force without the need for additional housing. There continues to be a shortage of childcare facilities, although this shortfall was being addressed in 2009/10, with the support of industry.

Recreation

The region is highly dependent on outdoor sporting and recreation activities. Because of the climate, water plays an important role in recreation facility provision – the coast and swimming pools. The Pilbara has five Olympic-size swimming pools for a population that would normally justify one! Each town has a well-equipped and well-maintained sports field complex – irrigated and well lit for evening use.

Challenges and Choices

The disconnect between population and economic activity

There has been a growing lack of connection in WA, between the growing economic activity in its north, and the expanding population base in its south. Cost pressures, labour shortages and developing technologies are creating a major physical separation between the site of wealth creation (predominantly up north in the Pilbara) and settlement (Perth and the south-west) (Pickford, 2009). Much of the recent investment in residential development in Perth and the south-west is being funded by people working away and living temporarily in the Pilbara.

Search for new models

To date, developers of the Pilbara region have generally adopted a mining-town mentality, being subject to boom-and-bust cycles, closely aligned to the fortunes of global commodity markets. Key issues that have recently exercised the minds of decision makers in the resource companies, governments and local communities have included:

- the need to attract a workforce and staff retention;
- the need to build community by reducing the reliance on 'FIFO' workforces;
- the implications of proposed remote operation of mine sites and railways;
- the need for greater investment in community facilities and urban infrastructure;
- initiatives fostering greater indigenous engagement in mining activities;
- third-party access to the region's rail systems (third-party access refers to the provision of access to a company-owned rail network by a competing company); and
- opportunities for greater economic diversification through supply-chain completion, tourism (Fig. 4.5), governance and services.

Feedback from other models of regional development are being looked at by local councils in the Pilbara region. They are examining places and experiences at diverse locations – from Dubai to Darwin, and the towns of North Queensland, such as Cairns, Townsville, Mackay and Rockhampton.

Fig. 4.5. The high quality landscape resource of the interior with tourist and conservation potential (photograph courtesy of Government of Western Australia).

Community benefit from mineral exploitation

Following a long period of lobbying for greater government investment in the region's communities, to make them more attractive places in which to live, the current state government came into power on the back of a campaign agenda to provide more 'royalties for the regions'. Thus at the start of 2010 there was the expectation that a greater proportion of the royalties generated by resource development in the Pilbara region would be invested directly in the region.

Evaluation

The West Australian Government, after a period in which it adopted a laissez-faire approach to development, is taking a more proactive stance towards the development of the Pilbara region. To address WA's disconnection between wealth creation and settlement growth, it has recently launched the 'Pilbara Cities' initiative, which focuses upon the revitalization of Karratha, Port Hedland, Newman and Tom Price. There is a growing impetus to establish a critical mass of population in the Pilbara, with a more diverse and sustainable economic base. It has been suggested that the state government will need to make a decision about a Pilbara city development, which could be almost as momentous as that made by the British Admiralty in the 1820s, when it advocated the establishment of the Swan River colony at Perth.

In many case studies in this book, the development of a region has been based on tourism, as the prime generating factor. In the case of the Pilbara, its development has been propelled by the development of its rich mineral resources. This has required the development of roads and urban infrastructure, which has, as a by-product, made the region accessible for tourism. While the development of this region's tourism has in recent times been stunted by the loss of visitor accommodation to 'FIFO' workforces, the Pilbara has great potential to become a major tourist destination – possibly rivalling the Queensland Sunshine Coast. It has an array of natural and cultural tourism assets: (i) the raw natural beauty of the Hamersley and Chichester mountain ranges; (ii) its pristine coastline with its island archipelagos, abundant aquatic life and marine parks; (iii) the appeal of quality wilderness in its National Parks and conservation reserves; and (iv) indigenous cultural tourism – not to mention mine-based industrial tourism! If Sharm el Sheikh, set in Egypt's arid Sinai Peninsula, can be developed as a major international tourism magnet – why not the Pilbara, which already has a domestic tourism pull to 'grey nomads'?

The way that Pilbara has been developed is not following a crude classical 'Klondike Model', but shows long-term community interest of existing and future residents, and the need strategically to settle the north-west of Australia, leading to a new set of requirements in regional development.

5 The Netherlands: a European Case Study of a Nation Planning with an Over Abundance of Water

Introduction

The Netherlands is a densely populated country of 16.5 million people on a land area of some 41,526 km². It is a flatland, much of it well below sea level, protected by dykes and pumping systems, having had a 700-year historic battle to protect itself from the sea and rivers. It has added to its land stock through reclamation from the sea, from swamps and from marshland. The population is concentrated in the west of the country on the core of the Randstad ('rim or edge city'), a circular rim made up of a linked cluster of its major cities, ports, towns, transport and industrial foci. There are four large cities within the Randstad, of which one, Amsterdam, the great historical trading city with a resident population of about one million, has long had international tourist appeal. The country is divided into some 11 provinces and some 850 municipalities (or Gementeen).

Government

In terms of government, the Netherlands has a constitutional monarchy and a two-chamber parliament called the States General. The first chamber is indirectly elected from members of the Provincial Councils, while the second chamber is directly elected by national universal election.

The Dutch Rijkswaterstaat, or State Water Authority, is sometimes called 'a state within a state' and has powers to control the complex hydrology of the state, with is sea defences, systems of drainage, locks, sluices, pumping stations, etc., that are vital to the continued and safe economic life of the country, much of who's surface sits below sea level.

The Netherlands and Israel are mirror opposites, in terms of their relationship to water abundance and water shortage, and the means of survival in a land which is either water abundant or has a national water shortage.

There is a great historical paradox as far as the Netherlands is concerned, in relationship to its acceptance of a high degree of state interference and controls related to survival and yet it is fundamentally an individualist, commercial and aggressively trading society. The Netherlands is a Christian nation, which has historically been divided between its Catholic and Protestant sectors of the population, but both share an overwhelming Protestant work ethic so that religion and values relate closely to an urge to work, to achieve, to cooperate and to accept the notion of work, and rest from it, but have a more reluctant view of 'indulgent tourism' as opposed to rest and relaxation from work.

Stage and state of development – motivations for planning

While there is a long history of the development of water planning in the Netherlands its other fundamental planning is for control of land use, for transportation and the economy. Recreation and tourism planning is of a much more recent vintage. The general planning system evolved in the period before the Second World War, but became fully developed and operational in the post-war reconstruction period. The fully developed planning system can be said to have had its major phase

of development from the 1960s through to 2005. A new planning system started in 2006 and these two systems are compared.

The Old Planning System 1960s–2005: Basic Problems

While regional park and forest recreational provision in the Netherlands to meet majority recreation needs were extensively developed, the national park and national landscape park systems needed further development and were already under review by the 1970s (see Fig. 5.1). Parts of the coastal beach/dune

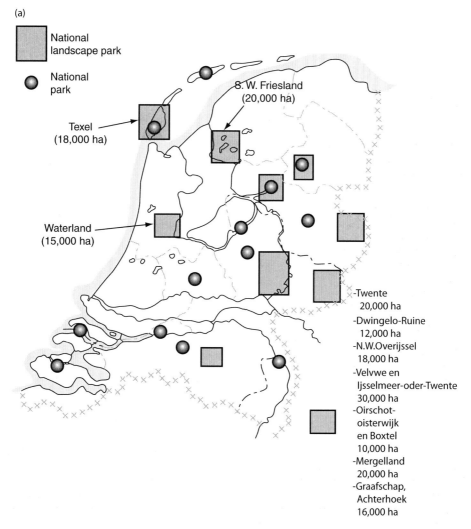

Fig. 5.1. The old system, 1960s–2005: Dutch strategic and management planning. (a) national parks and national landscape parks.

(b)

Fig. 5.1. Continued. (b) national parkland (the old system).

resources were under great pressure as well, especially near the developed seaside resorts.

Integrated management mechanisms were lacking for the provision of domestic urban leisure. The management systems, such as for the so-called Recreational Communities (Recreatiegemeenschap), needed simplifying as they were complex, too top-heavy and hyper-democratic organizations. The general planning system in the country was a system designed to be one of regulation and control. This went from national reports (Notas) laying down all of the related systems for land use, transportation and conservation, at the national scale, via provincial plans (known as 'Streekplanen'), down to the local or municipality level, where a system of detailed strict control (known as local statutory municipal plans or 'Bestemmingsplanen') were applied.

(c)

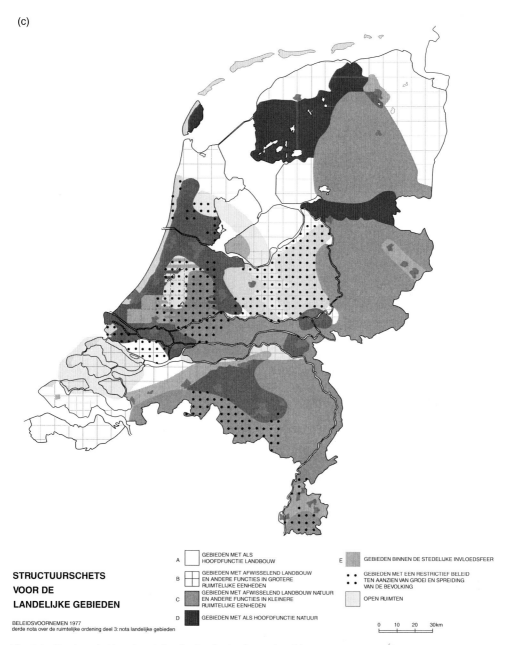

STRUCTUURSCHETS
VOOR DE
LANDELIJKE GEBIEDEN

BELEIDSVOORNEMEN 1977
derde nota over de ruimtelijke ordening deel 3: nota landelijke gebieden

A GEBIEDEN MET ALS HOOFDFUNCTIE LANDBOUW

B GEBIEDEN MET AFWISSELEND LANDBOUW EN ANDERE FUNCTIES IN GROTERE RUIMTELIJKE EENHEDEN

C GEBIEDEN MET AFWISSELEND LANDBOUW NATUUR EN ANDERE FUNCTIES IN KLEINERE RUIMTELIJKE EENHEDEN

D GEBIEDEN MET ALS HOOFDFUNCTIE NATUUR

E GEBIEDEN BINNEN DE STEDELIJKE INVLOEDSFEER

•• GEBIEDEN MET EEN RESTRICTIEF BELEID TEN AANZIEN VAN GROEI EN SPREIDING VAN DE BEVOLKING

OPEN RUIMTEN

0   10   20   30km

Fig. 5.1. Continued. (c) national sketch plan for land use (the old system) (courtesy of RPD).

These local plans defined the use of every plot of land, whether it was for residential, industrial, recreational, tourist, military or any other use, and specified detailed recreational uses such as camping and caravan sites, as well as recreational forests. In the old system the constraint of affluence affected budgets, attitudes and non-sharing, as did the division of the country into two primary religious communities, one Catholic and one Protestant, which constrained everything by duplication of facilities, and a consequent shortage of some other community budgets. The traditions of natural resource management (of forests, lands and waters) were stronger than the traditions and abilities of people or visitor management within the Netherlands (see Fig. 5.2).

Resources for tourism and recreation, upon which the tourist products are based in the Netherlands comprise:

(a)

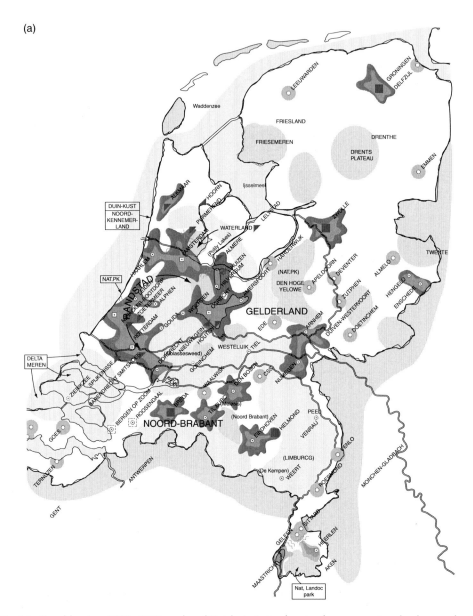

Fig. 5.2. The old system 1960s–2005: scales of Dutch strategic planning for conservation, land use and recreation. (a) national structure plan for urban development, conservation and recreation.

(b)

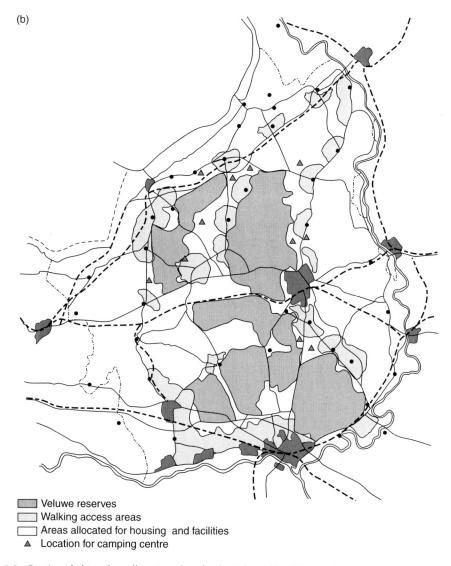

Veluwe reserves
Walking access areas
Areas allocated for housing and facilities
▲ Location for camping centre

Fig. 5.2. Continued. (b) outline allocation plans for the Veluwe (the old system).

- Historic cities like Amsterdam and the large number of historic towns like Delft, many of which are ports. These have urban built heritage, museums, parks and attractions and also cater extensively for sports.
- The sea coast and the seaside resorts.
- The countryside resources including the Veluwe, the Heuvelrug, the tulip bulb fields, the Friesian lakes, the islands beyond the Wadden See, Dutch State Forests and regions like Drenthe.
- Water resources including canals, canal trips, fishing, boating, the great rivers, sailing/boating holidays, etc.
- Theme parks and man-made attractions.

The importance of the heaths, woodlands and dune landscapes of the centrally located Veluwe as a major land resource for outdoor recreation and tourism is especially

(c)

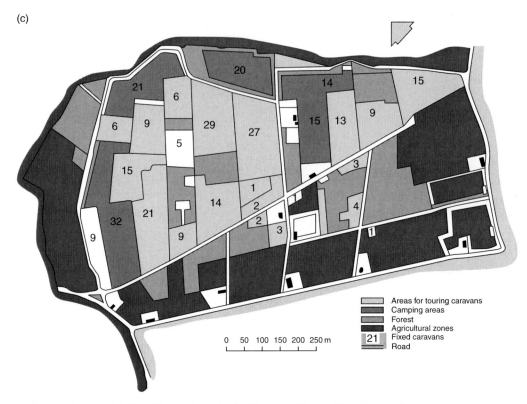

Fig. 5.2. Continued. (c) local (recreation) plan for Noenes in Haaren (the old system).

important for Dutch domestic visits. In the old system there were 5-yearly Open Air Recreation and Tourism Plans which were very important in relation to the tourism and recreation sector.

Who are the tourists?

While international tourists are drawn in large numbers to the historic cities and some of the larger seaside resorts within the Netherlands, it is the domestic tourists who largely use the countryside and inland water resources of the country. Domestic bed nights account for over 80% of all the tourist bed nights spent in the Netherlands and roughly half of the long holidays are spent in chalets, bungalows and holiday villages, while almost a half of the long holidays are spent in tents or caravans on so-called camping and caravan sites.

Development planning for tourism and recreation 1960s–2005

The system of development for tourism and recreation

During this earlier period planning for recreation and tourism in the Netherlands was primarily related to three arms of government:

1. Financial allocations (e.g. £30 million in 1975) and intentions for outdoor recreation planning in the countryside, which were in the 1960s and 1970s vested in the Ministry of Culture, Recreation and Social Welfare (CRM) at the central government level. The Ministry also had interests in nature conservation and urban cultural provisions – this was all to change later.

2. The general overview of national planning whereby recreational and heritage resource conservation objectives were linked to other development, was vested centrally in the

(d)

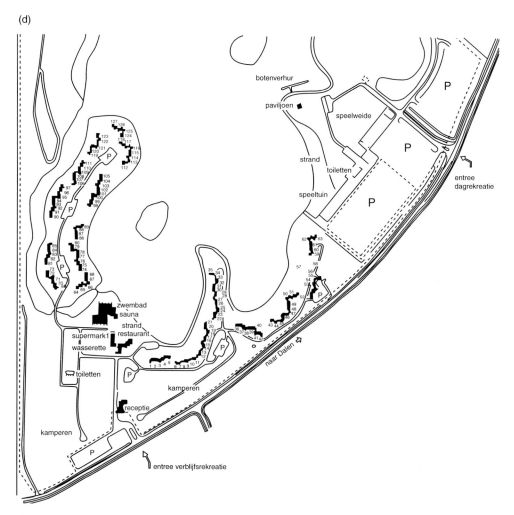

Fig. 5.2. Continued. (d) site plan (old system) showing the high quality waterside recreational villages of Sporthuis Centrum (courtesy of RPD).

Ministry of Housing and Planning. Figure 5.1c shows an indicative National Structure Plan for the Netherlands as prepared under the Derda Nota (or Third National Report) in the 1976/77 period. This defined the land uses and key water uses and can be related to the other maps in Fig. 5.1, which show the systems of national parks and the proposals in that period for the development of further national parks as well as a system of national landscape parks.

3. Planning for tourism was vested in the Ministry of Economic Affairs nationally. Tourism marketing abroad was looked after by the Nederlands Bureaux voor Toerisme (NBT), the national tourist board, which was financed by the Ministry of Economic Affairs. Tourism information services to both foreign and domestic tourists were offered by the local tourist information offices (the VVVs) – the VVV system of 400–500 units had national, provincial and local or municipal components, and the system was responsible for the national network of tourist information centres. This system was partly funded by the public sector and partly by the commercial sector.

The system of planning and development was organized at three levels (national, provincial and local or municipal levels), but via a structure which was far more complex than they seemed to be. This is all illustrated in Fig. 5.3.

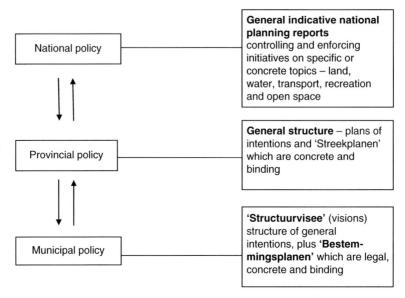

Fig. 5.3. The structure of the old planning control system 1960s–2005 (courtesy of Delta Commissie).

The sector of tourism in the Netherlands and attitudes to recreational development

The strong Calvinist or Protestant work ethic in Dutch society (as already mentioned) sees active outdoor recreation as important and valued as a process of refreshing and renewing people for their work life, which was seen as fundamental. Therefore, substantial financial and land space allocations and planning for nature conservation, national outdoor recreation in the countryside and upon the water were seen as very important by the Dutch population.

Anti-tourist lobbies and feelings were strong in the public sector in the 1970s, and resource allocation to tourism was poor, political powers were kept weak and there was an uphill battle to get things done in this area by the public sector, as the assumption was that it was a commercial-sector field. The tourist industry as far as the public sector was concerned in the Netherlands had a slightly besieged quality about it. On the other hand, leisure services tended to be separate functional services, and integrated leisure-services planning in urban areas was undeveloped in this period.

The very strong pressures for action in the recreation and tourism field were particularly focused upon: (i) heritage conservation; (ii) nature resource protection; (iii) recreational

forest provision; (iv) water recreation provision; and (v) the maintenance of environmental quality. Developers felt constrained by the power of the green mafia (or series of voluntary-sector pressure groups) in this period. In the old system the conservation-planning idea was under-developed, the tourism and recreation lobby was relatively weak compared with the nature conservation lobby (which was relatively strong), while the green forces for environmental protection were relatively weak and ineffective in the 1970s but grew stronger between the 1970s and 1990s.

Research base of policy and action

In the old system, the CRM was the major sponsor of research on recreation, cultural provisions and nature conservation. State support was given to agencies such as Breda's National Institute for Recreation and Tourism Research. There were three specialist state research institutes with regard to natural systems, and contract research was sponsored in the universities with regard to leisure and recreation. Independent research was done at places like the Institute of Land and Water Management at Wageningen Agricultural University. Research was also done by special foundations (e.g. Stichting Recreatie) and dissemination was done by them as well as by government ministries, and at day conferences run by the voluntary-sector ANWB (the national motoring organization which started as a cycling organization).

Evaluation

The Netherlands appeared to have good planning in this period with a plan-making and plan-adoption tradition. Planning for outdoor recreation provision in particular was in a state of organized complexity, despite the centralized major responsibilities for it being vested in the CRM.

A large amount of good countryside and coastal provisions for active and passive recreation were realized by bodies such as the State Forestry Service (Staatsbosbeheer) and the Polder Development Authority. Urban provisions were more unbalanced, and by the 1970s tourism plans for regions were more of an idea rather than a reality. In the 1980s TROPS, or Tourist Recreation Plans, were developed for the provincial and subregional level but these tended to be guidance or indicative documents rather than statutory documents.

While in the old system, water planning as a prime national system was taken for granted, the focus in the planning control systems was upon not only water planning, but also upon the controlled use of land, transportation and outdoor recreation planning, plus the conservation of high quality landscape resources. While planning for outdoor recreation was seen as an integral part of the planning system, tourism was seen separately as a market force which was dealt with primarily by the private sector. The hotels, restaurants and catering sector (or as it is known in the Netherlands 'Horeca') is largely a private-sector system with some public-sector involvement with regard to standards, consumer protection, health and public safeguards. The system of planning was a comprehensive one but it was defensive and reactive and is now seen to have been slow and somewhat inflexible. Dissatisfaction over time led to a major fundamental review and the introduction of a new planning system starting in 2006.

The quality of natural resource management work upon conservation and recreation zones in the polders, in the countryside and in the coastal dune parks, as well as in the national landscape parks and national parks, plus work in the forest parks, was of an extraordinary high quality. Dutch residents obtained great satisfaction from the large-scale outdoor recreation provision made, especially by the public sector.

General Approaches to Planning in the Netherlands

Economic planning and the role of tourism

The very small tourism unit or division within the Ministry of Economic Affairs had its origins in a hotels directorate in the trade division of that Ministry in 1948. Its original task had been the reconstruction of hotels destroyed by war. In 1959 the tourism division was linked to wholesale and retail trade. By 1978 two divisions existed in the Ministry relating to tourism: (i) for tourism and the international balance of payment returns; and (ii) for hotels, restaurants, cafés, transport and services. The Ministry of Economic Affairs' investment in tourist infrastructure was related very much to a stop-go policy with periods of spending and no spending. Much of the tourist infrastructure was provided by other arms of government, such as by Ministries responsible for transport and water engineering. For a period, a selective investment regulation act governed hotel investment in the country. Dutch economic planning was both aspatial nationally, and spatial in provincial policy terms.

Physical planning in the Netherlands and planning for recreation

National planning for recreation conservation was covered in such national reports as the Derda Nota (see Fig. 5.1) or the Third National Report on National Planning which integrated the intentions of the CRM with those of the Rijks Planning Dienst (RPD) or State Planning

Service and there was a National Coordinating Committee on Open-air Recreation.

State and provincial budgets were allocated for provisions which resulted from general recreation plans or subject plans for recreation at the regional scale, and municipal authorities planned their own provisions and funding. Area planning for recreation was undertaken by special Area Recreation Authorities or Recreatiegemeenschappen (see Fig. 5.4), complicated bodies which were run by several local authorities and representatives of provincial and other government and tourism interests. In Fig. 5.2 examples are shown of the National Structure Plan for Urban Development Conservation and Recreation in the Netherlands and within that the location of the Veluwe (Fig. 5.2b), which was the subject of a 'Facetstreekplan', which was then managed by a Recreatiegemeenschap. Examples in Fig. 5.2 also show a 'Bestemmingsplan', for an area which is largely for recreational land uses

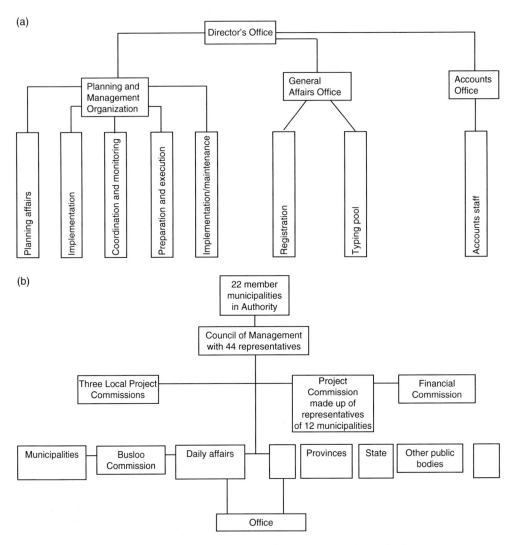

Fig. 5.4. Old and new Dutch systems: Recreatiegemeenschap (Area Recreation Authority) – management and democratic accountability of the authority. (a) Organization of the Recreation Planning Office; (b) governmental and other membership of the Recreation Authority (courtesy of Veluwe Authority).

in this particular instance at Noenes (Fig. 5.2c). An example is also given of a development by the Sporthuis Centrum organization and this is for the recreational village known as Huttenheugte (Fig. 5.2d).

Levels of planning

Several types of plan for recreation evolved depending on a number of mechanisms used, for example: (i) urban regional recreation plans, such as that developed for the Rijnmond region, centring on Rotterdam and upon the Great Waterway, and implemented by a mixture of provincial and municipal funds; and (ii) recreational community plans (Recreatiegemeenschappen) such as for the Veluwe recreation community of local authorities employing a very complex and difficult system for implementation in management. Regional action was selective so that it was not effective for the Amsterdam region but was for the Rotterdam region. Provisions designed for domestic recreation also came to be used extensively by large numbers of foreign day visitors and tourists, particularly from neighbouring Germany.

Water management and control as a critical planning system

As much of the Netherlands is a controlled hydrological system, leisure provision, tourist provision and conservation action is often a by-product of water defence, new land development and water management schemes. Thus many key provisions have been developed, owned and managed by bodies like the National Water Authority, the Polder Authorities, the Ministry of Agriculture and extraordinary consortia of interests in complicated management systems.

The Rijkswaterstaat or State Public Works Department for Water is officially responsible for: (i) the infrastructure of a waterways network suitable for a given volume of freight traffic; and (ii) the safe and efficient handling of water traffic (commercial and recreational). Water supply and management, shipping, conservation and recreation are all separately managed, and surprisingly there is no single agency which is an arbiter for all conflicts in this field.

Conservation of the built and natural environments

Antiquities and historic monuments

Ancient monuments in the Netherlands are protected by a range of bodies, there being no equivalent of the type of body like the UK National Trust, nor one universally responsible department of antiquities. Public sites, voluntary-sector and private-sector sites make up a complex system. There are publicly protected archaeological sites, and conserved historic villages, such as Orvelte in the Drenthe region.

Historic settlements and urban built heritage conservation

Legislation on conservation and renewal in the Netherlands is fairly satisfactory, but budgets are totally inadequate as are the instruments and this is why much urban renovation is so-called 'gentrification', or loss of the original population and gain of new higher income populations. Physical stock, continuity, retention and improvement are at the expense of social change.

National parks, national landscape parks and sites

In the old system, the provision of a network of national parks and national landscape parks was partly developed and under review. The voluntary sector had a notable role in national park and forest management and also in countryside interpretation and education, but the pressures were great and provisions inadequate, thus it became important in the new period to develop a more extensive system of national parks, and linkages between this whole conservation system.

Demand and supply

Two hundred million people live within a 250 km radius of the Rhine-Maas Estuary and the Dutch sea coast features with their backing national parks and national forests are only a few hours away by road for some 13 million people who live in the Rhine Ruhr area of Germany. The State Forest Service,

(Staatsbosbeheer), which was part of the Ministry of Agriculture, had a prime national role which continues, in developing and managing forests, essentially for recreation purposes.

Potential for tourism and for change in the old system

A speculative commercial boom in tourism started in the 1960s in the Netherlands, but it was ill-informed, badly advised economically and resulted in too many large hotels being erected in the wrong locations, targeted at the wrong markets. Corrective action came in the 1970s and 1980s.

There was a general lack of confidence in the role and work of the Ministry of Economic Affairs, which was responsible in part for tourism, and showed a limited ability to understand or to initiate tourism. The only hope for tourism planning in the 1960s and 1970s was via the CRM which then had certain links to the NBT and to the State Planning Service.

The New Planning System: 2006–2020

The new system was developed as a reaction to the old one and involved some three planning agents: (i) the national government; (ii) provincial authorities; and (iii) the municipalities (see Fig. 5.5). At provincial level each province was to have two types of plan, one Veranderingen Transformation and secondly an Inpassingsplan Integration. These were to replace the Streekplan and other provincial plans. At the municipal or local level the Bestemmingsplan was to be retained but now this did not require approval by the provincial authority as it could be approved at the local level, and also mapping at all levels was to be digital mapping so that there could be an interactive mapping structure for all levels of the nation. Each agent was to be responsible for and accountable for its actions. There was to be decentralization as far as possible and central decision making was to be made only when absolutely essential. Thus, the new system was to be positive, focused and selective, as compared to the old system which was seen as negative, controlling and comprehensive.

The new planning system is set out in a document published in 2006 entitled *National Spatial Strategy – Creating Space for Development* (it was adopted in 2008). This was published by the Ministry of Housing, Spatial Planning and the Environment (VROM), together with the Ministry of Agriculture, Nature and Food Quality, the Ministry of Transport, Public Works and Water Management, and finally the Ministry of Economic Affairs. The structure of the document comprises an introduction followed by planning objectives, the philosophy of the government's tools of implementation, the concentration of urban development and infrastructure, going with and anticipating the flow, investing in quality of nature, developing landscape with quality, development perspectives for the regions, specific themes, and then basic quality standards. Policy is defined up to the year 2020, with prospects up to the year 2030.

This 2006 document was based upon the fundamental strategy which replaced the former Fourth National Policy document and the Second National Structure Plan for Green Areas. The principal change in this whole approach was in the 'how' rather than the 'what' to do. Fewer rules and regulations were to be set by central government and more was to be focused on development planning, and less upon development-control planning. The pivotal role for land use plans shifted in emphasis from planning or control to development itself, with proposals for economic development and infrastructure development. The *National Spatial Strategy* set which basic values (i.e. basic quality standards) were to be guaranteed everywhere, and which spatial structures would entail greater responsibility for national government. Nature and landscape were to be carefully evaluated with buffer zones and green spaces in and around cities, and the focus was upon basic quality standards, first for environmental and safety reasons, and secondly in order to maintain a high quality landscape, in a densely settled and pressurized country.

With regard to water, nature and landscape, the national spatial structure comprises the major rivers, the Wadden See, the

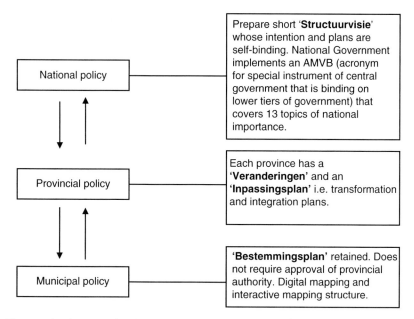

Prepare short '**Structuurvisie**' whose intention and plans are self-binding. National Government implements an AMVB (acronym for special instrument of central government that is binding on lower tiers of government) that covers 13 topics of national importance.

National policy

Each province has a '**Veranderingen**' and an '**Inpassingsplan**' i.e. transformation and integration plans.

Provincial policy

'**Bestemmingsplan**' retained. Does not require approval of provincial authority. Digital mapping and interactive mapping structure.

Municipal policy

Fig. 5.5. The new development planning system 2006–2020 (courtesy of Delta Commissie).

Ijsselmeer, coastal, bird and habitat directive areas, and protected nature areas, the national ecological network and main ecological links plus UNESCO World Heritage areas and national landscapes. A layer approach is used in the Netherlands, whereby land use in the country consists of three layers: (i) surface (i.e. water, soil, flora and fauna); (ii) networks (i.e. all forms of infrastructure that is visible overground and invisible hidden underground); and (iii) occupation (i.e. spatial patterns due to human use). They consider all three layers and constraints are placed upon land use and its future use, sustainable or otherwise.

The *National Spatial Strategy* is linked to key new tools legally: (i) an amended Spatial Planning Act; (ii) a new Rural Planning Act as a successor to the Land Use Act; (iii) new Land Policy; and (iv) a second urban renewal investment budget plus rural areas investment budget. Thus it can be seen that the focus has shifted towards tools. The agenda for a 'vibrant dynamic countryside' was published at the same time as the *National Spatial Strategy*. The recognition of simplicity of networks, with only the main seaport, one main airport, so called 'brain tools ports' (for research and

development) and 'green ports' (i.e. knowledge-based intensive horticulture and agrobusinesses). High speed rail links were to be developed to the north and the west of the country. Green spaces were to be safeguarded in and around the urban areas, so that adequate provision for green recreation would be made in and around cities, and sufficient land reserved for green areas and other recreation opportunities, while creating sustainable recreation landscapes. A special role was to be given to national buffer zones regarding their possible use both for recreation and for agriculture. The approach therefore has both so-called 'green and blue priorities', that is to say a land-based open space on the one hand, and water-based recreation on the other, with access by foot and by bike to these areas. With regard to environment and safety, European norms for nitrogen dioxide (NO_2) were expected to be achieved by 2015 (i.e. a European air-quality directive). With regard to noise pollution the Dutch Government was to be dealing with major noise problems along the motorways and railways before 2020. A special water policy was to involve a three-step strategy for water quantity, in particular for: (i) retaining it: (ii) storing it; and

(iii) discharging it. A three-step strategy for water quality was to involve: (i) preventing pollution; (ii) separating the clean from the polluted waters; and (iii) purifying the water. The National Spatial Planning Key Decision Map 6 in the Report shows areas under the EU's Bird and Habitat Directive and its Nature Protection Act.

Map 7 in the report shows National Spatial Planning key decisions and this includes: (i) defining or delimiting national landscapes at the green heart of the country (i.e. the green heart of the Randstad); (ii) the new Dutch waterline defences; (iii) the national landscapes not yet formally delimited but about to be; (iv) national policy in investing in the quality of nature; (v) national government, provincial and municipal responsibilities for different types of protected nature resources; and (vi) national government funding with provincial implementation. The Netherlands is committed to designating large areas with internationally important ecosystems, and it has a National Parks Policy aimed at creating 18 new national parks, as pearls within the linked chain of the National Ecological Network. The current National Ecological Network in the Netherlands is far too fragmented and so the main aim is to create some 12 main ecological links, allowing for easier and more movement of animals and insects between areas by 2018.

Species policy, that is protecting plants and animals outside of national ecological networks, is defined and there are some 18 areas to be defined as National Landscapes as well, and 'within National Landscapes special attention is also needed for nature in relation to cultural history, landscape, and for tourism and recreation'. With regard to noise control, noise contours are plotted around Amsterdam's Schipol Airport and no new housing is permitted in areas which are heavily affected by airport noise. The 'green ports' are the internal agricultural development areas for greenhouse agriculture and flower bulb cultivation, in other words – areas of very intensive agricultural development. The National Spatial Planning Key Decision on Map 8 of the Report includes protected ground water areas for industry and drinking water supply. Water sports routes are also defined, because these give through- routes for motorboats and sailing boats.

Specific attention is given to five policy themes in the strategy: (i) the supply of construction materials; (ii) military areas; (iii) energy supply/electricity; (iv) energy supply for natural gas extraction and storage; and (v) subterranean spatial policy (i.e. below-ground pipeline systems, drinking water and industrial water supply). The national policy refers to and implements some seven earlier accepted documents which are:

- the Second National Structure Plan for Green Areas;
- the Second National Structure Plan for Military Areas;
- the Second National Traffic and Transport Structure Plan;
- the Third Policy Document on Coastal Areas;
- the Third Policy Document on the Wadden See;
- the Third National Structure Plan for Electricity Supply; and
- the Fifth National Policy Document on Spatial Planning.

The report thus includes and specifies some five forms of planning:

1. Water Planning quality and quantity control.
2. Land use planning, including recreation and nature conservation.
3. Transportation planning.
4. Environmental quality planning, involving air quality, noise quality, water quality and other specific qualities.
5. Recreation and tourism by the recreation planning sector and tourism by the commercial sector.

Furthermore, control and legal systems, hierarchy, and timeframes are given, and for once sustainability parameters are defined for realms such as those of water, air quality, environmental quality, life quality and sustainable transport.

Summary

1. The Dutch Tourism System is a tripartite one which is based on: (i) the tourism unit which is part of a Directorate General within the Dutch Ministry of Economic Affairs; (ii) the NBT which

is responsible for international marketing of Dutch tourism; and (iii) the VVV system, a network of national provincial and local tourist information, marketing and booking offices.

2. The tourist and recreation resources are dependent upon the national provisions of national parks, national landscapes, recreation areas, woodlands and water areas for domestic active outdoor recreation.

3. Conservation of the natural and built heritage of the Netherlands is largely managed by the public and voluntary sectors.

4. The assumption is that investment in provision of urban hotels, attractions, restaurants and catering provision will all be made by the commercial sector (known in the Netherlands as the 'Horeca' sector this comprises hotels, restaurants and catering).

Evaluation

It is early yet to evaluate the new Dutch system, but as an approach it seems a remarkably fine model for all other countries to emulate, whereby the roles of national government are limited to essential areas, that are agreed between all branches of central government. A set of policies are there which are aimed on the one hand to aid the effective competitive economic position of a nation and therefore carry out the range of economic developments in urban industry, intensive agriculture and research-based economic developments, which put a nation in a favoured position. At the same time, on the other hand, the system expands upon the provision of national parks and national landscape parks, by putting in place an elaborate system of nature protection by full development of a national ecological network, which is a remarkable model for any nation. There is also a concern for major development projects to both achieve the necessary developments (e.g. the expansion of

Amsterdam airport, at Schiphol) but at the same time recognizing the noise impacts so preventing housing developments in those areas that would be blighted by the extended development of the airport. In all ways this is a sensible, rational model for a democratic state, which simultaneously harnesses an effective range of development intentions, but ensures they are compatible with the maintenance of the ecology of the nation, the protection of nature and the development of a landscape park system. Thereby in the heritage cities and towns, the coastal zones, the water areas and the countryside, a well-balanced and highly developed system is created for both domestic and international tourism, as well as primarily meeting the expanding needs of domestic recreation.

Paradoxically, the early post-war Netherlands was far more sustainable environmentally, than is the position by the 2000s. As far as transport was concerned, it had relied on cycle use, the excellent rail system, with connecting coach services, and a negligible number of private cars. Since then the great expansion of the Dutch motorway network and the fundamental shift to reliance on a huge stock of private cars has created congestion, severe noise and air pollution, aiding global warming, without achieving the dreams of total mobility and freedom to which travellers aspired.

The Netherlands has achieved a range of sustainable tourism products which include provision of a separate nationwide system of cycle trails, complete with cycle parks and direct access to the sea coast and nature reserves. A range of sailing, camping and canal boat holiday offers, give water-based sustainable alternatives – easily accessible via the rail and coach travel services. Only the growing aircraft-based and car-based alternatives for travel diminish the value of the impressive Dutch stock of sustainable travel products.

6 Israel: a Middle Eastern Case Study of Planning in a Mediterranean/ Desert Edge Location (RMP)

Introduction

Israel is an East Mediterranean democratic state, on the edge of a desert zone. In 2008 it was a country with a population of 7.25 million people, a mixed economy, a high economic growth rate, highly urbanized and with a notable tourism growth rate, despite its complex security situation. It is a small country of some 20,000 km² (8000 square miles) within its pre-1967 boundaries. It is a new nation state, formally established in 1948, on a large part of the territory of the former British Mandatory Palestine.

The partition of Palestine, determined by the UN in 1947, led to the Jewish Community of Palestine creating a state of 600,000 Jews, and for part of the Arab Palestinian population that remained in their homes. For an immigrant nation to develop in this land, with its very limited water resources, the challenges for the new country were to plan the land, settlement, economy and water resources, for it to become viable as a nation. The new country, with ancient roots in its territory, had to deal subsequently with a half century of mass migration, in a perilous defence situation, for much of its life.

The pervading national interest in archaeology, and the built relics of the nation's biblical past in this area, have a special culturally unifying role, nationally, and a political role

in terms of self-image and external image, in a nation that has the most diverse population of any country, despite their supposed unity in being Jewish. The considerable allocation of national resources to the renovation, restoration, management and interpretation of built heritage sites, is all the more significant in a country which allocates about half its national budget to military defence. Even in defence though, there are links, as army officers in their commissioning ceremony, take their oath at the historic mountain-top site of Massada, where 2000 years ago 1000 defenders committed suicide rather than surrender to the Romans. The land has a 6000-year settlement history. Thus in conservation, cultural and recreational terms, built heritage sites have a special significance for a diverse immigrant nation needing unifying elements. In addition, this is the Holy Land to adherents of five world religions: Christianity, Islam, Judaism, Bahai and Samaritanism.

Israel is a small country, but its land is extraordinarily complex in physical, geographical, environmental and climatic terms – ranging from wet hill country in the north, to dry desert in the far south, and from coastal plains to deep hot valleys and mountains. In 60 years the nation has had to settle millions of immigrants, create an extended settlement system, build an economy and cope with both development planning and conservation planning. Tourism developed slowly, but latterly impressively within this period. Internally, national road and rail systems have been extended, a range of development towns built, seaports and airports created, and externally air links, sea links and recently land links have opened to Egypt and Jordan.

Settlement and Heritage Resources

Apart from inherited natural resources of varied landscapes, topography and flora and fauna, which differ over short distances, re-afforestation has added 122 million trees to a previously deforested land. The built heritage resources for conservation, culture and tourism are remarkable. The three main cities of Tel Aviv – Yafo, Jerusalem and Haifa – all have biblical associations with their sites, and Jerusalem especially has the sacred sites of three world religions. Smaller cities like Beersheva, Nazareth, Tiberias, Safed and Acre, all have important historic associations. Historic sites of the land are associated with 35 centuries of recorded history. Biblical sites and holy places of the five religions listed earlier, are here.

Development towns – such as Arad, in the North Negev, which is a spa town, Eilat, on the Red Sea, now a major seaside resort, and Ashdod, a major new port-city – break away from the mould of new towns as placeless housing centres for immigrants. Spas, based on natural resource assets, have been developed at Tiberias, the new Dead Sea resorts, as well as at Arad. The big cities of Tel Aviv and Jerusalem have had a great stock of hotels, restaurants and diverse attractions (from museums and theatres to night clubs, discos and bars) developed in them. Eilat alone, as a resort-city, has 11,000 hotel bedrooms!

The funding of all this development, creating a substantial society in a 60-year period, would not have been possible if done alone by this small nation. There have been three hidden partners in this process: (i) the worldwide Jewish Diaspora, which has charitably funded things such as land purchase, tree planting, sponsoring of university and hospital development; (ii) the US Government's major

subsidies for immigrant absorption and national defence; and (iii) international speculative capital investment by the commercial sector in hotels, marina and spa development.

The Antiquities Law protects all listed historic sites in the country that date from ancient times up to 19th-century sites. A special study on 19th and 20th century settlement sites (up to 1947) has been accepted and most of these sites are now being protected.

A great amount of archaeological work and of excavation has taken place since 1967 – systematic digs, surveys, studies and work done in Jerusalem, the Negev and further afield. Sites such as Qumran, Avdat, Hazor and Massada are now better understood and more fully interpreted. National and local surveys continue, and key finds are to be seen in excellent museums such as the Israel Museum and the Rockefeller Museum – both in Jerusalem.

While heritage sites have been classified and looked after by the Department of Antiquities, and subsequently 42 key sites managed by the National Parks Authority, established in 1963, the fate of historic town cores has been mixed. While the cores of Acre/Acco, Jaffa/Yafo and part of the Old City of Jerusalem have been carefully renovated, it is different elsewhere. Central Bethshan, Tiberias and Nazareth's renovation and redevelopment has been inadequately controlled and is most unfortunate.

National Planning for Settlement, Water Supply and Communications

Physical planning started in 1948, with national strategies for settlement, communications and water supply. The aim was to spread the population over the national territory, and stop over concentration in the central coastal belt from Tel Aviv north to Haifa. In 1953 construction started on the National Water Carrier, so that the concentrated water resources of the River Jordan and the Sea of Galilee (Lake Kinneret), in the wet north, could be carried south and linked with the waters of the River Yarkon, by Tel Aviv, then be taken on to the North Negev desert, enabling its agricultural development and the creation of several cities there. Of the country's total annual renewable water resources stated to be 56 billion ft³, 75% was to become used for irrigation, so that by 1970 over 400,000 acres of land were irrigated farmland. Today, with over ten million people living between the Mediterranean and the Jordan, in Israel and Palestine, water resources are exceeded despite supplementation and seawater desalinization. There is a problem of saltwater invasion into the water table of the coastal plain. A Jordan Valley Authority, modelled on the Tennessee Valley Authority, was long ago suggested by the great US consultant Professor Lowdermilk. It merits reconsideration today.

In the early 1960s both National Park Authorities and Nature Reserve Authorities were created, before the second National Physical Master Plan was launched in 1964. While open space, conservation and tourism elements were in this physical planning, it was not until 1976 that the major Outline Tourism Plan was devised. Development planning was critical to the physical development of the state, but its economic planning lagged behind this. A big problem of the first 25 years of the state was the centralized planning of a country which, though it had a mixed economy, was for long dominated by the thinking and organizations of its Labour Government, with its socialist trade union organization (Histadrut) and its health service (kupat cholim) and its building and commercial arms. Liberalization of the economy and society took decades to happen.

Communications were focused for long on developing the road system partly because the Jewish community in Palestine had run its own bus services, while the British Mandatory Authority ran the railways. Belatedly, Israel developed a modern rail system between its main cities. The Mandatory Government had developed Haifa port, and this was much later supplemented by new ports at Ashdod on the Mediterranean, and Eilat on the Red Sea. The sole major international airport at Lydda/Lod was greatly extended and developed in three phases.

The aims of national planning in Israel have long been to settle the national territory more evenly, but despite all the controls and incentives used in 60 years of development, the great land resource to the south in the Negev, with 60% of the nation's territory, is the least settled. It is the driest and hottest area of the country, and most of its population is in a number of development towns, such as Beersheva with about 200,000 residents, Eilat with 60,000 and smaller development towns each of about 20,000 in Arad, Dimona and Yeruham (the two latter cases are places where residents were housed when they came off immigrant ships or flights, and from which they would like to escape to the big cities). With all of these problems of physical and economic development, immigrant absorption and continuing defence problems, it is clear why tourism planning was a delayed priority.

National Planning for Tourism Development and Heritage Resource Conservation

In 1948 some 4500 tourists visited the infant state of less than 0.7 million population. By 1950 some 33,000 tourists were visiting a state of new immigrants, now 1.5 million in number. Some 60 years later some three million tourists were coming to an Israel State (in 2007/8) of 7.25 million! How has this all happened?

From scratch Israel had many potential advantages for tourism development:

- its appeal for religious pilgrims of several religions;
- its unique range of built heritage and historic associations;
- natural heritage variety and climatic advantage;
- sea coast and lake resort appeal for active sports, beach and sun tourism;
- spa waters and remedial muds for 'wellness tourism';
- youth market appeal to work on kibbutzim, as volunteers, or use the field study centres or appeal for Diaspora Jewish visitors to come on educational tourist visits to see 'the Jewish State'; and
- a VFR component to tourism.

Given peace and stability, tourism could also be a source of earning hard currency, and aid the balance of payments via this key invisible export.

The system which emerged for Development Planning for Tourism and Recreation started with the National Physical Plan of 1948. This provided guidelines for the conservation of natural heritage (National Parks and nature reserves), conservation of built heritage (defining key sites) and defining major tourism development locations. As early as 1967 the idea of a separate National Master Plan for Tourism was mooted, but a provisional plan was not ready until 1972, and a final agreed National Master Plan for Tourism and Recreation (based on Leitersdorf and Goldenburg's 1976 work) prepared for the Ministry of Industry, Trade and Tourism. Within this combined Ministry, tourism planning was done by the Government Tourist Organization. Tourism achieved ministerial status early in government.

Until 1967, basic fears regarding national security inhibited tourist development and appeal to international investors. Post the Six Day War, government economic incentives to invest in the development of Israel tourism infrastructure, especially hotels, became a notable feature. As shown in Fig. 6.1, locational incentives were given to invest in four categories of development area.

What is vital to note is that the tourism planning of the 1970–1980 period provided all the basic plans, whose realization, in building development terms, are still taking place on the ground in resorts like Eilat, the Dead Sea spas and the new city-break hotels of Tel Aviv, Haifa and Jerusalem. General tourists, business tourists, conference tourists and the new short-break international urban tourists, together enable a high occupancy rate in the big city hotels. This is vital to the economic sustainability of a sizeable hotel sector in a relatively small, if in part densely settled country.

This led to a huge scale of international and domestic investment in hotel, marina and resort attractions, which were realized in priority locations. Some ten international hotel chains established themselves in Eilat, Tel Aviv and Jerusalem, with three major local hotel chains also expanding greatly as well. These added to the stock of national kibbutz guesthouses, resort villages, field schools and youth hostels.

The mature system of tourism planning in Israel, by the 1970s had several elements:

- National and regional tourism planning relating to choice of locations for, and types of, tourism development, plus key associated conservation activities and grant levels.
- The Israel Tourist Development Corporation selling bonds abroad to raise capital for tourism development in Israel.
- Regional development projects – integrated multi-purpose regional projects – included specific tourist elements.
- Development Corporations had tourist and related functions.
- Development companies were the special companies which renovated the historic core of old Jaffa, and of Acre, plus the Jewish Quarter of the Old City of Jerusalem.
- Site development projects, for example hotels, beach developments, marinas, or a foreshore development project – such as the marinas plus the hotels area of North Beach, Eilat.

The 1976 Plan achieved a better spread of major Tourism Development Zones around the country, with Eilat as a major Red Sea resort, hotel spa developments at new Dead Sea resorts, key new developments at Tiberias in the north, Arad in the North Negev, plus consolidation of the tourist functions of Jerusalem and Tel Aviv in the heart of the country. Tourism was welcomed not only as a boost to the economy, but also because it was a 'clean' and 'soft' industry, which promoted the state and its image. The hotel-building phase boosted service sector employment and training systems nationally. Health tourism, holiday tourism and conference tourism grew quickly, and soon outstripped pilgrimage tourism, as growth sectors.

Five capacity problems arose from this process:

1. The limits of water resources, whereby tourism was competing with agriculture and other development, for such resources.
2. Ecological capacity questions affected sites on the Sea of Galilee, and especially those on the Red Sea, where coral protection from pollution became a management issue.

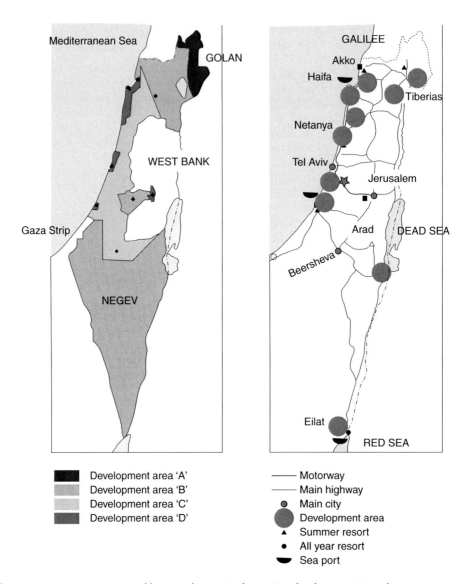

Fig. 6.1. Economic incentives and locational strategies for tourism development in Israel.

3. Perceptual capacity problems, as in a small country it became harder to find 'wilderness zones' and 'quiet' away from development.

4. National Park capacity problems meant that overcrowding at some sites damaged their conservation, and additional new parks were required to ease pressures.

5. Urban site capacity problems arose, in some very popular and highly accessible locations. Historic Jaffa, so close to the core of metropolitan Tel Aviv, suffered notably.

Conservation work of five types is done in Israel:

• Conservation and management of special habitats and ecosystems by the Nature Reserves Authority.

• Conservation and management of listed built and/or natural heritage sites (e.g. Massada, Sachne, Caesaria) prepared in the past by the Ministry of Education and Culture, then managed by the National Parks Authority (Fig. 6.2).

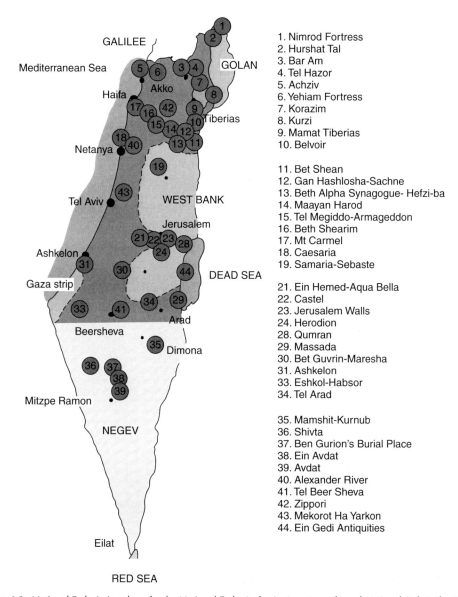

GALILEE

Mediterranean Sea

GOLAN

Haifa

Akko

Tiberias

Netanya

Tel Aviv WEST BANK

Jerusalem

Ashkelon

DEAD SEA

Gaza strip

Arad

Beersheva

Dimona

Mitzpe Ramon

NEGEV

Eilat

RED SEA

1. Nimrod Fortress
2. Hurshat Tal
3. Bar Am
4. Tel Hazor
5. Achziv
6. Yehiam Fortress
7. Korazim
8. Kurzi
9. Mamat Tiberias
10. Belvoir

11. Bet Shean
12. Gan Hashlosha-Sachne
13. Beth Alpha Synagogue- Hefzi-ba
14. Maayan Harod
15. Tel Megiddo-Armageddon
16. Beth Shearim
17. Mt Carmel
18. Caesaria
19. Samaria-Sebaste

21. Ein Hemed-Aqua Bella
22. Castel
23. Jerusalem Walls
24. Herodion
28. Qumran
29. Massada
30. Bet Guvrin-Maresha
31. Ashkelon
33. Eshkol-Habsor
34. Tel Arad

35. Mamshit-Kurnub
36. Shivta
37. Ben Gurion's Burial Place
38. Ein Avdat
39. Avdat
40. Alexander River
41. Tel Beer Sheva
42. Zippori
43. Mekorot Ha Yarkon
44. Ein Gedi Antiquities

Fig. 6.2. National Parks in Israel run by the National Parks Authority (courtesy of Israel National Park Authority).

- Conservation and renovation of urban built heritage areas for tourist reasons (e.g. central Jaffa and central Acre).
- Conservation and restoration of historic quarters for cultural, political and incidental tourist reasons (e.g. the Old City of Jerusalem; Fig. 6.3).
- Renovation and improvement of areas and/or individual buildings by the pri-

vate sector (e.g. the German Colony in Haifa, Old Tel Aviv, and the Yemin Moshe Quarter of Jerusalem).

Uneven provisions and uneven visitor pressures upon resources led to the growth both of voluntary sector bodies to act, and new public sector bodies (such as the Environmental Protection Service, 1972) to emerge or act/react to mistakes made and

(a)

Fig. 6.3. Examples of built heritage conservation. (a) The reconstruction of the historic Jewish Quarter of the Old City of Jerusalem.

inadequacies in the system. Older voluntary sector bodies like the Society for the Protection of Nature and Malraz (a council for the prevention of noise and air pollution) were added to by the creation of the Council for a Beautiful Israel, the Association for Environmental Planning and the International Committee on Jerusalem (to protect its special physical character).

Katz and Gurevitch's (1975) book *The Secularization of Leisure: Culture and Communication in Israel* also points to the many complex changes in the approach to resident leisure provision compared with the provisions for international tourism. The good provisions for management of heritage sites, which are often exemplary in the planning and provisions even if relatively starved of resources, says much for the work of the National Parks Authority.

The case studies of Jaffa's renovated historic core, and that of the renovated Jewish Quarter of the Old City of Jerusalem (which had been badly damaged by the occupying Jordanian Foreign Legion), show the best of urban renovation work done in historic cores of cities in Israel. The Jerusalem work had required a special Act of Parliament (Knesset) and involved the Government establishing a 'company for the reconstruction and development of the Jewish Quarter in the Old City of Jerusalem'. The plan involved recreating housing for 2600 people, plus another 1500 in religious and educational establishments. A large commercial component related to tourism purposes was involved, for example in the restoration of the Roman Cardo, and of a big square by the Western Wall of the Temple (the 'Wailing Wall').

(b)

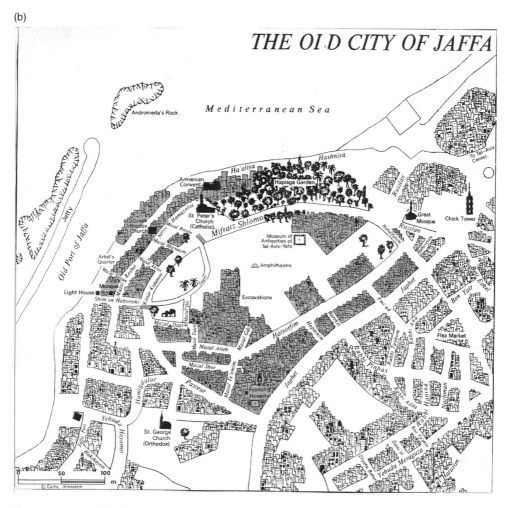

Fig. 6.3. Continued. (b) the renovation of the historic core of Old Jaffa in Tel Aviv.

Evaluation

In the context of tourism development and heritage conservation, Israel presents an interesting paradox. It is a country whose ethos is one which is hell-bent on 'development' and upon 'progress', very akin to that of the USA. However, its search for national unity, continuity and identity, makes it simultaneously obsessed with its ancient past, as well as the trauma of the European Holocaust in the 20th century. Thus 'Yad Vashem' – its great Holocaust Museum and Centre in Jerusalem – is its national shrine, but the resources going into tourism development are disproportionately greater than those going into heritage conservation.

The systems set up are complex and good, but under-funded, because of the drain of public budgets on defence. Yet the great diversity of the population of the state, even within its majority Jewish population is such, that paradoxically it is the external threat alone, which unites the nation. Threats from Iran to wipe out Israel fundamentally unite the nation's 5.5 million Jews in 2008, who recall that in the 1940s some six million Jews were exterminated by the Third Reich in its 'Final Solution' of the 'Jewish Question'. The issue of security is thus an all-pervading one in Israel.

(c)

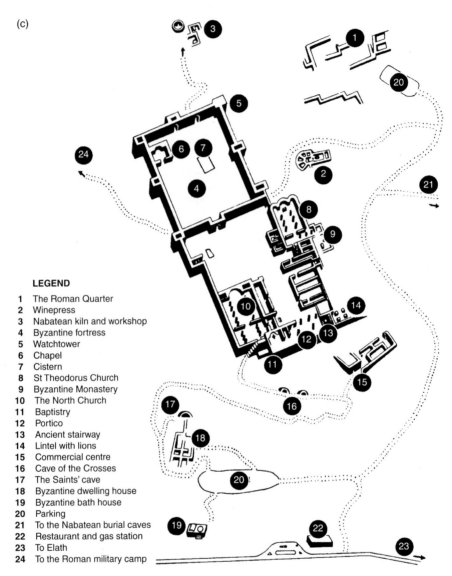

LEGEND

1   The Roman Quarter
2   Winepress
3   Nabatean kiln and workshop
4   Byzantine fortress
5   Watchtower
6   Chapel
7   Cistern
8   St Theodorus Church
9   Byzantine Monastery
10 The North Church
11 Baptistry
12 Portico
13 Ancient stairway
14 Lintel with lions
15 Commercial centre
16 Cave of the Crosses
17 The Saints' cave
18 Byzantine dwelling house
19 Byzantine bath house
20 Parking
21 To the Nabatean burial caves
22 Restaurant and gas station
23 To Elath
24 To the Roman military camp

Fig. 6.3. Continued. (c) Avdat–the Nabbatean city–conserved and interpreted by the National Park Authority (courtesy of Israel National Park Authority).

The range of products offered by Israel today in the tourism field is very impressive, and the standard of service offered has improved greatly. A big range of markets can be satisfied by what is on offer, but pricing may need to be reviewed as Israeli tourist products are comparatively pricey, and there is the issue of access to the country as access is basically limited to entry by air as sea access is not good and land access via complex border crossings from Arab States time-consuming.

The sustainability of Israel's international tourism model is at present far too dependent upon air travel, which needs radical technological and fuel changes, if it is to be sustainable. Israeli tourism is currently fundamentally dependent upon European and American markets. It functions like an island nation, which uses its air links, and has abandoned its earlier strong passenger-ship sea links to Europe. If future peaceful normalization of the Levant took place, then both Israel and the Lebanon would be the natural destinations for both Middle East and East European tourists. The under-development of the Palestinian Territories and their interdependence in future with Israeli tourism, must await hopefully the day when two states – one Israeli and one Palestinian – can cooperate in tourism planning and water planning in the mutual interest of the survival of the two peoples. With regard to sustainable tourism products, walking or trekking holidays, based upon the 'Israel National Trail' and forest trail systems, are highly developed, as is camel trekking in the desert. Kibbutz work-volunteer holi-days, using rail or coach access, are popu-lar, and there is growing use of the railways, which are now well used and increasingly modernized.

7 Denmark: a Scandinavian Case Study of Regional Conservation Planning for Tourism and Recreation 1960–1980 (RMP)

Introduction

Denmark is a flat and low-lying nation of some 43,000 km² or 16,631 square miles in area (i.e. about twice the size of Israel) and in 2000 it had a population of about 5.3 million inhabitants. With its peninsular and complex set of islands, it sits at the entry to the Baltic Sea, and is the bridge between Scandinavia and the European mainland. It is a sophisticated and highly developed society and a largely rural nation with a few big cities, and a dominant capital city region in Greater Copenhagen (see Fig. 7.1).

Coastal regions and islands characterize the nation's landscapes and are the places where problems of conflicts of land use and user-pressures are evident, and warrant interventionist responses. Landscape and nature conservation are critical to tourism. Tourism and resident recreation depends upon the conservation of the natural resources of coast, beaches, scenic landscapes, general countryside and urban built heritage environments. Nature conservation includes the protection and maintenance of high quality living natural resources of air, water, land and related flora and fauna, integrated within their dynamic ecosystems.

Though a sophisticated nation, Denmark was late in creating its effective system for national conservation planning, which emerged

in the 1960–1980 period, and is a clear and helpful model to other states which may be late in tackling such national needs. Environmental conservation is a big field, ranging from the built and cultural heritage to the natural heritage. The maintenance of the integrity of such resources is critical to Man's survival and identity, to his education, health and well-being. In considering these factors in the Danish case, the focus is upon the countryside aspects of nature conservation, tourism and resident recreation.

Environmental resources give rise to tourism and recreation, in their many forms. Conversely, tourism and recreation may generate the provision of infrastructure, environmental services and built facilities. The essential question, though, is to what extent are recreational activities of tourists and residents compatible with, or even destructive of the host environment upon which they depend, and whose resources must be conserved, if their activities are to be sustainable.

In the 1960s Denmark was a highly developed country in terms of its levels of development planning on the one hand, but on the other hand it was belated in some aspects of conservation planning. It already had significant experience of physical planning at the national, regional and local scales. Foundations for conservation planning were laid by a national landscape classification

Fig. 7.1. Map of Denmark (courtesy of Århus Regional Authority).

task, which gave guidance for the choice of areas for National Parks, nature parks and conservation areas. By the 1960s, a first attempt at national land use zoning tried to define specific zones for landscape conservation, for agriculture, for summer-house development and for urban expansion.

Conservation planning thus set out with a difficult task in Denmark. Regional work in the Copenhagen and Århus regions, demonstrated how National and Area Nature Conservancy Offices had an important role to play in this sphere. The Danish Forestry Commission is primarily an organization which conserves the limited stock of existing forests. Tourist, recreational and conservation interests are brought together in a body like Friluftsradet, whose composition is explained later. Conservation agencies as such, were given a major and formally recognized role in this process.

Unlike their counterparts in the UK, Greece, France and Israel in the 1970 period, the state tourist organizations in Denmark, were not planning bodies, and were not involved in conservation. The Danish National Tourist Board, under the Ministry of Commerce, was essentially concerned with overseas marketing and promotion, while the regional boards had marketing, activity promotion and coordinating roles. Thus, the tourist bodies were not part of the conservation-planning process.

Silkeborg Lake District National Park

The Silkeborg Lake District National Park, in central Jutland, to the west of the city of Århus, is a useful test case for examining how the conservation of heritage natural countryside resources in Denmark, came to be reconciled with development of tourist and recreation development pressures, within a Danish National Park. National Parks were a new element in Danish countryside conservation planning, as they were first introduced as late as the mid-1960s. In making a late start, however, the Danes took the opportunity to learn from the mistakes of others, and to try and plan in an innovative way.

Within Silkeborg Lake District National Park, some 10% of the land was in state-owned forests, which are managed and conserved by the state, and the remaining 90% of the land was in private ownership. This constraint of land ownership is akin to the situation in British National Parks, and very different to the total state ownership of National Park land in countries like Slovakia, Poland and the USA. This factor greatly constrained the form and extent of planned intervention, and the resulting planning and management strategies used.

Preliminary planning of the National Park was undertaken in the County Nature Conservancy Office in Århus, where a team of some 17 staff were engaged. The National Park Plan defines conservation areas and pocket zones for development. The planning of the National Park was not conceived in isolation, but formed an integrated part of a regional planning process for conservation and recreation. Silkeborg is at the edge of the Århus Region, and was part of the 1976 Preliminary Regional Plan.

The Århus Regional Sketch Plan for Conservation and Recreation provides specific development zones for:

- town development areas;
- holiday development zones;
- camping and caravanning sites;
- scouting centres;
- hotels and free-standing facilities; and
- visitor centres with a focus on natural history and countryside interpretation.

Recreation and tourism development in the Plan were defined in detail; a range of activities and facilities were specified, such as boating, which was long established on the Lakes, linked to touring and to short-stays. Some 500 canoes were made available to hire, plus paddleboats for family groups, the very old and the very young. Disused railway lines were re-used to create independent trail systems for cyclists and walkers (on tracks 1.20 m in width), and trails for horse-riders (1 m wide). The trails were signposted, and were in part planted and paved. Another linear provision was a 2.5 mile 'veteran railway', with an old train on tracks to offer recreational trips in summer and at Christmas. The train provision is in the National Park, as is a system of small, limited-capacity car parks. These were constructed in woodland locations, visually discreet, and with a capacity well below that of the host environment.

Hotels and inns servicing visitors to the region, plus camping and caravan sites were to be provided commercially, at specified locations. The Regional Authority acts to improve bathing spots, create the visitor centres and construct birdwatching hides. It also set up forest drives and walks, and developed a 'high' viewpoint on the 'mountain' – a hill 174 m high in this rolling, but low landscape. Marketing and promotion of the tourist and recreation opportunities were to be done by the commercial sector and by the regional tourist organization. Camping and caravanning provision was deliberately limited, with the largest single site restricted to a capacity of 600 units. The first major visitor centre, south of Roerbaek, was receiving 500 visiting cars per day, in peak season, within a few years of its opening.

The management of the Danish National Parks themselves is based on a theory of nature park conservation, used earlier in France, where key reserves are identified which are fragile and need protection. To protect them they are surrounded by concentric management zones, which range from 'inner core areas', which are virtually closed to visitors, via 'protected areas' with limited entry, through to 'edge where visitors are encouraged'.

Evaluation

Though late in the field of regional conservation planning and National Park planning, the Danes learned from the successes and mistakes of other countries. They devised simple and clear principles of conservation and development, which were incorporated into their plans and management schemes. Though the IUCN criteria for National Parks could not be achieved in Denmark, a realistic way of applying good conservation management theories in a region with very small public land-holdings was achieved.

A Nationwide System of Regional Planning for Conservation and Recreation

As already indicated in the test case of the Århus Region and its National Park planning, these became integrated into Regional Plans for Conservation and Recreation, and this became a national system in the 1970s. Regions were redefined in the 1970s, with their number being reduced from 27 to 12. All the new regions were to be required to plan for recreation and for tourism, as well as for landscape and nature conservation. The new conservation planning was to be linked to and complement the general physical planning of each region. General physical planning was already done by the Regional Planning Departments, while the new recreation and conservation planning was to be undertaken by Regional Nature Conservation Authorities. The Århus regional approach that has already been presented will now be compared with that for the Copenhagen Region, which is the prime and most intensively developed region in Denmark.

General background to Danish planning

The process of urbanization and industrialization, with their impacts upon the coasts and countryside of Denmark had led to the setting up in 1961 of a national planning committee. It was responsible for producing the zone plan of 1962. This was a nationwide physical or outline sketch plan defining both zones for development and zones for conservation, in relation to primary activities. Debates nationally about the best choices of land use had led to the need to obtain a detailed picture of the country's landscape and recreation resources. This in turn led to the official development of a methodology for analysing landscape, and consequently for conducting a systematic analysis of the national natural resources of the Danish landscape. In 1967 the National Nature Conservation Committee published their landscape evaluation map for the whole country, which led to modifications and publication of further studies in 1971 and 1972.

The methodology applied nationally, as well as for test regions such as Århus, focused upon natural science interests, cultural history, aesthetic assessments, recreational potential and integrated analysis, all on a simple map. In this way academic assessment was translated into working analyses which could aid policy. Three zones of countryside were defined, and a critical basis laid for the new style regional conservation plans and physical plans produced from the late 1970s onwards in Denmark, and including within them a recreational sketch plan or ideas for each region.

The Copenhagen Region

The Copenhagen Region has been the test bed for all planning in Denmark. In 1959 a 'Conservation Planning Committee' reviewed nature conservation and recreation in the capital region's coast and countryside, under new legislation introduced in that year. Key subsequent legislation in 1969 (i.e. the Urban and Rural Zones Act) encouraged planning for recreational interest of the population and preservation of scenic values, while another Act in 1972 allowed for land acquisition for recreational purposes. In that year, two other Acts (a 'Regional Planning Act' and 'Regional

Planning in the Metropolitan Area Act') provided a basis for linking regional planning,
recreation planning and nature conservation. The Copenhagen Region in the idea
sketch of 1973 was given a basis for both
'allocations of area for conservation and
open-air activities'. The plan was based on
an assessment of landscape resources and a
ranking of scenic values, recreational activities on land and on water, and area vulnerability to development.

The resultant sketch plan included proposals for regional parks, district parks and
linear parks, nature conservation areas, landscape and heritage conservation areas, as well
as recreational areas and marinas. After the
1972 Acts, conservation planning led to continuous cooperation between the Regional
Nature Conservation Planning Committee on
the one hand, and the Regional Planning
Authority, which prepared the official Regional
Plan, on the other. The role of regional parks,
the concept of 'support points' and 'controlled
coastal conservation' as well as development,
were all recognized.

The Århus Region

As already indicated in relation to the planning of the Silkeborg Lake District National
Park, Danish National Park planning was
integrated into wider conservation-planning
activity for a whole region. This took place
under a County Nature Conservation
Planning Committee, whose work was
twinned with that of the Regional Planning
Committee. Thus in the instance of the Århus
Region, a nine-volume series of reports on
general physical planning for the region
were prepared, and were the subject of a
major programme of public consultation.
The content of these documents complemented that of the regional Conservation
Plan, published in 1976 and covering all the
territory of that region. The Conservation
Plan defined national and regional conservation areas and parks, and linked back to
basic recreational development proposals
contained in the Regional Plan. The twin
focus which emerged, therefore, was for an

emphasis on conservation of natural heritage resources in the Conservation Plan, and
a balancing treatment of development, in the
Regional Physical Plan. The partial 1980
Regional Physical Plan gave way to an integrated approach, in the 1993 Regional Plan
for Development, Conservation, Recreation
and Tourism.

Some 11% of Denmark is forest, but in
the Silkeborg Lake District some 18% of the
area is forested. The forests often form the
core of the 'nature parks' in the Århus
Region, with protected but scarcely used,
and relatively inaccessible, core zones. As
already indicated, these areas were graded
outwards towards the areas of greater use,
with increased accessibility, and therefore
higher densities of use for recreation and
tourism, at the outer edges. The plans are
clear, and related to ongoing management
strategies on the ground.

Evaluation

The regional plans for Copenhagen, Århus and
elsewhere, showed a meticulous concern for
balancing the needs for conservation, with those
of recreation and the whole range of land uses
and transportation corridors. Their twinned
approach was: (i) for conservation, recreation
and tourism; and (ii) for general physical and
economic development planning.

Friluftsradet

In the contexts of conservation and development planning, a Danish innovation was that
of Friluftsradet. It is an organization in which
all voluntary sector interests, para-public and
special interest groups involved in recreation,
tourism and conservation are represented. It
is a 'Parliament of all the user and protection-
ist groups'. By uniting so many diverse interests, it can fund staff and consultants to do
advocacy work, including resource invento-
ries, capacity and management studies.
Friluftsradet contributes to regional conservation, and physical plans, and works in
association with IUCN.

Conclusions

Neither Denmark, nor any other single country can be held up as an exemplary model as to how to plan, theorize or to manage planning for conservation, recreation and tourism. However, from the twin-planning Danish approach, despite its late start, the simple concepts employed, and the safeguarding mechanisms used (Friluftsradet on the one hand, and the Ombudsman, on the other) Denmark can give several useful pointers at the regional and national scales – especially in conservation planning – to others who may be even later starters in this field than them!

8 Maldives' Tourism Development: a Test Case in the Indian Ocean for Conservation and Economic Development in an Islamic State (RMP towards STP)

Introduction

The Maldives is an island nation of 1190 tiny islands, spread over 26 atolls, some 340 km south-west of India, on the Equator, in the Indian Ocean. In 2008 the republic had a resident population of 300,000, living on 185 of the islands. The other defined islands are used for economic purposes, such as for tourism and agriculture.

Tourism activity started by an Italian tour operator in 1972 led to a transformation, over time, of the national economy, which formerly had depended upon fisheries and agriculture, and came to depend upon international tourism as its prime foreign currency earner. By 2008 some 89 'resort islands' had been developed in the Maldives, and two more were being planned. These had a total resort bed capacity of over 17,000, and if the hotels and other bed capacity are added, the state has a total tourist bed capacity of over 20,000, serving over 600,000 visiting international tourists p.a.

As an Islamic republic, the government of the Maldives was keen to get economic benefits from tourism, but wanted to retain its cultural integrity, as it wished to keep 'its residents culturally protected from tourism influences'. Thus, early on it decided upon the separation of use of islands, into those which were to be exclusively for Maldivian residents, and those which were to be used as tourist resorts. Maldivians were to be permitted to work upon the resort islands, but were normally expected to sleep and live upon their own islands.

Tourism Development

The natural heritage resource assets of the islands were the basis of their appeal for tourism development. The tropical climate, the coral-based islands, with their beautiful palms, lagoons, white sandy beaches and incredibly rich fish life in the pure waters, and the pure air were the magnets drawing tourists here for water sports, beach life, great diving, peace and beauty. The islands are spread over 26 atolls and stretch for some 820 km north to south, and are about 130 km at their widest point. The islands are very small, none being larger than 4.5 miles in length, nor reaching an altitude of more than 2 m above sea level. They are subject to monsoons and tsunamis; many of the islands were badly damaged by the Great Asian Tsunami of 2005. The only sizeable town is the capital Malé, which is the seat of government, and main centre of trade, education and commerce. It has a population variously stated in official publications to be about 75,000 or 100,000 residents.

The development of tourism is vested in the Ministry of Tourism and Civil Aviation of the Republic of the Maldives, and the key governing legislation (according to three official documents of 2008) is the Maldives Tourism Act (Law No. 2/99). This Act provides for the:

> determination of zones and islands for the development of tourism in the Maldives: the leasing of islands (to foreign investors) for development of tourist resorts, the leasing of land for development as tourist hotels, and tourist guesthouses, the leasing of places for development as marinas, the management of all such facilities, and the operation of tourist vessels, diving centres, and travel agencies, and the regulation of persons providing such services.

The stated goals and objectives of tourism in the Maldives include:

> ensuring the equitable distribution of the economic benefits of tourism to the society, and making tourism a vehicle for the protection and conservation of nature and natural resources, and the revitalisation and preservation of the nation's cultural assets.

How this was all to be realized, was not specifically set out! In the 2007 Tourism Yearbook of the Ministry of Tourism and Civil Aviation of the Republic of Maldives, it is indicated that despite the great physical damage done by the 2005 tsunami, the tourist industry recovered in 2006, and had remarkably successful results again. The urgent repair and reconstruction of damaged resorts was done, and compensatory marketing and promotion intensified. In 2006 there was a 52.3% growth in returns, over those for 2005.

In 2006 the release was announced of some 35 new islands to be made available for resort development. The decision was made to create a Maldives Tourism Development Corporation, with 45% government and 55% publicly owned shares. Growing demand for more tourist beds had led to more action in infrastructure development. Central tourism training development went together with new tourism training facilities in the resorts themselves.

Communications

The transport infrastructure development has been impressive. The early development of Hulhule as an international airport island with sea ferry connections (via Dhonis) to Malé, and to resort islands, has now led on to the main airport having both a full ferry port and a sea-plane base attached. So there are now aeroplane connections and two companies offering sea-plane connections to a number of secondary airports on the other atolls, as well as traditional Dhoni boat and fast boat connections from the airports both to resort and to resident islands.

Early air connections to Europe, Australasia and Japan were vital to the tourism development of the Maldives. By 2006, some 16 international charter airlines were serving the Maldives. A national airline service had been created to handle internal transfers within the Maldives. High tourist growth rates and high occupancy rates in resorts were notable, and were echoed in high aircraft occupancy rates as well. By 2006, it was decided to develop direct international flights to the Southern Zone of the Maldives, so that no longer were all flights having to go via the international airport at Malé on Hulhule.

A 2007 Third Master Plan for Tourism aimed to increase national bed capacity for tourists to 33,000 by 2011. New accommodation was to be provided in new resort-island development, in hotels, guesthouses and on 'live-aboard' safari or small cruise vessels. To increase local economic benefit, in this new phase of development, most new resorts are to be leased to local companies. Currently only 47% of resorts are operated by local companies, and the majority are operated by foreign companies, or foreign shareholding companies.

Tourist arrivals remain mainly European in origin with Italy as the top generator-country, followed by the UK and then Germany. Australasia and Japan are also significant markets. To gain the economic benefit from this process for residents, a bed tax is levied on all foreign tourists, and a departure tax is paid by each foreign tourist flying out of Malé International Airport. The award-winning character of Maldives resorts, spas and diving centres reflects the growing popularity and appeal of the high quality tourist products offered by this nation.

> In three and a half decades the (tourist) industry has become the main source of income of the people of the Maldives. Tourism is also the country's biggest foreign currency earner and the single largest contributor to the GDP…
>
> (www.tourism.gov.mv; accessed 1 October 2010)

Heritage Conservation

In the 1970s and 1980s protection and respect for the nation's Islamic heritage, life and values was seen as important as protection of the rich natural heritage – which is the primary source of appeal for the Maldives as a tourist destination. The purity of air and water, the rich biodiversity of the seas were recognized for their vital importance, and are the subject both of legal protection and of strict guidance and control of visitors' actions.

Maldivian culture has a deep-rooted respect for its host environment. Its Law on Protection and Preservation of the Environment defines 25 'marine protected areas'. Protected marine life legislation prohibits the fishing and collection of eight species:

- black coral;
- triton shell (conch shells);
- giant clams;
- berried and small lobsters;
- turtles;
- Napoleon wrasse;
- dolphins; and
- whale sharks.

Some four types of destructive fishing methods were banned from 1998 onwards and 1996 legislation established 15 important marine dive sites in the marine protected areas. Three islands outside of the marine protected areas were also conserved and protected from exploitation.

Legislation in 1996 and 1999 defined 23 bird species protected in the Maldives, and prohibited the catching, maltreating, trading or keeping in captivity, egg removal and destruction of nesting-grounds from 2001 onwards.

To respect host culture and the natural environment, visitor codes of do's and don'ts are and were given to tourists and as respect has grown, visitors acting and dressed appropriately may now also visit Malé (which was originally not open to casual visitors) and some residential islands, briefly.

On the basis of evidence seen by the author and respected other official observers of the Maldives scene, a high quality of environmental protection has been achieved throughout the Maldives, and as yet, there have not been law cases of foreigners showing any lack of respect for local social mores. This problem has however occurred in Dubai, in Saudi Arabia and other Islamic states but has not yet occurred in the Maldives.

Constraints

In the period that Maldivian tourism has existed (since the early 1970s), there have been a number of constraints which have affected Maldivian tourist development, but which the nation has nevertheless coped with effectively. This period has been one that has seen regional health risks (such as avian influenza, which affected Asia) and terrorism (which has occurred in neighbouring Sri Lanka, India and parts of the Indian Ocean near Somalia) that have not reached the Maldives. Visitor perceptions and attitudes have had to be addressed on these issues, as well as upon the tsunami, which did have disastrous effects in the Maldives in 2005, and caused enormous environmental damage.

The question of global warming and of sea rise is a critical one for an island nation whose altitudes range from 1 to 2 m above sea level. Some rash trade journals have already 'written-off' the Maldives, Bangladesh and other low-lying nations as 'likely to disappear' under the future rising seawaters. Rising oil prices and the carbon footprint of dependence on current aircraft access to markets is an even more serious immediate worry. The scale of tourist development on the islands relative to freshwater resources, the density of visitors to residents, and their carbon footprint are bigger and real issues.

Economic transformation of the nation, due to income from tourism is astounding: having worked in the Maldives in the 1970s–1980s period, one must accept the changed quality of life for locals and the physical transformation of the capital city, Malé, from being an unhealthy, shabby, port town to now being a modern city with decent services of all types and impressive physical development and facilities (Fig. 8.1).

The training and re-education of fishing and farming people into a service nation of tourist-industry providers is a major feature of a nation which has seen gains and losses from this process.

Resort Development

Foreign capital and know-how combined with local adaptability, local building, fishing and agricultural skills, and government incentives have achieved a national transformation, and the creation of some 91 resorts, generally with small groups of small buildings on each of these resort islands, which take advantage of the peace, the diving, spa, boating, culinary and other offers in the Maldives. Often 'water-bungalows' offer visitors their own temporary home in a distinct and self-contained unit, on a deck in the sea with a gang plank and jetty access to the shore, to link their central dining and other recreational facilities such as shops, special baths, spas and bars.

Scale of Changes and Impacts

What is unclear as it is not explained in the Tourism Development Plan, nor answered in replies to e-mails on technical matters sent to the Ministry in Malé, is any indication of the scale of thresholds or maximum capacities of the number of visitors that the nation can physically handle. Some 600,000 visitors p.a. produce a great deal of human solid and liquid wastes as well as of refuse. It is unclear which technical systems will be used in future on each island to dispose of these wastes in a way which will not disturb the purity of the waters, nor pollute the very limited land resource. The ultimate limits of freshwater supply are not clear, nor the costs and implications of future desalinization of seawater. This sort of information is vital for assessing the realities of long-term 'success and failure' in handling tourism, as much as the sus-

tainability of the host culture, under pressure, and the non-sustainable international air travel to the Maldives.

Evaluation

From what has been stated in the preceding section (on the scale of change and impacts) it is hard to assess in detail, technically, the sustainability of all the physical changes to the Maldives. What is clear is that the economic impacts to the nation have been extraordinary – changing its communication system, updating, enlarging and modernizing its capital city, opening up its society to the world, but seemingly not causing severe cultural impacts to the host's society, or that could become a cause of rioting or of public disturbance. Visitors are better behaved, and seemingly more respectful of the host culture here than in many other developing societies affected by international tourism.

In 2008 the Maldives received a Grand Award from the Pacific Area Travel Association for education and training in the work done on Cinnamon Island Alidhoo, in the Maldives, where a model approach to community participation in development, learning and training was being achieved.

The physical geography of this island nation and its low elevation (maximum of 2m) above sea level creates great risks of tsunamis, as was seen in 2005, when much of the nation was submerged and the scale of damage was enormous. The risks associated with global warming, and possible sea rise, the geological features of this world region, and likely repeats of tsunamis, must be a source of fundamental concern to present and future Maldivian governments.

What has been achieved in 30 years is impressive and domestic empowerment and benefits appear to be steadily increasing which is a critical factor. Having produced an educated population that welcomes the scale, form and levels of benefit arising from tourism is a vital factor towards achieving the sustainability of tourism in this nation. It does assume though, that future sea and air transport to the Maldives will undergo technological changes, which will radically reduce their carbon footprint.

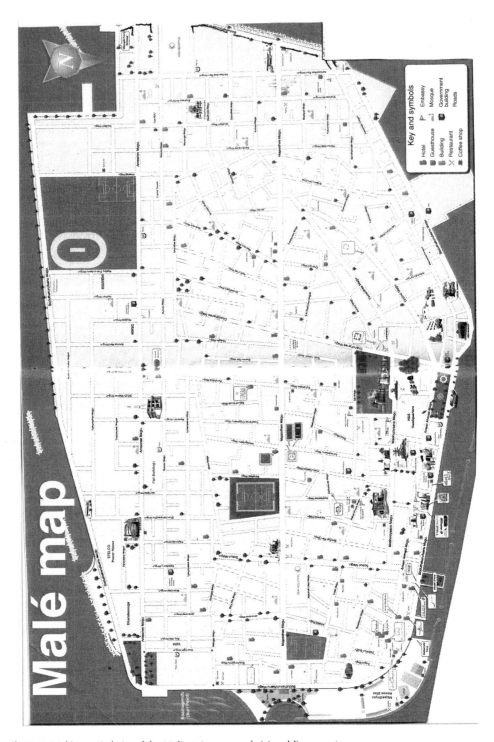

Fig. 8.1. Malé – capital city of the Malives (courtesy of visitmaldives.com).

9 Sustainable Transport to Tourist Destination Countries

Introduction

You cannot have tourism without travel, and therefore the forms of travel used to get to and from destination nations is a vital component in assessing the sustainability of international tourism products. How far are the current forms of transport to and from tourist destinations sustainable? What are the transport modes which are employed in the modal mix, and what impact upon the environment does the choice of different travel modes, such as ships, planes, cars, buses and trains, have upon the environment? Which have less impact and which more?

According to Peeters *et al.* (2004) some 65% of intra-EU tourist trips in 2000 were by car and less than 10% of them were by air. Peeters *et al.* also reviewed rail journeys within the European context but despite their comparative environmental impact advantages, only in three instances do cross-national border rail movements account for 20% or more of such journeys. The comparative energy use levels of the different travel modes and their environmental impacts must be scientifically assessed and evaluated if Man is to make responsible choices in terms of the use of sustainable tourism transport. This has been a very big issue since 2003 and was raised by the Stern Review (2006). A large body of the world's scientists now ascribe the

rate and scale of world climatic change as due to Man, as a causal factor in carbon production and damage to the natural systems. Destruction of forest cover and other human actions such as transport based on using fossil fuels exacerbate these issues.

In this chapter most of the discussion focuses on Europe and North America, the destinations for which we have the best tourist statistics available. It is known that the current primary means of transport access to destination is by private car. Europe attracts 57% of international worldwide tourist arrivals. Though China has the largest domestic population and domestic tourism (and it may be the largest tourist destination), the relevant statistics are not available.

The risk of terrorism

The risk of terrorism has become a notable factor in the last 20 years and this is not only related to terrorist actions at tourist destinations, whether they be in Egypt, India, Spain or Bali, but also to terrorist actions affecting tourism transport (planes, ships and trains) en route to such tourist destinations.

Terrorism has been increasingly targeting tourist transport, regardless of its sustainability. The attack upon the aircraft which went into New York's Twin Towers resulting in 3000 deaths raises planning issues for high-rise development in cities such as Shanghai, Sao Paolo, Tokyo and Sydney, regarding their air defence systems. The attacks on London's underground and buses resulted in some 57 deaths and pose issues with regard to travel safety for underground systems that exist in cities such as Moscow, Paris, Montreal and others. The attack on Madrid's central railway station, which resulted in 200 deaths, raises defence issues elsewhere. An earlier phase in the blowing up of tourist aircraft both on the ground and in the air seems to have abated.

The risk of natural disaster

Natural disasters not only affect destinations but also transport to and from such destinations and during tourist stays. Floods and hurricanes have affected centres such as Shanghai and New Orleans while fires affect the Mediterranean and North American and Australasian destinations. Tsunamis have affected the Maldives, Sumatra and other destinations, while earthquakes have regularly affected countries such as Italy, Chile, Japan and New Zealand – the resort of Napier in New Zealand was destroyed by a combined earthquake and tidal wave. Monsoons affect destinations such as Mumbai (was Bombay), while volcanic eruptions have affected Naples and the Naples Bay Area where the ancient resort of Pompeii was located.

Which Forms of International Transport Are Used Now?

According to Peeters *et al.* (2004) transport used for tourist reasons is divided into some five modes:

- air transport;
- rail transport;
- sea-ferry transport;
- coaches (i.e. road-based coaches); and
- private cars.

Transport to and from tourist destinations is a vital element of assessment in considering the sustainability of tourism to and at any specific destination. According to Gössling and Peeters (2007) air transport is the most environmentally harmful form of tourism regardless of plane loading or high occupancy levels of the aircraft.

Within Europe the private car was the dominant transport mode within the EU for outbound tourism trips, in the year 2000, for some 60% of domestic tourism and for 65% of intra-European movements.

Cruising

The recent growth of large-scale sea cruising and the huge size of cruise ships which can accommodate up to 4000 passengers each, raise issues with regard to the physical pollution caused by such vessels, as well as the visual pollution of such large ships in small destinations. Cruise ships also raise many risks in relation to future international terrorism.

Rail access

European rail transport's share of the total travel market decreased in the period 1970–2000, dropping from 10% down to 6% of the total (due to the explosive growth of car and air transport). According to Peeters *et al.* (2004), there was a 38% actual increase in rail transport use between 1970 and 2000, while the use of coach transport in the same period increased by 53%, private car transport increased by 154%, and air transport increased by 753%.

There are many constraints upon the environmentally desirable increase in rail access to tourist destinations. These relate to: (i) costs; (ii) social attitudes; and (iii) the variable levels of new investment in high speed rail provision. France, Spain, Germany and Japan, for example, have invested massively in the sphere. According to a *Times* report of 29 June 2009 (Keeley, 2009), the Spanish Government was planning to invest €119 billion by the year 2020 in rail infrastructure alone (exclusive of the additional cost of rail rolling stock). The UK has as yet only built a short stretch of high speed rail connection from Central London to the Channel Tunnel in order to connect to the European Continental Rail Systems. The UK proposals for a high speed rail network were published in 2010.

The Environmental Impacts of Transport Used

Peeters *et al.* (2004) defines some five groups of 'environmental impacts of transport'. These are as follows:

1. Global impacts like climate change caused by emission of carbon dioxide and other greenhouse gases (GHGs).
2. Continental impacts such as acidification ('acid rain') due to emissions of SO_2 plus NO_x.
3. Reduced air quality and related human health impacts caused by emissions of particles from diesel engines, but also by the emission of CC, NO_x and SO_2.
4. Damage to nature and landscape caused by redevelopment of nature areas or valuable landscapes, through infrastructure development and large parking lots in vulnerable landscapes.
5. Noise pollution.

Long-haul air transport is a big danger. Evidence from a study of tourism transport to Amsterdam in the Netherlands, indicated that some 70% of the environmental pressure of inbound tourism was due to air transport use, but long-haul air tourists accounted for only 25% of Amsterdam's tourism revenues. Thus the ecological cost was very great though the economic benefits from such movements were relatively limited.

Peeters also emphasizes that air transport has the largest impact upon climate change, while private car transport causes the largest impacts upon air quality and sea ferries cause the impacts upon acidification. According to Gössling and Peeters (2007) it is air travel which generates the most emissions, and which most damages the environment as aeroplanes are at least 10–12 km in height above the Earth, in the upper troposphere and the lower stratosphere, where the impacts that affect the Earth's surface are greatest.

The Stern Review (2006) stated that 'human induced climate change is caused by the emissions of carbon dioxide and other greenhouse gases (GHGs) that have accumulated in the atmosphere, mainly over the past 100 years'. Stern also stated that we must face 'the economics of moving to a low-carbon global economy'.

High speed rail transport is highly desirable because it has less impact on the environment than other transport forms (see Table 9.1), and the fact that it takes travellers from one city centre to another, thereby reducing local transfer changes and impacts. Environmental impacts, however, also have to be related to the cost levels of transport to the user, as while there has been a phase of competitive cheap or low-cost airline provision and offers, with great consumer appeal, low-cost rail offers tend to be restricted to specific categories of domestic travel users rather than to international tourists.

Long distance rail offers

By 2009, two brochures – *Great Rail Journeys* (offering medium-haul holidays in Europe) and *Worldwide Holidays by Rail* (offering long-haul rail trips) – were being marketed for the 25th year in succession. These offers by rail range from trips including one night sleeping on board the train, up to journeys where 12 nights or more are spent on board the train. Within Europe, rail holiday offers range

Table 9.1. The impact of different modes of transport in terms of their carbon footprint.

Low impact modes	Medium impact modes	High impact modes
Electric car	Ferry ship	Petrol car
Train		Aircraft
Coach or bus		Large cruise ship
Cycle		
Sail		
Canoe		
On foot		

from journeys from London to Venice, and either on to Rome or Istanbul, or from London to Moscow as an alternative, while south–north holidays are offered for the full length of Norway or Sweden. At the other ends of the Earth, north–south New Zealand rail journeys are on offer, and in Japan there are high speed rail offers on 'bullet trains' from Tokyo to Hiroshima. Long-distance rail journeys are a mix currently of the use of fast through or express trains, and of high speed train offers.

The long-haul offers by rail, give viable alternatives to air trips, where they are across continuous tracts of continental land. Some short under-sea tunnel and/or bridge crossings link rail in the UK to continental Europe, or Scandinavian mainland rail networks, across and down to Denmark. Thus coast-to-coast offers across Canada or the USA rank together with great trans-Asian routes, such as the Trans-Siberian rail journeys from Moscow to Vladivostock on the Pacific Ocean. That journey includes 12 nights on the train! There are extraordinary trans-India, trans-China and Tibet, as well as cross-Australian trips (both south–north and east–west). Only for trans-ocean crossings must sea or air transport be used, and usually given the limits of time available, and budget constraints upon the travellers, this means air transport use.

In 2011 the choice between rail and air transport to the traveller is affected by the issues of time availability for such a journey, and the comparative cost – financially and environmentally – of the different travel modes. Air journeys are much faster but have a far greater carbon footprint, while rail journeys take much more time and cost more to purchase but have a lower environmental impact (Table 9.1). Since 1960 sea-passenger liner alternatives to air transport have greatly diminished in availability. Only the North Atlantic still offers some sea choices, but increasingly these have cruising characteristics. Up until the late 1950s most travellers from North West Europe to Australia and New Zealand, as well as to South Africa, went by sea-passenger liners, with some of the longer journeys taking up

to 5 weeks in time! The demise of the sea-passenger liner and the emergence of a huge worldwide cruise market is a significant change.

Offers such as those in the *Great Rail Journeys* brochure are now linked to 'responsible tourism', and help for agencies such as the Forest Stewardship Council. To quote the 2009 publication:

Offset your CO_2 emissions:

When it comes to carbon dioxide, we all unknowingly over-indulge. Each time we heat our homes or drive the car, CO_2 is added to the atmosphere. To reduce greenhouse gas emissions like CO_2, and prevent further damage to the atmosphere we all need to work towards a low-carbon life style. The responsibility applies as much when we travel and particularly when we fly. As well as taking steps to reduce your 'carbon footprint' you can neutralize or 'offset' the adverse impact of your flight. Carbon offsetting means donating money to projects, specifically set up with the aim of reducing the level of CO_2 in the atmosphere on your behalf, thus making your air trip 'carbon-neutral'. In this way we can counteract the damage we cause. The projects include:

- Renewable energy – this replaces non-renewable fuel such as coal.
- Energy efficiency – this reduces the amount of fuel needed.
- Forest restoration – this absorbs CO_2 from the atmosphere as the trees grow.

Future Transport Alternatives: Cost/Impact/Choice

Even before considering sustainability, transport questions have to consider issues of accessibility and affordability to know the real costs both to the users and to the environment. Issues of equity such as affordability and disparities of access to transport are raised as well as the general health and safety issues. Europeans are now making more and more transport trips, but these are of shorter duration in terms of time.

Eco-travel and ecotourism

Many so-called ecotourism products offered are at long-haul destinations, access to which is generally by air, using very large amounts of kerosene or petrol in order to get there. So-called ecotourism products that do not use eco-travel are not therefore ecotourism! The desirability of future long-haul travel wherever possible being by rail as opposed to by air transport is evidenced by Peeters and other writers, who indicate that in intra-European travel, if one compares a 500 km return trip by rail with an 8000 km return trip by air, the GHG emissions of the flights will be 168 times larger, than those for the rail journey though the air journey is only 16 times as long. Thus long-haul air journeys have GHG emissions over ten times as great as those produced by equivalent rail journeys.

Satterthwaite (2004) pointed to the fact of car use being eight times as great in US cities as in wealthy Asian cities and that even in European cities it is 3.5 times as great as Asian cities in this respect. European cities have about 2.5 times as much use of public transport as US cities do and have about half the car ownership levels found in American cities. Air travel contributes to 60–95% of each trip's contribution to global warming according to Peeters *et al.* (2004). Between 2000 and 2020 they estimate that the growth rate for air transport in Europe for example will increase most and then rail and car transport, while ferry and coach transport will increase the least. Thus though it may be considered desirable to have use of transport modes ranked according to their minimal impacts upon the environment and upon global warming, the reality is likely to be otherwise.

Fuel-cell cars, hydrogenous fuel and sustainable energy sources (sun, wind, water, biofuels) will certainly reduce environmental impacts of transport in the future according to Peeters *et al.* (2004). While technological developments in rail vehicles aim to double the energy efficiency of such transport in the next 30 years, unfortunately the likelihood of rail becoming a dominant transport mode is a very low possibility.

The Issues Raised and Scientific Evidence

1. There is a vital need to shift from the use of the private car and of air transport, over to the use of rail and coach modes, if we are to reduce greatly the negative environmental impacts of tourism transport.

2. There is a need to increase the average length of stay of tourists, and to reduce the number of trips made, at a time when tourist stays are actually becoming shorter in length and the trips becoming more frequent.

3. Uneven competition between air, rail and road travel modes and the new low-cost airlines create many extra hidden costs and damages to society.

4. Changes to non-petrol-based transport, such as the so-called electric and other non-petrol cars, can reduce pollution and improve environmental well-being and reduce the damage to climate.

5. There is a need to change public perceptions about air travel and its causal role in climate change. Work by Gössling emphasizes this.

6. There is an urgent need for technological revolutions in the development of non-petrol-based cars and aircraft that use less energy. While a number of electric battery cell and other non-petrol-based cars are now produced, their very high purchase cost will mean there is at least a 10-year wait before their general introduction.

Conclusions and Evaluation

The scale of continuing use of petrol-based private cars and of aircraft for tourism is such that GHG emissions, air and noise pollution and other serious causal risks to climate change, will generate governmental pricing and global emission trading system responses, that will not solve the problem. For example air passage duty (APD) will greatly increase flight costs but will not solve the problem.

The range of factors acting against the desirable shift to rail and coach transport are noted, but despite all the negative impacts stated, air transport is likely to be the winner in this game of competitive travel modes. European and national governments, if they do wish to limit GHG emissions, may have to speed up the development of cleaner technologies for air transport and seriously review taxation subsidy and cost incentives in the modal split between choices of transport if sustainability is to be achieved. Heavy taxing of air flight users may damage commercial provider air companies but not have the requisite environmental benefits, as stated by Peeters *et al.* in 2004 'the environmental impacts of inter-continental tourism are large, compared to their economic value', hence the need is somehow to reduce such damaging travel.

Part II

Regional Tourism Planning and Natural Resource Planning

---

10 Introduction to Mountain Region Planning for Conservation and Tourism

International Experience of Mountain Region Planning for Sustainable Resource Conservation and Tourism

The concept of natural upland zone protection is particularly linked internationally with the history of the National Park movement, whose effective origins were in the middle of the 19th century. The North American movement is both seminal and well documented. The rustic philosophy of Thoreau, Audubon and Emerson, the vision and zeal of Muir, the understanding of Leopold, the thrust of Roosevelt, the energy and force of Marshall, contributed to the evolution not only of the US National Parks, but also of forests and wilderness systems, and to the wider development of a multi-functional approach to the uplands. Mountain areas, deserts, rainforests and other ecosystem types were all eventually to have characteristic extensive examples conserved, in order to:

1. Protect and conserve them in their natural state, to keep their landscape characteristics, protecting their flora and fauna and ensuring their inviolability against the forces of development.
2. Provide areas which may be scientifically observed, studied and understood.
3. Maintain ecosystems in their equilibrium state, or regenerate their natural landscape state, which may have been adjusted in the past by Man.
4. Provide incidental recreational or tourist experiences of these environments in their natural state for Man to experience the beauty and wonder of nature and the environment in its 'wild state'.

The forces – poetic, conservationist, ecological, amenity and political – behind the American movement have their echoes across the world in the amenity movements in Britain and Australia, and bodies such as the Tatra Society in Poland. In the Tatra Society mountaineers, naturalists and nationalists combined to try and achieve a National Park in the Tatras well over a century ago, modelled on the Yellowstone National Park in the USA (Fig. 10.1).

The 27-mile long Tatra Alpine chain is the smallest Alpine zone in Europe, and encapsulates all the problems as well as the assets of such regions. Today, mountain region planning for conservation, tourism and a range of economic activities is a complex and demanding process. National Parks are often only a small part of such uplands, but enclosed protective zones, many categories of park type and other heritage protection categories have needed to be introduced and defined as part of the emergence of a 'parks system concept' for each individual nation's countryside and coast. Mountain zones have come to be seen

(a)

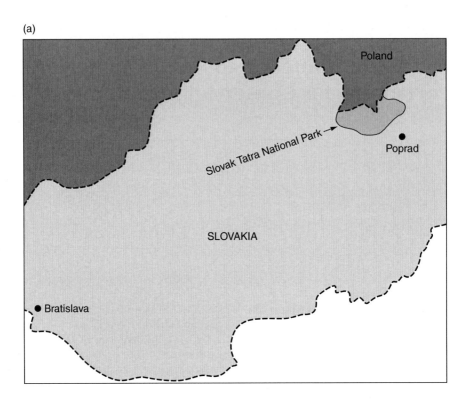

(b)

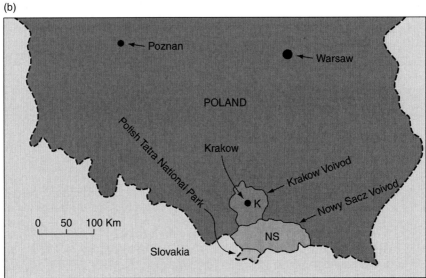

Fig. 10.1. Location of the two Tatra National Parks: (a) Slovak Tatra National Park; and (b) Polish Tatra National Park.

as resource zones, rich in development potential, as well as important as locations of heritage resources to conserve. One is reminded, however, of Aldo Leopold's comment in 1925 that: 'Our tendency is not to call things resources until the supply runs short.' With 21st-century developing nations characterized by their galloping resource consumption, mountain regions are at risk as places from which timber, water, minerals and other resources may be extracted, where nuclear and hydro-electric or wind-generated power stations are sited, defence systems and mechanisms concealed or nuclear wastes dumped.

The increase of accessibility has ended the past protection of sensitive resources by remoteness alone, and rural depopulation has often generated strong economic development attitudes to such 'peripheral regions'. It has emerged that economic planning, physical planning and conservation planning have come to work together: (i) economic planning to deal with 'uneven' development (among other things); (ii) physical planning to deal with locational questions and to resolve conflicts in land use (by planning in advance of crises); and (iii) conservation planning of the zones of national heritage of mountain and coastal ecosystems, and their associated landscapes, flora and fauna. Latterly national systems and programmes of environmental protection and management have also become involved to protect these areas from the polluting effects of man's economic activities. And finally there is the need to meet urban man's need for rest, recreation, therapy and restoration to well-being, which has led to the extensive use of upland, as well as of coastal destinations for holiday, day-visitor recreation and health therapy purposes. Thus mountain regions, seemingly in contrast to the problems and conflicts located in our cities, represent other equally difficult basic sets of problems that require resolution.

Defining and Solving the Alpine Problem: a European Dimension

Mountain region planning must not be seen, however, only in the context of environmental and nature conservation, with tourism and recreation taking a secondary role. A complex matrix of factors are involved – trading off local community interests against those of a national and international character. The sets of factors were first carefully presented in the Council of Europe's 1978 seminar at Grindelwald in Switzerland, on the 'Pressures and Regional Planning Problems in Mountain Areas'. The report of that seminar stated that:

> The Alpine Region is the largest mountain region in Central Europe…Virtually all the essential problems of the European mountain areas can be studied by the example of the Alpine Region. Owing to the central location of the Alpine Region between the big agglomerations in Europe some problems occur practically in model form in this region.
> (Council of Europe, 1978)

> One of these problems is the increasing 'external determination' in the Alpine Region by the surrounding agglomerations.

'External determination' in this context means that from the viewpoint of the agglomerations, the rural areas are seen as only a complementary and supply area (e.g. supply of labour force, recreation area, raw materials, drinking water and energy, to secure further growth of the big cities). In particular the shifting of decision-making processes from the Alpine Region into the centres of economic and political power (e.g. investment decisions on the establishment of tourist centres, large cabin cableways, motorways, power plants, major industrial plants, long-distance drinking water supply and second homes).

Thus – who defines the problem of the mountain regions is seen as critical as to the weightings given – for there is a balance of benefits and of losses in the set of demands, and the needs relating to these regions, and to the capacity limits of resource supply and potentials of such areas.

Policy makers in major population centres, distant from such regions, may sometimes view them as areas of relative low-density settlement, or of comparatively residual populations. However, such populations are critical – whether for the management and protection of heritage resources, for resource development and resource management activities, or for the servicing of tourism and recreation.

Grindelwald inverted this viewing process, and looked first at the needs of the alpine residents. Plus the residential functions, population and settlement were all examined in relation to the viable future of the resident populations. Seven million people live in Europe's Alps, and the work function involves 2.8 million work places there. Agriculture, fishing, industry, energy, water as well as services, provide an employment base. The resident population has supply functions and needs, cultural functions, and characteristics which need protection, especially from the impacts of tourism and tourism development.

Externally generated demands upon the Alpine zone include those for:

- day and weekend recreation;
- tourism;
- second homes;
- retirement; and
- transit travel.

The external demands continue to develop in relation to resources – the need for: (i) food; (ii) timber; (iii) hydro-power production; (iv) water supply and use; and (v) mineral extraction. The social, political and economic significance of such questions may force a low priority to be given to the fundamental conservation roles of protecting ecology, balancing and protecting landscapes, scenery, flora and fauna. Critical land areas may still not be protected as national parks or as nature reserves.

In choosing case studies, therefore, a strong weight is given to the polarities of conservation and development functions, which must be accommodated, and how far legal and financial instruments, organizations, planning, development and management systems are set up, plus devising their aims, and setting about achieving them. Some attention is therefore given to what and who causes the problems in the mountain regions, how issues are tackled, and with what effect. Who benefits, and who loses from such interventions?

In attempting to solve the problems of the mountain regions, it can thus be seen that such regions may have three basic functions:

- that of providing living space, and meeting the needs of their local populations;
- that of providing 'complementary space' and resources for the population in the non-Alpine locations (i.e. development and use functions); and

- that of critically maintaining ecological balance and the preservation and protection of vital natural heritage resources.

The planning and management of these regions must therefore attempt to achieve the reconciliation of conflicting multiple objectives (i.e. the strains or conflicts between goals or objectives). The findings of the 1978 Grindelwald seminar and of the 1976 Bari Conference of European Ministers Responsible for Regional Planning and many subsequent conferences exemplify this point well.

Political commitment to the mix of conservation and development aims is insufficient. The following may all be required: (i) problem analysis; (ii) effective local population participation in decision making; and (iii) introduction of viable organizational, legal, financial and planning involvements. Regional planning has spatial, economic and cultural dimensions, plus development and conservation facets. Different locations may require different weights or emphasis to be given to:

- conservation functions; or
- development functions; or
- a mix of functions related to manageable concepts of sustainable capacity.

The different weights, given in different political systems and at different stages of economic development, are therefore highly relevant to our interests.

Conclusions About Alpine Sustainability from International Experience

Having synthesized a wide range of international experience in this field, several basic points may be made, namely that:

1. There are various mechanisms of planning and the relevant types of regional and area planning will include dimensions of physical or spatial planning, transportation planning, conservation planning of natural heritage resources, and management, economic and development planning (including investment planning and resource development), as well as environmental protection planning.

2. Conservation policies focus on the conservation of key ecosystems, landscapes, flora and fauna, as well as protection of natural heritage resources from redevelopment, damage or destruction (i.e. conserving environmental heritage be it built and/or natural as well as cultural heritage). Development policies will include zoning, resource capacity planning, the balanced development of infrastructure and superstructure, the careful planning and limits of development of settlements – their size, scale and character – and prevention of an inter-regional or inter-resort competitive 'arms race in tourism' development. Programmes are thus critical for harmonization of plans and areas for tourism development, social and economic development, with the plans and programmes set up to meet the needs of conserving heritage landscape and nature.

3. Sets of incentives and controls may be required to give statutory effect to plan intentions, if the legal and financial instruments are to convert paper plans into ongoing implementation and realization of policy intent. Furthermore, planning systems will need to be complemented by systems of managing areas – be they in conservation or in development schemes. Management planning is becoming an overwhelming need in this sphere internationally.

4. Theories and concepts to guide our approaches to landscape conservation, area and site development are rapidly being made more explicit now. The emergence of sophisticated techniques in the late 20th century include: (i) cost–benefit analysis; (ii) planning balance sheets; (iii) Environmental Impact Statements; (iv) interaction matrices; (v) Ultimate Environmental Thresholds (UETs) and capacities; and (vi) Tourism Carrying Capacity Analysis. IUCN, WWF and similar bodies are helping to evolve these in relation to current concepts of sustainable environment management.

Economic theorists like Malisz, Clawson, Hill, Mishan, Lichfield, Archer and Markovic, all applied economic theory more specifically to the economics of tourism and of conservation, while sociology theorists belatedly turned to the social and psychological parameters of the field. It is useful to be reminded by Swiss academics like the late Professor Krippendorf, when he addressed the issue of tourist policy in mountain regions in his book *Les Devoreurs des Paysages*, that:

> The paramount objective of tourist policy consists in the long-term securing of physical and mental recreation as well as regeneration and social activities for as broad a spectrum of the population as possible in an unspoilt landscape and in settlements adapted to the requirements of both landscape and visitors with due regard to the long-term interests of the local inhabitants.
>
> (Krippendorf, 1977)

11 Introduction to the High Tatras and the Slovak High Tatras Case Study

Use of the two East European examples was thought to be of especial interest for several reasons. The processes of urbanization and industrialization in Slovakia and Poland occurred later than in many other European countries and the major phase of it took place in the communist period. Precious and limited upland resources historically had a cultural significance to both societies, and required legislation, planning and management action before all the conservation and development requirements expected of them could be fulfilled and reconciled. That provided contrast and comparison of these two approaches to the Tatras (sharing the same sort of political system until the 1990s) to the concepts and approaches used in the more familiar classical capitalist economy of the USA, and the mixed economies of Western Europe would, it was hoped, reveal certain fundamental questions and answers.

The High Tatras are a tiny and precious Alpine resource unique in importance and character to Poland especially, which is essentially a large extensive lowland country. The High Tatras formed by comparison a special and highly ranked part of the extensive upland resources of Slovakia. Two nations which were of the same political hue, shared this one small special natural resource zone. Different approaches in organizational, conceptual and technical terms were used by the

two nations, in the planning and management of this shared resource. The two approaches should make interesting comparisons, and jointly provide a comparative model of how far the values and approaches to upland planning of East European societies in the communist period, relate to or differ from those which are used in the mixed economies of capitalist societies.

The Resource Base of the Twin-nation Upland Zone: Location and Extent

The High Tatras are the highest part of the 1200 km-long chain of the Carpathian Mountains, which lie to the north of the River Danube's lowlands, in Central Europe. The entire Tatras Mountain Range is small, totalling only some 800 km^2 in area, of which 650 km^2 is located in Slovakia, and 150 km^2 in Poland. The Tatras subdivide into three units:

- the western part ('Zapadne Tatry');
- the central part ('Vysoke Tatry'), or the High Tatras; and
- the eastern part ('Belianske Tatry').

The western and central parts form the border between Slovakia and Poland. The High Tatras have an area of 260 km^2 which make them the smallest of the world's Alps.

The principal ridge of mountains is only some 26.5 km in length and some 17 km in width at the widest point. Some four-fifths of the High Tatras lie within Slovakia while only one-fifth is in Poland. They form the northern mountain boundary of part of Eastern Slovakia and the mountains also form part of the central section of Poland's southern frontier.

Both for Slovakia and Poland, the Tatras represent the key high Alpine zones within each country. However, for Poland they rank as a unique resource, while for Slovakia they are an Alpine resource of international importance.

Physical characteristics

Some 300 mountain peaks, towers and high ridges are contained within the High Tatras, together with some 35 high mountains, valleys and hollows, while some 15 mountain lakes are found at an altitude of over 2000 m. Of the mountains themselves, 25 are over 2500 m, and of these six are over 2600 m high. The two key highest peaks are Gerlachovsky Stit (Mount Gerlach) at 2665 m and Mount Lomnicky at 2626 m. The cluster of peaks form a tight chain, which rises suddenly over the Poprad basin in Slovakia with no intervening passage of foothills. The rocky peaks loom above a dark green zone of dwarf pine forests, and a lower zone of coniferous woods into which nestle to the south a line of small health spa settlements and recreation resorts which grew based upon their spa waters, scenery and winter sports.

Flora and fauna

The mountains of the High Tatras and their associated valleys, terraces, tarns and streams are remarkable not only for their great scenic value, but also for the extent and quality of their fauna and flora. Since 1813 when a book entitled *Principal Flora of the Carpathians* was published, botanists have come here to study the rich mountain flora, which includes Swiss stone pine, miniature willow, spruce, rowans, glacial buttercups, crocus, edelweiss,

primulas and gentians. Animal and birdlife is equally rich, including marmots, bear, boar, chamois, bison, roe deer, lynx, wolf and wildcat; as well as eagles and stork. Salmon trout and crayfish are found in the streams. Geological, geomorphological, hydrological and climatic characteristics make this area of great national value both to Slovaks and Poles for scientific study and nature conservation.

The Slovak Part of the High Tatras: Historical Development of Recreation and Tourism

From the data given it will be obvious that the Tatras were to become of great importance both for scenic and for conservation purposes. However, long before scenic tourism, and the development of active winter sports the special qualities of local spa waters, sulfur and other baths and the fine quality of the mountain air drew visitors to this region.

The region has a very long cultural history of human settlement and activities. Prehistoric refuges for Man existed here. As early as the Iron Age metal producing took place in the valleys of the Tatras, where later primitive iron kilns and charcoal production occurred. It was not until the Middle Ages that an intensification of settlement was notable, first to the south of the mountain range, and later to the north of them. Economic activities came to be those of grazing, timber cutting causing deforestation, and shepherding, mining and environmental degradation, with hunting in the forests. Recreational activities first grew out of economic pastimes: the making of mining hammers in the first half of the 16th century gave rise to making climbing sticks, while shepherds crooks or sticks and poachers guns, came later. In 1565 there was a key pioneering trip of the people of Kezmarok to the lake of Zeline Pleso. There is evidence of 17th century recreational trips and tours – and this marked the start of educational and recreational activity in the Tatras. The date of the first recorded mountain climbing in the Tatras was 1615.

The small Tatra spa town of Stary Smokevec was founded as early as 1797, at a height of 1010 m, and is the oldest tourist settlement in the mountains. Other resorts essentially developed as health resorts of the Austro-Hungarian Empire, as railways in the 19th century made the region more accessible to the growing centres of urban population elsewhere. While the 18th century had seen the development of climbing and study trips by priests, mineralogists and botanists, it was not until 1772 that a nobleman had gone climbing for 'fun'. In 1793, the first gamekeepers' and hunters' huts were erected while the first isolated recreational chalets were built in 1797.

Nineteenth-century developments followed an interesting sequence: in 1835, Mount Krivan was used as a symbol of Slovak nationhood, so groups made 'cultural' trips to it. By 1863, with levels of visiting increasing, the first tourist chalet was built up in the High Tatras. From 1871 onwards was the start of the 19th-century's tourism development boom, for the railway was built from Bohumin to Kosice, and the area was suddenly linked into the main European railway system, giving rise locally to spa and general health resort developments. The settlements of Tatranska and Lomnica (at 850 m) and Strbske Pleso, date from 1892. The development of scenic tourism, then of mountaineering and skiing led onto the phased opening up of skiing, climbing and of viewing zones in mountain areas near these three resorts, with access via cog railways and later on by cable cars.

To the relic 'grand hotels' of the Imperial heyday, were added a few later hotels, and in the communist period a batch of trade union sanatoria, tourist hotels and hostels were built. These were part of the planned development of selected zones, balancing active resource conservation zones elsewhere. Connecting road and airport developments took place.

The lake of Strbske Pleso, the most visited in the Slovak Tatras, is linked by transport routes to a key post-war winter sports development zone, where new skiing, ski jumping and other associated sports facilities were provided. This was recognized formally in 1970 by the holding of the World Championship in Skiing, in Classical Disciplines at the new centre; ski jumps, lifts, tows, new hotels and car parks were all constructed.

Prior to the 1960s the area had a few old resorts. As a result of 1960s' regional planning, there was both expansion of the old resorts, and the creation of new ones, over a wider territory with major 'trade union holiday house holidays' for workers from the cities. Hotels of this type were built in no less than eight locations. State-provided sanatoria, bath houses, spa mineral springs and mud treatment centres were developed in four of the centres in the Tatras. Thus spa attractions, as much as general sporting recreation and tourist attractions retained their functional importance in the region.

National Park development

As early as the 1870s, a movement started by small pressure groups to create a 'reservation' on the Slovak and Polish Tatras. Plans did not become more concrete until the 1920s, but their fulfilment was ruled out by lack of legislation and by opposition from those with powerful hunting interests and private owners of large-scale forests, lands, tourist and health therapy establishments. The area suffered degradation of its forest and mineral resources during the Second World War, and it was not until after that that the first formally protected 'State Protected National Reserve' was realized.

The Slovak High Tatra National Park Preservation is the largest wildlife reserve of Slovakia, set up in 1949 under a Slovak law of December 1948. An area of 50,000 ha (or 500 km^2) was designated, all of the land within it was nationalized, a special management agency was created, and the flora and fauna resources were thus placed under the formal protection of the state.

Outside the area of the park proper, is a 'protected zone' covering 700 km^2. The National Park has a special administrative body, and is guided by the Consultative Body for the Tatra National Park (TNP or TANAP). In addition, there is a Tatra National Committee that acts as a safeguarding watchdog upon nature conservation management.

Within the park a system of 350 km of trails were signposted and recognized, with some seven high peaks made accessible by mountain trail. Associated isolated cabins, refuges and hospices were created. A major long distance path, the Magistraba, was developed along valleys and peak ridges for some 64 km. This provides the opportunity for a 3-day hike in good weather conditions.

There are extensive mountain (conservation) zones, accessible only to hardy walkers, climbers and cross-country skiers, while the majority of the peaks require skills in order to reach them. Only a few peaks and selected pockets have been opened up by good foot trails or by a suspension, cog railway or other forms of mechanical access, for scenic viewing purposes, and to enable skiers to start their downhill runs.

The three small settlements Tatranska Lomnica, Stary Smokovec and Strbske Pleso, long-connected by tram or light rail through to Poprad, are all linked by a post-war road called the 'Road of Liberty'. This allows coach and car-based tourists to go to the resorts, camping zones, view points, small car parks and simple picnic places. New buildings and facilities were concentrated in small zones, adjacent to the three existing settlements, such as at Nowy Smokovec. Until the 1990s, the strategy provided sustainable development as most travel was by rail and coach, and visitor numbers were kept well below the areas' capacity levels which had been pre-planned.

New winter facilities were concentrated in and near Strbske Pleso, and the National Parks Museum and Mountain Rescue Service headquarters were both placed at Tatranska Lomnica. New hotels and hostels were paid for in the communist period by the hotel, tourist or trade union bodies.

Active cultural heritage conservation, including folk heritage, was seen as an element of the planning strategy. Conservation of wooden architecture in its traditional vernacular form was taken as far as the conservation of whole settlements, such as Zdiar, while folk dress, wooden crafts, weaving, fabric printing and leather crafts were all treated as economic activities which are linked to tourism. In addition, tourist activity (based on the use of coaches) gave access to nearby historic towns such as Kezmarok and Levoca, the Castle of Spis and historic rural hostelries and restaurants. Political conditions in this period, the limits of intra-national tourism in the European communist bloc prior to 1989, and the slow start of Western European tourism access to the Slovak Tatras gave the region time to plan in advance of crisis conditions.

Development Planning and Heritage Conservation Planning in the Slovak High Tatras

The 'Countryside Plan' for the High Tatra region was first prepared in the late 1960s and early 1970s by the Czechoslovak Institute for Urbanism and Regional Planning (URBION) in Bratislava, in its Department for Tourism and Nature Conservation. Advice was given by consultants and specialist institutions. Implementation was vested in the State Planning Commission, the Regional National Council, and the Chief Architect's Office for the High Tatras National Park Authority.

As stated already the Slovak High Tatras represent an extraordinary set of natural and cultural resources for conservation. However, the zone is both a meeting point and a focus of conflicts of interests and uses, requiring formal reconciliation via planning. The 1974 tourism report by URBION included analyses and proposals both for the High Tatra Countryside Plan, and for the associated development and management projects for the adjacent subregions in the protected zone. The High Tatras were seen to serve three primary functions:

- recreation and tourist travel;
- reserved areas for preserving the pristine natural features of these high-altitude regions and their study; and
- special therapeutic treatment.

Conflicts were recognized, but it was seen that:

> It is indispensable to assist suitable conditions for all these functions to develop if the value of the territory is to be permanently maintained

and if this permanent value is further to figure in the invisible export found within the framework of tourist travel.

The planning approach thus set out to optimize meeting the demands of all the three main functions, that is: (i) nature conservation; (ii) tourist development; and (iii) health sanatorium provision. Territorial or physical planning was given a higher ranked role in this area than economic investment or development planning, which was made secondary to it. Thus the Countryside Plan preparation for the National Park, plus management and development plans for associated areas, and levels of planning were all first vested in a single institute, which had all the technical skills, a permanent technical staff of 110 and ready access to the services and skills of 300 other experts in associated scientific and academic institutes.

Regional and national government accepted the theoretical and methodological approaches put forward by URBION as the binding basis for all follow-up actions. A high-ranking significance was given to the High Tatras because of the outstanding quality of the area for the three sets of interests, and the special social and economic gains that resulted from conservation, use, and selected development activities there. The development potential for winter sports especially, was seen to have great advantages, and yet also represented an insurmountable challenge.

The High Tatras were divided into seven distinct areas for tourism and recreational activity and two areas for 'sanatorium therapy purposes'. Scientific research on high altitude fauna and flora was started, reserves established, zones of different character defined, and carrying capacities were set.

Visitor accommodation capacity was to be fixed and limited in advance:

- 10,000 beds were to be the limit for tourists and recreationists; and
- 3000 beds to be provided for health/ therapeutic needs in relatively high altitude locations.

Accommodation, location and distribution was planned so that 'the activity radius of

(or generated by) individual accommodation complexes or centres ends at the borders of the strictly reserved (or totally conserved) zones. Buffer or "filtration" zones of silence (were to be) created in between the individual centres'. The Countryside Plan for the National Park was linked to the planning and management of the adjacent foothill zones including their settlements' principal communication routes, forestry, agricultural, development and recreation functions. Socio-cultural and historic heritage functions and sites were specially protected. The 'honey pot' or magnet function of settlements was to draw off recreational and tourist pressures from sensitive uplands, and a communication strategy devised to 'control destination capacity by the controlling of accessibility' (Fig. 11.1). Scenic routes had few strictly controlled stopping points.

Environmental quality protection and enhancement aspects of the Countryside Plan were especially interesting: air, water and landscape resource protection policies were devised, to prevent undesirable impacts. Countryside Plan goals included 'rendering the high altitude region of the Tatras entirely dust-free and smoke-free'. District heating schemes in adjacent regions were switched over to gas and electricity so that smoke pollution generated in industrial regions did not affect the Tatras, and power lines were forbidden in the mountain zone.

Evaluation

By the 1970s, in terms of the relationship of legal, administrative and technical processes, the integrated planning activities for the Slovak Tatras was an East European model of great quality. Fundamentally the basis of Slovak tourism was that of domestic demand, and at the basis of its foreign tourism were visits from and to other socialist or communist countries. Domestic tourism developments were dealt with in five year plans. Travel agencies arranged classical recreational holidays, as well as short-term trips with a cultural function. Even by the 1970s, official government documents gave as much emphasis to the economic role of tourism as to its

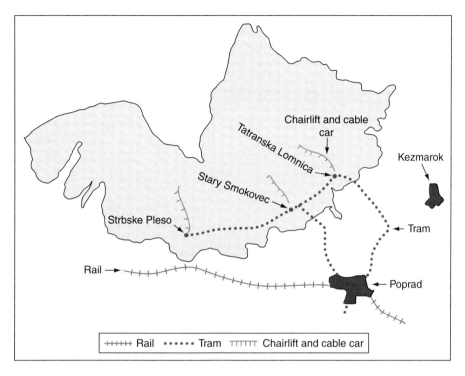

Fig. 11.1. Strategic planning for National Park sustainability – visitor capacity to the National Park was controlled by transport accessibility.

health, recreational, educational and cultural facets. The Tatra National Park was a peak tourist attraction drawing some 3.5 million tourists in the summer season alone in that period. Promotional investment in accommodation both for balance of payment reasons and for social reasons was seen to aid tourism. The Slovak High Tatras territory was thus approached in a very sophisticated way whereby every vegetation zone was treated as part of an ecosystem management and wildlife management approach in the Alpine and sub-Alpine zones. The statutes covering the National Park covered both the National Park proper and the adjacent protection zones within which economic and physical development activities were strictly controlled so as to protect the biological and aesthetic qualities of the National Park itself. In addition special temporary protection zones to cover mineral springs and their environs, which have spa functions, were specified by legislation introduced by the Ministry of Health. To aid carrying capacity control objectives and

to facilitate a more even spread of visitors over the whole region counter magnets were established at various points outside the High Tatras region itself to attract tourists and active sports people. They were established on the lower border zone of mountain areas and such concentrations were to serve intensive and extensive recreation. Some seven new settlement complexes were developed elsewhere in the region to draw off pressures from the established resorts.

The Liberty Road became converted into a high capacity public transport route with inner and outer Tatra circular routes connected by radial link routes, with parking places from which there was public transport access to the edge of the development zones. Thus by doubling the area of land provided for recreational use from 9000 to 18,000 ha, URBION planned to reduce recreational capacities from 8.4/ha to 6.6/ha by the year 2000. This allowed for the visitor rate to increase from 77,000/day to 125,000/day, related to a regional tourist capacity set at a maximum of

45,000 beds. In terms of timing of visits, incentive and controls were put in place to slightly reduce peak season visiting, increase off-season visiting, and transfer pressures to new visitor locations away from the limited territory of the High Tatras. Thus in conclusion, it may be said that a well-conserved natural heritage of unique quality, fulfilled conservation and health provision goals together with a delayed entry into mass international tourism. This gave TANAP or the Slovak High Tatra's Natural National Park in its wider region the chance to plan and devise development and management systems, in advance of the coming of large, and otherwise unmanageable, tourist pressures.

12   The Polish Part of the High Tatras: the High Tatras and the Zakopane Areas

Introduction: Location and Physical Factors

The Zakopane subregion, formally comprising Poland's only true Alpine mountainous area that contains the Tatra National Park established in 1954, and the hilly sub-Tatra agricultural and recreational region, together made up about 1/13th of the Krakow region of Poland located in the far south of the country. The whole Krakow region formerly covered 15,500 km² or 5% of the total area of Poland. In 1960 the population of approximately 2.5 million was heavily concentrated in the northern half of the region, most distant from the mountain resort of Zakopane. A new and smaller rural region or voivod, called 'Nowy Sacz' was brought into being, with an east–west orientation and linking the Tatras to other frontier zones. Post-1975 this region's focus was tourism. A National Ministry of Administration, Regional Economy and Environmental Protection was also created in 1975. The Zakopane subregion focuses upon the mountain resort of Zakopane with a population of over 30,000 and is in an international frontier-area zone. It contains high mountains (over 2700 m high), deep valleys and lakes and is intensively used for active winter sports and recreation. It has wild areas similar to those in the Slovak Tatras and is equally notable for its rich flora and fauna.

Heavy snows, a long winter and poorer quality mountain soils characterize this subregion. The Zakopane area also has a vibrant traditional mountaineers or Goralski culture, with distinctive architecture, dress, music, dance and cuisine.

Motivation for Change

This was an area of conflicts between large-scale popular Polish desires for mountain recreational activities, spa and tourist development, and the needs for nature protection, health and study. The Zakopane or sub-Tatra region has 26% of its area covered by forests. Winter recreation was over-concentrated in one small area of the mountains until the mid-1960s. Recreational growth nationally had to be controlled and directed in order to prevent the destruction of nature. Areas near the mountains needed protection from heavy visitor impacts; facilities therefore needed to be concentrated away from the mountains, but with access routes, and with predetermined and managed sustainable capacity levels. The lessons of visitor pressures upon the one sizeable mountain resort of Zakopane motivated strong planning policies for the Polish Tatra mountains, and these were coordinated with the policies for the Slovak part of the Tatras, across the international frontier, prior to 1968. However, the Polish Tatras differ from their Slovak neighbour as they cover a much smaller area, and Zakopane is the only large settlement in the Polish Tatras and it has a northern aspect whereas the Slovak Tatras have a series of south-facing smaller settlements.

Infrastructure and Superstructure

The Tatra National Park in the extreme south of Poland has good communications to the north (i.e. to Krakow and the rest of the country) via rail and road. An international airport is located at Krakow and there are coach routes as well as private car traffic on the main roads connecting Krakow and Zakopane. Also within the National Park there is the similar system of generous hiking trails as found in the neighbouring Slovak park plus provisions for car parking, cycling, and ski lifts and rack railways to climbing and skiing areas as well as opportunities for biking, climbing, skiing, bathing and spa treatment. In the Polish Tatras, as in their Slovak neighbour, there is a generous provision of a range of accommodation extending from hotels, pensions and hospices, plus private mountain peoples' homes with rooms to let as well as camping sites, mountain chalets and huts, and a limited number of sanatoria and spas within the mountains themselves. In the postwar period both in the Polish and in the Slovak National Parks it became clear that to prevent damage from over-visitation capacity had to be controlled by limiting access via transportation routes as well as limiting the quantity of accommodation provided.

Characteristic Problems to be Tackled

1. How to conserve and protect unique cultural and environmental resources on a small land area, which is under severe pressure.
2. How to create a balance between rationally expanded tourist facilities, and a range of development, with the strong nature conservancy requirements for parts of the National Park which is the most beautiful Alpine zone in Poland and where nature had to be protected.
3. How to spread the pressures of tourist activity more extensively in order to ease the over-use of the immediate facility of Zakopane town, which is intensively visited.
4. How to find ways of using tourism expansion for domestic and international visitors, as a major means of boosting the regional economy, which until 1975 had been largely dependent on the Krakow region's industrial base. Optimal growth of the regional income required realization of considerable and real tourist and recreational potential.
5. How to rationalize, in advance, subregional land use and the communications patterns as a means of gaining maximum benefits, but preventing critical conflicts of land use.
6. How to establish the sustainable accommodation capacity in terms of hostel beds and camping site provisions in the mountain area proper, commensurate with sound nature conservation protection.
7. How to maintain ecosystem equilibrium, establishing the carrying capacity of different land areas, and managing them optimally.

Agencies and Proposals

The regional or voivodic planning office was at first responsible in the 1963–1965 period for the preparation of the subregional plan, and the start of its implementation. Planning both at the subregional level and at the National Park level was undertaken. The plan for the sub-Tatras aimed at the balanced development and physical planning of an upland tourist region, with forestry, hydro-power and nature conservation components. By 1963 there were already one million people p.a. visiting the Tatras. This soon rose to 1.5 million visitors annually. The southern third of the whole Krakow region prior to 1975, was zoned as a National Recreation Zone, including over 23 so-called 'health resorts'. The sub-Tatras fitted into this broader regional context of growth. Tourism, recreation and conservation were the primary functions of the new voivod of Nowy Sacz, to which the whole Polish Tatras area was re-allocated.

The Tatra National Park Agency (TNPA) in Zakopane was a branch office of the Polish National Ministry of Forests, which was the sole source of park finance. The TNPA managed 21,164 ha (beyond the Reglami or boundary path to the park) of nationally owned land in the park, including 11,314 ha of reserves. It had an office staff of 73 and employed 200 ground workers which included foresters and botanists and 40 specially trained National Park rangers.

The 1965 approved plan for the National Park prepared by Professor Kruczala and staff of the Krakow Regional Office, working formally in association with consultants, was approved by the Prime Minister's Office which then allocated funding via the Ministry of Forests to the TNPA. The Polish Academy of Science via its special advisers in nature conservation, located in the science institutes of Krakow, supplemented the available local technical skills which were needed.

Shelters in the park were built by the Polish National Tourist Company 'Petet' and chalets were provided by the voluntary sector PTTK organization.

Plans

Via the formally approved Detailed Territory Development Plan of 1965, the Tatra Mountain National Park was treated as a mixed use concept – for environmental and wildlife conservation, wilderness and new forests. Five edge-area pockets of intensive winter and summer recreational facilities were to replace the existing concentration on a single valley complex based upon the one major resort. Four additional tourist-flow valleys were created (Fig. 12.1). A linear development area, as a counter-magnet for tourism and recreation was to be created outside, and well away from the territory of the Tatra National Park. The cost of building developments were met by hotel, trade union, regional and other agencies, employing their own or consultant architects.

As indicated in the Polish national study in Chapter 3, until 1975 territorial plans and

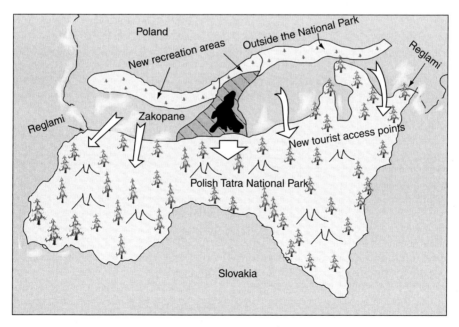

Fig. 12.1. The setting of Zakopane and the strategy to relieve visitor pressures on it by creating new National Park entry points and new 'honey pots'. The Reglami is the boundary path to the park.

regional plans were prepared at the regional or voivodic level. Subregional or district spatial plans were relevant to the special case of the Tatras region. The category of 'Detailed Regional Plan' was applied to the Tatras because the Tatras had a set of technical problems, and also represented a resource of national importance in terms of tourism, recreation and spa provision. The plans for the sub-Tatras and for the National Park grew out of the 'Master Regional Plan' for the Krakow region.

Between the mid-1960s and mid-1970s, major changes in national and regional administration occurred in Poland, and these affected the jurisdiction and boundaries relating to the Tatras subregion. Furthermore, land ownership, management and planning variables differed fundamentally here from those in other communist countries.

Thus in this context, national ownership of National Park lands was critical, as was the exercise of planning and development powers outside of the National Park in areas which were not in state ownership.

Implementation

Rapid realization of developments and investment plans of the 1960s was due to the national priority that was given to the Tatras in the state budget via the National Ministry of Forests, in recognition of the national importance accorded to the Tatras for tourism. Additional tourist and sports facilities were planned to have a 'honey pot' function. Limits were set in relation to the sustainable capacity of mountain areas, to be used for active sport and tourism. Transportation facilities in the hill country zone next to the mountains had to be greatly extended. The spread of activity and of investment was in order to relieve excessive pressure upon Zakopane town and its surroundings. Intensive agriculture was restricted to the limited localities with good soils, and these areas were encouraged to supply industrial and tourist destination zones with vegetables, fruit, fresh milk and other perishable foodstuffs.

The 'Tatra National Park Plan' method and 'Comprehensive Management Strategy' prepared in Krakow (see Fig. 12.2), show the relevance of the method and strategy, not only for the Tatras but also more generally because of their wider technical importance.

Management Strategy and Techniques

In a 1968 paper by Dr J. Kozlowski an explanation was given of the evolution of the Tatra Management Plan and the research behind it. The Tatras was a new and experimental test case in this field, because Polish National Park planning was a new field. Indeed, despite the legal statutes establishing National Parks in the post-war period, the Poles lacked a precise definition for all their functions and objectives. Consequently, planning offices and universities reluctantly moved into this new phase of development working upon National Park management planning.

The National Park Plan was the first instance of 'threshold theory' or 'threshold analysis' theory being applied in this context of preparing a spatial management plan for a set of conserved natural resources; the technique had been developed to deal with planning for urban expansion and for bridging physical and economic planning.

In this new Tatra study 'amenity thresholds' were related to some three sets of criteria:

- the degree of uniqueness of quality of a resource;
- the degree of transformation or reversibility of a change to a resource; and
- the degree of resistance of a resource to an activity.

Qualitative assessment preceded quantitative analysis. These studies were prerequisites for establishing sustainable carrying capacities for defined points, sub-areas and routes covering the territory of the Tatra National Park.

While in the USA at this time, carrying capacity had been seen as a sociology determinant with a definable density at which the user's perception of, or response to, 'wilderness' fails, in Poland it was essentially treated

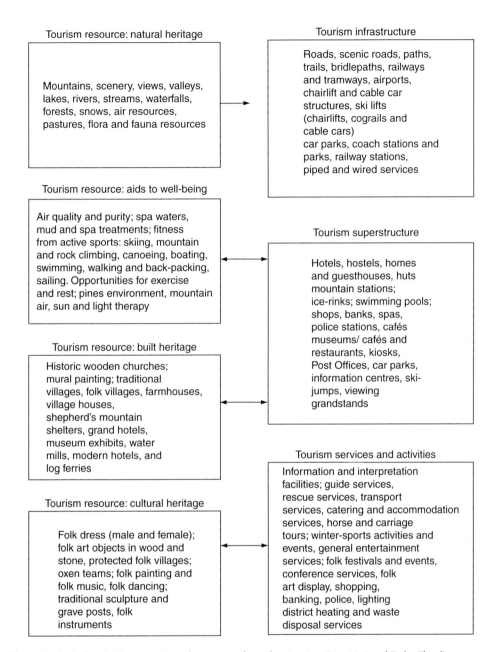

Fig. 12.2. An indicative interpretation of an approach to planning two Tatra National Parks. The diagram shows the various aspects of the tourism package that need to be considered in the planning process. Arrows indicate different aspects that affect one another.

as an ecological or ultimate environmental capacity, the point at which environmental impact damage or deterioration occurs – first affecting the equilibrium of the natural system and consequently marring the tourist response to it. The Model Work Method, and optimal approach, drew upon the 'Delphi Method' of brainstorming a scientific problem, as well as upon accurate site surveys involving observation measurements. Daily carrying capacities were specifically subdivided into: (i) trail capacities; (ii) point capacities; and (iii) generated movements to locations. The National Park area was covered by 120 site survey points, for which preliminary sustainable carrying capacity guestimates were made, these all being threshold points on trails or at accommodation points. Total entry numbers, site numbers, and environmental or amenity thresholds, helped to work out the optimal number of visitors, and thus to establish the level of sustainable carrying capacities per day. Through a process of aggregation the researchers were thus able to establish a total National Park optimum carrying capacity, in terms of numbers.

The relationship of site capacity to accessibility, and to access channel capacity thus were key determinants of management control in conserving heritage natural resources, and this idea and approach recurs in this book. The Tatras study contributes noticeably to the testing of these management theories via the use of simulation models.

The beautiful mountain lake of Morskie Oko, accessible by a 10 km access road, was found to be suffering from excess visitor impacts and this generated pollution, and disturbed the balance of its natural ecosystem. Simulation models were used to test out management approaches, related to variable tourist traffic capacity levels, for this one valley and road to the lake, as well as separate models for all tourist traffic movements in the National Park. From the simulation and testing process it was found that a level of 3500 visitors/day was the optimal level to maintain the quality of this famous lake. Computer-based simulation models were run for the whole National Park with all its 17 entry points over a 14-month period. These studies led to an optimal daily visitor limit of 10,000 persons being set for the National Park. However, 23,000 visitors/day were already being recorded, and as a result of political pressures the compromise capacity of 20,000 visitors/day was set, as an accepted compromise between all parties.

A formal methodology for elaborating the Tatra National Park Plan was devised learning from this trial research and its applications and feeding back from experience nationally and internationally (see Fig.12.3) The indicated method was based on a three-phase approach incorporating normative and optional model elements. A process of social surveys, consultations and participation resulted in multi-level analyses and multi-functional models were introduced. Spatial plans and alternative models were used en route in order to define an optimal model.

The elaboration of the Management Plan took place between 1975 and 1977. The work was based on existing legislation affecting the Krakow voivod earlier, and later the Nowy Sacz. The technical volumes and planned documents proved to be encyclopaedic, and yet most of the approved plan was implemented by 1980. The complex and detailed Management Plan for the reserves gave working guidance to the staff of the TNPA. In terms of approach, the emphasis was to be on: (i) foot-trail tourism; (ii) self-regulation; and (iii) a system of planned carrying capacities, linking sites, route accessibility, levels of accommodation provision, and with locations for specific activities and specific services, all of which were listed. The research institute involved published all the documents, which came to be of national and international significance.

The Evaluation of the Polish National Park Approach

The Tatra National Park was one of 11 National Parks in Poland at that period, but now a much more complex and elaborate park system exists. By 1972 approximately 2.5 million visitors p.a were recorded in the Tatra National Park compared with the 1965 projection of 1.5 million. Special cleaning action had to take place; recreation 'decentralization' was planned, with the promotion of underused National Parks to hive off the excess pressures placed upon the Tatra National Park itself and later upon the adjacent areas. The possibility of road closure was discussed. Good work was done at several levels of government in order to get a coherent view of park systems and their surroundings rather than simply of the area of National Parks, so that the roles of various types of countryside,

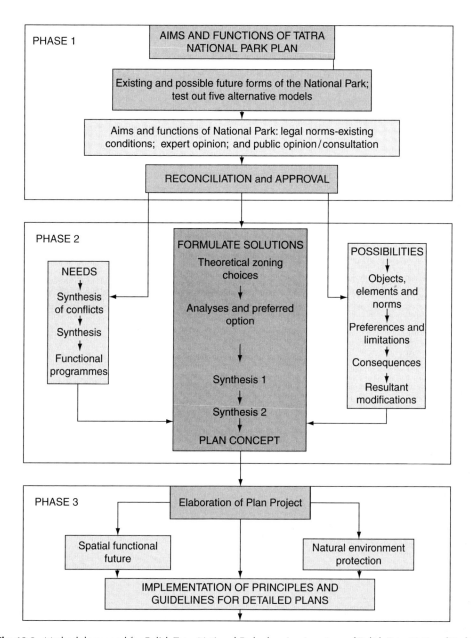

Fig. 12.3. Methodology used for Polish Tatra National Park planning (courtesy of Polish Tatra National Park).

landscape and nature protection and conservation on the one hand, plus of tourism and recreation development on the other, could be achieved.

Polish National Park practice benefitted not only from the input of research work in the universities, but also from the work of a number of specialist institutions, such as the Polish Institute for Environmental Protection after 1973 and the Polish Institute for Sustainable Development after the 1980s. Polish planners recognized that the planning of mountain regions and National Parks cannot be done in isolation from the larger physical and economic systems of which they form a part. Carrying capacity, attraction and accessibility thus came to be viewed in the context of strategic national planning. National parks and nature reserves were placed at one end of a spectrum of conservation measures and types which were to be graded, and related to protection aims and capacity controls. Urban parks and tourism development points were thus seen to form part of a complementary spectrum of positive provisions for tourism and recreation, which aim to optimize attraction and capacity. The simple statement of moral and societal purposes in what was then a centralized communist state with overtly stated views on 'social improvement and health improvement' and upon the roles of rest and regeneration of workers, were associated with landscape conservation, and these helped to clarify needs, roles and goals in approaching the multiple objectives of mountain region planning.

Evaluation of Polish Tatra National Park Planning in its Wider Context

Polish National Parks planning came to be seen increasingly in the context of national and regional strategies comprising nature reserves, parks, forest, protected areas and buffer zones. Such work was twinned with the national reviews and plans for recreational development, tourist facilities and routes. The Polish Tatras in particular provided a critical test bed for the most complex experimental planning and management work done in the conserved upland zones of Poland.

13 Subregional Resource Conservation Planning: the Firth of Clyde 1970 – the First New European Strategy for Integrated Leisure and Tourism Development

Introduction

In 1969, the then voluntary-sector Scottish Tourist Board (STB) commissioned a second-stage study of the Firth of Clyde or Clyde coast area, by an academic team of 12 to do a major report on the future of this vital Scottish region, relative to its supply and demand for tourism and recreation at a critical point in time. The Firth of Clyde is strategically located in the Central Belt of Scotland, and is the location of the majority of the supply of recreation and tourist resources for the Clyde region. At the time of the study, the Clyde region, including the Glasgow City region and the Clyde coast, was split into two from a tourism-planning point of view, and in local government terms was split up into a large number of local authorities. In proposals of the Wheatley Royal Commission on local government (Wheatley, 1969), which was to be later implemented in Scotland creating the Strathclyde region, these two tourist regions were brought together in a single body. However, at the time of the study the Clyde coast region had no statutory significance, and was a loose collection of local authorities and very large numbers of private interests. The resultant 250 page report on the Firth of Clyde carried out by the team at Heriot-Watt University and the Edinburgh College of Art, showed a highly innovative approach, with many of

the elements it included of a nature that have still not yet been adopted in normal practice by 2011.

First it is necessary to introduce the study region itself. The Clyde coast region focuses on the estuary of the River Clyde and includes the islands of Arran and Bute, the Cowal Peninsula of Argyll, and the coastal region of Ayrshire through to the town of Gourock, at the entrance to the Clyde. This historically is a water-focused region, upon which Glaswegians have for the last 100 years or more, had the tradition of going 'doon the watter'. They sailed via a fleet of river steamers to the island resorts and coastal resorts developed from the 19th century onwards. The resorts provided the resource supply to satisfy the recreational and tourist demands of the 2.5 million people residing in the Clyde Valley region centring upon Glasgow. The Clyde Valley region is a great industrialized city region largely developed in the 19th century, living within a classic valley region profile based upon the River Clyde, famed for its shipbuilding, for this is where the world's great ocean liners, warships and cargo ships were built.

Glasgow itself, the location of demand for tourism and recreation in the Firth of Clyde region, is an immigrant city of Highland Protestant Scots and Irish Catholics, with their two great football teams of Rangers and

Celtic, and an urban leisure-based tradition of music-hall humour, drinking in bars, and the climax of annual holidays that involved going 'doon the watter' to the seaside resorts on the islands of Bute, Cumbrae and Arran, and the coastal resorts of Ayrshire.

The late 1960s was a major time of change with the decline of the shipbuilding industry on the Clyde, urban renewal in Glasgow with the knocking down of the Gorbals, and the start of British uptake on air-package holidays overseas. The class-based traditional Scots' holidays were also changing, and there was a need for a major review of this region's future recreation and tourism economies.

Justification

This case study is included because the Clyde Study created a remarkable timely opportunity to look at the development of a regional strategy for resource conservation and tourism development, involving a radical look at alternative approaches to change, and to assessing the whole range of existing and potential resources of a region. The desirable notion was introduced of planning creatively and systemically for the whole of a region's resources, related to transport, economic means and the implementation of a large-scale pattern of change.

Thus the aims of the Clyde Study were to review existing and potential resources for leisure and tourism, for the residents of this major Scottish region, and also to look at

the economic potential for future external demand both from the UK and from overseas. Such demand could contribute to the economic well-being of this region, which was undergoing economic structural change. The STB wanted ways to be found of reviewing systematically all the resources of this complex region, their capacities, and their competitive ability, as well as their accessibility. An evaluation was asked for of new development possibilities and help to change the opportunities, and to improve the quality of life for the residents of this wider region and of the tourists visiting it.

In summary, it can be said that there was a threefold aim in this study:

1. To devise a system of regional review of the resource potentials, examine the types of resource, look at accessibility, capacity and investment.
2. To identify the potentials, and indicate a range of development projects and their realization, with detailed valuation of the financial cost of realizing such projects, the practicality and their capacities.
3. To model alternative strategies for the development of the region, of resources to be conserved, and to identify the type and location of key priority development projects.

The study team first established certain principles (as shown in Figs 13.1 and 13.2), assuming that the capacity of terminal resources could be controlled by controlling accessibility to such destination locations. Secondly, they realized that the Firth of Clyde region had to be related very closely to the Glasgow City region

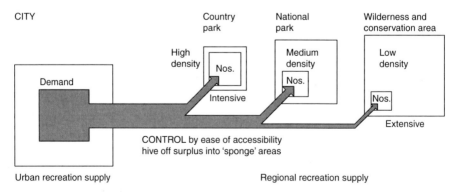

Fig. 13.1. Control by accessibility: fitting resource capacity and visitor numbers (Source: Travis and Consulting Team, 1970).

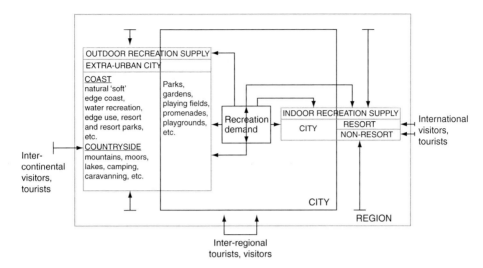

Fig. 13.2. Theoretical model of recreation demand and supply in a city region (Source: Travis and Consulting Team, 1970).

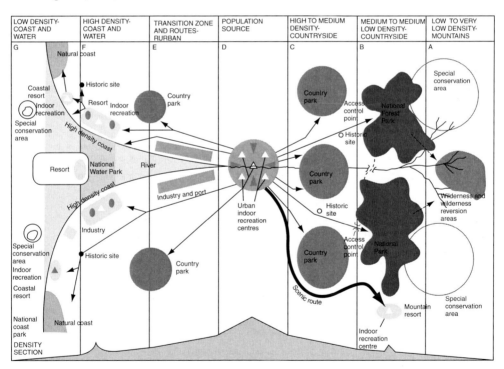

Fig. 13.3. Theoretical model for planning the recreation and tourist resources of the Clyde Valley region (Source: Travis and Consulting Team, 1970).

because these two subregions were interdependent, as shown in the theoretical model of demand and supply given in Fig. 13.2 and then applied diagrammatically to these two adjacent regions as shown in Fig. 13.3.

However, before one could approach strategic development it was considered necessary to devise a system of classifying tourism and recreation resources and in this context, it drew upon the seminal work in the USA of the Outdoor Recreation Resources Review Commission (ORRRC), directed by Senator Rockefeller. However, that sixfold classification system was devised to meet the needs for policy planning in the USA, and it was decided to adjust and modify their approach so that it would be appropriate for use in British, and more specifically Scottish, circumstances. The team devised a new resource classification system based on that of the ORRRC and called it the Clyde Recreation Resource Classification (CRRC) system (see Fig. 13.4). The report spelt out this classification system in great detail and illustrated examples of all the categories, but this is only given in summary form in this book. On the basis of a large amount of fieldwork, desk research, use of the new classification system and consultation with a large number of stakeholders, the team devised three test 'recreational strategies' based on different assumptions about the future of the region. These in turn were tested against a large number of criteria, the result of which was that strategy 'C' came out in the report as the preferred strategy for tourism and recreation development proposed for the Firth of Clyde region.

Model Studies

As there were a large number of local authorities in the area, it was subdivided into a series of subregions, approximating to the interests of local authorities, so that the requested seven model studies could be related to actual situations and real needs at locations within the Firth of Clyde study area.

Model study 1 was a marina development, the Kip Marina, proposed for Inverkip in subregion number 1. It examined all the land, water and technical requirements and the phasing of the development and estimated costs. Figure 13.5 presents a summary map of the proposals.

Model study 2 was the development of a new indoor recreation centre proposed for the new town of Irvine in subregion 2a. It was proposed that such a multi-use recreation centre could be built adjacent to the new town

centre and thus satisfy resident recreation in the new town, and because of its near-beach location, provide important wet-weather recreation opportunities for tourists visiting the Irvine beach development (Type 'A' in the CRRC; see Fig. 13.4).

Model study 3 related to scenic routes and the selected example was for an area in the Kyles of Bute in subregion 6. All the complex requirements for scenic roads, their siting, location, provision of associated services and management were spelt out in the report.

Model study 4 was a heritage site, Burns' Cottage in the village of Alloway, the birthplace of Robert Burns, located in subregion 2b. Meticulous studies were done of how to: (i) accommodate tourist visits in the village; (ii) maintain the fabric of the historic cottage itself; (iii) provide appropriate car parking, new buildings and temporary exhibitions; and (iv) deal both with the Burns' site as a key national heritage site in itself, and set out the idea of developing a Burns' Trail in Scotland as a major tourist proposal.

Model study 5 was to demonstrate the approach to improving old resorts, as many of the resorts in the region were old, tired and in need of physical renovation as well as in modification of their attractions, traffic management, parking and other facilities. The resort of Rothesay on the Isle of Bute was chosen, and detailed studies were made for the central area of the town, showing suggested new developments, including: (i) a Clyde steamer museum; (ii) a pedestrianized shopping centre; and (iii) a new traffic-free heart for the resort. Guidance was given on how to upgrade and adjust a resort for modern circumstances. This is shown in Fig. 13.6 and is located in subregion 5.

Model study 6, namely for outdoor recreation in a National Park type area, was applied to the Isle of Arran because this island in the estuary of the Clyde has all the landscape features of Scotland in miniature located within a small area. Thus it provided an opportunity to look in great detail at the management of land resources, flora and fauna, and all the issues of conservation in a land-based context and a maritime environment, in a potential Clyde National

CLYDE RECREATION RESOURCE CLASSIFICATION

*Footnote: Outdoor Recreation Resources Review Commission (Rockefeller) Classification

*ORRRC CLASS	Comments and reason for modification for the Clyde	Clyde Recreation Resource Classification (CRRC)
CLASS I HIGH DENSITY RECREATION AREAS Areas intensively developed and managed for mass use	Need to integrate resort recreation resources, indoor and outdoor recreation resources in one major category wherein the full range of mass recreation and high density resources are brought together	TYPE 'A' DEVELOPED OR PRO-POSED RESORTS: URBAN INDOOR AND OUTDOOR RECREATION RESOURCES
CLASS II GENERAL OUTDOOR RECREATION AREAS Areas subject to sub-stantial development for a wide variety of specific recreation uses	Need to relate to British legislation, need to maximize the use of a range of linear and pocket resources both by design and by management	TYPE 'B' COUNTRY PARKS AND POCKET RESOURCES: MAJOR SCENIC ROUTES WITH FACILITIES: LINEAR ROUTE RESOURCES
CLASS III NATURAL ENVIRON-MENT AREAS Various types of areas that are suitable for recreation in a natural environment and usually in combination with other uses	Need to create a much broader range of categories to meet British and especially Scottish conditions. Need to plan for a series of multiple use concepts of different sorts. Need to safe-guard and protect attractive woodland and private farmland areas from excess recreational pressures, and to allow for economic changes in these spheres	TYPE 'C' NATIONAL WATERPARKS, NATIONAL FOREST PARKS AND AREAS OF NATIONAL PARK-TYPE CHARACTER
CLASS IV UNIQUE NATURAL AREAS Areas of outstanding scenic splendour, natural wonder or scientific importance	Need to recognize specific measures and means of rural conservation of what is good; need to separate nature conservation from other forms of rural conservation; need to take action over elements, areas or lines of blight and convert them into assets in a high quality landscape	TYPE 'D' SPECIAL CONSERVATION AREAS: RURAL ACTION AREAS FOR CONSERVATION
CLASS V PRIMITIVE AREAS Undisturbed roadless areas characterized by natural, wild conditions including wilderness areas	Need to recognize difference in scale of primitive areas in UK and USA and the difficulty of achieving even micro-wilderness areas in our highly urbanized society. Recognize the need, but modify the concept and its scale and timing to suit Scottish conditions	TYPE 'E' WILDERNESS MANAGEMENT AREAS
CLASS VI HISTORIC CULTURE SITES Sites of major historic or cultural significance, either local, regional or national	Need for more comprehensive category to deal with difference in concept, means and jurisdiction under range of public legislation as well as under private initiative. Use of the term 'Heritage' already used in Eire and the USA is more appropriate than that of 'Historic'	TYPE 'F' HERITAGE SITES
NIL	Need to include transportation elements in recreation resource planning system because of significance of access, capacity and control theories	TRANSPORTATION CHANNELS AND INTER-CHANGE POINTS
NIL	Need to relate recreation to other economic activities and to locations of population which generate recreation demand	ECONOMIC ACTIVITY FOCI

Fig. 13.4. The Clyde Recreation Resource Classification (CRRC) (Source: Travis and Consulting Team, 1970).

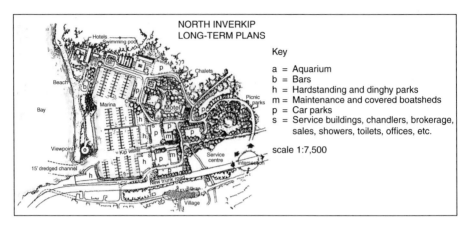

Fig. 13.5. Model study 1: Kip Marina development (at Inverkip) in subregion 1 (Source: Travis and Consulting Team, 1970).

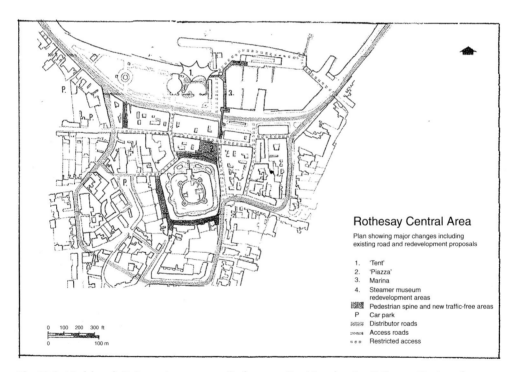

Fig. 13.6. Model study 5: Resort improvement (Rothesay on Bute) in subregion 5 (Source: Travis and Consulting Team, 1970).

Waterpark. The overall strategy for development and conservation for the Isle of Arran, in subregion 4, is shown in Fig. 13.7.

Finally, model study 7 examined the coastal control policies in the environs of a country park, and the area chosen to apply this to was Culzean Castle and country park and the South Ayr coast located in subregion 3. This provided an opportunity to look at many issues relating to attractions, developed coast, soft and hard coastline, issues of camping and caravan sites, and the relationship with travel

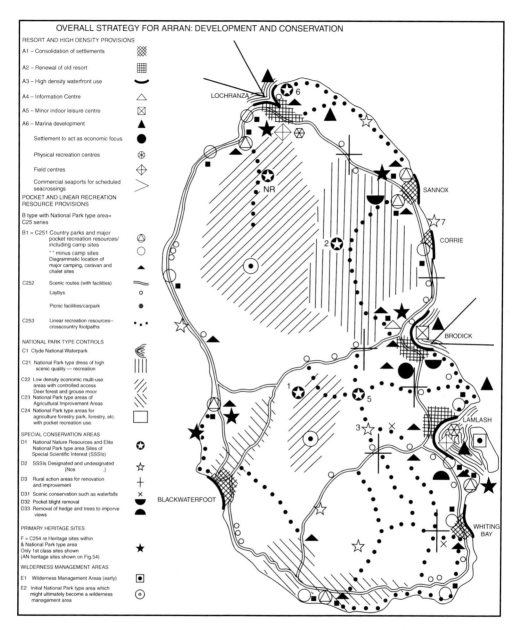

Fig. 13.7. Model study 6: Outdoor recreation in a National Park type area (Isle of Arran) in subregion 4 (Source: Travis and Consulting Team, 1970).

routes. The diagrammatic plan of the study area is given in Fig. 13.8.

Evaluation

Perhaps it is important to ask why this study was innovative and important. There are several reasons for this including:

1. It was innovative because it was the first example of a total regional system for recreation, tourism development and conservation in a classic valley region, being done within the UK.

2. It was the first area for which a new resource policy classification system was devised and applied in Western Europe.

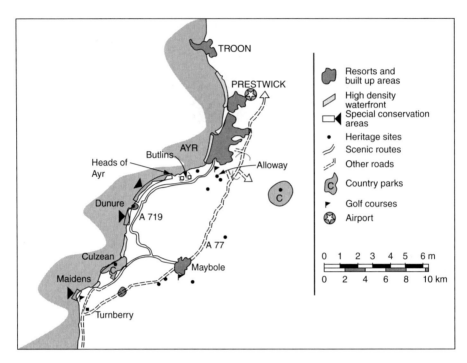

Fig. 13.8. Model study 7: Coastal control policies in the environs of a country park (Culzean and the South Ayr coast) in subregion 3 (Source: Travis and Consulting Team, 1970).

3. It tested out the whole notion of control by accessibility and examining the capacity both of routes and of terminal capacity.
4. It introduced the idea of preparing and formally testing alternative strategies.
5. The notion was used of having test projects based on key themes, which had multiple applications throughout the study region.

Perhaps the study was done a little too early in time, in so far that the full region for which it was prepared (i.e. the Strathclyde Urban Region Authority) did not formally come into legal being until sometime afterwards. There was therefore the problem of no single agency existing at the time to realize the proposals for the region's comprehensive conservation and development. However, where specific projects had started, for example with the regional parks in the area, in the absence of other guidelines, this document was used for subsequent developments. It also provided models that were used elsewhere in Scotland, as well as partially in the region for which they were designed.

The CRRC system has not yet been adopted either in Scotland or elsewhere in the UK, but the problem remains that such a classification system is still needed. There are many economic studies contained within the Clyde Study, which are of great interest and importance, but are too detailed to include here, but again they form part of the innovative approach used. In 1969–1970 testing for sustainability was not done, but the essential nature of the proposals, both in strategy 'C' and in the model studies, is such that they can be adjusted and adapted to criteria of sustainability, and so in no sense are they dated.

The failure in this approach and in many others was the absence of a formal delivery system. It remains the problem with consultancy studies that if they are not commissioned by an implementation agency, there is a real problem in realization of what are often practical, innovative and advantageous sets of conservation and development proposals, which can place a region in a good competitive position with competing tourist destination regions elsewhere.

Scotland belatedly started introducing National Parks in 2002 and 2003, one of which was Loch Lomond and the Trossachs, located at the edge of the study region, and now functioning as a National Park, as is the Cairngorm National Park in the north of Scotland. However, no action has been taken as far as the National Park type approach suggested for the Isle of Arran, as many local residents and other interest groups resist the idea of such formal mechanisms as they believe it will limit their freedom. However, what does remain from this study is an enormous wealth of ideas, techniques and approaches which remain progressive and useful in the field of tourism planning and management today.

14 Upland Classical National Park Eco-model: the Plitvice Lakes National Park, Croatia 1990

Introduction

The Plitvice Lakes National Park is the most famous and most popular of Croatia's eight National Parks, having been first declared as a National Park in 1949. It is a 19,500 ha domain, located in Croatia and created out of an extraordinary stretch of wild countryside, including mountains, forests and valleys, focused upon an elaborate lake system in the Karst limestone uplands. In 1979 it was declared a UNESCO World Heritage Site and has a unique set of natural attractions. It is two-thirds wooded uplands and about one-sixth meadows and lake. The system of 16 stepped lakes is divided by travertine barriers (see Fig. 14.1). The area overlaps the jurisdiction of some four local authorities. Plitvice is a model of the best of European countryside management practice, and this has been evolved in the context of regional resource reviews.

According to a former park manager, Mr Kramaric:

> The National Park has a very small core zone of natural phenomena of quality (1.6% of total area); this has a big surrounding buffer zone of forested areas. Tourism has essentially been related to the high capacity core area – the rest of the park is a refuge for all wildlife, and aims to stay focused upon nature conservation and scientific work. Secondary attractions are the virgin native forests and the wet and also the dry meadows, plus the rich wildlife and flora.

Countryside Management by a Profit-making, Multi-functional Public Corporation

In the period immediately prior to the Yugoslav Civil War, the National Park Authority was generating an annual income equivalent to £27.5 million and had a trading profit of some £6 million p.a. in 1990. It was employing a permanent staff of 1800 and up to 450 extra staff in the peak season. The park was opened in 1949. It operates its own eco-transport, catering, interpretation, sales and conservation services, but also runs its own hotels and camping sites. Two of the hotels are located at a distant location from the park, while two others are located on its edges, and some three hotels are located in its core area.

Outside of the North American continent, Plitvice is probably unique in its range of roles in countryside planning, management, conservation, hotellery and commerce, production and service roles. The public corporation managing the park produces and services different sectors, ranging from nature conservation, forestry and protection; to site transport, hotel management and campsite

(a)

(b)

Fig. 14.1. Plitvice Lakes National Park – location (a) and physical character (b).

creation and management; to agriculture and forest industries, engineering services, information and retailing services. Its management is a 'bottom-up, not a top-down affair'. The Board of the corporation functions as a totally independent body, raises its own revenues in the marketplace and is free to spend income as it alone decides.

Transport Planning and Visitor Management

The National Park first removed private traffic from its lakeside roads. Now only one road actually crosses Plitvice itself, and the corporation hopes soon to have totally transferred the major road system to a wide bypassing loop located outside the National Park. At the two entrances into the core zone, all vehicle parking is concentrated, and visitors are then transferred on to walks, or alternatively on to panoramic electric buses which ply the near-lakeside road, or the electro-boats on the lake, which are silent, electric and non-polluting. It is intended for all of the eco-transport in the National Park to be part of a sustainable management programme. Fencing off the National Park, enables its gating, zoning and management of visitor numbers, and creation of protection zones. Transport and pedestrian planning and management, spatial and wildlife management are all a working reality. In 1986 the National Park had a planned capacity set at 1,200,000 visits p.a. By 1990, after the war, some 682,000 visits p.a. were being handled already. Car parking spaces are limited deliberately to 3500 in number, and coach spaces are set at a maximum of 100. A capacity of 10,000 visitors/day has been set, relative to the two entry-control points, in order to sustain resource quality. Variable charging rates are made at the entry. (In the 1980s/1990s the entry cost varied from £3 to £8.75.) This all reinforced the joint 'carrot and stick' approach, or system of incentives and controls used in management.

Visitor impacts, in terms of litter, wear, wastes and damage, were overcome by a generous repairs and maintenance budget. The 2250 jobs directly generated in the National Park ranged from maintenance to forestry, information, transport, retailing, hotels and catering services. Local jobs are created essentially to employ local people. Detrimental environmental impacts to date have been due to acid rain generated in distant industrial regions, rather than to tourism.

Capital Development Funding

The National Park corporation is a business which contributes money to national government and receives no public income. Its £27.5 million budget in 1990 was derived from gating fees, accommodation and catering sales, plus retailing income. Development and maintenance are the biggest outlays of the corporation and are much larger than the £5.7 million outlay on annual salaries. A trading profit equal to £6 million p.a. was being achieved in 1990, and this meant that annual investment plans, as well as the Five Year Management Plan, had an effective cutting edge.

Design and Physical Management

Within the 250 ha core area for tourism, there are 7 km of minibus routes, and each of the six buses or trains within the park has a capacity of 750 people. The 20 km of raised footpaths are located in the core area and are the heart of the system. The decked paths are deliberately placed at 30 cm above the orchid-filled meadows. So visitors see the natural richness but are physically separated from the meadows and their flowers which are thus protected. The wooden deck system is constructed simply and seems to work well. A trial 0.5 km was tested out first, before general adoption was approved by the scientists and conservationists in the park. Interpretation and presentation was given careful attention – signposts and markers, complement publications and guides in some 13 languages, ranging from Croatian and English, to Japanese, Arabic and Hebrew! There are sophisticated audio visual systems, and personal guides and interpretive planning systems are also offered to the visitor.

Conservation and UNESCO World Heritage Site Status

It is not only the extraordinary lake system, but also the quality of the indigenous fauna and flora, which are protected that make Plitvice so important. This ranges from its large population of brown bears through to its lynxes, wolves, deer and wild boar populations. Many bird species are represented here, including a range of woodpeckers, as are the extraordinary numbers of orchids and other remarkable flowers in the water meadows. The management standard of the conservation activity is at an outstanding level.

The Quality of Planning, Design and Management

More strategic work and scientific work and research has been carried out on and in Plitvice than in any other National Park in Europe. Detailed scientific knowledge about its hydrological system, the chemical changes and the flora and fauna has been gained, alongside the engineering innovation, such as the walkway system, whose calcified supports carry it for great lengths across the sensitive wetlands.

Because Plitvice is among the most successful economic enterprises in the former Yugoslavia and now in Croatia, it shows how conservation and tourism can mutually reinforce one another. This National Park has many practical lessons to offer others. It is, however, very different from places like the English Peak District, where we will see later in this book (Chapter 16, Case Study 2) there are complex challenges upon an extraordinary mix of resources in an unfenced environment.

In 1990 Plitvice as a public corporation demonstrated a management answer. As the park was a totally fenced and gated resource zone under singular ownership, the corpora-

tion had the power to charge entry and the freedom to manage revenues and to generate its own capital budgets. Thus it used conservation to create a major tourist industry for a poor and marginal area within upland Croatia. The quality of planning, management and operation of this National Park as a conservation agency, tourism provider and as a business, is the economic focus for the region which it dominates. The National Park creates the income and economy for its own subregion and is a major source of taxes for the local authorities. Thus it actually contributes to the public sector and does not take money away from it.

The biggest achievement of this National Park is that all the earlier inappropriate development has been moved out of the park proper. For example, camp sites, which were originally located by the lake, were first moved to the park entrance, and are now located outside of the park itself. All new hotels will be built outside of the National Park's boundaries. Employees who live in the village inside the park, were by 1990 already being moved to better housing in a new village being developed outside of the National Park. Life for locals and for visitors was and is getting better! Shortly after the on-site evaluation studies were being done by the author in 1990, the National Park was militarily invaded and was physically damaged. Later, in the period after the end of the Yugoslav Civil War, it had to be extensively renovated and structures rebuilt.

Access to and enjoyment of a well-managed, high quality, countryside resource needs to be paid for:

*   directly – via an entry charge at the gates of a fenced-in park – run by a public corporation as in the case of Plitvice, by the state, or by a voluntary sector foundation as is seen in the Dutch Hoge Veluwe National Park; or
*   by a private estate as demonstrated at Villandry in France.

15 Community-based Desert Ecotourism, Ancient Cities and Nomadic Cultures

Introduction

The historical association of sand and rock deserts is with explorers and famed hardy travellers, rather than with modern international tourists, thus in the desert context we think of figures such as Lawrence of Arabia, or Wilfred Thesiger books such as *Arabian Sands*, or Laurens van der Post's *Bushmen of the Kalahari*.

The Desert Resource: the Sahara

Known as the 'Great Desert' in Arabic, the Sahara is the world's largest hot desert, and covers most of North Africa, including many nations – two of which, Algeria and Egypt, will be referred to in more detail. The Sahara is a sand and rock desert only exceeded in size by that of Antarctica's cold or ice desert. Its area is over 9 million km², or 3.5 million square miles. It extends from the edges of the Atlantic Ocean in the west, includes part of the Mediterranean coast and continues beyond the Suez Canal to the Red Sea. In area it is almost as large as continental USA.

In composition it varies from desert mountains to sand seas, dune fields, great sand dunes, to salt flats and to stony desert. Its indigenous peoples include many of the Berber-speaking tribes of North Africa, and range from Arabized Berbers in the Moroccan Atlas, to the Tuareg tribes in its centre and south, as well as the Bedouin to the east, extending into Sinai, the Negev and the Jordanian Desert. It is estimated that about 2.5 million people live in the Sahara – mostly in Egypt, Morocco, Mauritania and Algeria. Tamanrasset is one of the most important cities of the Sahara located in southern Algeria, and will be covered in the Algerian study. The southern Algerian Sahara is in the hyper-arid zone with minimal rainfall, rare vegetation, mountains and hamadas, wadis, sand dunes, sand seas and salt flats.

The Nomadic peoples of the desert are unique in: (i) their strict codes of hospitality to strangers; (ii) their naturally hostile environments; (iii) the appeal of their people; and (iv) the wild beauty of the harsh natural climates they endure with their temperature extremes and the shortage of water and shade. Adding to the appeal and pull of these remarkable peoples are the wealth of ancient ruined cities in desert oases, and conserved heritage sites such as Roman Timgad (or Leptis Magna) in Libya, Babylon in Iraq, and Petra with its great Nabbatean culture, in Jordan.

The deserts are changing – they are spreading in area, and yet resource development is spreading into the deserts, to obtain its oil resource and extract its natural gas and minerals. Oil wealth, particularly in the Middle East, has created new great modern cities on the desert edges, and some of these in turn have come to act as hosts to international tourism, for example Dubai on the Persian Gulf, or resorts such as Hurghada on Egypt's mainland Red Sea coast, and Sharm el Sheikh in Egyptian Sinai.

Modern urban desert-edge resorts have locations that enable 'add-ons' to their mass tourism attractions by offering short safaris by camel, but more typically by jeep or four-wheel drive to historic cities, to supplement their urban pastimes. Such tourism is not eco-tourism, as it is not sustainable and is not really community based.

Supply and Demand: the 'Sun Belt' for Winter Tourism

As shown in Fig. 15.1, a 'winter sun belt', where North West Europeans take their holidays, extends from Madeira and the Canaries, via southern Algeria and Egypt to the Red Sea, where resorts such as Hurghada, Sharm el Sheikh, Aqaba and Eilat are all located.

These resorts in the 'sun belt' compete with each other, and the competition is partly based on: (i) travel time by air, from North West Europe; (ii) comparative cost of packages there; and (iii) competitive quality of appeal. None of these centres in themselves represent community-based ecotourism, but as will be seen in the case studies later, they are often the stepping-off points for associated desert zones, where community-based ecotourism is developing, particularly in the Middle East and to a lesser extent in the central Sahara.

Community-based Ecotourism

It is important to define terms such as 'ecotourism' very clearly so that there is no misunderstanding. In this context it is appropriate to quote the work of Dr R. Denman (2001), who in the WWF international publication entitled *Guidelines for Community-based Ecotourism Development* gave the following useful definition:

> Ecotourism is a frequently debated term. Sometimes it is used simply to identify a form of tourism where the motivation of visitors,

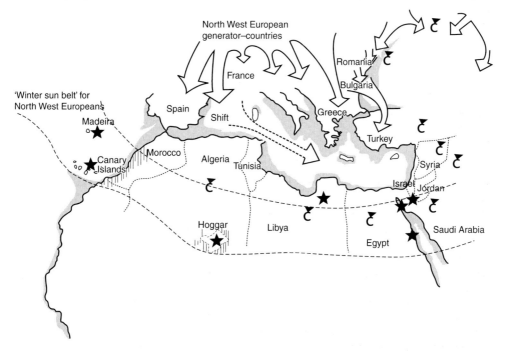

Fig. 15.1. Shifts in summer and winter tourism for North West European markets.

and the sales pitch to them, centres upon the observation of nature. Increasingly, this general sector of the market is called 'Nature Tourism'. True 'ecotourism', however, requires a pro-active approach that seeks to mitigate the negative, and enhance the positive impacts of Nature Tourism. The International Ecotourism Society defined ecotourism as responsible travel to natural areas that conserves the environment, and sustains the well-being of local people.

Denman then goes on to postulate that 'community-based ecotourism' is a 'form of ecotourism where the local community has substantial control over, and involvement in, its development and management, and a major portion of the benefits remain within the community'.

How far is real community-based desert ecotourism developing, when, where, with what degree of integrity and by whom? There seem to be natural opportunities, such as those associated with heritage trails, for developing such community-based ecotourism world-wide, for example the Silk Road to Tashkent, the Golden Road to Samarkand, the Chinese Silk Road to Xinjiang, and on from Kashgar to what was once known as 'forbidden Tibet'! In the deserts of the Middle East the Spice or Incense Trail, that extends from Dohar to Shibam in the Hadramaut, on via the Yemen and Saudi Arabia to Nabbatean Petra in Jordan, via the ruined Nabbatean cities of the Negev Desert in Israel to Gaza. This has had a long historical appeal to writers and explorers.

The recent attempt on British television to reveal the Spice Trail, in late August and September 2009 by Kate Humble and the BBC team, showed that today security problems, terrorism and political barriers, limit what can be done and experienced on such a trail. However, the thrill of destinations like the mud skyscraper desert city of Shibam and the great temples of Petra, left British viewers greatly tempted to venture forth.

In this book, some case studies in four test countries are being examined to see how far the beginning of community-based desert ecotourism is emerging across the great Sahara Desert, as well as in the Negev and the Jordanian Desert.

Case Study 1: Petra, Wadi Rum and Aqaba, Jordan

The Kingdom of Hashemite Jordan is a state, which is the historic home of tribal Bedouin, with a large adventitious urban population made up of Palestinian and Iraqi migrants. In the southern part of the Kingdom are found two key heritage sites:

- the great Nabbatean city of Petra – a UNESCO World Heritage Site; and
- Wadi Rum, a desert valley of great beauty and with much archaeological interest and key historic associations.

While modern international tourism to Jordan is focused upon its capital city of Amman and the port city of Aqaba (with about 90,000 population), which has a hotels resort and sea-diving facilities, visits to Petra and Wadi Rum are seen as essential add-on attraction elements. It is essential however, to examine how far Bedouin ecotourism is evolving in relation to Petra, Aqaba and Wadi Rum. Therefore, past evaluative visits made to Jordan have been supplemented by desk research, both online and from published sources. Jordanian tourism representatives were also interviewed at their stand at the World Travel Market in London.

The Petra heritage site, which merits at least a 3-day tourist visit, normally gets a 1-day visit from international tourists, or even only a part-day visit. Tourists staying overnight use accommodation located on the edges of Petra, or in Wadi Musa, or in Aqaba. The norm in accommodation used, is excellent quality modern hotels, often linked to international chains. An interesting and hopeful alternative to the norm is the 'Taybet Zaman' – a renovated, stone-built, 19th-century Jordanian village near Petra, offering traditional elements like a Souk (market), a traditional bakery, olive press, museum and even a Nabbatean pool. Modern comfort and services, and local staff, offer luxury ecotourism.

The guiding and transfers in Petra, and the aids to climbing, trekking and sports in Wadi Rum, are all done by local Bedu, whose roots are in this area. It is difficult for a foreign tourist who is a non-Muslim, non-Arabic-speaking visitor to obtain traditional home-based or guesthouse based Bedu stays.

Some halfway answers are available: one can camp on the beach at Aqaba, and this combined with heritage site visits, by bike rental or on foot with a Bedu guide, can lead to traditional dining in a Bedouin tent – especially in somewhere like Wadi Rum. When in Wadi Rum, one is obliged to take a Bedouin guide, if on a hiking tour. You can stay commercially in a Bedouin camp overnight – to dine, sleep, socialize, enjoy coffee, music and talk, and can link this to a short or long camel trek, if that can be managed!

Case Study 2: Tamanrasset and the Hoggar Mountains of the Sahara, Southern Algeria

Algeria, with a population of nearly 33 million in 2009 and a land area of 2.3 million km^2, is a large nation, much of whose territory is an arid region. The Sahara Desert comprises 80% of the Algerian land area south of the Saharan Atlas mountain range. The Hoggar Mountains, the highland area of the central Sahara, are a wildly configured area of rocky desert and mountains, the highest of which is Mount Tahat, 2918 m (nearly 9000 ft) high.

The central part of southern Algeria is the home of the Tuareg tribes and people, with whom the author spent a working week in the 1980s, as part of a UN/WTO mission, on the development of alternative tourism. The Tuaregs are a proud, trading, nomadic desert people, who historically traded by camel trains, taking a range of spices, goods, products and services across Central Africa.

First, the French Government, and then later the independent Government of Algeria have proceeded with the enforced urbanization of these nomadic people, to control and to police their activities. Cameleers are increasingly changing over to four-wheel drives for desert trading purposes. However, the Tuareg also provide the drivers, cameleers and guides to the Hoggar and Tassili – the two mountain areas of the south Sahara, which are the destinations for a limited number of hardy tourists.

Tamanrasset, with a population of 120,000 in 2009, has grown into the largest settlement in southern Algeria and the central Sahara, as a result of the Tuareg urbanization programme. It is the trading and shopping centre, and the main centre for tourist accommodation in the region. It is linked by domestic air services, and also by rough dust road to Algiers, the capital city located far to the north, on the Mediterranean. Tamanrasset is basically an oasis, which was the resting or stopping point for ancient camel caravan trains and desert traders of the Sahara. The Tuaregs have a strong identity, who converse in their own Berber tongue, as well as speaking French and Arabic. Visitors can still delight in the Tuareg camel racing at dusk, to the memorable sounds of their ululating womenfolk, and the music, shooting, shouting, coffee and storytelling at night. Visits to desert waterholes and to the tomb of Tin Hinan are local highlights.

Evaluation

All the tourist accommodation is locally provided and owned, or in one instance (that of Hotel Tahat) is owned by the Algerian state, but all is simple, and there is no presence – as yet – of international hotel chains. There are fewer than a dozen visitor accommodation options in Tamanrasset, and these range from the state-owned Hotel Tahat (of about two-star standard), to one or two cheap so-called hotels, a few guesthouses, and camp sites to huts. Facilities are basic, and the impure water can only be drunk safely with the addition of purification tablets. Ecotourism, camel, jeep and four-wheel drive trekking in the Hoggar Mountains is offered by Tuareg cameleers (without camels), and as virtually all the modest accommodation is locally owned and offered, it is community based. The switchover from camel use to petrol-based vehicles, thus limits the sustainability, as does the fact that most visitors come by air to Tamanrasset. In these uncertain times in Algeria, traditional Italian motorbike-based tourists from Europe are now rarely seen riding through the desert dust clouds from Algiers en route to Lagos in

Nigeria, as they were still doing in the 1980s. Scenery, culture and wilderness in southern Algeria still have great appeal, but the constraint is one of personal insecurity.

Case Study 3: Incense Trail of Nabbatean Cities in the Negev, Southern Israel

UNESCO declared the 2400 km Incense Trail from Dohar, via the Hadramaut, the Yemen, Saudi Arabia, Jordan and Israel, to the Palestinian port of Gaza, a World Heritage Route. Israel later formally tackled its 150 km section of the Incense Trail, covering the Negev's ruined Nabbatean city sites of Mamshit, Ovdat, Shivta and Halutza, to Gaza, in Palestinian Autonomous Territory. The managed sites in Israel are run by the National Park Authority (NPA) and the IUCN whose work was commented upon in Chapter 1. The Negev Desert comprises some 60% of the land area of Israel and is its vital land resource.

However, though the heritage sites are managed by the NPA, there is no formally organized community-based ecotourism in the Negev, which is specifically focused upon the Incense Trail.

What does however exist in the Negev Desert, are three or four disparate ventures, reflecting an ecotourism approach:

1. The Bedouin tourism elements – including the Rahat Bedouin Heritage Centre in the Bedouin town of Rahat in the northern Negev, also the Bedouin Centre at Lahav in the Negev, and Bedouin dining opportunities in places such as at the Timna heritage site and the Beersheva Market. Though it is possible to have Bedouin dining entertainment, and even to purchase fine handmade fabrics, Bedouin home-stays for tourists in Israel do not yet appear to be on offer.
2. Desert kibbutz stays – in guesthouses or in volunteer work schemes, in several settlements in the open desert, the Arava Desert valley and in the desert mountains. The special appeal of the southern Arava is based on its Timna heritage site, the Hai Bar Nature Reserve, rift valley landscape and some six settlements with experimental ecotourism provisions.

3. Desert research study visits – to Sde Boqer, with its college, its Desert Research Institute and also to experimental settlements in the Arava valley including Yahel, Yotvata, Elifaz, environmental study-focused Neot Semadar and the ecological community of Lotan. Experimental desert architecture and even one desert solar neighbourhood are found in the Sde Boqer area.
4. Walking holidays – or 'Tiyulim' across the desert, via a National Foot Trail – takes walkers through the Great Crater, and the remote small development town of Mitzpe Ramon, with opportunities to stay with families or at small inns, reminiscent of the historic 'Chans' available in the past to Arab travellers.

Eilat, as the main international seaside resort of Israel, is located on the Red Sea, and on the edge of the southern Negev. Travel companies located in Eilat offer short safaris mainly by jeep, four-wheel drives or quad bikes, (rarely by camel) into the city's desert surroundings. These trips are not ecotourism, as the stays are hotel-based and not home-based.

Fleischer and Pizam, writing in 1997 about rural tourism in Israel, noted its significant growth in the first half of the 1990s, with an explosion in bed-and-breakfast provision and a great increase in community-based rural stays in all parts of the country. Some 14 so-called 'tourism incubators' (centres for rural tourism training and counselling) now exist throughout the country – including its desert area.

Case Study 4: Egyptian Ecotourism and Desert Tourism

Egyptian Sinai

During the Israeli military occupation of the Sinai Peninsula, it paradoxically started international desert tourism there, at a number of small settlements, extending from Eilat via Taba and Nuweiba, down to Sharm el Sheikh. After the return of Egyptian sovereignty to the Sinai, these resorts were much more fully developed by Egypt, and became the basis of a new region in Egypt to host international tourism.

In southern Sinai, these resorts range from the large town built at Sharm, up to much smaller settlements up the Gulf of Aqaba, and are linked to a number of attractions, such as visits to St Catherine's Monastery inland by Mount Sinai, to the Ras Muhammed Nature Reserve with its mangrove swamps and coral reefs of the Gulf. However, this development in the south and east of Sinai has been hotel-based and has not attempted home-based ecotourism, though it does use Bedouin staff to enable safari visits, as is also the case in Israel and Jordan. In Northern Sinai however, the larger desert settlement of Al Arish with 100,000 residents has become the base for much quieter, low-key Egyptian domestic tourism, with little international add-on tourism. Here the guesthouse and home-based ecotourism for the Egyptian domestic market is beginning to take place.

The Egyptian Western Desert/part of the Sahara

Egypt's great Western Desert, which forms part of the Sahara, includes some five major oases at Siwa, Baharia, Farafra, Dakhla and Kharga. The first serious Egyptian ecotourism developments taking place in the Sahara have been focused upon two locations, namely Siwa and Dakhla.

1. The Siwa Oasis is some 80 km across and has mineral springs and two salt lakes. Here tourists can stay in the Siwa Eco-Lodge which is built in traditional style, aimed at sustainable tourism and at giving guests optimal contact with nature. The architecture, furniture and furnishings are traditional and hand-crafted, foodstuffs are locally grown and organic, and no electricity is used.

2. The Dakhla Oasis has a desert lodge and there is also a special development called 'Qassa El Bawrity' at the Bahariyya Oasis. Sahara EDK (Sahara Egyptian Desert Keepers) is, I quote: 'A cohesive body of desert tourism experts that share experiences and knowledge in order to elevate Egypt's desert tourism to the highest possible eco-standards' – an impressive intent. Package offers include:

- 10-day trips from Cairo to Siwa, and on to the Great Sand Sea, and the Qattara Depression, finishing with a call at Marsa Matruh, before returning to Cairo; and
- 7-day trips from Cairo to the White Desert, using four-wheel drives (which now replace camels), to Farafra and Dakhla to Qasr (a medieval medina) and on to the great temples of Dush and Luxor.

While choices are given of camel trekking or four-wheel drive, most international tourists prefer safaris by four-wheel drive, jeep or quad bike. Camping, trekking and birdwatching are some of the activities which are included in these oasis visits and stops. To date, it is in the Western Desert of Egypt where the most interesting early experiments of integrity in this field of home-based, desert ecotourism are being attempted.

16   Introduction to UK Upland Planning for Countryside Conservation, Recreation and Tourism

The roots of 21st-century UK planning for countryside conservation, recreation and tourism are in two 19th-century movements that are linked: (i) the Romantic Movement; and (ii) the movement for public access to the hills and countryside. Though 1872 had seen the world's first National Park created at Yellowstone in the USA, it was not until 1929 that the UK Government first reviewed the idea of National Parks in Britain, and this was in response to pressure from bodies such as the Campaign for the Protection of Rural England (CPRE). In 1932 a great mass trespass on Kinder Scout in the Peak District had taken place, in order to fight for the right of public access to the uplands. From 1943 to 1945, John Dower drafted proposals for some ten British National Parks to be created in England and Wales, and this was presented to the Standing Committee for National Parks. However, it was not until 1945 that the Dower Report was published, and finally 1949 saw the UK Government pass the National Parks and Access to the Countryside Act. The first British National Park to be designated was the Peak District National Park in 1951. This was created some 79 years after Yellowstone, and was very much a test bed for this field of action in the UK.

Twin pressures for the 1949 legislation were: (i) the express needs for recreational and tourist access to the countryside; and

(ii) the need for protection of beautiful upland countryside from development and from blight. John Dower, who had shaped the UK's idea of a National Park, presented one which was unacceptable to the IUCN's classic category II definition, but was more appropriate for IUCN's category V protected area. He stated that:

> A national park is an extensive area of beautiful and relatively wild country in which, for the nation's benefit, and by appropriate national decision and action, (a) the characteristic landscape beauty is strictly preserved, (b) access and facilities for public open air enjoyment are amply provided, (c) wildlife and buildings and places of architectural and historic interest are suitably protected, while (d) established farming use is effectively maintained.

By the mid-20th century, when the UK started to establish its own National Parks, it was already a highly urbanized country, with essentially humanized landscapes, and apart from some pockets in North Wales and Scotland, it lacked those 'vast expanses of virgin lands', which were found in the American Rockies or the mountains and savannahs of some parts of Africa and Asia. By 2009, the UK was a nation of over 61 million people, and though the extent of countryside conservation had extended, it was hardly able to meet the enormously increased recreation and tourist pressures placed upon its highly pressurized coast and countryside. The UK's approaches to landscape protection and land management of such areas have been bound to reflect very difficult compromises in all ways.

Case Study 1: National Park Planning and Management

By 2009 some 12 National Parks had been established in England and Wales comprising almost 15,000 km² in area (Fig. 16.1). In addition two National Parks had been created in Scotland (of approximately 5700 km²), and a further two were being considered for England. The 14 existing National Parks in the UK covered over 20,000 km², over 8% of the UK's territory, and nine of these cover upland regions. Originally when they were first created, the National Parks were to be run jointly by local planning authorities, who were to share the costs with the government; subsequently this changed and a sequence of agencies (National Parks Commission, Countryside Commissions, etc.) took on responsibility for the overall management of the National Parks system.

UK National Parks characteristically have encouraged the use of a multi-mechanism approach to countryside conservation, management and planning. In addition to National Parks, a wider system of countryside conservation was devised including heritage coasts and several other elements:

- Some 31 Areas of Outstanding Natural Beauty (AONBs) covering about 9% of the land area were established in England and Wales and were to be run by the local planning authorities.
- A network of country parks was formed to meet urban-generated recreation needs within the countryside.
- Green Belts were established in order to contain or separate major urban areas and prevent them from growing into each other.
- Long-distance footpaths, such as the Pennine Way, were established.

- Urban fringe provisions and experiments were set up to absorb urban pressures and to deflect excess recreational tourism demands away from the National Parks, AONBs and other areas of sensitive character and limited visitor capacity.

This set of provisions are complemented by the important conservation activities of bodies like the Nature Conservancy Council – later to be replaced by English Nature and Scottish Nature – which enabled National Nature Reserves, nature reserves and Sites of Special Scientific Interest (SSSIs) to be protected. Complementary bodies like the Forestry Commission established Forest Parks, later Community Forests and a National Forest, while incidental water recreational provisions were made by bodies such as the Regional Water Boards, which later became privatized, and by the British Waterways Board which had responsibility for canals.

In the UK, countryside conservation and planning within National Parks and other mechanisms was tied back to the system of statutory town and country planning. This was so that the control of development, conservation measures, action on amenity, tourism and recreation provision could be linked to plan preparation, development control and management systems. Already by 1974, the Sandford Report started to reveal the range, scale and levels of conflicts and problems which were already facing the upland regions which had been designated as National Parks, or other conserved areas in England and Wales (Lord Sandford, 1974).

These conflicts were not only between conservation and recreational tourism, but also between both of these functions and a wide range of other economic demands which were made upon the areas. Some of the English National Parks, for example the Peak District, lie within 10 miles of major metropolitan areas, and individual parks were already found to be getting up to 100,000 visitors/day, and since then have grown to receiving as many as 22 million visitors p.a. in the case of the Lake District. By 2009, in a nation with a population of 61 million, with approaching half that number of private cars, the problems of the National Parks are

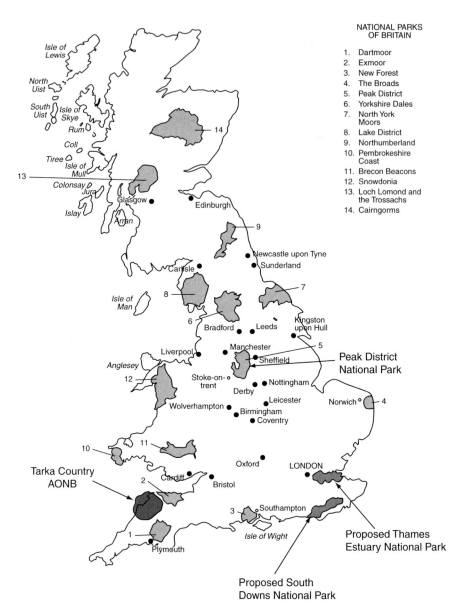

Fig. 16.1. National Parks of the UK in 2009. AONB, Area of Outstanding Natural Beauty (courtesy of Roly Smith and the AA).

generated not only by the great pressures of private mobility, but also by the limits of capacity of the National Parks as destination areas.

In the UK, as in the Netherlands, early 21st-century thinking and practice has also come to embrace the notion of nationwide, regional and local 'green infrastructure' providing a living network of green spaces, water and environmental systems in, around and beyond urban areas. Sometimes these are based on river basins, or networks that link Community Forests and intra-metropolitan valley and trails networks. At the regional scale in the UK this is seen in recent strategies such as the '6Cs Green Infrastructure Strategy' for the East Midlands, the 'On Trent' river basin initiative, while current US theory and practice is reflected in Benedict and Mac-Mahon's (2006) book *Green Infrastructure*.

Other land-use conflicts arose in the past, because of demands for mineral workings and sites for power stations, reservoir develop-ment, power lines and defence structures. With all these demands placed upon them, quality countryside was at risk. Therefore to review the detailed working of this system, two sample areas in the UK are looked at in more detail. First, the Derwent Valley area of the Peak District National Park in England, and secondly the Tarka Project within an AONB in Devon in England. The Peak District National Park and the Tarka country area are roughly the same size – about 500 square miles in extent – but the Upper Derwent Valley is only a small part of the Peak District being about 40 square miles in area so is a small, compact, and very special case for study.

Case Study 2:
The Upper Derwent Valley in the Peak District National Park

This is a highly accessible valley system, with large reservoirs, high quality landscapes, farmland, woodland and moorland. It is an area which is under enormous visitor pres-sure from nearby urban areas. Over 1.25 mil-lion visits were being made by visitors to this valley annually, and so this fine and delicate natural environment was found to be at risk from the pressures of private vehicles and recreational visitors regularly invading it. The visitor impacts upon the natural envi-ronment, upon wildlife, and upon the route networks, were such within the National Park that strong action was needed to man-age visitors and traffic, in order to protect the area, and to manage it better in the interests of local residents as well. The key challenge was how to get a number of parties with overlapping responsibilities to handle visitor management jointly by coordinated action.

The Peak District National Park Authority was the body which acted as the catalyst in this case, taking the lead in bringing together the three major landowners involved: (i) Severn Trent PLC (a water company); (ii) the National Trust; and (iii) Forestry Enterprise. The aim was to get them to accept and cooperate in a new partnership, together with local govern-ment authorities, parishes and other wider community stakeholders, in a coordinated management scheme for the area (Fig. 16.2). Integrated traffic and transport management was proposed, based on setting a desirable capacity for this destination. Furthermore twice-yearly stakeholder group meetings were agreed, with a joint budget as a coordinating tool, plus monitoring.

The start date for the first project was 1980–1981. Traffic congestion was very severe in the area, and a plan, plus a multi-party development budget was created to realize a new set of visitor and traffic arrangements in the Derwent Valley in 1981. An initial joint budget of £750,000 was established, suffi-cient to fund the provision of a central car park, do road and other works, plus the road closures.

Subsequent annual budgets for mainte-nance and management were built up to about £110,000 p.a. by the 1990s. The aims increasingly came to be focused on achieving a modal shift from visitors using cars to trains or buses to get to the area, and when they arrived there, to give incentives to leave their cars at appropriate car parks, and then travel by minibus, bicycle or on foot.

The scheme used a mix of controls and incentives, or 'sticks and carrots'. Some two roads totalling over 7 miles in length were closed, either part time or full time, improved off-road parking was created, and alternative means of access were given – 'park-and-ride' provision via minibus and bicycle or foot trails created as part of the new sustainable access system. This included: (i) 'clearways'; (ii) improved bus connections; (iii) new cycle hire; (iv) bicycles put on trains; and (v) special actions on the Hope Valley railway line. Free welcome leaflets, the sale of guidebooks, the provision of eight informa-tion boards and the opening of a visitor infor-mation centre were all complementary parts of the management strategy. By 1998 the annual budget bid, which by then included

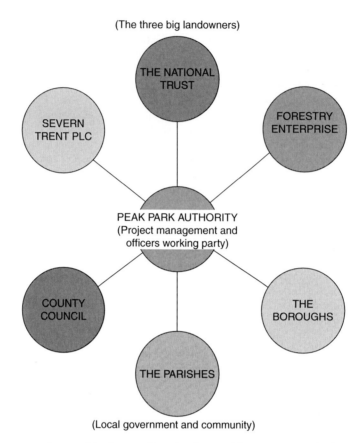

(The three big landowners)

THE NATIONAL TRUST

SEVERN TRENT PLC

FORESTRY ENTERPRISE

PEAK PARK AUTHORITY
(Project management and officers working party)

COUNTY COUNCIL

THE BOROUGHS

THE PARISHES

(Local government and community)

Fig. 16.2. The system of partnerships for coordinated action on visitor management in the Upper Derwent Valley of the Peak District National Park.

European, regional and local funding, had grown to nearly £250,000 from all sources.

By 1990, the Upper Derwent Valley Scheme was already winning awards, in recognition of what the project was already achieving in terms of improved management. The formerly trafficked roads were being returned to people as pleasant places where wildlife could now survive. Visitor surveys were started, and in the 1990s a formal evaluation was started of a process which has continued for some 20 years.

The achievements to date of this scheme include the provision of:

- traffic-free roads;
- connecting bus services from the surrounding cities;
- seven new and improved car parks to accommodate about 470 cars and three

coaches and some four special parking areas;
- special access for anglers and carefully managed trout fishing;
- three official picnic areas;
- 18 miles of extra routes, mainly as walking trails, but some for horse riding and cycling;
- a National Park Ranger Service in the area; and
- environmental improvements, so that wildlife benefits have been achieved and ecological and archaeological surveys have been conducted.

In addition, there have been 13,000 cycle hires a year from the cycle centre and over 70,000 visits p.a. to the information centre.

There are key lessons to be learned from the Upper Derwent Valley experiment. The first is of joint working and joint funding, for essentially this involved partnership schemes involving major landowners and the local community. This is the multiple stakeholder model required if you are to achieve socially acceptable changes in natural resource projects. Partnerships politically and practically achieve much more than any one party can, working alone. Secondly, intervention is necessary, as is commitment and sustained action, if sustainability is to be attempted in tourism and recreation provision, where pressurized visitor traffic is noticeably affecting and damaging a beautiful area, with wildlife assets. Conservation action and integrated transport planning action were the twin policy bundles which were both needed in this planning for environmental sustainability. And finally, a key lesson was that when experiments were being undertaken it was necessary to monitor them, and adjust management action to the feedback. The Derwent experiment provides some interesting contrasts with that of the Tarka Project.

Case Study 3:
The Tarka Project in Devon

The problem in this instance was dealing with a relatively large rural area (about 500 square miles), which was undergoing notable economic changes, including those of industrial change and decline, and it was a place where small-scale tourism was only slowly overtaking agriculture in importance. The challenge was one of creating twin and integrated strategies for nature conservation, and also for recreation and tourism – which were to benefit the host rural community. The idea behind this scheme was the use of the story of Tarka in Henry Williamson's novel *Tarka the Otter* which had been created about 70 years earlier, and was now to be used as a linking identity or branding for the area.

Devon County Council was the initiator or the catalyst in this case, which again employed a partnership approach with the backing at that time of the Countryside Commission at the national level and four district councils at the local level. The Tarka Project was set up in 1989 and was functioning from 1990 onwards. The organizational response to all the local prob-

lems found, was to set up over time some five mechanisms, namely:

- The Tarka Trail;
- The Tarka Railway Line;
- The Tarka Country Tourism Association;
- The Tarka Country (or branding); and
- The Tarka Trust for Conservation and the Tarka Conservation Fund.

A development budget in the early phase included many items such as the £500,000 for acquiring part of the existing railway line from British Rail, by the County Council. The key issue over time was the development of joint budgets, with many parties contributing to them, but generally the County Council itself being the leader and leading contributor, for example giving £300,000 out of a total joint annual budget for management and development of £600,000. Furthermore, continuity was achieved via joint budgets and the appointment of a special staffing project officer – the 'Otter Officer' or the 'Conservation Officer' – this was done jointly with private funding, and also tourism staffing which was done with joint commercial funding.

The project became a framework for initiatives about: (i) rural communities; (ii) rural economic diversification; (iii) the creation of new employment opportunities; and (iv) the protection and enrichment of wildlife, natural beauty and the special character of North Devon. While the Upper Derwent Valley had had a problem surplus of visitors to deal with, North Devon by comparison was an under-visited area, and needed to get a spread of new visitors, in order to get resultant economic benefits across the area. The desire to create sustainable access meant that alternative transport promotion was necessary, with the creation of 180-mile Tarka Trail in a 'figure of 8'. Part of this trail was to be a cycle way, part a walkway, and part a rail route. At the start of the project only 1% of Devon's visitors came to the Tarka Country, and the aim was to boost the area's share of Devon tourism.

A marketing strategy and an interpretation strategy were prepared, and much advice was given to farmers, landowners, as well as to visitors. Visitor penetration of the area steadily increased, and the spread of walkers and cyclists locationally, as well as in terms of their added numbers, was indeed significant.

The results of the initial phase of the project were: (i) the old railway line was bought for a nominal sum; (ii) most of the Tarka Trail and Line was created; (iii) access systems were secured; and (iv) the logo was adopted widely, so that the branding intention for the area did start to get acceptance.

Evaluation

When the author did a detailed review of the project some 7 years after its start, due to all the effort and the continuity over this longer than expected period, much was found to have been achieved:

1. Increased visitation was a notable reality: in the period from August 1995 to September 1996 some 483,000 walkers and cyclists visited the area and 150,000 cycle journeys were made on the Tarka Trail.
2. Five new cycle-hire businesses had been created and had survived economically.
3. There was a 5.9% increase in tourist night stays achieved in the Tarka Country between 1985 and 1995, a period when the total numbers of tourist visits to Devon actually declined by 1.5%.

4. Over 500 full-time equivalent jobs had been created in the area.
5. Tourist expenditure was estimated to have generated about £18.6 million in economic impacts in the area.
6. A high media profile had been achieved for the area, and Tarka branding had become generally used locally, with no less than three sets of awards having been won by the project by that date.

Wider lessons from the Tarka Project are, first, that it took about 10 years' funding and continuity, to reach a critical mass of the project, and not just 3 years, as was first anticipated. Secondly, partnership, branding and a range of complementary mechanisms were essential to convert the project into a set of new realities. The use of the 'otter image' was found to be 'warm, good, and positive', aiding the tasks of conservation, as well as linking to the Tarka Trail concept, which became the 'centrepiece of the recreational infrastructure'.

Despite essential differences in scale and purpose, these two English case studies, one from the Derwent Valley and the other from the Tarka Project, clearly demonstrate the principle of sustainability in tourism resource management and access.

17 Post-industrial Regional Tourism Planning: the South Wales Valleys – Strategy for Development and Conservation in the 1980s

The Challenge

In 1983, when the Wales Tourist Board commissioned the study of the South Wales urbanized valleys, which had been the main Welsh centre of coal mining, it raised the key question as to how to approach an 'unconventional destination'. This was to be a 'new tourist destination', but it was in fact a bold and outworn industrial area, with a vital working-class culture, lacking the notion that it could possibly become a place that visitors would choose to come to, for their holidays! The economic reason behind the study was the closure of coal mines, and the loss of jobs was driving the push to get new employment in clean, light industries and in tourism, to sustain the large population of 'the Valleys' who did not wish to leave their homes there.

The critical need was to create a distinctive and appealing destination, based on the unique blend of: (i) a strong and proud industrial people; (ii) a changing landscape; and (iii) a heritage of industrial archaeology and vital culture. This area could not, and should not, become a 'Costa Brava', nor even a 'Switzerland', but how should it be changed, and into what? Could this host industrial culture enable a new type of community-based urban-hosted tourism? Could it give economic and social benefits to the hosts, and provide attractive and memorable experiences for the visitors? This was the challenge of the proposition.

Responsive Approach of the Study Team

The self-set goals of the academic study team tackling the 'Valleys' problems' were:

- to further the economic, social and environmental well-being of those who live in the Valleys;
- to provide new jobs, in or associated with tourism and other developments for the Valleys' residents;
- to create a legitimate range of tourist products and experiences of integrity to visiting tourists and day trippers;
- to identify, nurture and protect the region's strong heritage of culture, customs, traditions and associations, its built environment, its industrial archaeology and its forgotten high quality natural resources;
- to create opportunities for local people – not only via jobs, but also through enhanced quality of life, via the provision of new sports, recreational and tourist activities, associated with the leisure and tourism industries; and
- to guide development and conservation activities sensitively, in ways that

harmonize with local traditions, identity and environment, to celebrate and exaggerate local identity and not to deny it.

This was the very demanding brief which the team set for itself, with limited time and budgetary means to complete. It resulted in a 330-page report, based on exhaustive research and consultations. It was publicly launched with much media attention to a major conference of all the local authorities, associations and interest groups represented, at a location in the Valleys, and not in Cardiff!

Inventorization of Existing and Potential Tourism Resources

After examination of regional definition and constituent local authority boundaries, the Valley system was identified and related to: (i) existing and proposed systems of transport and communications; (ii) the supply of tourist accommodation and examination of tourist services; and (iii) a review of changes in employment, unemployment and employment which was specifically applicable to tourism.

Unusually, questions of perception, images and attitudes were examined, as well as the relationship of tourism to host cultures and tourism cultures. These provided attitudinal parameters with which to view the later tourism inventorization programme.

The tourism inventory included the following:

1. Built resources of industrial archaeology and heritage – these were recorded in meticulous detail, valley by valley, including mapping all the resources of industry, monuments, trails, bridges, canals, railways, tram roads, quarries, workers' and owners' housing areas.
2. The museums and galleries resource of the Valleys.
3. The architectural and built heritage – this included records of castles, abbeys, cathedrals and chapels, plus all historic sites and historic buildings (Fig. 17.1).
4. Indoor leisure provision – these were reviewed and mapped as a resource.
5. Cultural heritage resources – these were examined in detail including cultural factors

which could and could not be mapped, relating to language, ethnicity, population composition, historical and geographical richness as well as education, work and life values. Further, records were made of all of the associations with personalities from the worlds of politics, writing and poetry, music, theatre, opera, cinema, media, crafts, and especially 'famous sons and daughters' of the Valleys. A wider 'cultural heritage' was thus considered than had been attempted previously.
6. Natural resources – these were reviewed, inventorized and mapped. They included not only those of the familiar economic exploitation sense such as coal, but also the natural resources of countryside and coast (the landscape elements, flora and fauna, forestry resources, country parks, trails and way-marked paths, gardens, reservoirs, lakes, canals, waterfalls and the river system, plus resource-based sports and pastimes).
7. The 'forgotten resource' of the 'Welsh diaspora' – this is because Wales, like Scotland, Ireland, Italy and other lands, has historically lost many of its sons and daughters to outward migration as a result of economic push-and-pull factors.
8. New resource potentials – these were preceded by examination of visitor levels to the six existing primary visitor attractions within the region.

Basic Principles and Strategic Assumptions

It was assumed that we would work hard to avoid developing placeless major attractions, that could already be found at such destinations as Blackpool, Benidorm and Barry Island, but it was important that the area should be itself, and develop as a secondary set of locations of tourist attractions and events that complement those existing in Cardiff, the coastal resorts and in the adjacent Brecon Beacons National Park.

With regard to Cardiff and the coast, Cardiff City – as the Welsh capital and the focus of administrative, commercial and cultural activities – is within an hour and a half's travel time of nearly all locations in the

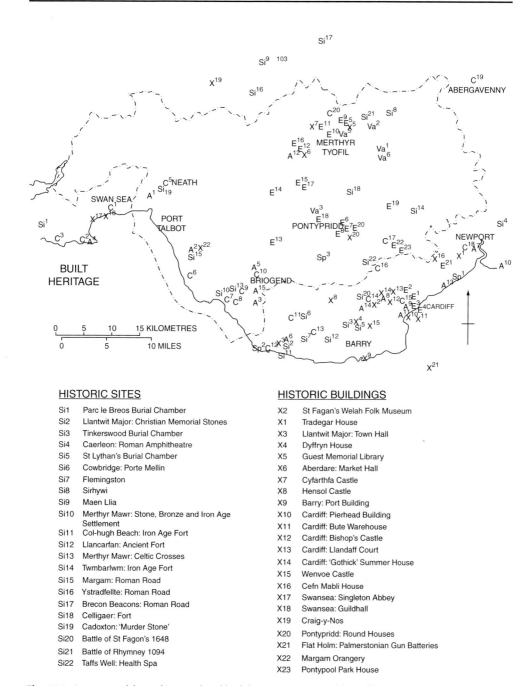

Fig. 17.1. Inventory of the architectural and built heritage resource of the Valleys (Source: Travis and Consulting Team, 1983).

HISTORIC SITES

Si1	Parc le Breos Burial Chamber
Si2	Llantwit Major: Christian Memorial Stones
Si3	Tinkerswood Burial Chamber
Si4	Caerleon: Roman Amphitheatre
Si5	St Lythan's Burial Chamber
Si6	Cowbridge: Porte Mellin
Si7	Flemingston
Si8	Sirhywi
Si9	Maen Llia
Si10	Merthyr Mawr: Stone, Bronze and Iron Age Settlement
Si11	Col-hugh Beach: Iron Age Fort
Si12	Llancarfan: Ancient Fort
Si13	Merthyr Mawr: Celtic Crosses
Si14	Twmbarlwm: Iron Age Fort
Si15	Margam: Roman Road
Si16	Ystradfellte: Roman Road
Si17	Brecon Beacons: Roman Road
Si18	Celligaer: Fort
Si19	Cadoxton: 'Murder Stone'
Si20	Battle of St Fagon's 1648
Si21	Battle of Rhymney 1094
Si22	Taffs Well: Health Spa

HISTORIC BUILDINGS

X2	St Fagan's Welsh Folk Museum
X1	Tradegar House
X3	Llantwit Major: Town Hall
X4	Dyffryn House
X5	Guest Memorial Library
X6	Aberdare: Market Hall
X7	Cyfarthfa Castle
X8	Hensol Castle
X9	Barry: Port Building
X10	Cardiff: Pierhead Building
X11	Cardiff: Bute Warehouse
X12	Cardiff: Bishop's Castle
X13	Cardiff: Llandaff Court
X14	Cardiff: 'Gothick' Summer House
X15	Wenvoe Castle
X16	Cefn Mabli House
X17	Swansea: Singleton Abbey
X18	Swansea: Guildhall
X19	Craig-y-Nos
X20	Pontypridd: Round Houses
X21	Flat Holm: Palmerstonian Gun Batteries
X22	Margam Orangery
X23	Pontypool Park House

Valleys. Cardiff is already the locus of concentrated new hotel development, tourist and recreational developments (especially around the new Cardiff Bay). The Valleys will remain secondary to Cardiff, as it is a major magnet for hotels, attractions and many types of tourism. Proximity to Cardiff can however positively aid the Valleys.

Brecon town and the Brecon Beacons National Park sit immediately north of the Valleys, and represent prime, high quality countryside, scenic, active outdoor recreation and existing tourist destinations. The Valleys can complement the Brecon Beacons and should not try to compete with the National Park, nor Cardiff, nor the coastal resorts like Barry Island and Porthcawl.

The attractions that the Valleys already have can be an 'add-on' to those of Cardiff, and of the Brecon Beacons National Park. Strengthened and improved existing Valleys' attractions, as well as new attractions there, can complement and succeed as part of the elaborate package of tourist offers in South Wales. Festivals and home-stays for unlinked tourists and for VFRs can be a basis for real growth in the Valleys tourist industry.

Strategy

The strategic guidelines for tourism development and conservation, shown in Fig. 17.2,

recognize Cardiff, Swansea and Newport as tourist destinations in their own right, which can also serve as three 'gateways' to the Valleys' tourism, starting as add-on attractions to those in the coastal cities and the Brecon Beacons National Park, and slowly developing beyond their secondary status in tourism.

Eight potential tourist destination areas (DAs) are identified at: (i) Cwmbran – Cwm Carn; (ii) Abergavenny – Blaenavon; (iii) Tredegar – Ebbw Vale; (iv) Merthyr; (v) Glyn Neath; (vi) Vale of Neath; (vii) Margam – Afan Argoed; and (viii) the Rhondda. Detailed developments and conservation specifications for each of these DAs were set out in the report and in addition the scenic and touring potentials of the new forests of South Wales are indicated on Fig. 17.2 (the forests of Margam, Cymmer, Rhondda and Cwm Carn). In additional some six development projects were proposed.

New lead-in 'gateway zones' were proposed at the southern and eastern entry points to the Valleys – to serve those coming in via

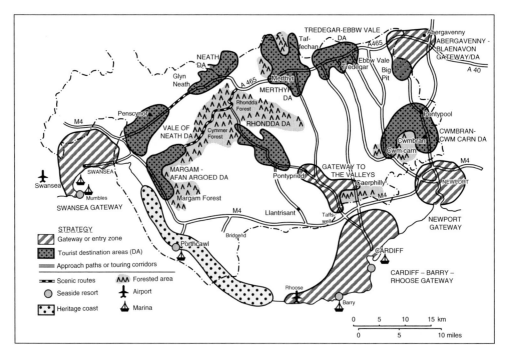

Fig. 17.2. Strategic guidelines for tourism development and conservation (Source: Travis and Consulting Team, 1983).

Cardiff and from the English Midlands. The complementary role of the Glamorgan Heritage Coast to the south, and the Brecon Beacons National Park to the north, was recognized. Hotel provision remained concentrated in Cardiff, but upgraded bed-and-breakfast and farm-stay provision and improved café and restaurant dining opportunities for Valley locations were proposed.

Development Project Proposals

Arising from the realization of resource potentials and market demands, several new development projects were proposed, including:

- An Industrial Folk Festival, based upon the Rhondda Valley, using home hospitality, improved existing event locations such as Miners Institutes, new trails, a launch of new tourist information centres, and a locus for the great brass bands and choral tradition, of the region.
- An interpretation centre – to tell 'the story of the coal trade, and the social and economic history of coal'.
- A study centre on trade unions and political history.

- A youth activity centre and a trekking centre for upland visits, to be located at Pont Nedd Fechan.
- A 'Gateway to the Valleys' visitor centre, with petrol filling stations, tourist information centre, cafés and toilets.

Evaluation

The absence of a Regional Authority, and the diminishing development role of the Wales Tourist Board, led to a continuing myopic role of the competing, small-scale and introverted local authorities – who failed to see the need for a wider strategic approach, and the need for a mix of complementary, rather than competing developments. Key attractions like the Big Pit Coal Mining Museum and the Rhondda Heritage Centre have continued their successful roles, but sadly the idea of clustered developments and provisions is still neither understood, nor applied in South Wales. The forest walks, rides and driving trails have grown in popularity, but major development proposals will probably have to wait for a time when further economic and physical decline has occurred, before their vital role is recognized and accepted.

18 Nature and Culture: Developing a Rural Region's Heritage Trails Through Dolenjska and Bela Krajina in Slovenia

Marko Koscak and Anthony S. Travis

Introduction

This joint rural case study is one of a region in Slovenia, where we can track the 15-year process, from preliminary idea in the early 1990s to the full operational reality by 2005, of sustainable tourism in a strategically located, destination region.

This study is divided into five sections:

- origins and catalysts;
- integrated rural community development project;
- international team of consultants for the Heritage Trail;
- stages of commercial product adaptation and implementation; and
- evaluation.

Origins and Catalysts

The 30-year period from 1960 to 1990 saw distinct phases of evolution in tourism planning and conservation thinking and actions in the Western world. This led to concepts and processes of sustainable tourism planning. By the end of the 1980s a UK National Task Force on 'Tourism and the Environment' was set up, in order to provide sustainable tourism guidelines for three problem categories:

- the countryside;
- heritage sites; and
- historic cities and towns.

Travis was commissioned to direct a consultancy team, which acted as research provider to the Task Force. This enabled a synthesis of the collective experience of writing about sustainable tourism planning, in three language groups – English, French and German. Michael Dower chaired the Countryside Working Party, and the roles of these two participants (i.e. Dower and Travis) were to take on significance for Slovenia – as will be seen later in the story. International cooperation in tourism research and development between the UK and Slovenia was a vital component in this story.

When, in 1991 Marko Koscak, a senior engineer/planner from Dolenjska, was given official Slovene sponsorship to come to the UK for a special programme of intensive study on sustainable rural tourism, it was to Birmingham that he came, because of Travis's long working association with Slovenia. Dr Koscak worked with Travis in the Midlands getting direct feedback from the Task Force phase, and having exposure to best UK practice. Professor Dower was interviewed by Koscak in one of the meetings. Koscak is the continuous thread through this story, with Travis participating in phases of it, while Dower re-appears officially in the major Heritage Trail period.

Fig. 18.1. Location of Slovene Dolenjska–Bela Krajina Heritage Trail.

Several key actors and catalysts can be identified in this story: (i) the National Ministry of Agriculture (in Slovenia); (ii) the Bavarian Ministry for Agriculture; (iii) the Faculty of Architecture at the University of Ljubljana; (iv) the European Commission's Tourism Directorate; (v) a Regional Chamber of Commerce; (vi) a commercial tourism operator; and (vii) later a market research consultant. The location of the study area is shown in Fig.18.1.

Integrated Rural Community Development Project

On his return to Slovenia in 1991, Koscak was employed as a planner with the Trebnje Local Authority, in the Novo Mesto region. He was also an external consultant to the Slovene Ministry of Agriculture from 1991. From 1999 to 2001 Koscak was a full-time adviser to the Government of the Republic of Slovenia, in rural development. This was on the programme for 'Integrated Rural Development and Village Renovation' (CRPOV), which

started in 1990, and was associated with the Food and Agriculture Organization of the United Nations (FAO) and with the Bavarian Ministry for Agriculture. Bavaria helped in the initial phase of transferring experience and know-how. CRPOV was based on a 'bottom-up approach', involving an initial 14 local project areas, in 1991. Two villages were located in Trebnje Municipality, and around 500 local residents were involved in the project. During this period around 250 local projects were developed in Slovenia, primarily aimed at development possibilities for rural economic diversification.

The community development role of CRPOV involved many local village meetings, linked to the economic need for diversification of the rural economy. CRPOV worked together with an expert team on strategy and action. Critically, our case study of a rural region sits strategically between Ljubljana and Zagreb, on the international motorway from Belgrade to Ljubljana. This has a high location potential for selling locally sourced food and wine products, as well as craft and tourism products. Tourism is based on the appeal of a gentle landscape of hills and river valleys for walking, horse-riding, cycling, angling, rafting or the simple enjoyment of its unspoilt character.

CRPOV led the way to rural product development and as a by-product, community-based sustainable tourism. Such tourism requires partnership and cooperation between the public, private and the NGO voluntary sectors. Cooperation of this sort was not common in the period 1992–1995 in Slovene tourism. It was clear, however, that sustainability – in Slovenia or anywhere else – requires community involvement, and the commitment of local actors and producers. The appeal of such action is to add tourism products to the other rural products, which they complement.

Community-based rural development is thus an ideal starting point for sustainability, whether in agriculture, and/or tourism. This creates an 'environment' in which new opportunities can occur for: (i) economic diversification; (ii) new job creation; (iii) added value to agricultural products; (iv) local guiding; and (v) new farm services. In this process, institutions like an agricultural extension service play a very important role, in terms of capacity building and of human resource development.

CRPOV resulted in the creation of a tourism product, by offering a themed 'commercial package', by linking with Slovene Railways, in developing a 1-day tour. This theme was the main idea of a Development Strategy, one result of which was an 18 km-long Baraga Walking Trail. Initially, this product was offered to school pupils. The response was limited, as there was no commercial partner to market and sell the product on the domestic market. However, there were improvements in infrastructure, and in housing, plus local training schemes to create business opportunities. In 1996, the project was given an award in Munich, as part of ARGE – 'Landentwicklung und Dorfeneurung' Development Competition. This was also a confidence-building phase for rural people locally, later enabling them to become part of a broader, regional project with its tourism elements.

The Wine Trail was a parallel project to CRPOV, at the national level. The idea behind it was to promote wine, plus the culture, customs and traditions of the wine-making areas of Slovenia. The effort resulted in 25 wine trails, created all round the country.

International Team of Consultants for the Heritage Trail

This background of CRPOV and the wine trails prompted Koscak and his Slovene colleagues to accept an invitation by a consortium, who in 1996 secured EU funding, to launch two pilot projects in Slovenia and Bulgaria, to create heritage trails. The consortium included: (i) Ecotourism Ltd, a British consultancy firm; (ii) PRISMA, a Greek consultancy firm; and (iii) ECOVAST, the European Council for the Village and Small Town, of which Dower was then Secretary General. He introduced the consortium to Koscak, who then persuaded the Novo Mesto Chamber of Commerce to act as the local partner of the consortium for the Slovene initiative. The team on the Slovene project consisted of: (i) Duncan Fisher of Ecotourism Ltd as project leader; (ii) Dr Harold Goodwin, carrying capacity expert; (iii) Peter Nizette as marketing expert; (iv) John Sell and Jane Wade as experts on product development; (v) Michael Dower as planner; and (vi) Marko Koscak as local project manager. All of these were supported by regional and national institutions in the field of natural and cultural heritage.

The UK/Slovene Heritage Trail team conducted a tourist resource inventorization and selection, based upon natural, built and living cultural heritage resources of the selected region. Some 150 sites were identified and proposed by the different partners involved in the participation process, for the Heritage Trail. From this large number, 28 sites were selected to be networked in a trail system for the area. The idea was to develop a tourist product which can offer opportunities for stays of up to 7 days in the region. Two key forms of access were used for the clustering of attractions:

(i) a 'garland structure' model; and (ii) a 'flower structure' model (see Fig. 18.2). These alternative models enabled visitors to travel out either from many decentralized accommodation bases or from a single centralized accommodation base. Existing tourist assets and potentials were the basis of these groupings.

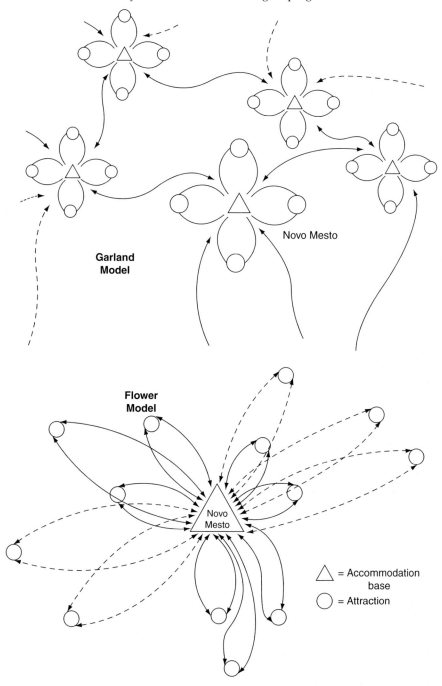

Fig. 18.2. Alternative models of rural development.

A major result of this work was the creation of a regional partnership of 26 organizations, from the public, private and NGO sectors, which signed an agreement to cooperate in the Heritage Trail's implementation phases of marketing and product development. This partnership, working under the umbrella of the Regional Chamber of Commerce, lasted nearly 10 years. It supports, coordinates and brings together the provider partners. Work in general consists of marketing activities, product development and training activities, where different combinations of partners, institutions and individuals are involved.

For marketing purposes, a commercial partner, Kompas Novo Mesto, was brought into the partnership in 2001, as it was necessary to have a much 'stronger attack' on foreign markets. Kompas was to act as the marketing agency, on behalf of the Heritage Trail partnership. Although the official launch of the product was in 1997, at the World Travel Market (WTM) in London, followed in 1998 by a presentation at the ITB tourism fair in Berlin, there was no significant response. Foreign markets at that time had limited awareness about any Slovene tourist products, other than the constantly featured 'traditional Slovene tourist icons', such as Lake Bled, Kranjska Gora ski resort, Postojna Cave and Portoroz seaside resort.

The effective commercial launch of the Heritage Trail internationally with a foreign tourist industry adviser, and a much more professional coordinated national approach, was delayed until 2002, in London. There, at the WTM, the launch had the active support of the Slovene Tourism Board, plus other relevant institutions.

Stages of Commercial Product Adaptation and Implementation

After the launch of the Heritage Trail to the domestic market, the international launch of the Trail was at the World Travel Market in 2002, but this did not give rise to responses by foreign tour operators and travel agents. It became clear that external help was needed to find such foreign trade partners, and identify the niche markets selected and targeted. Travis became employed in this role.

From Travis's market research on Slovenia's key foreign markets, the special interest markets with a focus on either cultural tourism or nature tourism (ecotourism) were selected. Independent and some major commercial operators were to be approached by phone, fax or online. Two hundred firms were identified in seven European countries. Of these, 60 firms were contacted by at least two contact modes, but only six showed some interest.

The problem revealed was that though there is much interest in Slovenia as a high-growth destination country, it is seen by the international industry as a country with four major attractions or 'tourist icons', already mentioned. For a long time, Slovene overseas marketing focused only upon these well-known destinations.

By 2003, low-cost airlines made Slovenia easily accessible to high-spend foreign markets. Air travel cannot be a basis for sustainability, but may have to be used to 'open-up a destination' to international markets in the first place. Sustainable rail travel access must be the aim! The Heritage Trail product offered was being linked to an 'air gateway' at Ljubljana or Klagenfurt, with access routing via Ljubljana. In-depth contact with key operators by phone showed that there were two viable special-interest packages, which could appeal commercially:

1. A Heritage Trail add-on package to offers at Bled or Ljubljana.
2. An integrated new 'Highlights of Slovenia' holiday, which started with 25% of the time at two existing icons (namely Bled and Ljubljana), then the remaining 75% time allocation spent on the Heritage Trail.

Testing of this product, with the two alternative packages, with a group of six UK professionals was extremely successful. A second tour with tour operators from Germany and the UK in 2004 was less successful. In 2005 a specialist walking-tour firm assembled its bespoke and individualized Heritage Trail offer, and independent tour operator firms started preparing for launching the two individualized alternative packages online.

Site design, management and animation

The detailed design of the heritage sites on the Trail is of note; on-site information boards of standardized design were made and installed at all sites, with car parking where appropriate, and in selected cases toilets and other appropriate services provided.

Animation of the sites is impressive, as they are used for museum events, dance and song presentations, horse-riding, cycling stops, traditional cooking and craft displays, talks and historical re-enactments. Thus good design of elements is combined with lively animation, to bring all the locations to life.

Evaluation

Because the heritage-resource-based tourism phase was preceded by the work on integrated rural community development, there was a community-based approach to development. In this context, tourism was a part of the economic mix. This created a real hope of sustainability, via the local communities' support for a new mixed economy. Sustainable development can underpin successful tourism, if the right strategy is chosen.

Heritage-resource-based tourism development, if it is to be sustainable, must:

- show respect for the carrying capacity of resource zones – be they robust or fragile; and
- have rural community involvement and commitment to tourism, because they have a stake in it, and have net gains from it.

Much tourism development arises because the destination creates potential tourism products, because they want economic gain from them. Rural tourism products have to be adjusted to fit niche market demands that are highly competitive sectors internationally.

Thus, market awareness and understanding must be built in early in the development process, or it becomes much longer and harder.

New tourist destinations are very difficult to launch internationally, even if they have high accessibility, unless they can be linked to existing icons or magnets. This new Slovene offer had to be adjusted, to do just that.

The identification of 'gateways' is critical in new product formulation. Whether this be a selected airport, sea port, railway station or whatever. If the gateway is the airport of an attractive heritage city (like Ljubljana), then both add-on package possibilities, as well as links to a popular 'short city-break' destination, add great value.

Continuity of personnel in a development process is of real importance: Dr Koscak's initiating and continuity role was critical, as were the continuing interactions with external partners, who were supportive and shared a belief in the integrity of the development, over a long period of time.

This model ultimately is a sustainable one because it has multiple stakeholders and is community based, and has the equal support of small rural operatives and major agencies. The support from several levels – local, regional, national and international – enabled this 15-year development cycle to be achieved. The prime dependence upon a domestic market, with limited carbon footprint, aids the sustainability of the Heritage Trail.

Commercial assessment

The Kompas agency prepared and monitored the number of commercial visitors coming to the Heritage Trail for the period from 2002 until 2007. The commercial visit levels were estimated to be some 30–40% of the total visitor numbers to the Trail. While in 2002 some 354 domestic visitors made commercial visits to the Heritage Trail, 99 foreign tourists also came as commercial visitors. By 2007, some 1987 domestic commercial visitors were visiting the Trail, and some 559 foreign paying tourists were coming as well. Of a total of 2546 paying visitors coming to the Trail in the region of Dolenjska and Bela Krajina, some 1987 were from Slovenia, 129 from Italy, 88 from Austria, 54 from France, 31 from Croatia, 25 from Germany, 20 from Macedonia, 14 from Serbia, and 12 from Greece. The commercial benefits of this process are felt by the owners of guesthouses and farm-stays, as well as shopkeepers, guides, food and craft shops. It demonstrates the economic benefits of such a community-based, rural tourism Heritage Trail.

19 Host Cultures and Tourism: Is a Culture Sustainable?

Introduction

It is vital to study the impacts of tourism upon host communities, as well as upon host cultures. Our aims thus are socio-scientific in that we need to observe, to understand, as well as to interpret and analyse, in this field. However, in addition, arising from such study, it is also necessary to do policy analysis of the work of related government and agencies affecting tourism, and the nature of change and policy recommendations, in order to suggest who should do what, where, in which different ways, so as to minimize the social disbenefits of tourism's impacts, and to optimize potential social benefits arising from tourism. Thus contemporary evaluation in this field, shares those of the Vienna Centre Study's interest in causes, phenomena, experience and effects of tourism; and in theories that help to understand these. First, however, it is necessary to define some of the key terms employed:

'Culture' was defined by Tylor in 1871 as: 'Culture or civilisation, taken in its wide ethnographic sense, is that complex whole which includes knowledge, belief, arts, morals, law, custom, and any other capabilities and habits acquired by man as a member of society.'

Malinowski in 1931 gave a more universal and less anthropocentric definition: 'A culture is a functioning, active, efficient, well-organized unity, which must be analysed into component institutions, in relation to one another, and in relation to the environment, man-made as well as natural.'

In the author's report on Wales in 1983, the word 'culture' was taken to mean: 'the system of values, beliefs, behaviours, morals, and other social phenomena shared by a group of people, based on their common experience of life, language, and history' (Jones and Travis, 1983).

Realm

The study of the social, cultural and linguistic impacts of tourism is a very recent field in terms of its development: it is younger and less developed than the field of economic and environmental impacts of tourism. Because some of the key work internationally has been done by social anthropologists, and to a lesser extent by sociologists, it has related to a Third World context, rather than to the developed world.

In approaching the general question of tourism's impacts on social, cultural and linguistic characteristics of any nation or region, it is first necessary to establish the state of knowledge worldwide with regard to this field. Only in this way may we try to establish any common features of tourism's socio-cultural impacts or how far it demon-strates either distinct or markedly different features in this specific realm.

What is clear about the social and cul-tural impacts of tourism is that it is a recent and new field of research interest, following well behind the much earlier academic atten-tion given to fields – such as the economics of tourism, economic impacts, and the phys-ical and environmental impacts of tourism. Key book sources appeared as late as around 1980, for example *Hosts and Guests: the Anthropology of Tourism* (Smith, 1978), *Social and Cultural Dimensions of Tourism* (Noronha, 1979) and *Tourism: Economic, Physical and Social Impacts* (Mathieson and Wall, 1982). The sources agree that this field of concern relates to the effects of tourism upon the tourist, upon the host society and cultures, as well as the inter-relationship of tourists and hosts.

The attitudes towards tourism, its value and effects, vary greatly. While the Helsinki Conference which was dealing with human rights, optimistically suggested that 'Tourism helped the development of mutual under-standing among peoples and contributed to economic, social, and cultural progress', commentators like Turner and Ash (1975) contrastingly stated that: 'International tour-ism tends to lead to the systematic destruc-tion of everything that is beautiful in the world.' Erik Cohen, sociologist and anthro-pologist, wrote in 1979 that:

> The tourist…is a superficial nitwit, easy to please as well as to cheat. Isolated in the environmental bubble of tourist hotels, restaurants, and other touristic establishments… easy-going, superficial creature, with only slight contact with, and even a slighter understanding of his surroundings.

These black-and-white alternatives are highly emotive, and therefore every effort has to be made to present what hard evidence does exist, both of the positive and of the negative social impacts of tourism. As Mathieson and Wall (1982) stated there is a strong skewing of evidence in favour of the economic benefits of tourism, and conversely a skew towards the social and cultural disbenefits of tourism's impacts.

Much depends, however, on how far one takes evidence from the developed or developing world, and how far one is deal-ing with social and economic differences between the host and the visitor popula-tions. Furthermore, state attitudes towards tourist development, vary considerably. Many Nation States, given limited economic choices, go for tourism development, with little prior impact assessment, some eco-nomic, and no social or cultural assessment. The variations in host state roles in control-ling, encouraging, discouraging tourism, its forms, scale and rate of growth, may be significant factors in the subsequent eva-luation of tourism's social impacts on that society. When in the 1980s, a phase of research about tourism's social impacts was started, it was coloured by the research work of the 1960s and 1970s – when economic costs and benefits were fairly closely looked at, but the socio-cultural assumptions made were fairly simple.

It is intended therefore to look more closely at this field, separating out the social, the socio-cultural, linguistic and political impacts of tourism on the host environment. It is of special note that, when examining the impacts of tourism in developed countries like the UK, one may be examining 'regu-lated' networks, in Jafari's (1982) sense. This is because there are key interventionist roles that can be vested in bodies such as national tourism organizations (NTOs), as compared with a free reign of uncontrolled market forces, which is the situation in some Third World countries, which increasingly host international tourism. These relationships of cultures are indicated in Fig. 19.1.

The Social and Demographic Impacts of Tourism

In any situation examined, the size, distribu-tion and composition of the host population, and the scale and rate of build up of the visi-tor population and its distribution will be sig-nificant. As indicated by Valene Smith in 1978, the variation between the early 'explorer' phase, with few and adapting guests, through to the charter phase, with mass movements and

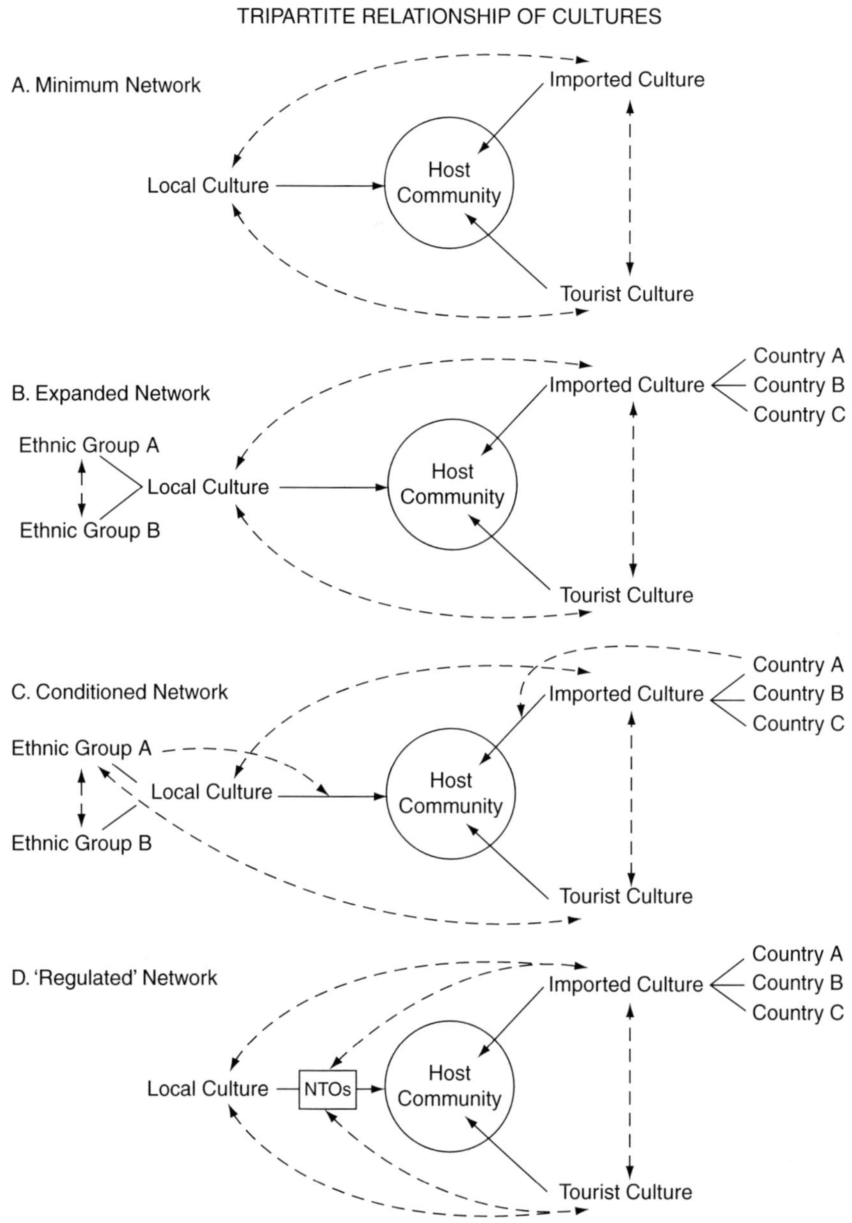

TRIPARTITE RELATIONSHIP OF CULTURES

Fig. 19.1. Tripartite relationship of cultures (Source: Jafari, 1982).

even saturation conditions, will create very different circumstances, and greatly contrasted impacts (see Fig. 19.2).

Many of the studies undertaken in the past, related to the 'opening up' of under-developed or developing societies to visitors from the developed world (see van Egmond, 2007).

In these circumstances, many social effects arise from tourism's major impacts upon the local economy. Typical social impacts, in such instances are:

• The creation of more new jobs for women, and young people.

Frequency of types of tourists and their adaptations to local norms.

Types of tourist	Numbers of tourists	Adaptations of local norms
Explorer	Very limited	Accepts fully
Elite	Rarely seen	Adapts fully
Off-beat	Uncommon but seen	Adapts well
Unusual	Occasional	Adapts somewhat
Incipient mass	Steady flow	Seeks Western amenities
Mass	Continuous flow	Expects Western amenities
Charter	Massive arrivals	Demands Western amenities

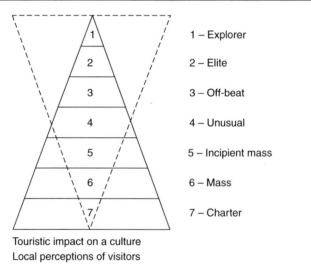

1 – Explorer

2 – Elite

3 – Off-beat

4 – Unusual

5 – Incipient mass

6 – Mass

7 – Charter

Touristic impact on a culture
Local perceptions of visitors

Fig. 19.2. Tourist impacts and visitor perceptions (Source: Smith, 1978).

- Changes in the size and composition of the host population.
- Occupational changes, with development of a money economy (where one may not have previously existed), and a more diversified economy.
- Growth of jobs in services, shopping, catering, local transport and crafts, and the emergence of tourism or culture brokers in the local economy.
- Lifestyle changes occur, though sometimes local culture, imported culture and tourist culture may be separate and distinct, interactions between them occur (see Fig. 19.1).

- Social well-being or at least improved economic well-being of some of the hosts occurs – if the forms of tourism relate to direct economic returns to local householders, if they rent rooms, or space, as compared with situations where foreign capital and foreign hotels and hoteliers take over, and economic returns go abroad.

While Roxburgh, as early as 1979, suggested that: 'People in the Third World manifest their free choice in a market place dominated by the values of the countries of advanced capital; they do so by purchasing those commodities which are dysfunctional for balanced economic development.'

Graburn in 1983 had, however, contrastingly wrote that: 'Tourism should not be linked to Capitalism...but to disposable income, increased education, and cultural self-confidence, and the push-pull factors of touristic opportunities, and motivations, spreading across national and political boundaries.' What is critical is how far the economic effects of tourism lead to improved social well-being of the host population, with: (i) local rather than foreign ownership; (ii) improved employment; and (iii) improved health conditions. If income differential between host and guest continues to grow, rather than to diminish, this sows seeds of conflict, as much as do negative cultural and linguistic impacts (see Noronha, 1979).

The 'demonstration effect' of visitors on a host destination and social life, can lead not only to changes in consumption, dress, diet and lifestyle, but can lead to inflation in the host economy. Tourists often generate demands for imported foods, goods and services – and these lead to difficult social, as well as economic impacts.

The social impact of tourism may have a beneficial effect on the status of women, who may get some degree of economic independence via jobs in the money economy. This may alleviate a suppressed social position, but it is suggested in some studies, can also affect marital stability.

Social costs and benefits arise from the impacts of tourism, but public health and hygiene gains at new destinations may go together with new imported diseases. The growth of venereal disease (VD), and more recently the growth of Acquired Immune Deficiency Syndrome (AIDS), in Indian and Pacific destinations have been attributed to tourism by a number of commentators.

A noticeable social and economic impact in the Third World significantly attributable to tourism is the localized growth of population. Young, uneducated and poor women in Korea, Thailand, the Philippines, Taiwan and Sri Lanka, now find employment in large numbers in prostitution, catering to tourist demands. Japanese, German, Dutch and Swiss specialist firms sell 'sex tourism' packages to Far East destinations, on a large scale. A range of studies authenticates the economic, social and moral effects of this phenomenon (see O'Grady, 1981).

According to a number of published statistics, retirement and second-home foreign population growth in some Mediterranean destinations has given rise to major social changes in these tourist destination areas.

Socio-cultural Impacts of Tourism

An extensive literature now exists on the socio-cultural impacts of tourism, mainly relating to the impact of First World tourists upon the Third World. Pizam and Milman in 1984 wrote that:

> Social and cultural impacts of tourism are the ways in which tourism is contributing to changes in value systems, individual behaviour, family relationships, collective lifestyles, moral conduct, creative expressions, traditional ceremonies, and community organizations. In other words, they are the effects on the people of host communities, of their direct and indirect associations with tourists.

Thus much depends on the state and stage of cultural development, both of the host society and of the tourist cultures which may affect it. While there is the pull of various forms of culture of the host society – such as its archaeological, architectural, artistic and craft traditions, host culture, lifestyle and customs, plus host traditions (in the forms of festivals, ceremonies, beliefs, dances and events) – tourists, in being drawn to these, exert effects:

1. Tourists as generators of cultural changes or the acculturation effect – Cultures interact with each other, and much will depend upon the robustness of a host culture, on host self-confidence and self-belief, in such a situation. While on the one hand Farb (1969) optimistically suggested: 'Every culture is composed of multitudes of cultural elements such as religious beliefs, social practices, tools, weapons, and so forth...these elements are in a continual process of interaction: new syntheses and combinations are constantly being produced'; Furnham (1984), on the

other hand, sees culture shock, bewilderment and disenchantment in the tourist encounter, as much for the ill-prepared tourist, as for the confused host!

2. Inter-cultural communication, informal and formal, whereby via the marketing of host culture, culture is sold as a commodity – Commercialization and commodification of culture via tourism creates limited social interaction between hosts and foreign tourists. The relationship is one of unequal coexistence, in which tourism is providing an 'alternative sugar crop'. According to Adler (1981) the socio-cultural problem arises from a fundamental non-fit of the expectations of tourists and of hosts. He claims the tourists want escape, change, new impressions, to experience a lot, to escape monotony and everyday constraints, and to satisfy unsatisfied needs. Thus tourists, he claims, make the trip destination and the people there, into a means to satisfy such ends: therefore, contact between host/guest reduces the relationship to that of a commodity. Music, dances, art, religion, any ceremony can be packaged and 'commodified' if the commercial sector sees visitor perceptions and demands at this level. The money culture then sadly commodifies 'hospitality' itself, and this may change part of tourism.

Greenwood (1972) has written up a process of cultural *commoditization* in the Basque region of Spain, where 'Fuentarrabia is more an enterprise than a town... and promised to become indistinguishable from all other tourist towns on the coast of Spain.' While religious rituals have been commoditized in Tonga, dance has been in Spain, and traditional spectacles are commercialized in Italy, Tonga and elsewhere.

Culturally, the demonstration effect of tourism is that it may induce unattainable economic and social aspirations, resulting in prostitution in Asia to serve tourist demands, and economic crimes like mugging, theft and pick-pocketing in Hawaii and coast of Spain – but, without the hosts achieving their cultural and social aims. Bali (to which more reference will be made later) has a robust culture and cultural self-belief – and has demonstrated, according to several authors, that the demonstration effect does not necessarily apply, and

has adapted foreign ideas to its own culture, using a clear logic and 'an intelligent par of adaptation'.

Tourism is blamed for changes in social mores and in moral conduct: relative to the growth of prostitution, crime, gambling, vandalism and religious decline. Few of the many studies using such evidence – compare O'Grady (1981) with Adler (1981) – include empirical evidence, and fewer still look at how far urbanization, media influences, economic crises and other factors, may be part causes of these phenomena.

It is not necessarily the superficial changes in the cultural expressions that may count most – changes in status, mores, lifestyles, cuisine, customs and ceremonies – but changes in the underlying values, social relationships and in the strength, quality and integrity of people's lives at a destination that counts.

Writers like MacCannell (1976) and Graburn (1983) pay much attention to the tourist culture and experience – seeing tourism 'as the sacred journey' or tourism paying 'mutual respect for society', but are still worried with the problem of authenticity of experience, and of encounter, for they see much of tourism as 'staged authenticity'. Much of the challenge to tourist boards and to the commercial travel industry is thus how far in packaging and commoditizing culture and tourist experiences, can creative interaction and positive benefits of a socio-cultural, as well as of an economic nature, be nurtured.

The Impacts of Tourism on Language

As indicated in Mathieson and Wall (1982) few studies have addressed the impact of tourism on language, and language-based aspects of culture, at host destinations.

White's (1974) studies in Switzerland came to the conclusion that:

> tourism...may be highly disturbing to established social patterns and the maintenance of a vibrant local social and cultural identity. The evidence (of Switzerland) is that tourism generally acts as a destructive force in this sphere, and one that must be weighed against the desire for general economic development.

In studies of Swiss valleys that vary in tourist impact, he postulates direct correlations, and implies a causal relationship between scale of tourism entry, and level in decline of the host minority language. Studies in other minority-language areas – such as in Gaelic-speaking parts of Scotland and minority areas in Austria and Spain – indicate similar dangers.

White (1974) notes that:

> the effect of tourism on language change and patterns of socio-linguistic use in eastern Switzerland, emphasizes the role of this sector as an agent of diffusion of both social and cultural information, and attitudes. This is particularly important for rural areas, since for many parts of Europe tourism is the only modern economic sector in which development is feasible...In this present paper it is notable that the decline of Romansch (a Swiss minority language) speaking in the study area, is coincident with the growth of tourism, although other factors have also been present, such as changes in the education system... The most economically beneficial and socially least disruptive type of tourism is that of locally-based accommodation provision, such as farmhouse guests, camping sites, and Youth Hostels.

Language differences between hosts and guests may be minimal, or significant: Catalan – a minority language – is a majority language in its own territory. How far a minority language is spoken by thousands or by millions of people in its own territory seems to be another important variable. There seem to be high risks for minority languages spoken by small minorities, especially if a major world language is spoken by the visitor groups. The scale and vitality of any language, the amount of new writing and responsiveness in it, requires close examination.

Noronha (1979) has suggested that there are three stages of tourism development: (i) discovery; (ii) local response and initiative; and (iii) institutionalized tourism (institutionalization). Applying this to the language dimension, the acculturation effects will grow – especially if economic incentives in phase (ii) mean a need to use a guest's language, (as opposed to the host language), increasingly for language communication in economic encounters. Borrowing from a visitor's

language grows in such encounters, it is postulated. Tourism's impacts on host language and change will grow with increased economic exchange and economic change generally – through the 'demonstration effect' of tourism and through more direct social contacts (however superficial) with increased numbers of visitors.

Labov's 1963 and 1966 research work, done in relation to the Martha's Vineyard area of Massachusetts in the USA, relates to the social and socio-linguistic reactions of residents (at a tourist destination) to in-migrants and to tourists. What happens in relation to public contact language domains (where locals and visitors come into contact) is that some residents use their local tongue or dialect in front of visitors very assertively, and others deny the use of their local form of expression in front of visitors.

The Political Impact of Tourism on Destinations

The political impact of tourism on destinations is a subject which is not normally addressed, but is an aspect of the socio-cultural impacts of tourism that at least merits mention. Much literature has indicated that tourism is seen as very positive in this sphere as a freeing, liberalizing and modernizing force, particularly in very conservative and traditional host societies. Writers like Meleghy et al. (1985) looking at the Tyrol, in Austria, wrote that: 'It is only by introducing tourism, that certain pre-capitalist traditional enclaves of society are caught up by modernisation and capitalist development.' Yet they conclude that: 'Provided that development is relatively slow and of an equable nature, tourism can integrate itself into traditional structures; instead of causing their destruction, it can make their survival possible.'

Not only in helping to ease the difficult role of women in some societies, but also because of the economic structural effects aiding the young, aiding commerce, and acting against some traditional institutions does tourism thus aid processes of change, innovation, political development and modernization. It may socio-culturally have some destabilizing effect, yet creatively aid non-revolutionary political change.

Doxey's writings in 1975 and 1976, show how an index of 'tourist irritation', or irritation with and by tourists, leads to host responses. They in turn sometimes lead to political responses.

Political problems arise, according to some evidence (Smith, 1978; Cohen, 1979; Noronha, 1979) from cultural differences between the hosts and tourists, over issues such as: (i) nudity on beaches; (ii) overt sexual behaviour and intimacy in public places; (iii) levels of dress, or undress, in religious places which may be viewed by tourists simply as 'tourist attractions'; and (iv) noise levels, litter, pollution or overcrowding generated by tourism. Tourism as a source of local economic inflation – and of crime waves – is identified as a causal factor, in some host locations.

The Skew of Research Evidence on Socio-cultural Impacts

As will be evident from the summary foregoing text in this chapter, the weight of evidence is skewed heavily in the direction of the negative social and cultural impacts of tourism. Much of the work which has been done has related to tourism impacts in Third World countries. Thus, the north–south dialogue and the centre–periphery arguments work on the nature of 'under-development' links in closely to this literature. It makes all the more necessary the obtaining of first-hand data – direct empirical data – to get an adequate measure, and relevant measured response, from tourists and host on the key issues.

The circumstances of the 'encounter' also need close examination – do guests and hosts meet in the home, or are they ghettoized in separate locations? Are guests integrated with the hosts (as in Senegal) or deliberately isolated from the host community (as in Gambia, and in the past in the Maldives)? All these questions need addressing.

As a preliminary guidelines checklist of the wider range of positive and negative impacts of tourism on the social and cultural aspects of a tourist destination, this chapter concludes with an extract from a listing produced by the author for UNEP (Travis, 1984) that was published in the UNEP Industry and Environment journal.

Listing of socio-cultural benefits which may affect a tourist destination:

(A) *Cultural development and exchange*
Increased knowledge of host culture by visitors. Awareness of its music, cuisine and arts, and possibly some knowledge of language.

(B) *Social chance and choice*

Increased social and job chance; increased social contacts; new ways of life; increased interest and variety; increased goods and activities choice; increased chances for women; possible independence for biological households; increased job generation gives social option to migration; production of an 'open society'; changes and improvements in diet.

(C) *Image*

Improved reputation and visibility of host community to outsiders; increased knowledge elsewhere about the destination.

(D) *Host culture*

Develops because of demand for traditional entertainment; demand for traditional arts, architecture, crafts and music; 'Good' local gastronomy boosted; appreciation of one's own and other socio-cultural elements.

(E) *Health*

Improved public health, hygiene and sanitation standards; improved health services, sewage and waste treatment; environmental services upgraded.

(F) *Social and amenity involvement*

By provision of services, amenities and facilities not otherwise available to hosts – and social and activity choices therefore arising from them.

(G) *Education and conservation*

Education and learning aided. Training opportunities developed. Boosts for heritage protection, interpretation and management.

(H) *Understanding boosted*

Cultural interchange of hosts and guests, peace and understanding aided; breakdown of language barriers, of social and class barriers, of religious barriers, and of racial barriers; new experiences possible, access to new ideas, lifestyles and cultures.

(I) *Political changes*

Repressive political systems may be modified as a result of large-scale movements of people, goods and ideas to tourist destinations. The young, the radicals, and forces for change may be aided by tourism.

Listing of socio-cultural costs which may affect a tourist destination:

(A) *Cultural impacts*

– Host culture destruction; host culture debasement.

– Unacceptable rate and scale of cultural conflict and change.

– Damage to cultural systems, and to cultural resources. Minority languages at destinations placed at risk. Changes in sexual habits and roles.

– Demonstration Effect: residents copy behaviour, values, norms of visitors.

(B) *Social stability*

– Loss of original state and stability. Loss of cultural pride. Status of relationship between hosts and guest cultures changes.

– Changes in community cohesion, disruption of kinship and community ties.

– Groups likely to gain from change in conflict with existing old, conservative order. Simplicity gives way to complexity.

(C) *Consumerism*

– Consumption changes, introduction or expansion of gambling, prostitution, drunkenness and other excess; vice and drugs, theft and petty crimes grow.

– Rich visitors come to poor communities – creating tension, increased differences – haves/have-nots; envy, dislike, hatred.

– Cultural commercialization, and commodification of society.

– Commercialization of the arts; folk art becomes airport junk-art.

– Increased role and ascendance of commercial interests.

– Increased living costs, growth of money economy and of materialism and consumerism.

(D) *Law and order*

Increase of social conflicts, development of irritations, antagonism and interest groups; increase in crime, social tensions, dangers, more policing, more control necessary. Growth of prostitution, gambling, with or without licensing – socio-economic conflicts and attacks.

(E) *Social links and choice*

– Short-term and transient social relationships with visitors are not real and meaningful links.

– No visitor understanding or knowledge of hosts, their culture and language.

– Misunderstanding. Hostility, debasement. Destruction of social spontaneity. Costlier living, diminished housing chances, lead to more overcrowding, social tension in families.

(F) *Health*

New diseases introduced, plus more of old diseases.

(G) *Meanings*

Increasingly mass entry of visitors makes contact and meaning diminish. Commercialization of religion and rituals, decline of traditional religion. Pressure to change social values, dress, mores, habits and behavioural norms.

(H) *Political*

Tourism neo-colonialism, political conflict encouraged. Destabilization. Migrant workers introduced – increased political and economic conflicts – social implications.

20 Mid-Wales Festival of the Countryside: a Model of Events to Reinforce Rural Culture and Life

Arwel Jones

Aims

The original idea was of a region-wide and summer-long 'Festival of the Countryside', and was suggested by the Development Board for Rural Wales (DBRW), as a contribution towards: (i) arresting the decline in rural population and economic infrastructure; (ii) solving the conflict of interests threatening the future countryside; and (iii) providing for the increasing demand for rural holidays and recreational activity. The event became the Mid-Wales Festival of the Countryside – a joint venture between Cynefin (an organization set up in 1982 to encourage intelligent use of the environment), DBRW and the Countryside Commission Office for Wales. The area to be covered by the Festival was 4800 km², or 40% of the land area of Wales. The Festival proposal represented a major innovation in the development of what was then called 'green tourism', a sustainable form of community-based rural tourism aimed at nurturing the natural environment and a vibrant rural way of life.

In 1984, DBRW's main intention was 'to bring the countryside to the forefront of the region's marketing profile', by creating a region-wide programme of rural activities. Cynefin identified additional aims, namely: (i) to convey, in an interesting and coherent way, the messages of the countryside and of conservation; (ii) to satisfy the varied recreational demands of residents and of visitors; and (iii) to stimulate the rural economy and boost revenues for providers of rural attractions. The Countryside Commission was keen to improve and extend the provision of responsible recreational and educational opportunities for all. It was hoped that people would care more for their environment as a result of what they saw and did through the Festival's activities.

Description

The Festival, as it developed, contained a wide range of activities, ranging from a badger watch to farm visits, conservation lectures, white-water rafting, plus touring arts and crafts exhibitions.

All information and editorial was prepared for the annual programme, which was published in magazine form, and which brought existing activities and events, together with new ones. Large numbers of copies (100,000 in 1988; 40,000 in 1989; and 60,000 in 1990) were widely distributed through Tourist Information Centres, libraries and other outlets in Mid-Wales, the Welsh Borders and selected other locations (e.g. Stratford upon Avon and London). During the period of the Festival (from June to September inclusive), the magazine's distribution was supplemented by the use of local posters, handbills and media publicity.

The Festival team provided support and advice throughout the year. Potential event organizers were encouraged to develop ideas with the team, possible sources of grant aid and supplementary advice were identified, and, where possible, direct financial or organizational support was given. 'Mini-festivals', such as the 'Lake Vyrnwy Festival' and the 'Dolgellau Farming Festival', were organized and funded by local groups (Fig. 20.1). Such events took place regularly throughout the summer, and provided promotional focal points for local involvement, attracting as they did significant numbers of visitors. The intention with every Festival local event was to hand over responsibility to an appropriate local body, at the right time.

The years of experimentation and establishment were 1985 and 1986, a time of finding out the limits of the possible, and of setting up the requisite communication networks. Initially, the Festival was organized by a part-time director and by part-time events organizers. In 1987, two full-time coordinators (on a British Trust for Conservation Volunteers Community Programme scheme) were appointed to work with the part-time director, and enabled the Festival to develop further. Five activity themes were devised: (i) 'Nature and Wildlife'; (ii) 'The Working Landscape'; (iii) 'Rural Rides'; (iv) 'Arts and Crafts'; and (v) 'History and Tradition'. Six geographical areas were identified (Snowdonia, Montgomeryshire, the Heart of Wales, the Brecon Beacons, Teifi Valley and Cardigan Bay) and different ways of promoting the Festival were explored, for example via the use of personalities, and of conferences.

At the end of 1988 a phase of consolidation, reappraisal and some restructuring, was entered. A new grant-aid formula was devised, one which introduced the active involvement of all eight local authorities, with matching funding from the Countryside Commission, and continuing support from DBRW. The number of Festival events had risen steadily from 300 to 400 in 1985, to over 700 in 1988, and direct attendance numbers grew from 90,000 in 1985 to 250,000 by 1988!

By 1989, the Festival had impressively started its fifth year of activity. The core team now comprised a part-time director, two full-time Festival coordinators, a driver provided by Cynefin, and a data support worker, on a casual basis. In 1989 the *Mid-Wales Companion* was published, a 220 page handbook on the wildlife, landscape, history and culture of the region, and a direct complement to the Festival.

Initially, the DBRW had provided significant funds to help the Festival – especially in its marketing, as it recognized the time required to establish a strong identity for it. In the first year the Countryside Commission's financial input was limited, as it was unable to match the monies of another central government body, but a part-time events organizer – with a research and experimentation budget – was provided by them. By 1989/90 operating costs were provided by the eight local authorities, the private sector (through Broxap and Corby Ltd), matched by the Countryside Commission, and DBRW. Advertising revenue from the magazine that was produced and linked merchandizing also provided some income.

Direct funding for some of the events in the programme (such as for those projects which were particularly innovative or financially risky) was provided through the Festival. Earlier, this had included the use of: (i) DBRW Social Development grants and Social Promotion support; (ii) Countryside Commission funding; (iii) Cynefin funding; and (iv) private-sector sponsorship. Such 'pump-priming' had always been on the understanding that events would eventually become largely self-financing.

A quantitative and qualitative monitoring of events, conducted from 1985 onwards, produced a range of comparative data about events and visitor numbers. In 1987, it was estimated that about 20 full-time job equivalents were created by the Festival's activities. The economic benefit generated by the Festival in 1988 was estimated to have produced a £5 million turnover in the Mid-Wales rural economy (using multipliers of numbers of day visits and tourists).

Recreational opportunities were increased by making existing facilities more available, developing new ones (such as farm

Fig. 20.1. Demonstrations of farm machinery (a) and sheep shearing (b) at the Dolgellau Farming Festival (photographs courtesy of Mid-Wales Festival of the Countryside).

open days), and supplementing National Park events. The magazine was used to carry educational messages and information. The Countryside Commission in England and Wales recognized the potential of rural events programmes, and came to support rural festivals and other 'green tourism' initiatives more actively.

The use of resources and the shared burden of funding and responsibility was in general thought to be very effective by the participating bodies. The small contribution of each local authority (from different departmental budgets – such as those from Planning, Tourism or the National Park Authority), when doubled by the contribution from the Countryside Commission, could jointly support a substantial programme. The 1989 budget of £51,000 was a modest sum for a major enterprise, especially when compared with the budgets allocated for capital projects, or for national marketing campaigns.

Constraints

The differing timescales used, and channels of responsibility of the various grant-aiding bodies, at times caused operational difficulties. In particular, the retrospective nature of some grant-aid arrangements frequently caused Cynefin to suffer cash-flow or short-term debt problems. This was overcome, to some extent, by creating a central reserve fund, devising more flexible funding mechanisms, and by close working relationships with the different funding bodies. Following DBRW's revised funding programme a new financial structure developed, and this meant that Cynefin became wholly responsible for most aspects of the Festival, including: (i) salaries; (ii) magazine production; and (iii) the administrative and distribution costs. There was still considerable support in kind from DBRW, the Countryside Commission and the Nature Conservancy Council (which had been the parent organization of Cynefin).

The level of support for the Festival by the staff of Tourist Information Centres was patchy. At first, the Festival's experimental nature did not guarantee their confidence, but the Festival team slowly increased confidence by their attention to detail, and quick responses to queries and difficulties which arose.

Evaluation

Initially, there was some cynicism about how far the different social, cultural and linguistic character of Wales would be a constraint upon such tourist development. The Festival team recognized the value of this diversity as a strength and an identity element. They worked positively to invest these dimensions into the Festival, thus Welsh cultural evenings and Welsh 'singalongs' were introduced. The possible conflict between tourism development and rural conservation was largely avoided by the effective cooperation of key agencies, and the careful development of an environmentally and culturally sensitive programme.

As in other imaginative events around the world, such as in the New Zealand hospitality schemes for cattle breeders, or Indian ecovillage festivals, the strengthening and reinforcement of local identity and character enhanced its appeal. Though the Festival was of limited life, it demonstrated how far a rural region can host a community-based set of events, which: (i) celebrate the host culture; (ii) reinforce its social and economic life; and (iii) increase the visitors' knowledge of, and respect for, the culture and identity of a marginal region.

21 Den Norske Turistforening – a Voluntary Sector Sustainable Programme in Norway

Jan Vidar Haukeland

Aims

Den Norske Turistforening (DNT) is a Norwegian voluntary sector agency that works to promote opportunities for a healthy and active outdoor life in the mountains by: (i) operating lodges; (ii) marking summer and winter trails; (iii) arranging guided tours and practical courses; and (iv) publishing a great deal of information.

Membership of the organization is open to all, and its main aims are:

- to let participants experience nature, in its untouched form;
- to activate travellers in a healthy way;
- to educate its members in different ways, through courses and through the provision of information; and
- to act as an interest organization, promoting better conditions for outdoor life ('Friluftsliv'), and thereby working actively for the protection of the natural environment.

The DNT has tried to avoid a 'mass character', in the sense that it has not accepted making access into mountains too easy a proposition (preventing road building, funicular lines and ski lifts). New members are welcome to be close to nature, but in a manner which does not destroy it.

Friluftsliv

DNT is linked to a Scandinavian, and especially Norwegian, philosophy of so-called 'Friluftsliv'. This is a form of Scandinavian outdoor resource management and use, which has special philosophical and spiritual dimensions. This deep tradition, deriving its inspiration from the Romantic Movement, is a desire for the individual and the family to get out into nature, and as Fridtjof Nansen said 'to have a sound spirit in a sound body' (Dahle, 1993). It is a process of 'living in harmony with Nature, and not winning a war against Nature,' as suggested by Thor Heyerdahl (Dahle, 1993).

In the Norwegian publication *Nature: the True Home of Culture* edited by Borge Dahle and published by the Norwegian University of Sport and Physical Education in 1993, a group of distinguished Norwegian thinkers and writers explored many of the philosophical and practical dimensions of Friluftsliv, or this approach to simple outdoor living. In Friluftsliv the individual or family travels by rail, or bike, or on foot, or goes on cross-country skis – straight from home to the destination areas, in order to explore nature on foot, on skis, on bike, in canoes, or in small groups with family or friends. It is a process of living simply, absorbing and being with nature, and getting physical and spiritual renewal from being with, and in nature.

Description of DNT

DNT is a Norwegian nationwide voluntary association for mountain hikers. It was founded in 1868 as a product of the National Romantic Movement that swept over Norway in the middle of the 19th century. Painters, poets and musicians at first prized the beauty of the countryside, and idealized – for some decades – the lifestyle of people living in remote rural areas. In the 1880s, new communications developed rapidly – canals, roads and railways – which made the inland and upland areas much more accessible to people living in towns and the coastal regions. Travel handbooks were published, and six very active regional branches of the organization were founded at the end of the 1880s.

The number of members by 2006 was 210,000 (one in ten from abroad), and there is a growing public interest in what the organization offers. Increasing concern about ecological issues, and a rising trend towards a healthy lifestyle, made the DNT more popular than ever.

The DNT has historically developed a network of lodges and chalets (about 450 in total) in the mountains, ranging from large, staffed lodges with more than 100 beds, to unstaffed huts with just four beds. The staffed lodges serve all meals, and the self-service chalets have food provisions in them that are for sale. There are also some unstaffed huts which do not have food provisions, but are otherwise fully equipped for the visitor.

A network of trails marked with cairns link the lodges together during the summer period – this network is all together 20,000 km in length. The cairns are normally marked with a 'T' painted in red. Except for the crossings of glaciers, guides are normally not necessary, provided that the tourists are equipped with special maps of the area being visited. During wintertime, some 7000 km of paths or trails are marked in the snow with wooden branches.

All members receive a handbook on mountain trekking, with information about different routes. In addition, members are sent an informative yearbook and a quarterly magazine. The information provided covers different topics, such as: (i) ecological issues relating to flora and fauna; (ii) plans for National Parks; and (iii) documentation about threats to the environment. Local history, local food and cultural aspects of the different regions are also a focus. Some of the chalets are in fact old transhumance locations, in the mountains, for summer dairying, and this brings the visitor into contact with an important part of traditional Norwegian farming culture.

Practical advice, like recommendations about which kind of equipment is needed, is given for those who plan to make a trip. The DNT organizes a number of activities including special courses both for summer and for winter seasons, for those who want to learn more about the mountains. There are also guided tours for special-interest groups – like glacier walking, mountain climbing, trout fishing, photography, nature study, geology and archaeology. Special programmes are set up for old age pensioners, parents with small children, and for young people. Advice is also given for those who want to experience other forms of rural touring – such as canoeing, mountain biking and touring with a tent.

Experiences and Challenges

The experience to date of DNT is very encouraging. It offers its members a tourist experience that is active, healthy and educational, and which is meaningful for the participants.

The consciousness among the Norwegian general public about the value of untouched nature, has been powerfully strengthened through DNT's actions. The organization has also played an active role in identifying environmental conflicts, and has engaged in issues concerning plans for: (i) road building; (ii) hydro-electric power plants; and (iii) the routing of gas pipelines from the North Sea to neighbouring countries. These are plans which would affect the core regions of the route network provided by DNT.

There is, of course, a contradiction in the aim of protecting the natural wilderness, for on the one hand DNT welcomes a growing number of mountain ramblers, and on the other hand they give rise to visitor impacts. However, only 50 km of the paths laid have been damaged by erosion – mainly due to the fact that the mountain area is so very extensive. In some vulnerable areas, the traffic is limited by the routes being made very demanding in terms of the skills required to negotiate them. The philosophy of the DNT historically was to protect some regions from use, in order to preserve the wilderness completely. However, those regions have now been developed for different purposes, by other interest groups, which has caused much more damage than mountain hiking would have done.

Evaluation

This leads to an important conclusion, namely that tourism in this specific form, might very well be an effective agent for environmental protection. The fact that great parts of the Norwegian mountain areas are used by the DNT makes the organization an important political force, and that might be a counterweight to other competitor and more damaging interests, in terms of possible environmental misuse. The DNT has a long tradition of treating both nature and local culture respectfully. Its internal culture also motivates newcomers to act thoughtfully in the countryside. They learn to use, but not to abuse the environment, and this appears to be a most fruitful strategy. By and large DNT is an agent of conservation rather than of development. The organization aids the process of sustainable management of Norway's high quality, upland landscapes. DNT backs local tourism business development that fosters outdoor activities, and living mountain habitats need viable villages.

22 Cycling in the Netherlands – a Sustainable Move Forward for a Whole Nation

Ton Van Egmond

Introduction

The Netherlands, or 'Holland' for many tourists, has special peculiar characteristics that partly aid and partly restrict tourism. With an area of 41,500 km², and 15.6 million inhabitants in 2000, the Netherlands has the highest density of population of any European country. Consequently, every square inch of territory is subject to planning control, and truly natural landscapes disappeared a long time ago. Man's hand is evident everywhere. Only the Wadden Sea, that part of the North Sea directly adjacent to the Dutch north coast, may be called 'natural'. The Netherlands are overcrowded – it is almost impossible to find places without people. The country has little to offer to the 'drifter' or to the 'primitive camper'. Camping is only allowed at camping sites with sanitary facilities and water supply. Nevertheless, the Netherlands offer excellent facilities in at least two spheres that relate to 'sustainable tourism' criteria: (i) in cycling; and (ii) in naturism. Cycling facilities in the Netherlands are an outstanding example of sustainable and responsible tourism.

Cycling has a long history in the Netherlands. In the past the bicycle was used purely as a means of transport, but during the last 50 years, cycling has become an overwhelmingly recreational pastime there. Cycling is favoured by: (i) the generally flat nature of the country; (ii) the relatively small-scale of the cities as well as of the countryside; and (iii) the mild climate.

Aims

Government, local government, the voluntary and commercial sectors in the Netherlands, all combine to create both the physical infrastructure, the maps, routes, signposts, packages, information and publicity that comprise a set of informal choices, as well as organized offers to cyclists, which are certainly unequalled in European terms. The aims are to offer a rich choice of active and healthy cycling opportunities in town and country, by coastal dunes or in woodlands, for day trips, weekend outings, as well as for domestic and international tourism. It is an alternative and sustainable form of tourism, which sets out to give choices to the majority, and not to just small minorities within the population.

Description

A physical system of over 10,000 km or 6200 miles of special and often physically separate cycle lanes and paths has been created, and most of this has been developed exclusively for recreational purposes. Thus the cyclists are insulated from other traffic, are able to enjoy in safety and in peace, both the beauty of the countryside, and way-side facilities, amenities, and linked accommodation available.

The promotion of cycling has been given high priority in Dutch Government policy for several years, both at national and at local scales. This has linked to the actions in the past of the Nederlands Bureaux voor Toerisme (NBT; the national tourist board), the national motoring organization (the ANWB, which started as a cycling organization) and local tourist information offices (the VVVs).

For the Dutch tourist, the ANWB has designated more than 60 cycling routes, which vary in length from 25 to 50 km. ANWB's dense network of cycling signposts on the ground are numbered, and these numbers relate to those found on the excellent, special cycling maps published and sold by the ANWB. Other organizations such as cyclists' associations have also designed special routes.

The NBT together with the VVVs arrange complete cycling holiday packages, which are marketed as normal commercial offers abroad and to the domestic market. These packages can be booked directly with the organizers concerned (often a provincial or regional VVV), or through the National Bookings Reservation Centre, or sometimes through local agents. This form of tourism offers significant components. A cycling holiday package includes as a rule: (i) sea or air travel to the cycle hire and collection point; (ii) middle-priced and/or tourist-class hotels; (iii) an information package with route description and maps; and (iv) a luggage delivery service. Examples of these offers are:

- the 'Holland Cross-Country Tour';
- the 'Castles Cycling Tour';
- the 'Saxon Farm Trip'; and
- the 'Tour of Old Dutch Towns'.

Inexpensive accommodation offers exist in the 50 youth hostels available nationally, or in guesthouses, pensions, or bed-and-breakfast places, at camping sites, and especially in the log cabins, which are usually found on camping sites. Camping on a farm is not common in the Netherlands, except for school groups and scouts, who are accommodated in special farmhouses. Cyclists are well catered for generally, with cycle sheds and cycle parks provided at bus and railway stations, beaches and by woodlands and parks. Cycle paths often give direct access to beaches, to naturist beaches and to camps, which are not directly accessible to motorists.

Experiences and Evaluation

While foreign visitors increasingly come to cycle in the Netherlands, more and more Dutch people are taking cycling holidays outside their own country. Dutch coach operators have developed the so-called 'cycle coach' – a coach with a trailer, in which some 40 bikes can be transported. Together with the already existing cycle trains, this cycle coach enables people to go for a cycling holiday in the South of France, or in Italy or Scandinavia. Dutch tour operators arrange camping trips and hotel trips by bicycle through the most beautiful parts of those countries.

As a successful form of sustainable tourism, cycling in the Netherlands reveals few dangers and problems. Taken in the round, cycling offers a cheap, easy, healthy and active outdoor recreational alternative to the motor car, for day trips, weekend outings and holidays. This is especially true in a highly urbanized country, where traffic jams, noise and pollution, are part of the normal set of domestic expectations. Cycling is small scale, often individual, or associated with small-group travel. It is quiet, and safe, sensitive to the physical environment, and is acceptable in socio-cultural terms. Cycling holidays, as a rule, use local accommodation, and this gives community benefit (i.e. it optimizes economic and social benefits to the host communities). It is a form of recreation, which makes it easier to experience the physical, social and cultural environments. It leads to physical well-being and in the context of sustainable and responsible tourism, the promotion of cycling should, no doubt, be pushed to the fore.

Part III

Coastal and Maritime Planning and Management

Coastal Planning Evolution: Introduction and Choice of Case Studies

After the Second World War and the immediate post-war reconstruction phase, North West Europe, with its highly urbanized population, increasingly looked to the coasts of the Mediterranean Sea for its 'Leisure Littoral' from the 1960s onwards. Thus coastal development became an increasingly competitive sphere – caught between the pressures for development (for tourism, for new urbanization, for economic development, for energy provision and ports) and the need for conservation both as a natural environment and as a place of biotic production. Since the 1960s the sea resource itself has increasingly been put under pressure from the dumping of urban waste and untreated sewage, oil spills and shipping pollution – all critical impacts for an enclosed and tide-less sea, such as the Mediterranean.

In Part III, various scales of change and intervention are examined – from regional coastal planning – as seen in the Yugoslav or Croatian Adriatic, compared with the appraisal of England's and Wales' coastlines – to Mediterranean basin planning of sea and coastlines, with the follow-up ventures of agency action by the Priority Actions Programme Regional Activity Centre (PAP/RAC) doing work on tourism carrying capacity assessment (TCCA), on sections of the Mediterranean's coastlines. Finally, there is a unique national case study – that of the Netherlands, dealing with the issue of global warming and its potential large-scale sea rise, which is tackled as a priority issue by a nation state which has much of its land lying below sea level.

23 Adriatic Coastal Development Planning by Federal Yugoslavia (Now Croatia), 1960–1980

Historical Perspective

Independent Croatia, formerly part of the Federal State of Yugoslavia, is today a nation of over 56,000 km², with a population of over 4.6 million, and a coastline of 6000 km and some 1000 islands. Croatia has over 3200 years of complex cultural and economic development, under changing external influences. The geopolitical roots of modern Croatia relate to the successive entry of Illyrians, Celts, Greeks, Romans, Avars, Slavs, Holy-Romans, Bulgars, Byzantines, Croats, Turks, Venetians, the Austro-Hungarian Empire, Italians and Germans. Croatia possesses most of the Adriatic coastline of the former Federal State of Yugoslavia.

The Adriatic Sea, and access to and from it, has been an influential highway – of people, ideas, exchange, trade, attack and invasion, and friendly entry. Historically, Greek colonization from the south, Roman from the west and Venetian from the north have all had their effects. Many influences have left their physical relics behind in the built heritage of the country, such as the great Roman Amphitheatre of Pula, or the structure of the Roman Palace built by Emperor Diocletian, who hailed from Dalmatia and created Split. Modern Split's city core still sits within the shell of that former palace.

Phases of Physical Planning for Tourism: Federal Yugoslavia 1960–1975

In the first half of the 1960s, international tourism to Yugoslavia increased by 26%. In 1954 the country had only 81,000 tourist beds. By 1980 it was to have over one million tourist beds! Starting in the 1960s, there were four phases of development, commencing with large-scale coastal development for tourism grouped around existing settlements in Istria. Over 30,000 tourist beds were developed in the vicinity of Rovinj, and over 10,000 by the settlement of Porec. Placeless development, on a huge scale, swamped part of the Istrian coast. For Yugoslavia, Istria was in this period what the Costa Brava was for early Spanish tourism development. A few kilometres away from the Adriatic coast however, a medieval rural world continued, and despite water development projects like that in the Mirna Valley in Istria, the coastal boom contrasted with inland rural poverty, and the pace of the oxen cart. Italian out-migration from Istria in the period after the Second World War led to uneven development, the need to repopulate, and even a struggle to find new economic roles for the hill towns of Istria such as Motovun, Buje and Groznjan. The coast-to-inland relationship in Istria was a big challenge, and though later, day visiting from the coastal resorts to inland attractions was developed by package tourist companies, such as Neckermann, this was more tokenism than serious action to get major favourable economic impacts on the interior.

Jadran I, II and III

A mixed economy, a strong planning tradition, and rapid growth of tourism, provided the reasons for a fascinating sequence of regional planning studies for the Yugoslav Adriatic coast. Jadran I (the South Adriatic Project of 1967–1969) was the first major physical development plan for a key coastal tourism region of Croatia. It was followed by Jadran II. Jadran II was the Upper Adriatic Project of 1970–1972, covering the adjacent region. From 1972 onwards, Jadran III elaborated the South and Upper Adriatic Projects further, in terms of the reconciliation of development with the protection and conservation of the natural environment, and the built environment.

The three studies reflect a maturing of theory, concept and techniques of planning and development, as well as a refinement of the ideas of the agencies and of the technical personnel involved. From regional and project development thinking, Yugoslavia, and essentially Croatia, moved towards integrated regional planning, which combined conservation management with social and economic development aims.

By the beginning of the 1970s, with foreign tourists generating 23 million bed nights in Yugoslavia (essentially Croatia), overt tourist demand was leading the supply of tourist infrastructure and superstructure, so that in relation to the Upper Adriatic Region, Jadran II, comments:

> Yugoslavia's natural conditions for the development of tourism initiated a foreign and home tourist traffic which did not wait for new roads to be built. The Adriatic as a tourism attraction broke through all barriers and made essential the building of hotels and infrastructure facilities.
> (Planning Institute of Croatia, 1972)

Furthermore, tourism was to be used as a trigger to the development of a compatible, multi-sectoral economic programme for the region. Jadran II therefore aimed:

> to find possibilities of using tourist activity as an initial factor of development and the relation of this activity with other economic activities…Thus Adriatic tourism should… become an initial factor of development and cohesive force, as an economic multiplier of possible development.
> (Planning Institute of Croatia, 1972)

It can be seen, therefore, that Jadran II fundamentally changed the traditional stance of regional planning, towards the manufacturing and service sectors, and represented an important new test case for tourism planning.

The third Adriatic study postulated that the disbenefits and diseconomies of tourism development can be dealt with at low cost – in a system of linked planning and management activities. It preceded EU thinking by 20 years. A sympathy with, and respect for, ecological concepts and the survival requirements of ecosystems was displayed in Jadran III. The study dealt with the later stages of change; not only planning and physical development phases, but also the ways of managing, monitoring and coping with the effects, as well as the planned results, of intervention. Jadran III aimed at: 'enforcing the development but overcoming the adverse impacts of the development, protection of environmental quality… and the preservation of resources' (Planning Institute of Croatia, 1974).

The year 1978 saw a new tourism peak achieved on the Adriatic coast, when some 34.8 million foreign tourist nights and 48.6 million domestic tourist nights were spent in Yugoslavia. This made environmental conservation a new imperative. The planners and managers reacted against the 'placeless' and non-descript architecture which was swamping coastal Yugoslavia. They wanted instead to: (i) protect the heritage and environment; and (ii) deal effectively with air and water pollution and with problems of nuisance and of noise. Dr Hitrec and Professor S. Markovic evaluated the evolution of this learning process in planning and tourism, both in their national and in international contexts. The conservation-planning philosophy as it developed for Yugoslav/Croatian tourism is impressively handled in M. Dragicevic's major study of 1978. Croatia's TOMAS Market Research (Tourismus Marketing Schweitz – the Swiss system used and adapted by the Croats) confirmed not only that their key tourist markets were German, Austrian, Italian and British, but also that 66% of the foreign tourists were attracted by the natural heritage assets, and that nearly all came to the Adriatic for rest and recreation.

Eco-Planning and Visitor Management, 1975–1985

Before the 1980s, Jadran II had laid down foundations for biosphere conservation in Croatia, and a qualitative approach to environmental planning. New growth markets, such as for naturism, were coming to the fore, and depended upon environmental quality. Responsive product offers in Croatia had to compete with those offered in France and Italy. After the boom in mass-packaged air travel in the 1960s, competing market demands were for new products in more distant locations, and environmental purity became a prerequisite for tourist destinations.

'Soft tourism' and 'responsible tourism' grew out of creative responses to the destructive impacts of uncontrolled mass tourism, which had damaged the coasts of Spain, Greece and Turkey. By the 1980s, fears of environmental degradation were evolving in tourist destination countries, and the prospect was of a short economic life for new destinations. It is from this phase that ideas and responses grew, during the 1990s particularly, about 'sustainable tourism'.

Professor S. Markovic and his team at Plitvice Lakes National Park in Croatia provided an inland pace setter in terms of an approach to sustainable planning. This case model is discussed in detail in Chapter 14. Croatia's three island National

Parks (at Kornati, Mljet and Brijuni) plus a coastal National Park at Paklenica, and three inland National Parks (Risnjak, Plitvice and Krka) became uniquely equipped to become a brand leader in the new field of ecotourism/nature tourism.

The Jadran Planning Phase provided Croatia with a set of developed coastal tourist destination areas around existing towns. The project scale of the later developments was reduced. Schemes were reasonably designed, but had management shortfalls: (i) visitors faced inflexible meal regimes, fixed times for eating, restricted food offers and poor culinary standards; (ii) there was a lack of tourist information and environmental interpretation; and (iii) visitors had difficulties in understanding a host society with values different to their own. By 1984 66% of Yugoslav's tourism was coastal, even in the year in which Sarajevo's winter Olympics were held.

Croatia was already competing in the sphere of 'nautical tourism' and 'flotilla sailing' with Greece, Turkey, France and Italy. New systems of marinas and moorings were created in Croatia. However, management and marketing were in the hands of big cumbersome tourism enterprises – like Kompas. In a fast, competitive international tourism industry, they functioned like 'slow-moving elephants'. Provider 'convenience' in Croatia, rather than a 'user-orientation' found in competitor countries, disadvantaged Croatian offers in this period, and were not to be overcome until the later period, after the achievement of Croatian independence.

From the late 1970s into the 1980s the Vienna Social Science Research Centre's Six Country Study into the 'Socio-cultural Impacts of Tourism', was conducted under the direction of the author and Professor Przeclawski (Przeclawski and Travis, 1985). A team from the Zagreb Institute of Tourism led the Croatian National Study, which was part of the Six Country Study. From it, a clear picture emerged of the strengths and weaknesses of Croatian tourism. What came out of that report was an overwhelmingly positive international response to the coastal tourism offer of Croatia.

Evaluation

The overwhelming range of experience from the three Jadran projects is positive, creative and innovative, and links very clearly to other follow-up actions. This is because the work conducted in Yugoslavia and Croatia's Jadran projects linked through to developments in the Split region, and it was at Split that the new Priority Actions Programme Regional Activity Centre (PAP/RAC) was to be created, where critical work was later to be done in the Mediterranean planning context (see Chapters 25 and 26). Also the key work on TCCA largely emerged from the initiatives of the Split PAP/RAC office. Thus later work done on the island of Vis in Croatia, as well as studies on the coasts of Albania, Italy, Egypt, Greece and Cyprus, gave new templates by the Croat planners, involved in this TCCA phase. By 2009, with Croatia functioning as an independent national state, much had changed in Croatian coastal planning, and the privatization of much of the tourist industry changed many parameters and assumptions. However, the continuing benefit of the foundation work done in the Jadran phase of projects placed coastal Croatia in a good competitive position for its future, in international tourism terms.

24 Planning the Coastline: England and Wales 1960–1970

Introduction

An interesting example of the UK evolutionary approach to coastal planning policy, can be seen in the period from 1963 to the early 1970s, when arising out of an initiative by the Ministry of Housing and local government in 1963 to ask local planning authorities to do a special study of their coastal areas, a process of coastal planning research and implementation evolved. The intent of the 1963 government circular was fourfold:

1. To get local planning authorities to see which parts of their coastline needed safeguarding, so that their natural attractions would be enjoyed.
2. To see which parts of the coasts should have facilities for holidaymakers, and where other developments should be concentrated.
3. To see which steps should be taken to restore amenities.
4. To see what areas of scientific interest existed and needed special consideration for conservation action.

By 1965, in a period when much economic change was occurring, there was deep concern emerging about coastal development, and action was required by maritime planning authorities and the National Parks Commission, which was then responsible for the countryside. Therefore the Government asked the National Parks Commission to arrange a series of regional conferences to supplement the work which had been started under the 1963 circular, and this was to be supplemented by cooperation and liaison with a whole range of other bodies in this sphere: (i) the British Tourist Authority on the issue of statistics; (ii) the Nature Conservancy Council on conservation matters; (iii) the Sports Council on outdoor recreation issues, plus contact with commercial and industrial organizations; and (iv) liaison with the National Trust about the 'Enterprise Neptune' venture it was conducting.

Thus the pattern which evolved, started with national liaison and information gathering via local planning authorities, it had then gone on to the National Parks Commission being asked to set up a set of regional conferences, and in turn these regional conferences provided vital feedback, so that eventually a national report was produced giving an overview of the whole situation, and making formal proposals.

Regional Report Phase

An example of the regional conferences organized by the National Parks Commission, in cooperation with the maritime planning authorities and other parties, is that which was conducted in 1967 on the subject of the coasts of Yorkshire and Lincolnshire. It was published as a report in 1968 (National Parks Commission, 1968a) and addressed some eight issues. One of the first of these was that it looked at various parts of the coast that were being intensively used as caravan and chalet sites, which were a major issue, in this instance. Within this region, the coastline was considered to be of regional not national importance, and that this was a coast which was being increasingly affected by the impacts of tourism and recreation demands, which themselves were changing. A switch had been taking place from hotels and boarding houses over to self-catering accommodation. In the period from 1950 to 1965 this region had seen a fourfold increase in caravans and chalets, from 4000 at the beginning of this period, to 16,000 at the end of it.

In addition, the tourism and recreation uses, were giving rise to a new growth phase of retirement at the coast, which was the cause of housing growth and service demands, and this needed to be assessed. Some 24 miles of coast within these two counties were already in an existing National Park, and therefore were already subject to protection. However, there were problems on this coast of clearing away derelict shack developments, and even some outworn military installations. Spurn Head, a major peninsula on the coast, proved to be an area of considerable scientific interest, and was one where there was a need to limit public access, in order to protect both the birdlife and the geology of this area.

This section of the coast also had very considerable pressures from recreational sailing, and the question was raised as to meeting the requirement for new marina development, and adequate moorings for the growing sailing phenomenon. On questions of costs to local authorities working on problems of the coast, there were matters of cost sharing, to deal with extensive and expensive problems of dune conservation, and also issues of conflicts between recreation, conservation and the roles of electricity generation and transmission in the coastal zone. Finally, of the issues revealed in the Yorkshire and Lincolnshire report, there was the question of access problems due to increasing railway closures and transport modal shifts. The growth of private-car ownership and use was changing the need for the amount and quality of road system, particularly that serving the coast, and the links between resorts and the inland, visitor-generating urban areas.

The Coastal Plan for England and Wales

By the end of the 1960s, the regional conferences and reports had been completed, and it was possible for the new body, the Countryside Commission, which had taken over from the National Parks Commission, to prepare a major report on coastal preservation and development in England and Wales. This was published in 1970, as *Planning of the Coastline*. This national report contains some eight chapters with the following conclusions and recommendations:

1. Trends in tourism and recreational use of the coast – With regard to this it was stated that the coast would remain the focus for 70% of holidays, but there was a need for recognition of the shift to self-catering accommodation both in coastal and in resort locations. The increase in private mobility by car showed that there was a great need for information and local surveys about visitor statistics, and general statistics as well as local statistics were needed in this sphere.
2. Resorts – With regard to resorts, there was a growing need for car-parking provision, and also a need to safeguard the resort function within England and Wales (i.e. to protect the resorts by emphasizing their individuality and the complementarity of the varied offers in different resorts). The retirement factor, which was seen to be growing, was in need of study, and there was also a need for government, commerce and society to come to a view on the changing role of resorts within the national economy.
3. New holiday centres – It was considered that action was needed to provide new caravan sites in the country, and a process of aiding improvement in their quality. The general switch to self-catering which was taking place in the tourism sector was recognized and the need for new holiday villages was emphasized. Related to this was the question of national highway developments, to cater for

the changing scale of movement by private car, from the inland cities to the resorts.

4. Regional parks – The issue of the relationship of regional parks, National Parks and country parks to the coast was raised, and the recreational potential of countryside at the coast was identified for review and proposals.

5. Removing the mess – It became clear from the series of regional studies in England and Wales, that there was a sizeable problem of the clearance of eyesores, made up of former military installations that were derelict, ruined shacks, wasteland areas, colliery wastes and some inappropriately sited defence lands. This raised the whole question of how far special budgets and Compulsory Purchase Orders might be required as part of actions by local planning authorities to clear these blighted areas and upgrade the environmental quality of such areas on the coast.

6. Coastal industries – The exploitation of oil and natural gas off the coast, and in the North Sea especially, was seen as being of very great importance to the nation economically and in terms of energy. Recognition was given as to how far the linkage of working areas on the coast to these oil and gas fields, were properly accommodated. In addition, recognition was given to the National Ports Council proposals for 'Maritime Industrial Development Areas' (MIDAs) to be created – the so-called MIDAs Programme of selected and limited areas, where new port and associated industrial development would be actively planned for on selected sections of the coast.

7. Planning policies for the under-developed coast – These policies were also spelt out in the report, precisely defining where protection policies would be required and addressing the issue of public access to protected areas, some of which might be in private ownership, and therefore required management agreements on such matters as public access for recreation.

8. Heritage Coasts – Some 34 areas of the highest quality scenery were identified as 'Heritage Coasts' in England and Wales (see Fig. 24.1). These were to be nationally designated and would require special treatment and planning if they were not already part of National Parks.

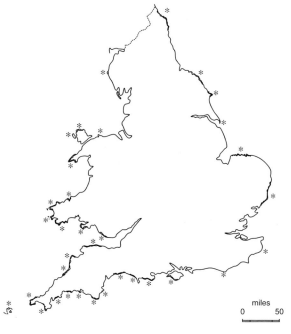

Fig. 24.1. Map showing the 34 areas identified as 'Heritage Coasts' in England and Wales (Source: Countryside Commission, 1991a).

Evaluation

A very large part of the ideas and proposals that arose from the regional studies and the national report were subsequently implemented over time. In particular the Heritage Coasts were created, and we have already seen an example of this in the Glamorgan Heritage Coast, referred to in the South-Wales Valleys Study, covered in Chapter 17 of this book. There has also been: (i) the development of coastal country parks and limited numbers of new holiday centres; (ii) extensive improvement in the location and screening of caravan parks; and (iii) large-scale removal of eyesores round the coast. The underdeveloped coast has been increasingly selectively subject to protection policies, and the continuing mix of policies for development and conservation have characterized active coastal planning in England and Wales.

The MIDAs have been created, but in fact the impacts of the working of off-coast oil and natural gas have been far greater than expected, even with controls on the coast. The biggest problem which has not been solved was that of the old coastal resorts of England and Wales which have continually had problems in terms of their economic base, their mix of activities, renovation and upgrading. This was mentioned in the report on the Firth of Clyde (Chapter 13) and will be discussed further in Chapter 45. The high-conflict estuarine areas of the coast, where economic development is in conflict with tourism, biotic production and wildlife conservation, is an issue which was under-explored in this earlier period, and came much to the fore later.

25 Mediterranean Action Plan and Blue Plan

Introduction

By the 1970s the UNEP had managed to galvanize all the nation states bordering the Mediterranean Sea to undertake a twin set of actions:

1. In 1975 to agree to undertake the Mediterranean Action Plan (MAP).
2. To approve a 'Blue Plan' – a project of prospective studies, designed to facilitate and to implement the MAP.

In 1976 at the UNEP conference in Barcelona on the MAP two key protocols were agreed:

- To prevent pollution of the Mediterranean by dumping from ships and from aircraft.
- To agree cooperation in combating pollution of the Mediterranean by oil and other harmful substances in cases of emergency.

The Blue Plan was for the Mediterranean basin area, and as an early follow-up to these actions of 1975 and 1976, some three international meetings were held, two in Geneva and one in Cannes, with a view to launching the plan and prospective studies, evaluating progress, and determining the focal points for the Blue Plan, so as to get the implementation of the programme underway.

The Blue Plan was to involve some five dimensions:

- To clarify the prospects in terms of evolutionary processes, and determine crisis scenarios.
- To deliberate or define the relationships in the components of the Mediterranean ecosystem.
- To determine action orientation.
- To create an open-ended situation.
- To determine the national and international scope of the Blue Plan.

By comparison with the Blue Plan, MAP was to have three components:

- Environmental assessment of the sea.
- Clarifying the legal framework and agreements.
- Environmental management and the socio-economic strategy.

The MAP was going to function through: (i) the governments of all the Mediterranean coastal states; (ii) inter-governmental meetings; (iii) the Executive Directorate of UNEP; (iv) Regional Activity Centres (RACs) established to work on aspects of MAP – the Oil Combating Centre in Malta, MEDEAS for Blue Plan at Sophia Antipolis in France, and the Priority Actions Programme (PAP) RAC at Split in Croatia.

Three phases of action were determined for the Blue Plan. The first phase was one of reconnaissance and information gathering.

The second phase involved analyses of the basin as a whole, looking at trends, scenarios and the risks involved. Finally the third phase was one of general coordination and dissemination of recommendations for governments to implement environmentally sound and sustainable development programmes (see Fig. 25.1).

The subjects to be investigated by Blue Plan included: (i) land–marine systems and subsystems; (ii) examination of water resources, competitive use and human priorities; (iii) industrial growth, strategies and services; (iv) energy; (v) health, population and population movements; (vi) use of space, urbanization and rural development; (vii) tourism, use of space and environment; (viii) intra-Mediterranean-economic relationships; (ix) transport and communications; (x) cultural heritage and cross-cultural relationships; (xi) environmental awareness and value systems; and (xii) the impact of non-Mediterranean influences upon the Mediterranean basin. It was seen that the Mediterranean ecosystem was functioning as two processes, namely as a consumption process on the one hand, and a pollution process on the other hand (Fig. 25.1c).

Management aims and sets of activities, plus system analyses were defined for the system and the programmes. Continuity and crisis scenarios were to be defined, and the institutional framework clarified. The financial bases were to be determined. The Blue Plan was not to have finance of its own, as it was seen to be part of the MAP, which in 1979/80 had a budget set of US$6.56 million. Some 25% of this budget came from UNEP, some 25% of its budget came from other UN agencies, and the remaining 50% of the budget was derived from the participating Mediterranean coastal states and the EU.

2006–2025 Perspectives

By 2006 the UNEP/MAP and Blue Plan/PAP/RAC had produced a major report entitled *A Sustainable Future for the Mediterranean: the Blue Plan's Environment and Development Outlook* (Benoit and Comeau, 2006). This was a summary of the published 2025 prospective for sustainable development in the Mediterranean, which had first been outlined in 2005. This report, produced in English and in French, gave the first feedback on all the summary responses to the requirements, which had been set out both by the Blue Plan and by the MAP, as well as defining scenarios and choices for the future. The Blue Plan report provided detailed data and analysis on all the interactions between population, settlements, economic activities, land, water and environment and focused upon six main issues: (i) water; (ii) energy; (iii) transport; (iv) urban areas; (v) rural areas; and (vi) coastal zones. It paid special attention to determining factors and to risks associated with a trend scenario, as well as upon strategic orientations proposed for moving to 'an alternative sustainable development scenario'. The report was requested by the Mediterranean 'riparian nations' and the EU. France, the European Commission and the European Environment Agency provided support. It is a collective work, drafted by the Blue Plan team, with the support of a steering committee, and with contributions from many experts from both shores.

The concept of sustainable development for the Mediterranean is used because the basin is a fragile ecoregion, with problems of degradation, and as it is one of the major world regions for north–south contact, and comprises a critical group of countries where stability and prosperity are required.

The appropriateness of such actions, by the year 2025

By 2000 already, the 22 riparian countries and territories, accounted for:

> 5.7% of the planet's emerged surfaces including deserts and mountain regions, 7% of the world's population with 427 million inhabitants, 32% of international tourism with 218 million visitors, and 13% of world gross domestic product, 60% of the world's 'water-poor' populations, and some 8.3% of the world's carbon dioxide emissions.
> (Benoit and Comeau, 2006)

Further, the percentage of carbon dioxide emissions was increasing.

The trend scenario was found to be one of gloomy prospects for 2025 because of global warming, droughts, earthquakes, floods and forest fires, which had marked the preceding

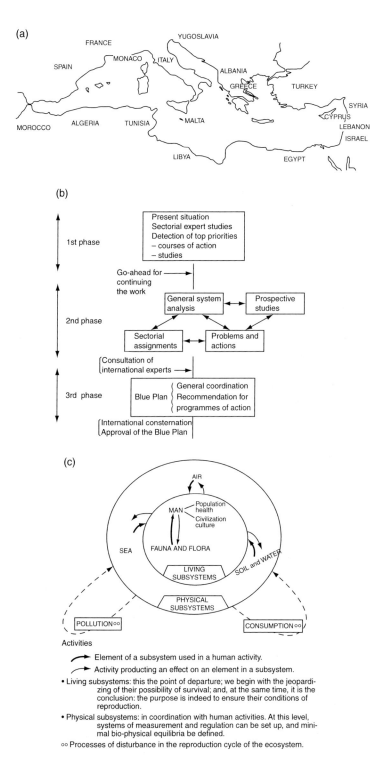

Fig. 25.1. The Mediterranean Action Plan (MAP) and Blue Plan: (a) the 'riparian nations' or participating coastal states 1979; (b) the three phases of the Blue Plan; and (c) systems analysis of Man's interactions with natural systems via processes of production, consumption and pollution (courtesy of MAP and Blue Plan).

decades. The growth of over-development was found to be increasing the Mediterranean's vulnerability to tsunamis. Global warming was expected to have long-term impacts on the basin and assumptions are made on the intensification of extreme climatic events. A differentiation was made between the north, south and east Mediterranean in respect of globalization and regional cooperation because the past 25 years had seen the collapse of the two block system (i.e. between capitalism and communism) and this had accelerated the pace of globalization within this world region. Several of the northern riparian countries of the Mediterranean have joined the EU and this has strengthened exchanges and progress. Changes in production and consumption of these EU countries remain unsustainable.

Southern and eastern countries of the Mediterranean, particularly in the Maghreb, mainly exchange with EU countries, and this process of Euro-Mediterranean interconnection and inter-dependencies is seen as likely to increase. In the last 20 years there has been a notable drop in fertility rates in southern and eastern Mediterranean countries which was much faster than that assumed earlier in the 1980s. It is assumed that for 2025 there will be a continuation of the demographic transition from the south Mediterranean, and therefore a convergence of fertility rates. Despite this population in the south and east Mediterranean have doubled over 30 years, to reach 234 million inhabitants by 2000, and are expected to increase by a further 96 million by 2025. Populations in Egypt and Turkey by then would total 95 and 87 million inhabitants, respectively (see Fig. 25.2).

On the northern rim of the basin however, the population has grown only by 14% over the same period, and is expected to increase by a mere four million by 2025. However, these population changes are associated with growing urbanization, growing water shortages, employment problems, poor economic performance, youth unemployment and continued north–south gaps. Economic growth remains uncertain for this period and environmental crises are there despite the expansion of policies. While environmental policies have been set up in all the countries, there have been tensions in regard to natural resources and environmental degradation, and these particularly affect the poor populations, and compromise economic and social development.

Constraints upon sustainability

There are six big problems defined, with regard to sustainability. The first of these issues is that of the limit on freshwater resources, and they are unequally shared, both in time and in space. Water demand is increasingly met by over abstraction on natural resources and the index of unsustainable water production on the Mediterranean catchment basin exceeds 10% in Israel, Cyprus and some Spanish regions, and some 20% in the Palestinian Territories. Energy problems, transport problems, waste disposal problems, sea pollution problems, the lack of and need for sustainable rural development policies, air pollution and health impacts, all combine to create very demanding circumstances, with which the basin is trying to cope. Attempts are being made to stop continuous degradation of coastal areas and ensure balanced development, but already the growing questions of coastal airports, river and urban waste disposal, heavily trafficked roads along the coasts of the Mediterranean and growing urbanization all challenge the ability to achieve satisfactory change.

Waste water treatment standard in coastal cities is still very mixed across the Mediterranean countries, and therefore there are limited hopes that the sustainable development policies defined, can be achieved. The MAP believes in a rationale of integration and anticipation. It wants to successfully decouple economic or urban growth from pressures on the environment. It wants to achieve an alternative scenario, which calls for a new type of Mediterranean thinking and acting, and achieving answers to the very specific constraints of the region. These include: (i) scarcity of water resources; (ii) climate change; (iii) natural hazards; and (iv) the need for solidarity between the coastal areas and their hinterlands. Mediterranean peoples have to cooperate on environmental and sustainable development issues but there are political and other factors which limit this intent.

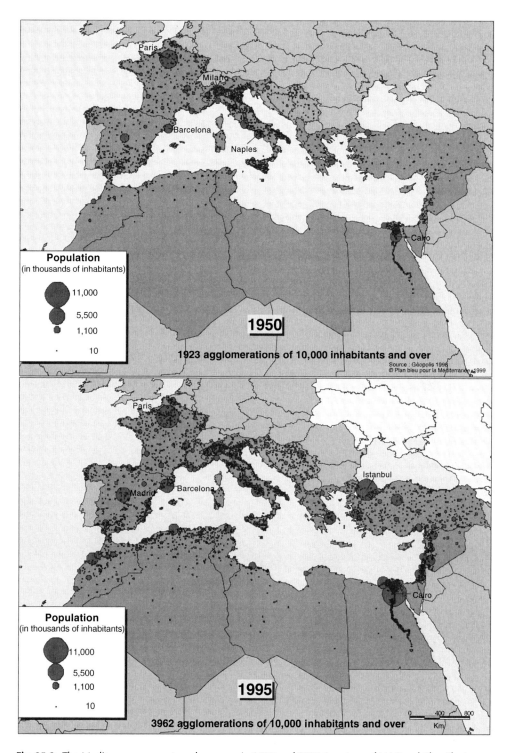

Fig. 25.2. The Mediterranean country urban areas in 1950 and 1995 (courtesy of MAP and Blue Plan).

Evaluation

Common and differentiated approaches are set out between clusters of countries and parts of the basin, and this means that there is a need for both national sustainable development policies, involving all the actors concerned, as well as some grouped policies (i.e. Euro-Mediterranean approach to cooperation policies). Tools for sustainable development strategies and policies are designed, and in relation to the period from 2006 to 2025, it was decided that the EU and the riparian countries only had two decades in which effectively to integrate sustainable development principles, in all their internal policies and partnerships, as a prerequisite for a new dynamic of growth 'cooperation and peace, respectful of the wealth of Mediterranean diversity' (Benoit and Comeau, 2006). Since the report was produced, the global banking crisis, and its effect on economic policies, further challenges the assumptions made in this key report. How far cooperation between countries, financial means available, and political will exists to upgrade and to harmonize standards across the Mediterranean basin is a huge, demanding and difficult set of questions to pose, let alone answer, in the near future. Progress to date gives rise to a pessimistic view of the future, despite all the mechanisms used.

26 Tourism Carrying Capacity Assessment in the Mediterranean 1980–2009

Ivica Trumbic

Introduction

By the year 2000 more than 65% of the world population was living within 100 km of its coastlines. This is where a large number of the world's great urban agglomerations have arisen. The Mediterranean Sea reflects this process of urban concentration on its coasts, which are also a magnetic destination for world tourism. The mainland and island coasts are thus pressurized places, where tourism competes with urban development, industry, energy development, biotic production, nature conservation and transport for limited space.

Carrying capacity of such coastal areas is limited, and has often been exceeded (Fig. 26.1). Over-use, or so-called 'saturation' of these destinations, has led to the need for conflict management and planning control, so as to try and achieve sustainable environments and sustainable tourism. The evolution and application of tourism carrying capacity assessment (TCCA) is a story of the development of a planning and management process (i.e. a procedure to deal with these conflicts to resolve the coastal tourism capacity problems).

It is 'coastal areas', as a geographically broad space which includes all terrestrial, transitional and marine ecosystems often extending to the nearest mountain range inland, rather than 'coastal zones', defined as a relatively narrow stretch of land affected by its proximity to the sea, which have proved to be the more useful subregions to which to apply the carrying capacity approach.

Though the use of measured tourism carrying capacity as a tool was developed in the 1960s, it was not until the 1980s that its value was formally recognized by the UN World Tourism Organization (UNWTO). In 1980, the Manila Declaration on World Tourism pointed to the growing problem of 'tourist saturation' and showed a resultant increased interest in the use of TCCA. In 1983, the UNWTO's report entitled *The Risks of Saturation in Tourist Carrying Capacity Over-use in Holiday Destinations* was published (UNWTO, 1983). As defined by UNWTO in that period, and subsequently accepted by many, the tourism carrying capacity is 'the maximum number of people that may visit a tourist destination at the same time, without causing destruction of the physical, economic and socio-cultural environment and an unacceptable decrease in the quality of the visitors' satisfaction'.

Not much later, resulting from the preliminary work of the Mediterranean Action Plan (MAP) published in the Blue Plan Report (MEDEAS-France, 1979), the MAP's Priority Actions Programme Regional Activity Centre (PAP/RAC) in Split, commissioned the *Guidelines for Carrying Capacity Assessment for Tourism*

Full saturation			Free development
Maximum			Intensive development
	Carrying capacity		Sustainable development
Minimum			Moderate option of alternative tourism
No tourism			Extreme option of alternative tourism

Fig. 26.1. Carrying capacity and sustainability (Source: PAP/RAC, 1997).

in Mediterranean Coastal Areas (PAP/RAC, 1997). The aim of the document was to describe a comprehensive procedure to analyse and assess tourism carrying capacity, and to incorporate it within the Integrated Coastal Zone Management (ICZM). It is a step-by-step process composed of the following phases: (i) documentation, inventorization and mapping; (ii) community participation; (iii) analysis; (iv) evaluation of a range of tourism development options, and selection of the preferred one; (v) definition of detailed development scenario; (vi) definition of the carrying capacity; (vii) integration of TCCA in ICZM; (viii) pre-feasibility studies, as the end phase of the TCCA process; and (ix) start of the tourism development planning process.

The core argument of the above guidelines is that the value of carrying capacity is assessed in the light of a choice of tourism development scenarios, and that it needs to be adjusted to the development requirements of different destinations. The examples of various types of tourism development may, thus, indicate the varying values of tourism carrying capacity with regard to the analysed physical, ecological, economic and socio-demographic components of the recipient environment.

The complementary management framework to TCCA is the ICZM, because it offers a good framework within which the principles of sustainable tourism development, where assessment of tourism carrying capacity is pivotal, can be applied together with those relating to all the other relevant sectors including water, soil, energy, fishing and transportation. The ICZM is an adaptive, multi-sectoral governance approach, which strives towards a balanced development, use and protection of

coastal environments. It is based on principles such as: (i) an holistic and ecosystem-based approach; (ii) good governance; (iii) inter- and intra-generational solidarity; (iv) safeguarding the distinctiveness of coasts; and (v) precautionary and preventative principle, which give a context for achieving the aims of sustainable tourism. The ICZM approach creates a constructive dialogue between the interests of authorities and multiple user-groups. It also prepares government representatives and other relevant actors for developing effective environmental legislation within their jurisdictions.

From Guidelines to Application

The first TCCA study following the PAP TCCA guidelines was prepared for the isolated Croatian Adriatic Island of Vis. The following values of carrying capacity were defined: (i) 16,000–20,000 stationary tourists for the intensive development scenario; (ii) 2500 for the alternative tourism scenario; and (iii) 4900 tourists for the sustainable development concept. The specific features of the island of Vis and its environment influenced the decision to choose a value nearer to the alternative tourism scenario. The results of the study were used during the preparation of the physical plan of the island.

In the central-eastern part of the island of Rhodes (Greece), the carrying capacity was assessed at approximately 30,000 tourist beds in an area of $400\,km^2$ and with 18,500 inhabitants (in 1991). The decision for sustainable tourism bordering to an intensive, yet controlled, development was influenced by the facts that: (i) tourism is highly developed in the island as a whole; (ii) the entire economy is oriented to tourism; and (iii) such development is allowed even within its socio-cultural perspective, since the population is ready and willing to accept the new strong development.

The 1994 ECOMOST Project (European Community Model of Sustainable Tourism; Hughes, 1994), promoted by the International Federation of Tour Operators, was a more detailed study using the concept of carrying capacity as the methodological basis. Its objective was to set measures which could curb the expansion of mass tourism in Mallorca (Spain) and the Island of Rhodes. It has set on enacting the active regional legislation on spatial development but, unfortunately, the main resistance came from municipalities. Because of that, in 1998 new complementary regulation had to be adopted by the Government of the Balearics, introducing a provisional 'moratorium' suspending any increase on tourism accommodation capacity until the new 'Tourism Law' was passed by the Parliament of the Balearics.

The PAP 1996 TCCA study for the 'take-off' tourism development zone Lalzit Bay in Albania (Travis and Klaric, 1996) proposed the following scenarios: (i) large-scale, high-capacity sustainable development; (ii) small-scale, low-capacity, but high-spend sustainable ecotourism; and (iii) medium-scale, optimal capacity, limited development. It considered the following elements:

- type, size and sensitivity of the tourist offer;
- national and regional tourism and environmental policy;
- type of tourism and level of tourism development in the regional context;
- interrelations between the region and the site; and
- political, cultural and economic preferences of the resident population.

Among other studies prepared in this early period, those that could be singled out for their specific characteristics were: (i) a zone in an early stage of tourism development (Fuka Matrouh, Egypt); (ii) a mature tourist destination (Calvia, Spain); and (iii) an isolated island (Elba, Italy). Comparison among these three studies shows the wide potential that TCCA has in generating site-specific sets of tourism development scenarios.

The TCCA for the Maltese islands was a milestone event. It is a comprehensive study undertaken by the National Tourist Organization of Malta and prepared by a multidisciplinary team composed of representatives of relevant national bodies. The main objective of the study was the formulation of the optimal level of future tourism development of the Maltese islands. The visitor population of the small Mediterranean island of Malta is about 1.2 million p.a. (approximately 11.3 million guest nights). Different scenarios were developed: (i) free development scenario; (ii) limited growth scenario; (iii) no growth scenario; and (iv) up-market scenario. The TCCA Committee established that the limited growth scenario for the next 10 years is the most viable option to be followed. Major factors influencing such a decision were the following:

- prevailing contribution of tourism to the Maltese economy;
- ideal occupancy rate for the industry's accommodation sector bearing in mind current and planned bed stock characteristics;
- seasonal spread of tourism demand to Malta;
- impact of tourist flows on utilities, attractions and facilities and environmental resources;
- changes in the Maltese demographic profile with the resulting social consequences;
- local population's perceptions of the tourism industry and their expectations; and
- visitor satisfaction levels may be reduced as a consequence of saturation, mainly during peak periods and in particular areas.

In terms of accommodation parameters, the Malta scenario directions were to:

- stabilize bed stock and not increase supply;
- improve the quality of service of existing establishments;

- increase the current occupancy rate;
- eventually be in a position to charge more feasible room rates; and
- develop specific types of accommodation.

The experiences accumulated during the first decade of the application of TCCA in the Mediterranean region were summarized in the *Guide to Good Practice in Tourism Carrying Capacity Assessment* published by PAP/RAC (2003). It has shown that the following lessons have been learned:

1. The decision-making process for TCCA can be undertaken using either a 'bottom-up' (better suited for highly developed areas) or a 'top-down' (in less developed tourism areas) approach.
2. The size of areas for TCCA differs, but the best results are achieved in middle-sized areas (micro-regions or subregions within a country) and with precise administrative boundaries.
3. The utilization of data is more dependent on the political and organizational framework where TCCAs are being applied, than on the quality of data used.
4. Use of indicators of sustainable development should be encouraged, particularly for the analysis of tourism development scenario.
5. The public participation process and public awareness are important for acceptance of the scenarios proposed.
6. Identification and selection of tourism development scenarios are crucial steps in the TCCA process.
7. Carrying capacity should always be based on the selected, presumably sustainable, tourism development option.
8. The integration of TCCA with other forms of planning, Integrated Coastal Area Management (ICAM) or structural planning, is necessary because it is giving a legal prerequisite to TCCA, although self-standing TCCA studies could also provide valuable input for guiding tourism development.
9. Implementation of TCCA will be more efficient in areas where public participation is more embedded in the resource management process.

A major contribution to the field of TCCA came in the form of the Coccossis and Mexa's book *The Challenge of Tourism Carrying Capacity Assessment: Theory and Practice* (2004). It argues that planning and management for tourism growth is becoming essential in the context of sustainable development, particularly because many tourist destinations are facing severe pressures from tourist flows and activities. The book examines the use of various tools to define, measure and evaluate tourism carrying capacity drawing on case studies from France, Spain, Italy, Greece, Croatia, Egypt, the UK, the Netherlands, Ireland, Belgium, Austria, Germany and Finland. It presents practical experiences of implementing the concept in various tourist destinations (i.e. historic towns, coastal zones and islands).

The last study to be prepared in the context of PAP activities was in Larnaca, Cyprus (Klaric, 2007) (Fig. 26.2). The main objectives were:

- Review and elaboration of the existing land use, tourism and infrastructure development and environmental problems in the coastal area of Larnaca district and especially southern Larnaca coastal area in relation to the prevailing international, national and local institutional and policy framework.
- Production of inputs useful for the general strategic and planning documents dealing with tourism in the Larnaca district and Cyprus as a whole.
- Development of guidelines for the implementation of TCCA methodology in Cyprus and their application to a pilot case study on the southern Larnaca coastal area in Larnaca district.
- Development and submission of a practical proposal for the incorporation of TCCA for Larnaca district within the Cyprus policy framework.

The methodology of the work included five phases and related activities:

1. Elaboration of the established and evolving methodologies and practices of TCCA in the Mediterranean and the EU, and their achievements and problems.
2. Collection and codification of all available information from the relevant governmental bodies setting out the current practices used,

Fig. 26.2. Main parameters and conditions of sustainable tourism development (Source: Klaric, 2007).

within the framework of decision making on tourism, land use planning, environmental management and infrastructure development in Cyprus in order to assess the carrying capacity of the coastal resources involved in such development. Based on this, there would be a review of the main deficiencies in the assessment of the carrying capacity of coastal resources in the legal framework in Cyprus.

3. Formulation of TCCA guidelines brief suitable to address existing and future environmental assessment issues in coastal development in Cyprus.

4. Implementation of a TCCA pilot application case study in Larnaca district with special emphasis on the southern Larnaca coastal area.

5. Formulation of proposals for the incorporation and operation of TCCA within the Cyprus policy framework to support sustainable use of coastal resources in Cyprus.

The latest addition to the field is the UNEP Division of Technology, Industry and Economics (DTIE) publication *Sustainable Coastal Tourism: an Integrated Planning and Management Approach* (Škaričić, 2009). It provides for a 'two-way' scheme allowing for the integration of tourism strategic planning into the wider process of ICZM on the one hand and, on the other, for the application of the ICZM approach in tourism development. The document has two main parts. Its main body tackles all the important issues related to coastal tourism and its positive and negative impacts on the natural environment and society, as well as various planning and management schemes for tourism, with particular reference to ICZM. Individual steps of the proposed process of strategic planning for coastal tourism, based on the concept of TCCA, are presented in an annex with all the details indicating when, how and by whom these steps are to be undertaken.

Evaluation

The experience in the first two decades of implementation of TCCA shows that the concept is an attractive one, because it easily catches the attention of major stakeholders and decision makers. However, practical approaches to actually defining it are met with a number of difficulties.

On the one hand, there are requests that TCCA's major output be a precise 'number' followed by the strict rules that would regulate the number of tourists in a certain regulation. On the other hand, more moderate proponents of TCCA state that it should be only a tool that would only guide tourist development in certain areas.

TCCA is particularly important in managing coastal areas, because it is the area where most of the tourism development takes place, where development expectations in many countries are at the highest level, but also the area where natural systems are extremely sensitive.

TCCA should be closely linked to the ICZM. Following this line of thinking, it is important to note that Mediterranean countries recently adopted a Protocol on ICZM (signed in Madrid in 2008). It is the first comprehensive legal ICZM framework ever adopted in the world. It offers a wide opportunity for sustainable coastal tourism based on the application of the carrying capacity concept.

27 'Working with the Sea': the 2008 Dutch National Response to Global Warming and Sea Rise

Introduction

In September 2008, the Delta Commission presented its formal advice to the Cabinet of the Dutch National Government, on the consequences of global warming affecting the rise in sea levels, and the resultant risks for life in the Netherlands. Its advice posed three issues:

1. Moral choices – There are moral choices, namely, do we continue to take collective responsibility for safety in relation to water levels, and their effect on people, the economy and the environment?

2. Aspirations – The sustainability principle of maintaining an attractive and safe living environment in the Netherlands, relates to the availability of quality of land surface, and of drinking water.

3. Implementation processes – If safety for the human population of the Netherlands remains a central objective, what integrated and new functional solutions are available, and by which means, and with what levels of flexibility, should this be tackled?

Report Content

The 140-page report in Dutch, whose translated title in English is *Working Together with the Sea*, presents mapped and statistical data, estimated costs, timed forecasts, plus strategic and design possibilities for action programmes (Delta Commissie, 2008). Its summary advice is that water security remains a crucial role 'involving as it does both protection against flooding and the security of our freshwater supplies'. The recommendations allow for phased, gradual flexible implementation, and the interventions proposed must be sustainable. A new Delta Programme was drafted, and was later to be anchored politically, financially and administratively in a new Delta Act of Parliament. The mission is seen as urgent, as 'the sea level is probably rising faster than has been assumed', and variations in river flow are expected to increase.

The Delta Commission's conclusion is that a regional sea level rise of 0.65–1.3 m should be expected for the year 2100, and from 2 to 4 m in 2200! This includes the effect of land subsidence. The Rivers Rhine and Meuse feeding into the Netherlands, from neighbouring lands, will be affected by temperature increase and changed patterns of precipitation – with decreased summer flows and increased winter flow. Around the year 2100, the maximum discharge of the Rhine is expected to be about 18,000 m^3/s, and the Meuse 4600 m^3/s. Rising sea levels will result in saltwater penetration via the rivers and ground water, and put much pressure upon natural supplies of freshwater. This will have damaging consequences for water supply, agriculture, shipping, and those economic sectors dependent upon cooling waters.

The costs of the Delta Programme in terms of extra annual costs in billions of Euros, with additional coastal space for other functions will be:

- €1.3–1.9 billion from 2010 to 2050; and
- €1.2–1.8 billion from 2050 to 2100.

Twelve recommendations are made for the future

The Delta Commission has developed an integrated vision for the future, extending to the year 2100 and beyond. Its twelve recommendations are:

1. Flood protection in dyked areas

Up to the year 2050 all present flood protection levels of all dyked areas nationally, must be improved by a factor of ten. New standards must be set by around year 2013. A Delta Dyke concept is provided for key areas, where even higher protection levels will be needed. Post-2050 the flood protection levels must be regularly updated.

2. New urban development plans

New urban development plans will decide whether to build in low-lying, flood-prone locations, and be subject to cost–benefit analyses.

3. Areas outside the dykes

New development in unprotected areas lying outside the dykes must not impede river discharge capacity or future levels of water in the lakes (Fig. 27.1 shows the water-planning zones). Residents/users must take responsible measures to protect against adverse consequences. The Government's role must be in the fields of public information, the setting of building standards, and in flood warning systems.

4. North Sea coast

Flood protection on the North Sea coast will be maintained by beach nourishments, possibly with relocation of tidal channels. Beach nourishment (or supplementation) must be done in such a way, that the coast can expand seawards in the next century. This will provide great added value to society. North Sea sand-extraction sites must be reserved in the short term – the ecological, economic and energy requirements needed to meet such large volumes for beach nourishment must be investigated.

5. Wadden Sea area

Beach nourishments or supplements along the North Sea coast may contribute to the adaptation of the Wadden Sea area to sea level rise. Monitoring the developments and analysis in the international context will be required. Protection of the island polders and the North Holland coast must remain assured.

6. Eastern Scheldt (South-western Delta)

Until 2050 the Eastern Scheldt storm-surge barrier is to retain its function (Fig. 27.2). Its disadvantage is the restriction it places upon tidal movement, and resultant loss of an intertidal zone. This will have to be compensated by bringing additional sand supplements from elsewhere.

Post-2050 the life span of the Eastern Scheldt storm-surge barrier will be extended by technical interventions. This can be done up to a sea level rise of about 1 m (in the year 2075 at the earliest). When the barrier is no longer adequate, a solution will be sought that largely restores the tidal dynamics with its natural estuarine regime, while maintaining safety against flooding.

7. Western Scheldt (South-western Delta)

The Western Scheldt (in the South-western Delta) must remain an open tidal system to maintain the valuable estuary, and for navigation to the Port of Antwerp. Safety against flooding must be maintained by enforcement of the dyke.

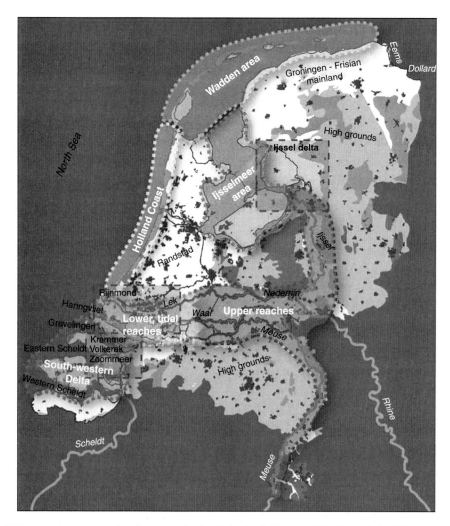

Fig. 27.1. Long-term, water-planning zones for the Netherlands (Source: Delta Commissie, 2008).

8. Krammer-Volkerak Zoommeer (South-western Delta)

Up until 2050 the Krammer-Volkerak Zoommeer, with the Grevelingen, and possibly also the Eastern Scheldt, can provide temporary storage for excess water coming from the Rhine and Meuse, when discharge to the sea is blocked by the storm-surge barriers being closed. A salinity gradient from freshwater to salt water, in this area, will provide a satisfactory way of solving the problem of water quality, and can offer new ecological opportunities. In this instance, an alternative supply of freshwater must be developed.

9. The major rivers area

Until 2050 the Meuse Works Programme must be implemented without delay. Subject to cost effectiveness, measures must be taken to accommodate discharges of 18,000 m^3/s from the Rhine, and 4600 m^3/s from the Meuse. This will require negotiations with neighbouring countries, and the 'European Directive on the Assessment and Management of Flood Risks', in order to harmonize the measures. Room must be reserved, and the necessary land purchased, so that the river system can safely discharge the 18,000 m^3/s of Rhine water, and 4600 m^3/s of Meuse water involved.

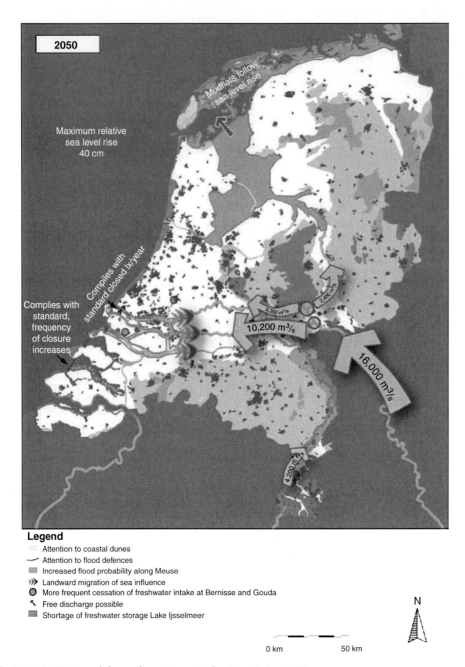

Fig. 27.2. 2050 Water defence plans (Source: Delta Commissie, 2008).

10. Rijnmond (the mouth of the River Rhine)

Until the year 2050, an open system (which can be closed in emergencies) offers the best answer for the Rijnmond against flooding, for freshwater supply, for urban development and for nature protection in this region. Extreme discharges of the rivers Rhine and Meuse will then have to be re-routed via the South-western Delta.

Freshwater for the West Netherlands will have to be supplied from the Ijsselmeer.

The necessary infrastructure to supply that will have to be built. Room must be created for local water storage in deep polders. Further research into the 'closable-open' Rijnmond system was seen to require an early start.

11. Ijsselmeer area

The level of Lake Ijsselmeer will be raised by a maximum of 1.5 m. This will allow gravity-feed drainage from the Ijsselmeer, into the Wadden Sea to beyond the year 2100. The level of the Markermeer Lake will not be raised. The Ijsselmeer retains its strategic function as a freshwater reservoir for the North Netherlands and, in view of the salt invasion of the Niewwe Waterweg, also for the West Netherlands.

Until 2050 there will be a need to implement measures to achieve the elevated water level, by gradual stages. The aim must be to achieve the largest possible freshwater reservoir by about the year 2050. There is a need to investigate measures to adapt the lower reaches of the River Ijssel and the Zwarte Water to a water level in the Ijsselmeer (i.e. 1.5 m higher than it is now).

Post-2050, depending upon the phased approach used, there may be a need for follow-up measures to implement a water level raised to a maximum of 1.5 m.

12. Political, legal and financial action

The political administrative organization of the Dutch water supply must be strengthened by providing cohesive national direction, and regional responsibility for implementation. It was recommended that for cohesion and progress a Ministerial Steering Committee be set up to be chaired by the Prime Minister or senior politician responsible, and including the Minister of Transport, Public Works and Water Management, and the Delta Director. Regional administrators could be involved in interpretation and implementation of individual regional assignments. A Permanent Parliamentary Committee on this subject was to be created.

It was recommended that funding should be guaranteed by:

* creating a Delta Fund, managed by the Minister of Finance;
* supplying the Delta Fund with a combination of loans from a range of sources; and
* making national funding available and setting draft rules for withdrawals from that fund.

A Delta Act will anchor political administrative organization and funding within the present political system, and current legal framework. This must include: (i) the Delta Fund and its supply; (ii) the Directors' tasks and authority; (iii) the setting up of the Delta Programme; (iv) the regulations for land acquisition; and (v) the rules of compensation for damages and graded loss of benefits, due to implementation of measures under the Delta Programme.

Evaluation

The Dutch Government's bold vision, imagination and practical realism in the context of global warming, presents a sobering presentation of how nations at risk due to expected sea rise, may act to continue to be sustainable, in extraordinary new global circumstances. The Netherlands has a long history of coping with demanding natural conditions, and using its wealth and technical engineering expertise, to protect and benefit its citizens. If global warming predictions prove to be right, then the heightened risks for poorer nations – such as Bangladesh, the Maldives and others – poses major political, financial and technical challenges – not only to such nations, but to the UN organization and its agencies. The low-lying coastal regions of developed nations need also to take note, and should be urgently assessing how far their flood defences and other such measures will cope with the predicted sea rises, now accepted by Dutch politicians. It is a major, challenging question now for the world community.

Part IV

Historic Cities and Sustainable Tourism Planning

———————————

28 Historic Cities as Sustainable Tourist Destinations

Introduction

At many points in the long history of cities, Man has produced a scale of city which was truly human: (i) it enabled ease of human face-to-face contact; (ii) its extent and spaces were scaled to the pedestrian; and (iii) there were views of nature in and beyond the settlement that gave him a sense of place, roots, peace, quiet and satisfaction. In medieval Siena, Venice, Florence or Dubrovnik, in the gardens of classical Kyoto, in the souks of the Islamic madinas, or in ancient Athens, Man was the module for the city.

Past City Image

The past image and identity of the city in the Western world is coloured by the writings, paintings, images and ideas of the late medieval and Renaissance periods. In the 19th century, innovators with utopian visions of the city sought again to discover and create the 'ideal city' whether in the form of a garden city or a philanthropic 'model workers' settlement'. Again, places were sought that fitted the scale of Man: towns that were small enough to 'hold in one's hand', contained places from which to view the countryside, woods, hills and sea beyond. Yet it is found

today that it is in the World Heritage Cities – such as Edinburgh, Prague, Salzburg or Washington, DC – that the ordered, varied, organic and beautiful city already exists. Heritage museum groupings, such as 'The Old Town' (Den Gamle By) of Århus in Denmark, recreate ideal forms for us, while we find that shopping in the Grand Bazaar in Istanbul gives the timeless, vital experience of what a city was, is and should be.

Future City Reality versus Possibilities

In the 21st century, the spiralling growth of 'megalopolises' – huge urban concentrations – has spread like a disease across the face of the planet. By 2015 it is estimated that the population of Tokyo will be over 30 million, Mumbai in India over 25 million, Lagos in Nigeria 25 million, Sao Paolo in Brazil 20 million, Dhaka in Bangladesh 20 million, Mexico City 20 million and Karachi in Pakistan 20 million. Their realities will be far from the 'ideal city', for often congestion, poverty, unemployment, frenetic competition, pollution, disease and personal danger characterize many of them. The challenge will be how to plan, to humanize them, make them work, and try to make life sustainable in them for their residents. They are distant from the case study given earlier, of London.

The focus of the chapters in Part IV on heritage cities gives the opportunity to see how, by which means and mechanisms and with what strategies, have attempts been made to conserve, adapt to new demands and needs, and try for long life as high quality cities. Can they be sustainable, and can their tourism be sustainable? Their experience and lessons are seen as vital feedback and guidance, not only to larger and less impressive cities, but also potentially for the world's megalopolises.

The major cities of Europe and North America have lived through at least six phases, in the last 200 years plus, namely:

1. Industrialization – The growth of industries based on the exploitation of natural resources, lead to big inward movements of rural populations. In turn this caused urbanization.

2. Urbanization – This was characterized by expanding towns with cheap development, low standards, competitive and high-risk environments, with dirty water, long work hours, diseases like cholera and tuberculosis, shortened lives and child labour. Some of these characteristics are seen in today's megalopolises.

3. Public heath, hygiene and public education responses – Over time it became clear that for such towns to be economically effective and survive, such responses were necessary to provide clean water, spacing of development with light, space, air, sun and health, and training for the labour force. Thus interventions were evolved to get efficient locations of workplaces and living, and transport to and from work, and to and from product markets. Industrial cities were thought to be sustainable.

4. Planning revolutions – The 20th century saw orderly layouts, greater efficiency of capitalist urban industrial systems for production and consumption, and improvements to provide adequate education, basic health, control of work hours and conditions, and good water and energy supply systems (the latter changing from coal, steam and gas, via electricity based on coal, petrol, to use of natural gas, nuclear power, and the start of sustainable energies).

5. Transport revolutions – Transport systems changed from those based on canals and rail, over to motorway use. There was a change from public transport to private road transport as a new dominant. The result was congestion, inefficiency, moves towards changing the modal split (the split between the amount of use of different forms of transport in a place, at one time), and a gradual awareness of carbon footprint of transport which led to the start of ideas on sustainable transport and sustainable development.

6. Leisure revolutions – Only late in the 19th century was some non-work time seen as necessary for refreshment of workers that would lead to gains in production. Better health, more time, more income and some surplus disposable income led to the leisure revolutions. From 1 or 2 weeks holiday p.a., we have moved to weekly leisure and several holidays each year, as a new norm. By the 1960s mass air travel led to the boom in international tourism, for much of the population, and over time the issue of capacity, quality of experience and impacts on destinations gave rise to the idea of sustainable tourism.

By the 21st century, with megalopolitan development, much of the world is returning to industrialization and urbanization!

Variation in City Size

Here in Part IV, five cities of very different population size and function, and variable quality of built, cultural and natural heritage resources, but similar in human scale (i.e. sympathetic to the size, scale and perceptions of Man), are examined. They are: (i) Edinburgh, a national capital with a population of over 400,000; (ii) Salzburg, a provincial city of 150,000, and one of great quality; (iii) Colonial Williamsburg, originally a tiny capital with a few thousand inhabitants, but today a vibrant 'museumized town' supporting a population of 20,000; (iv) Munich with a population of 1.3 million; and (v) Birmingham with a population of 1 million.

Sustainability Factors

Sustainable cities need roots and continuity, as well as having to face the inevitable elements of change. The physical and economic planning processes are a basic requirement for all cities – they are neither luxuries nor indulgences (see Fig. 28.1 for a model of the urban planning

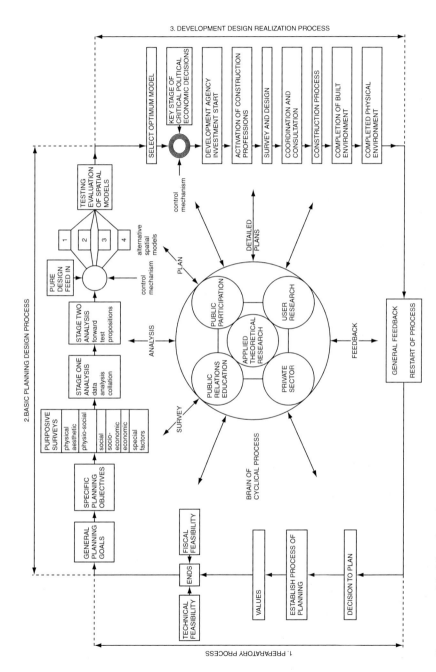

Fig. 28.1. Model of the urban planning process.

process). The shells of cities are washed through over time, by 'tides of activity', that pass through the built shell, and have to be accommodated. Cities have to deal with change over time, not only because of the natural physical ageing process of buildings and of plants, but because of changing functional requirements, including transport and tourism. The various forms of tourism also have their life cycles, and year-round tourism activity is required to keep a mix of tourism attractions and a range of tourist accommodation economically viable.

In planning and managing historic towns today, one needs to be conscious of the variable amount of tourism in each of them, for it is fundamental to the economy of some, and marginal to the life of others. Planning historic towns or cities for sustainability, thus involves:

- the conservation or physical sustainability of the fabric of the city;
- its fuel and energy efficiency;
- its economic and social recycling for tourism and other activities;
- the carbon footprint of its population, via consumption, production and transportation;
- cultural sustainability;
- provision of sustainable transport to and within the city; and
- host community benefit from tourism, within a set tourist capacity.

Thus the demanding planning and management processes are aimed at planning for sustainable development, and ultimately for sustainable tourism.

29 Edinburgh: Post-war Urban Planning and Conservation in a World Heritage City

Introduction: Edinburgh Planning and Tourism

'After London, the most popular destination for...foreign visitors in the UK is Edinburgh... It is the city's historical interest and associations which are mainly responsible for drawing people to it...Asked why they had come to Edinburgh, visitors gave three reasons...all dependent upon the preservation of the city's historical buildings' (see Figs 29.1 and 29.2). In this graphic way, Binney and Hanna writing in 1978 about Edinburgh provide a relevant lead in to linking the city's tourist function to its conserved heritage.

Edinburgh's proportionate pull for foreign tourists emphasizes both the quantitative as well as the qualitative significance of its attraction. Edinburgh tourism growth from the mid-1960s onwards, in terms of visitor numbers, movements, visitor expenditure, and the related growth of hotel building and tourism-related enterprises is well documented. However, it is not adequately tied back to the planning and protection of its built and cultural heritage resources, which are the generators of its tourism.

The Evolution of Edinburgh's Heritage Resources

Edinburgh is not just another city. It is truly unique in quality. It ranks among the shrinking list of fine total urban environments in the world. The extent alone of its high-quality architecture is remarkable...It must be considered in the same bracket as Siena, Prague, Venice, Amsterdam, Stockholm, and St. Petersburg.

(Travis, 1969/1970)

As James Bone commented: 'In a distant first impression of Edinburgh you are reminded less of man's handiwork than of a re-arrangement of nature' (cited in Travis, 1966; see Fig. 29.2).

It is a monument of world significance, because of its visual qualities, and the fact that physically it is the embodiment of so much history...Less than 10% of the area of Edinburgh however creates its significant external image.

(Travis, 1966)

Edinburgh is a world quality city, that is a place of extraordinary 'prospects' or set urban views.

The 1979 *AA Book of British Towns* similarly waxes lyrically that 'Edinburgh is one of the world's most attractive capitals, rich in vivid reminders of the past, and abundantly endowed with memorable buildings' (AA, 1979). Even such journalistic sources go on to define three sets of resources, which make the city so special for the visitor. First, its built resources including three key building

Fig. 29.1. Edinburgh – a city of 'prospects' and elegant skylines (photographs by Colin MacLeod).

complexes, namely: (i) Edinburgh Castle, the Royal Palace of Holy Rood House plus the new Scottish Parliament; (ii) the medieval Old Town; and (iii) its balancing planned Georgian New Town. Secondly, its natural resources of volcanic rocks, valleys, parks and gardens based upon them, plus its river and sea coast. Thirdly, its cultural resources partly reflected in the built heritage, but essentially tied to rich associations with remarkable personalities, past events and tales, and contemporary events and happenings (e.g. the Edinburgh Festival, the 'one-o'clock gun'

and actions of the Scottish Parliament) which reflect this continuing life.

From prehistoric settlement, via Roman settlement, medieval town, neoclassical planned town, 19th-century extensions, to 20th- and 21st-century additions and changes, Edinburgh has evolved sets of complementary heritage resources, which sit together magnificently, and form the urban theatrical stage on which it plays out its life today. The rare conditions of these resources today, their conservation, management and interpretation, are all aspects to which we now

Fig. 29.2. 'In a distant first impression of Edinburgh you are reminded less of man's handiwork, than a re-arrangement of nature' (photographs by Colin MacLeod).

turn. The fullest analysis of all the scenic, visual and heritage-resource characteristics of Edinburgh is found in a 1968 report by Lord Holford, as a background for the evolution of three-dimensional planning policies for the city.

Measurement of the pull of specific parts of those built-heritage resources are found in Binney and Hanna's (1978) work which stated:

the most heavily visited part of Edinburgh is the medieval area of the Royal Mile, which stretches from Edinburgh Castle to Holyrood House Palace via St. Giles Cathedral. But an addition, there is the New Town district which, with Bath, is the best-preserved example of Georgian town planning in Britain.

(An aerial view of the Georgian New Town is shown in Fig. 29.3.)

Fig. 29.3. Topography and city structure. Aerial view of the Georgian New Town alongside the medieval Old Town (Source: Youngson, 1966).

Socio-economic Structure of a Special City

Historically, Edinburgh's make up has been skewed in the white-collar direction. As early as the 17th century it was described as having overlapping circles of Court and Parliament (or the Law), the Church, the university and the medical world. Even in 2000, the Law, the Church, the universities and the medical fraternity were all notable interest groups in the life of the city. In terms of administration, the city historically has had a very mixed quality of local politicians. It took a strong provost and continuing dire health, plus law-and-order problems, to force the 18th-century local authority to authorize the building of the New Town. The modern history of planning, the festivals and tourism in Edinburgh, equally reflect the mixed calibre of local politicians, technical officers and external pressures upon the city council.

Pressure Groups and Change

A pro-tourism lobby was active in the post Second World War period. It comprised the brewers, hoteliers, shop-keeping-, transport- and banking-interests within Edinburgh. These groups all stood to gain economically from tourism, and from the Festival, which started in 1947. They formed informal alliances and covert pressure groups, promoting tourism and tourism-related developments, and backing for the Festival. The anti-tourism lobby, equally anti-Festival, has had representation of the Church, the Law and upper-income echelons of Edinburgh society – who were 'not in trade'.

Paradoxically, Edinburgh tourism gained most from the effectiveness of the environmental conservationist and the anti-change lobbies in Edinburgh, who worked separately, and reinforced each others' interests and activities.

The growth of pressure groups in the 1960s included residents' associations and powerful area groups. Supplementing the long-established Cockburn Association, Saltire Society and the post-war Civic Trust for Scotland, national bodies like the National Trust for Scotland in the voluntary sector and public-sector national bodies like the Countryside Commission for Scotland and the Nature Conservancy Council, had key roles.

The anti-change and anti-ring road lobbies (explained later) had strong overlaps with historical and conservationist groups, especially new residents' groups which came into being as a response to the threat of large-scale demolition, to make way for a new ring road's development. The emergence, roles and effects of these pressure groups led to beneficial environmental changes.

City Planning and Three-dimensional Urban Design

The planning and implementation of the 1767 plan for the New Town of Edinburgh placed the city in a world league for comprehensive three-dimensional planning (or civic design in the Grand Manner). Even in the Victorian era, when Edinburgh shared the philosophy of the 'market-place triumphant' in economic terms, its physical development – for some new parts of the town – echoed the Georgian tradition. By the turn of the 20th century, Patrick Geddes – the great Scots town planner – fought for a return to sensitive comprehensive planning in the city, but 40 years separated his 1909 pleas from the belated publication of Abercrombie and Plumstead's (1949) *A Civic Survey and Plan for the City and Royal Burgh of Edinburgh*.

The late 1930s had seen some architectural renovation work started in Edinburgh's medieval Old Town, but the 1940s saw notable decline in the overall fabric of the New Town, and even parts of the Old Town. Statutory town planning was introduced in 1947 and 1949 saw the introduction of Abercrombie's Edinburgh Plan. It provided Edinburgh's first set of three-dimensional civic design concepts since 1767. The city's official plan (i.e. the 1957 City Development Plan) was a modified version of the Abercrombie study. It was the First Review of the Development Plan, in 1965, that was to give rise to widespread public response. In that document the City Engineer included his proposals for an inner ring road, which generated strong anti-motorway development reactions and strong conservationist responses.

In Edinburgh, 1965–1968 was a period of: (i) public response and reaction to the ring-road development proposals; (ii) the lack of comprehensive planning; and (iii) the inadequacy of conservation activities. It effectively brought into the political arena, the lobbies, pressure groups and interest groups – starting with the anti-change, anti-ring road and conservationist groups, and later evolving into complex political alliances. The strong Edinburgh Amenity and Transport Association was established at this time.

A second phase in Edinburgh of creative local authority response to public action, covered the 1968–1972 period. During this time, the major *Report* by Lord Holford (1968) gave a three-dimensional base for development in the city. In 1970 there was a major conference on the conservation of the New Town, while the period starting in 1971 saw the publication of a succession of reports on transport planning by Professor Colin Buchanan, linked back to assumptions about urban conservation.

It is necessary to define three strands of planning, because there was not a return to a synthesis of these, until the 1970s. These strands are:

- urban architectural and three-dimensional civic design;
- land use and physical location planning; and
- traffic engineering and transport planning.

The 1965 First Review of the Development Plan had not synthesized physical location planning and transport planning – this was to come in the Buchanan phase, while Lord Holford's Report re-established the links between three-dimensional design and physical planning.

The recommendations of the Holford Report emphasized: (i) the retention and enhancement of identity and continuity in 'Conservation Areas'; (ii) protection of urban views or prospects and skylines; and (iii) the conservation of buildings. Height limits were to be placed on development, and a series of Central Area district conservation schemes were proposed. The study identified 'Clear Areas' where freedom to initiate high-rise development was in order, as opposed to Conservation Areas and 'Control Area' action.

Transport Planning and Public Participation

Resistance to major change in Edinburgh was undertaken by local people, in their interests. However, the effective results of this process of resistance and subsequent consultation and participation led to the retention and conservation of Edinburgh's physical character – the greatest asset of the city for tourist and resident alike.

The 1965 First Review of the Edinburgh Development Plan had included the City Engineer's proposal for an inner ring road. It was this ring-road proposal which gave rise to much opposition and the challenge ultimately led to the commissioning of independent consultants in 1968, to do a detailed planning and transport study of central Edinburgh. This complemented the pressure to get independent consultants to do three-dimensional planning for the city, as well.

The brief given to the transport consultants (Buchanan) in 1968 included the idea of a transport plan 'compatible with the retention and enhancement of the City's architectural and landscape heritage'. The tourist function was also mentioned at that stage namely:

> Edinburgh's importance as a tourist centre is second only to London in the UK, and it is also a major conference centre. The city is well endowed with cultural and entertainment facilities and the Edinburgh Festival is famous throughout Britain and the world. The sports facilities of the city have recently been enhanced by the construction of the Meadowbank Stadium, and the Royal

Commonwealth Pool for the 1970 Commonwealth Games.

The two 1971 Reports by the consultants first define the city's transport and environmental problems. The traffic problems included road congestion, parking inadequacy, servicing problems, environmental problems of shopping streets on main traffic arteries, severance of functionally cohesive areas, noise, fumes and vibration – all caused by traffic. Ultimately the ring-road idea was abandoned, and even the consultants' moderate proposals were only partially adopted and partially implemented.

The 'New Town' and Area Conservation Planning

Reference has already been made to the New Town of Edinburgh of 1767, planned by James Craig, to a neoclassical pattern, aimed to abate overcrowding in the medieval Old City, and following design precedents in Bath, London and Dublin. According to Desmond Hodges (Chairman of the Edinburgh New Town Conservation Committee 1975–1990) the New Town was developed as one of 'the largest unspoilt neoclassical developments in the world'. Small-scale conservation planning in Edinburgh had long been taking place. This process started in the 19th century, and continued through to 1939. Personalities like the great Professor Patrick Geddes and Sir Frank Mears were associated with this renovation process.

Legislative, fiscal and institutional means, developed in the 20-year period from 1947 to 1967, were to make area-based conservation feasible in Edinburgh. Bases for further initiatives came from: (i) the Planning Act of the late 1940s; (ii) the listing of historic buildings; (iii) the creation of an Historic Buildings Bureau; (iv) the National Buildings Record; and (v) the National Trust for Scotland. The Council for British Archaeology produced three key memoranda in the 1964–1966 period on the treatment of historic towns. The Civic Amenities Act of 1967 enabled the designation of Conservation Areas and this year was also the Bicentenary Year of the Edinburgh

New Town, and the year that the Scottish Civic Trust was formed.

From the 1940s to the 1960s growing problems were affecting the decaying shell of the New Town. These included: (i) commercial redevelopment; (ii) changes in the housing stock and traffic movement; and (iii) planning pressures. The threat of the inner-ring road proposals, insensitive new office block and parking garages, and threats of redevelopment on the city's south side by George Square led to residents' fears about the future, and new street associations, plus growing action by the Scottish Georgian Society and the Edinburgh Architectural Association resulted.

The 1968 Festival Exhibition '200 Summers in a City' for the Bicentenary Year, gave a boost to taking action about the New Town. Conservation needs were surveyed and a major conference on 'The Conservation of Georgian Edinburgh' took place in 1970. That conference recommended the setting up of a Joint Advisory Committee to conserve the New Town, at an estimated cost of £15 million over a 20-year period.

Action was to be taken to promote an interest in the quality of the New Town, to explain how to restore buildings to their original condition and appearance; public grants were to be recommended to enable owners to finance the renovation. It was to be a Voluntary Conservation Programme. Work went ahead, with grants in the first 2 years rising from under £5000 to over £150,000. By the end of 1975 over £500,000 in grant-aid work was committed. Edinburgh's New Town became the most significant element of the UK Pilot Projects in 1975 – European Architectural Heritage Year – a year that saw the end of this first experimental phase of the 20-year Conservation Programme for Edinburgh's New Town.

Tourism Planning and Leisure Services Management

Planning for tourism and the provision of leisure services represented further strands in the multi-sectoral planning activities in Edinburgh. In 1969 the voluntary sector Scottish Tourist Board, gave way to a new Statutory Board under the Development of Tourism Act.

Edinburgh City Council backed the Edinburgh Festival from its formulation in 1947 onwards, developed tourist information and publicity services and ran a city accommodation bureau for visitors. The city was very active in the fields of leisure services and tourism, before the tourism boom of the 1960s.

With the reorganization of Scottish local government in 1975 the new Lothian Regional Authority came into being, covering the Edinburgh region. A Lothian Leisure Services Department was established, with responsibility for the planning and management notably of leisure services, but also for tourism in the region. Later an Edinburgh and Lothians Tourist Board was created. Thus at the upper-tier level in the new two-tier local government system for the region, both leisure services and tourism activities were integrated, with links given to the separate planning department, which retained the major planning functions.

The Regional Council backed economic studies, provided a database for regional tourism and recreation planning, as well as undertaking strategic studies in these fields. The significance of tourism in the local economy needed to be measured. It was found then to directly support 6500 jobs in Edinburgh itself, generating £5 million in direct income to residents (from tourism) after all deductions were made, and a gross estimated annual expenditure in 1976 by holiday visitors to the city, of about £17.4 million of which £7.7 million was expenditure on hotels. While London had 65% of the share of foreign holiday visitor spending, Edinburgh had some 3% of the total. The tourism activity was to grow both in economic importance, and in the organization response to it. It was the later redefined Edinburgh Tourist Board which was to create the Edinburgh Convention Bureau, a body which planned and created in turn the Edinburgh International Conference Centre.

In a 1974 study, the author suggested that:

> A strategy for tourism and recreation must contain two bundles of physical policies: one set of proposals for development, and the other a set of proposals for the continuous

management of conserved resources which are to be protected. Thus proposals for active conservation by non-tourist agencies must be seen to be part of such a strategy.

(Travis, 1974)

This in fact did happen in Edinburgh and the Lothian region, partly through town planning and conservation planning.

Leisure visitor management was tested in the new Pentland Regional Park, as an important test case, while coastal resource management was also undertaken. However, planning and management of heritage interpretation only took place in some areas where town trails, guided walks and guided bus tours were provided.

Great historic cities like Edinburgh came to recognize both the demands for tourism, and the importance of appropriate resource supply to satisfy them. Residents gained from provisions made for tourists and vice versa. A set of facilities for the Commonwealth Games gave the city the key stock of resources for sport, which were to be used by: (i) residents; and (ii) visitors/tourists, who took up the remaining capacity.

However, fundamentally it is the conservation of urban built heritage resources, which proved to be critical to programmes of tourist development. A spate of hotel building in Edinburgh had to be underpinned by adequate conservation and interpretation activities, plus site management not only of the castle, but also of the Old and the New Towns. Resource protection was to give longevity to the reality of place, and to the life of 'the golden goose' of tourism, which lives off city heritage.

Evaluation

Tourism planning

Edinburgh is an optimistic case study – for in tourism planning, the national and regional institutional mechanisms that were developed became adequate and enabling, but the regional strategy unevenly developed its economic, physical and social dimensions.

Grants and trigger investments of the public sector in tourism proved to be of an important and major order: the hotels situation in Edinburgh changed beyond recognition. Self-catering accommodation opportunities developed more slowly. Public investment in the regional transport sector was significant, especially in the air and rail termini developments. Later urban transport developments were to be radically reviewed as well. Private investments in catering, commerce, travel agencies and tour operations were notable. Market investment by both the public and the private sectors was high. Investment in the adaptation and extension of museums and galleries was notable.

Conservation planning

The large scale of conservation work done and its effectiveness in the Georgian New Town, plus the virtual complete renovation of the Royal Mile in the Old Town and work on the cathedral and castle, has proved extremely impressive. Private investment plus public grant aid to other conservation areas in Edinburgh, meant that its built heritage and its landscape heritage stock are now in good shape. Desmond Hodges suggested that by 1975 some 8000 of the 11,000 residential properties in the urban central area were still in residential use. Conservation in the New Town was receiving two-thirds of its public grant from central government, and one-third from local government.

Conservation planning has thus been comparatively successful in Edinburgh, and this in turn reinforced and generated further tourism appeal. Tourism generated the means, which indirectly aided tourism via spending at the restaurants, theatres and shops in the conserved heritage stock of Edinburgh. Tourism complements local character and economic demands and converts commercial viability into profitability. Tourism thus aids Edinburgh conservation, and as commercial interpretation and management of that heritage was extended over time, this aided capacity protection, and generated further means which fed back into heritage conservation. The wider issue of event planning, and the spread of tourism activity outside of the Festival period, is a major issue – which is addressed in the next chapter of this book.

30 Urban Event Tourism: Edinburgh – the Festivals and Many 'Tourisms'

Introduction

Edinburgh's planning and conservation strategies were insufficient to develop an adequate basis for tourism developments in the city. By the 1980s it was seen that diversification of the Edinburgh tourist economy was essential, and in order to achieve economic viability there had to be adequate occupancy rates of hotels and other tourist accommodation, as well as an adequate take-up of attractions, on a year-round basis. The August Festivals' season or a summer season was not enough to sustain a city. It was vital also for the viability of attractions, and of many tourist services to develop a year-round tourist strategy.

The spread over the year potentially of conference, meetings and business tourism was seen as a vital aid. Cultural tourism, festival tourism, business tourism and governmental tourism had thus to be supplemented by a nurturing of conference, convention and meeting tourism, especially for off-season and shoulder seasons.

As in London, the high concentration of attractions and tourist accommodation were in the central area of Edinburgh (i.e. the Old Town and part of the New Town). A spatial strategy was required to achieve decentralization across the urban area. This was partly helped by the development of central Leith waterfront as a ship attraction, with its Ocean Terminal built next to the moored Britannia (see Fig. 30.1). A focus on the zoo, the development of mini hotel clusters en route to the airport, and the Forth Bridges, all helped this process. The four universities, with a very large student body almost equal to one-fifth of the city's population, was another important factor. University housing stock could be used by students in term time, and rented by visiting tourists out of term time. Aiding the spread of attractions and accommodation were the developments in local transport, such as the recent development of Edinburgh Trams linking the city to Leith in one direction, and to the airport in another.

The development of agencies also helped this process. The Scottish Tourist Board evolved into 'Visit Scotland'. In 1990, the Edinburgh Tourist Board became Edinburgh Marketing. The Edinburgh Convention Bureau's activities and the work of the Festival Office, led to the Edinburgh International Conference Centre being opened in 1995, and the city becoming 'the 1999 City of Architecture and Design'.

Tourist Attractions

By 2007 Edinburgh had over 100 tourist attractions but of these only some ten attractions were receiving over a quarter of a million

Fig. 30.1. New tourism attraction at Leith – Edinburgh's 'third town' – with the Britannia Ocean Terminal and the urban waterfront of the 'Shore' (photographs by Colin MacLeod).

visitors each p.a. In 2007 only two attractions were receiving over a million visitors, namely the National Gallery of Scotland Complex, which received 1.4 million, and Edinburgh Castle which in that year received 1.2 million visitors.

Visitor Patterns and Significance

By 1991, according to the UK Tourism Survey (UKTS) and International Passenger Survey (IPS), visitor spend in Edinburgh was already worth £290 million, and was generating over

16,000 full-time job equivalents from tourism. Domestic visitors were staying 3.5 days on average, and overseas visitors some 5.6 days on average. By 1997, Edinburgh offered some 22,000 plus tourist bed spaces, or approximately 9% of London's capacity. By the year 2006, 60% of UK trips to Edinburgh and the Lothians were for holiday purposes, compared with 22% for business and conference purposes, while 56% of overseas tourist trips were for holiday purposes, with 14% of their trips being for business or conference purposes. In both cases the VFR trade was significant, even more so for overseas tourists than for UK tourists. However, in terms of transport modal choice, while 86% of overseas tourists were arriving by air, the majority of UK tourists, some 49%, were arriving by private car, and 24% of UK tourists were arriving by train. Thus in terms of sustainability in terms of transport modes, UK tourists had a smaller carbon footprint than overseas tourists coming to Edinburgh.

The Edinburgh Festivals: from One to 13

While in 1947 the Edinburgh Festival was created, by the year 2008 Festivals Edinburgh and the Audience Business were working together to create a unique digital hub for what had become Edinburgh's 13 major festivals. Already by the later 1980s, the Fringe had become the largest of the events in the city, attracting 500,000 ticket sales for 990 events held at 140 venues. The second most popular event was the Science Festival, which by then was selling 201,000 tickets to 290 events, held at 41 venues. In comparison, the Military Tattoo sold 200,000 tickets for the single event that was always held at the one venue. However, in terms of value, at that time it was the level of expenditure on the Military Tattoo which came first representing an income of £19.57 million, the Fringe second with an income of £10.36 million, and the International Festival third with £6.91 million income. The tourist product of the city by 2008 related to activities in over 50 attractions.

The desire to get an annual spread of festivals over the whole year was achieved by 2008. The New Year's Eve or Hogmanay celebrations extend from the 29 December to the 1 January. This is followed by the Edinburgh International Science Festival that takes place in April, the Bank of Scotland 'Imaginate Festival' in late May and early June, the Edinburgh International Film Festival in June, the Edinburgh Jazz and Blues Festival from July to August and the Edinburgh Art Festival from late July to the end of August. The main festivals stay clustered in August and include the Edinburgh Military Tattoo, the Edinburgh Festival Fringe and the Edinburgh International Festival with three associated festivals including the Edinburgh Mela Festival and the Edinburgh International Book Festival. Other festivals extend through to the autumn and winter, so for example the Scottish International Storytelling Festival now takes place in late October into early November, and Edinburgh's Christmas Festival extends from late November to late December. Thus, though the main festivals stay clustered in August, the aim of spreading the festival programme across the year has succeeded.

The Fringe – a World Animation Leader

Of all the Edinburgh festivals, the most remarkable development is that of the 'Fringe' which includes a rich mix of drama, dance, comedy and street theatre. While in 1990 the Edinburgh Fringe had attracted an audience of 500,000 in ticket sales for 990 events held at 140 venues, this was to grow significantly by the 2007–2008 period. By then, ticket sales had risen to 1.7 million for 2050 events at 247 venues spread across Edinburgh. The scale and nature of this activity is so extraordinary that it requires detailed examination. How is it managed? Who does it target? And how does it succeed, year after year, in attracting such an enormous mixed-age audience, from across the globe?

To quote the Fringe organizers:

> the Fringe story began in 1947, when the Edinburgh International Festival was launched. It was seen as a post-war

initiative to re-unite Europe through culture, and was so successful that it inspired more performers than there was room for. Well aware that there would be a good crowd and focused press interest, six Scottish companies and two English decided to turn up uninvited and fend for themselves. In this way the Fringe story started.

(www.edfringe.com accessed 1 October 2010)

Because the gatecrashers to the official Festival enterprise continued in the second year a critic then dubbed their enterprise 'the Fringe of the Official Festival Drama', and so this is how the title and idea evolved. For the first 30 years the Fringe was small and intimate, but in the 1970s it started developing from its drama base into comedy, and in time the Fringe Society was founded. By 2008, the Fringe had a full-time staff of 14 and a very large staff – both full time and temporary – during the actual Festival period.

During the Festival period, they run a shop and box office, and a so-called 'Half Price Hut'. The growth of this idea became possible by expanding the range of venues to very large numbers, for performances right across the whole urban area of Edinburgh

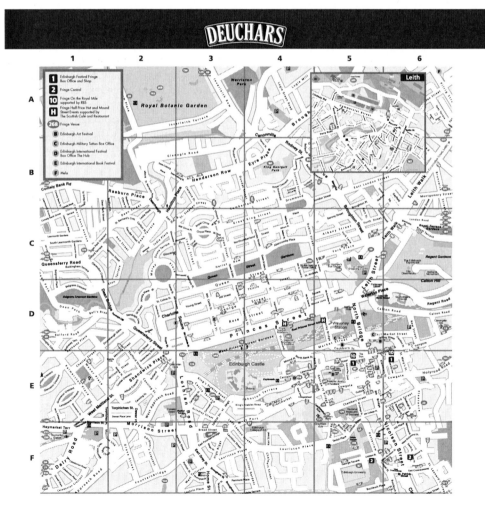

Fig. 30.2. Plan of the 343 plus venues used by the Edinburgh Fringe in 2010 (Source: courtesy of the Edinburgh Fringe).

and Leith, and it therefore came to exemplify a communitywide festival taking place, not only in theatres and halls, but in churches, cafés, shops, streets and anywhere that a small group could perform. Furthermore, its coverage came to include drama, comedy, children's shows, dance and physical theatre, events, exhibitions and music, musicals and opera as well as theatre and 'happenings'.

By 2008, 31,000 performances of 2088 shows were taking place in 247 venues. It was estimated that 18,792 performers actually took to the stage at the Fringe that year, and some 40% of the shows were world premieres, 60% were European premieres, and there were some 52 UK premieres. It is now estimated that the Fringe has a 75% market share of all attendances at Edinburgh's year-round festivals, and that it annually generates around £75 million for Edinburgh and the Scottish economy. The Fringe is not only for British innovators in the entertainment field, but also the locale for many European and American creative innovators; Edinburgh and the Fringe has come to be seen as the location for testing out audience reaction to an extraordinary range of creative endeavour. Furthermore, the fact that this has given rise to the use of a vast spread of venues in and around Edinburgh (Fig. 30.2) has meant that the whole Edinburgh community and groups within it – church groups and interest groups of many sorts – have both economic benefits and incentives to contribute, participate, increasingly use their facilities for the Fringe, and benefit from it directly and indirectly.

Evaluation

Of all the Edinburgh festivals, the Fringe is a remarkable world model, and world leader in terms of animation, community and worldwide involvement. It has taken on a special significance, almost worldwide, in terms of incentives and innovation for creative people in the festival realm, across the planet. The economic and cultural benefits have been measured, and a long life ahead would seem to be guaranteed for the Fringe. The Fringe creates 1380 full-time job equivalents in Edinburgh, and was already valued, in the formal 2004 study, as having £6.6 million worth of media coverage. By 2004 it was estimated that 70% of hotel occupancy in Edinburgh in August was due to the festivals, and most of all this was due to the Fringe.

31 Salzburg: Management and Tourism in an Austro-Hungarian Festival City

Introduction: Salzburg as a Heritage Resource

The extraordinarily beautiful and remarkably sited Austrian provincial city of Salzburg occupies a site which was first occupied by a Roman settlement. The modern settlement's origins go back to the year of its 7th-century foundation, but the character and layout of the historic inner town were determined by development spanning the periods from the medieval to the baroque epochs. Monasteries and convents founded in the medieval period led to clerical, political and commercial roles and initiatives, which were to redefine the city's character and functions.

The modern city, with a population of about 150,000, has its international image coloured by its key associations with Mozart and Schubert. However, much of its glorious heritage of built environment it owes to its Prince Archbishops. Given its high quality environment, it is not surprising that Humboldt deemed Salzburg to be one of the three most beautiful cities in the world, or that the city was chosen as one of Austria's three pilot projects for the European Architectural Heritage Year (EAHY) in 1975. Though Council of Europe initiatives in this field of urban conservation had started as early as 1963, it is also noticeable that Salzburg took formal action in terms of conservation earlier than the rest of Austria.

The physical heritage resources of Salzburg are of an outstanding quality, even in terms of international comparisons. No less than five significant elements of its structure may be identified:

- the historic inner or Old Town;
- the three wooded hills of Monchsberg, Kaputzinerberg and Rainberg;
- the fortress on its dominating rock (Fig. 31.1);
- the New Town, across the River Salzach, with its sets of bridges; and
- a suburban ring.

The Old Town and the wooded hills comprise the key heritage zone of Salzburg. Furthermore, the heritage resource is architectural in terms of the fortress, the cathedral and churches, palaces and Residenz, houses and museums, theatres and monuments. These buildings include those from the medieval period, the renaissance period, through to the baroque and later imperial periods.

It is not just buildings, but the total urban form of varied, rich and architectural mass and void, which Salzburg displays. Towers, domes, battlements, steeples and rooftops, decorate its beautiful skyline. Its ravine-like medieval streets contrast with squares, market places, arcades, gardens, courtyards, beer terraces, wine cellars and garden restaurants. Fountains, sculpture, monuments and decorative street

(a)

(b)

Fig. 31.1. Identification, recognition and renovation of historical monuments: (a) the fortress of Salzburg Castle (photograph by Peter Watt); (b) street signs (photograph courtesy of www.insidersguide-online.com).

(c)

Fig. 31.1. Continued. (c) historic painting of the Old Town and wooded hills.

signs make up the street furniture which identifies the spaces (Fig. 31.1). Beyond the townscape, a magnificent landscape setting, including mountains, like the nearby Untersberg, define perceptions of the city.

Salzburg: Street Furniture and Urban Squares

A three-volume *Austrian National Atlas of Conservation*, prepared between 1969 and 1977, covers the whole country and its townscapes including Salzburg. This work was done by the Architects' Department of the Federal Office for the Protection of Monuments. This is a mapped and photographic inventory of buildings and heritage areas, and provides the database from which local authorities can define needs, in terms of heritage protection measures. National and regional legislation provide for financial aid to carry out renovation and restoration work, by property owners and tenants of buildings who are listed by the Federal Office.

As indicated in the Austrian Report on 'Living Cultural Heritage', historical monuments in Austria are classified on the basis of:

• moveable monuments (including individual items like paintings and sculpture, and collections such as libraries); and
• non-moveable monuments (such as individual historic buildings and architectural complexes, up to the scale of a whole historic town centre).

The Austrian 1923 Conservation Act used this approach, also examining religious and non-religious monuments, as well as ownership categories. Threefold classification under the Hague Convention on the Protection of Cultural Property is also used. However, other legislation has adjusted Salzburg's approach to inventorization of resources, and the renovation of heritage areas.

Under the Provincial Parliamentary Act of 1967, the whole of the inner historic city core of Salzburg was declared a protected zone, which was to be the subject of conservation action. Within this defined area, it was aimed to keep the exteriors of all buildings, including courtyards, entrance areas, windows, archways, roof shape, form and colour, in their original state, with controls extended to building materials and the character of advertisements. Long before the work on the *Austrian National Atlas of Conservation*, an inventory was prepared of all buildings in the conservation area. Also all the works of art, and the elevations (or grounds) of buildings were catalogued in the whole Salzburg urban area.

To enable action on conservation, a special fund was created under the 1967 Act, to which the City Council contributed 60% of the budget and 40% came from the provincial authority. Formal and informal incentives were given to the public to engage in conservation activities, which were extended to include cleaning and clearing out of courtyards and spaces, to achieve a general upgrading of amenity and environmental standards. The work undertaken in the core of Salzburg under the 1967 Act comprised the Salzburg Pilot Project for the EAHY.

Agencies, Legislation and Decisions That Brought About Heritage Protection

In addition to normal town planning and building regulation work, a complex programme of work in Salzburg arose from federal, provincial and local authority initiatives in the realms of urban renewal, conservation management and cultural protection. Austrian Federal Ministries and agencies which brought about Salzburg heritage conservation work included: (i) the Ministry of Science and Research; and (ii) the Ministry of Construction and Technology.

The Ministry of Science and Research was responsible for cultural monuments and partly for conservation. A subdivision of this Ministry was the Federal Office for the Protection of Monuments. This Ministry had the right to designate 'renovation areas'. Linked to the Federal Office were three special technical departments, one of which – the Austrian Hague Convention Office – had an important conservation role. It defined the nature of cultural property, including for example, the definition of an 'historic core' such as that of Salzburg's, and categorized monuments as being of international, national or regional significance.

The Ministry of Construction and Technology dealt with maintenance and conservation work on buildings of cultural importance, owned by the state, and questions relating to preventing the impact of any road building upon the built environment, as well as the promotion of housing renewal and housing research. The comprehensive urban renewal of the Maxglan District and the project for the Mozarteum – both in Salzburg – derived from this Ministry.

Under the Urban Renewal Act of 1974, provincial authorities were generally given the right to designate 'renovation areas', while tax relief and financial aid to conservation was given in a Conservation Act, and in two Housing Acts of 1968 and 1969.

Reference has already been made to the 1967 Salzburg Provincial Legislation. This gave rise to the creation of a Commission for Salzburg's Old Quarter, which guided and directed the conservation process. A Salzburg Institute for Regional Research catalogued the city's cultural resources, while there were also active local pressure groups and conservation action groups. These included: (i) an Association for the Protection of Salzburg Landscape; (ii) a Salzburg Citizens' Association; (iii) a Diocesan Commission for Art and Monument Conservation; and (iv) a conservation publication. As a result of initiative, responsiveness and responsibility, the work done in Old Salzburg included pedestrianization, and not just minor renovation work.

Tourism in Salzburg

From 1988 to 1996, tourist bed spaces in Salzburg increased from 9600 to 9900 but visitor numbers dropped. Salzburg is an example of a city which was fairly successful in terms of its tourism economy, yet one in which the integrity of its cultural and environmental heritage was maintained. Tourism by 1988 was attracting 1.6 million visitor nights, spent in all forms of accommodation, but by 1997 this had dropped to 1.55 million nights. By 1997, there were 1.9 million domestic tourism arrivals p.a. recorded in Salzburg, compared with some 6.5 million foreign tourism arrivals, according to the FECTO Report of '98-99.

Salzburg caters for about five specific tourism markets, which relate closely to its heritage character, specific sets of activity, and its physical capacity to absorb these levels and numbers. The five tourism markets may be defined as:

- general holiday tourism (winter and summer);
- specific music-focused tourism (throughout the year);
- conference and congress tourism;
- general health tourism;
- health-treatment and convalescent-treatment tourism.

Music-focused tourism does not just rely on the Salzburg Festival alone, for in addition to the January Mozart Festival, there are Easter and Whitsun Festivals, Mozart and Chamber Music Weeks, and the 'Musical Spring', together providing all-round visitation. The cultural focus for music visitors, and other visitors, includes the programme of the Landestheatre and Marionette Theatre, as well as specific exhibitions and events at the museums and galleries, and performances in the cathedral and in the Residenz.

Conference and congress tourism focuses upon the Kongresshaus, and its excellent facilities and premises where international and national congresses, conferences, conventions and meetings are held. The range of size of halls can simultaneously accommodate groups as small as 60, or as large as 1000 people.

Health tourism is also important, as Salzburg is a spa with mud and health baths, medicinal mineral-water cures, hydrotherapy, saunas, Roman baths and other special treatments at the Paracelsuskurhaus – treatments which were first offered locally as early as the 1500s.

Salzburg's buoyant tourism does not suffer greatly from the problems of seasonality. Its central location and infrastructural developments mean that it is easily accessed from within Europe by railway, motorway and air transport throughout the year, and its scale and character of hotel development has been kept in balance with the tourist activity base. The lesson of Salzburg is to place limits on accommodation growth, and to focus upon the level and range of activities and facilities available to specific categories of tourist, who can find their fulfilment in its scenic, shopping, cultural, sporting, health and conference opportunities, as well as planned events.

Evaluation

The natural advantages of site, climate, physical and cultural heritage, and of character have been consciously optimized upon by Salzburg. The improvement through renovation of its inner historic core has gone hand in hand with limited pedestrianization, and means of boosting and spreading tourist and activity capacity. The day-tour hinterland is one of the Alps and lakes, in the Lake District of the Salzgammergut. However, the continental climate of Salzburg is a special advantage: one can count on snow in winter and sunshine and warmth in summer, and these affect activity patterns seasonally both outdoors and indoors.

The 'Festival City' of Salzburg offers a range of festivals, events and activities throughout the year. Edinburgh's problem of seasonality was earlier based on one concentrated festival but over time, Edinburgh developed events spread over the year, which Salzburg had already achieved. The value of tourism to both cities is notable. Edinburgh's boosting of investment in and development of the hotel sector has twinned investment in the renovation of its historic core.

The physical renovation process in Salzburg has been less extensive and expensive than that in Edinburgh, in terms of buildings, but in terms of pedestrianization, landscape treatment, attention to hanging shop signs and other details of street furniture, Salzburg's work on 'monuments and cultural conservation' is far richer and more rewarding for the visitor, than that of Edinburgh. Visitation in Salzburg is at a lower level than that of Edinburgh, but perhaps it views itself as more select. The open and warm hospitality received by the hotel visitor in Salzburg may also be related back to the human scale of this small and intimate city, as well as in its more modest environmental capacity terms.

For Mozart lovers, the quality of Mozartian events in Salzburg is incomparable: hearing Mozart's *Requiem Mass* in the brittle, icy air of the baroque cathedral interior in February, cannot be bettered. With respect to accommodation, the Austrian welcome given may be described as 'ingratiatingly lush' as compared to a rather cooler, but courteous welcome in Scotland. For 20 years Salzburg had a better spread of tourism over the calendar year than did Edinburgh, due to its range of musical and other events, but Edinburgh's tourist planners devised an event planning system which came to cover the whole year. In addition to being a thriving capital, Edinburgh also expanded not only its legal, but also its financial, commercial and educational sectors, to make it a rich destination for tourism. Salzburg cannot compete with Edinburgh's wider choice of tourist accommodation, dining out, drinking places, and its enormous worldwide range of entertainment, but it achieves an enormous amount for a high quality, traditional, provincial and relatively small, Austrian city.

32 Colonial Williamsburg: a Conserved and Renovated Settlement as a Managed Cultural, Educational and Tourist Centre

Introduction

Colonial Williamsburg is situated in Virginia, USA, to the east of Richmond, and to the west of Newport News. It is a town with a population equal to only 5% of that of Edinburgh, or 12% of that of Salzburg. It is small and very special. It is a small, totally restored 18th-century town, in essence a restored historic colonial capital settlement of an early British colony in Virginia. The purpose of conservation work at Colonial Williamsburg is best explained by quoting the words of the Board of Trustees. They aim:

> to recreate accurately the environment of the man and woman of 18th-century Williamsburg, and to bring about such an understanding of their lives and times that present and future generations may more vividly appreciate the contribution of these early Americans, to the ideals and culture of our country.
>
> (www.colonialwilliamsurg.com/ visit/ accessed 1 October 2010)

Williamsburg is an impressive example of the town scale of historic settlement conservation: it is a cultural and educational site, which generates major use for recreational and tourist purposes. As already mentioned, it is a small 18th-century colonial capital city, which is a large conserved historic site or a large outdoor museum. It is one of the largest 'living museums' of its type in the world. In international terms, it relates to, but is functionally fundamentally different from, the larger conserved Georgian Edinburgh, or the historic core of Salzburg. Williamsburg is managed *in toto* as a special museum; whereas the Edinburgh and Salzburg examples are normal living cities which have tourist functions, but are not managed as museums, nor are they managed by a Trust, which focuses upon their physical and cultural integrity.

This is a case study of a well-conserved and restored historic settlement, which can be highly instructive to tourism developers who may be involved in formulating action plans, for it provides attractions of high quality and integrity, whose appeal is both cultural and educational in the broadest sense. In visitor terms, developments such as that at Williamsburg can provide material of a satisfactory level for an advanced researcher, and yet equally provide an enjoyable but educational experience for the casual tourist, who is given a cursory glance back into a cultural history.

The Trust's Objectives

According to McCaskey, writing upon Williamsburg preservation back in 1970, the Trust's objectives are:

1. It teaches history and illustrates heritage.
2. It demonstrates a different lifestyle which can be enlightening to our society.

3. It offers beauty in a controlled environment under responsible management.
4. It promotes respect for the land and also for the environment.
5. Williamsburg helps to inspire hope for the future, particularly among the younger generation.

Environmental Conservation and Restoration

The buildings now standing along Williamsburg's streets and greens are some of the most important in the USA, in terms of restoration, renovation, research and tourism. In effect, they provide the basis of a city-wide heritage museum all set within a plan which was first conceived by Francis Nicholson, the Lieutenant Governor who laid out the new Capital of Williamsburg in the 18th century.

Nicholson envisaged a country town with public greens and with every house on the 1-mile long main street having at least half an acre of land. The fashions, be they of architecture or of dress, came from England, but they were adapted to the needs of Virginia, with its distinctive climate. Many of the public buildings, and a few of the private dwellings and shops were made of brick, but most of the town is built of wood – far less costly and less susceptible to dampness. The oldest of the public structures was the Wren Building of the College of William and Mary, which stands at the centre of the college yard and college life of what is now a small, but very important state university.

Eighteenth-century Williamsburg was, in essence, a carefully planned small town of over 500 buildings, with some of the most handsome buildings to be found in the colony of Virginia.

In terms of the definition of the problems and opportunities, this basic information provides the backcloth against which to view the programme of restoration which began in 1926, when the then Rector of Bruton Parish Church, living with the dream of preserving the city's historic buildings, discussed the matter with John D. Rockefeller Jnr. The Reverend Goodwin realized that many of the buildings which had been an integral part of the life of the colony of Virginia, and the foundation of the 'new nation', would soon disappear. With their shared goal, the two men began a relatively modest project to preserve a few of the more important buildings. As time progressed the scope widened, and now 85% of

18th-century Williamsburg is encompassed by the restoration work which has been undertaken. Mr Rockefeller donated funds, not only for the preservation of the original structures, and the reconstruction of those buildings that had vanished, but also for the construction of facilities to accommodate visitors and to interpret the story of Williamsburg. By the early 1970s some £36 million had already been invested in the museum and its associated works.

There is no doubt that the settlement restoration work in Williamsburg is one of the most extensive, comprehensively managed schemes yet undertaken anywhere. A very extensive piece of work which offered an opportunity to restore a complete settlement to its earlier physical state, and to preserve the beauty and charm of the old buildings and gardens of the site for purposes of display, learning and appreciation by the visiting public – in terms of its use, for educational and recreational visits, as well as for tourism.

The restoration of Colonial Williamsburg has made possible the preservation of some 88 original buildings, which were still standing when the work commenced (Fig. 32.1). They include the modest homes of craftsmen, a powder magazine, smoke houses, elegant town residences and the Public Records Office. Furthermore, these buildings are not museums in the more traditional use of that term; they are buildings in which the pattern of 18th-century life, including decor, furnishing and animation activities, is recreated for the visitor. Thus a feeling is created whereby the visitor is able to return to the time when the town of Williamsburg was the capital of a young colony. All the restored houses are used and lived in. Residents are given life-tenancy rights but have to meet special requirements laid down by the Foundation.

Restoration work has also included replacement of important buildings that had disappeared after the capital was moved to Richmond, Virginia in 1790. The 500 buildings which have been restored and reconstructed on original foundations have been done only after considerable documentary research and archaeological studies. This emphasizes the complete integrity of Colonial Williamsburg, and provides a very clear pointer to the possibilities which exist for reconstruction, though probably on a very much smaller scale at places in other parts of the world.

Fig. 32.1. Heritage conservation in Colonial Williamsburg (courtesy of US Travel Service).

Planning and Development

As shown in Figs 32.2 and 32.3, modern Williamsburg is a recreational/tourist attraction, which can now be divided into three concentric-ring principal areas:

- at the core the restored historic, traffic-free 175 acre colonial town;

- an encircling protective 3000 acre green belt; and

- the modern town with all its tourist-focused developments: the hotels, shops and restaurants to serve visitors, the visitor centres (which play such an important part in introducing all the concepts to the visitors) and the adjacent car parks and other traffic-related provisions.

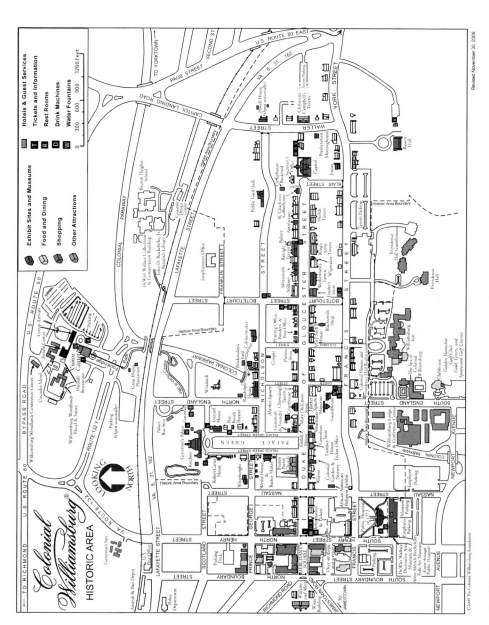

Fig.32.2. The historic core area of Colonial Williamsburg (courtesy of the Colonial Williamsburg Foundation).

The traffic-related provisions include a free coach-shuttle service, which carries visitors from the visitor centres in the outer zone, to the pedestrianized historic core (petrol-driven vehicles are excluded from the historic core). As some 92% of visitors come by private car, the traffic management arrangements in the system are critical.

Visitor Management

Due to the planning and management of the project, visitors can quickly appreciate historic Williamsburg as a planned town. They can witness the sense of order of the original 18th-century city plan, and that of the 20th-century development, beyond the green belt. The plan enables the core restored area to be protected, and set apart from modern Williamsburg, with its provision of over 7500 tourist bed spaces, and all the services and provisions necessary to cater for the influx of visitors.

With over one million visitors p.a., management arrangements have to be extensive. The creation of a very impressive visitor centre (with supplementary centres) in close proximity to, but located just outside and beyond the restored historic area, has eased traffic management problems.

This arrangement provides the opportunity for interpretation, introducing the concept of Williamsburg in audio-visual displays, and applying the planning concept of limiting visitor capacity in the historic core, to the planned through-put capacities of the visitor centres, and of the free coach-shuttle services. Consequently, Williamsburg has experienced as a highly sophisticated and well-planned tourist project, comprising all the distinct but complementary elements shown on the plan.

This effective method of visitor handling and traffic management, excluding all traffic other than the controlled coaches from the edges of the historic town, minimizes traffic loading in the vicinity of the sensitive historic area, which has no modern vehicular traffic in it. By the early 1970s the shuttle coach service was already handling a capacity of six million passenger journeys p.a.

Landscape Conservation

Williamsburg is not only a set of buildings, as there are also more than 150 gardens within the city, occupying 90 of its 175 acres, and of these some 85 gardens have been restored, on the basis of research, to their original colonial state including the original choice of trees, plants and paths of the 18th-century town. In particular, the Foundation gives much attention to protecting the trees from damage and disease, plus using nurseries to generate new stock, when replacement is required. As with landscape, the same level of care has been given to the conservation of the buildings' interior collections, so that the social history is interpreted and presented to the visitor, who is given a glimpse of daily life in the earlier colonial capital.

Animation

Williamsburg is also a place of work: 36 separate crafts are practised in the town, and of these some 16 colonial crafts were restored with craft workshops being created and staffed by 150 people. This is the most extensive animation project of its kind in the USA. The purpose is to show visitors how the colonial population worked, what they made and how they lived and dressed (Fig. 32.4). It also preserves craft techniques in danger of being lost forever. Skills on display to the general public include basket weaving, saddle making and the manufacture of musical instruments, rifles, furniture, boots, blankets, candles, pottery and jewellery. Visitors may watch all of these activities, without payment.

All of this has been achieved from very simple beginnings, when 80 years ago the first working blacksmith's forge was opened. Since then more and more crafts have been added, and research work has provided the basis to ensure continued integrity of what is displayed.

Costs and Benefits

None of this activity can come cheaply. By the 1970s Colonial Williamsburg already required

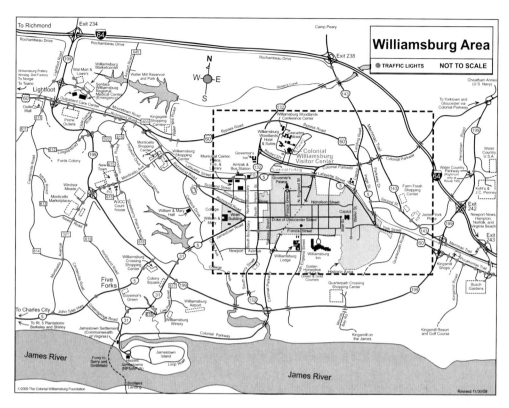

Fig. 32.3. The wider Williamsburg area (the historic core area shown is boxed) (courtesy of the Colonial Williamsburg Foundation).

Fig. 32.4. Visitors can watch displays showing how the colonial population worked, lived and dressed (courtesy of US Travel Service).

an annual operating capital of approximately £10 million. Over £36 million investment had been undertaken by then. Furthermore, the Colonial Williamsburg Foundation has its Board of Trustees, comprising a body of highly distinguished people, and an employed staff of some 3000. This includes 600 costumed individuals, who present and interpret the exhibitions and historic area to the public, and a balance of 2400 other people, who are employed in the operation of coaches, car parks, hotels, restaurants and shops. As a result Williamsburg's population has grown from 1000 in 1920 to over 20,000 by 1971 – the vast majority of people living in modern Williamsburg, whose economy is almost totally dependent on the related tourist industry. By 1971, the economic impact of tourism on the local economy was already of the order of £41 million p.a.

Evaluation: the Contribution of Colonial Williamsburg

Williamsburg is unique. It is doubtful whether a private enterprise heritage development on such a scale will ever be achieved again in the world. The integrity is evident of the research and study, the management arrangements, the staff training and retraining programmes and the quality and accuracy of all the conservation. Williamsburg is a tourist destination – and on average visitors make a 2-day stay. Reconstruction work is both honest and a means of cultural education and recreation.

Complex crowd-management techniques, 'the processing of visitors', the spreading of visitor numbers in time and in space, is all tackled professionally, without the visitor consciously realizing the extent of visitor management. Promotion and publicity, like the street cleaning and street-closure plans, are equally tackled with thoroughness and integrity.

Williamsburg is an attraction for educationists, cultural tourism and recreation. The majority of the off-season publicity for Williamsburg features the benefit of a 2-night stay, but with the development of other facilities and the scale of related tourist attractions in the region, including Busch Gardens Theme Park, Jamestown, Yorktown and Newport News, attempts were made to extend the length of stay and increase the beneficial economic impacts. It is the quality and integrity of Williamsburg's development and management, which is the vital focus. Williamsburg is a very special historic site, whose restoration is an international template of approach.

The wider contextual approach of Williamsburg is also of much interest. The original area of British settlement in Virginia dates back to 1607, and comprises a cluster of three settlements – Jamestown, Yorktown and Williamsburg – now linked together by a tree-planted Colonial Parkway, and jointly forming the Colonial National Historical Park. The strategic and conservation implications of this combination are all addressed later in this book in Chapter 39. The role of Colonial Williamsburg may change over time, but its contribution will remain a valuable one.

33 The Sustainable Historic City Centre: Munich as a Model

Introduction

The City of Munich, with a population of 1,300,000 in 2008, is the capital of the State or Land of Bavaria (Bayern) in the south of the Federal Republic of Germany. It is the administrative, commercial, legal and cultural hub of Southern Germany. In the post-war period it carried out a huge programme of central area renovation, which transformed the city core, in advance of the opening of the Olympic Games in the city.

In 1975–1977 a major research study for the UK Department of the Environment, was done by the author and J.R. Stewart, at the Centre for Urban and Regional Studies (CURS) at the University of Birmingham. Its subject was 'urban central area pedestrianization' involving detailed evaluative visits to eight German cities, conducting interviews there and making observations, as well as doing desk research. Munich, one of the cities visited, proved to be an outstanding example, and remains a model for good sustainable design in spatial management and transport terms, even today.

Process of Change

By 1976, the City of Munich had 3 years' experience of using and evaluating its newly completed pedestrian city centre. A special law had been required to create the pedestrian zone. The sequential approach followed by the city, in its development process, was as follows:

- to prepare a Central Area Plan;
- to define the pedestrian zone, linked not only to the Central Business District, but also to the conserved historic quarter, and to the cultural and recreational hub of the city;
- preparation of the S-Bahn (above-ground rail) and U-Bahn (underground or metro rail system) to serve the centre;
- to hold a design competition for the character of the pedestrian realm; and
- to accept and implement the winning and approved pedestrian zone design, once operation of the two new rail systems serving the centre, went ahead.

The pedestrian zone was not only planned in terms of its physical design, but also in terms of an 'events plan' for activities to occur in and on the pedestrian area (Fig. 33.1). Today the user can see the great difference to the building frontages on the formerly trafficked roads that previously characterized the centre. Negative vehicular space of the past, was replaced by a positive and safe, long-stay pedestrian activity area – not only in sun and rain, but also even in sub-zero conditions of snow and ice in midwinter.

Results

The qualitative improvement to the environment is marked, in terms of: (i) outdoor space; (ii) diminished noise and vibration; (iii) improved amenity; and (iv) improved treatment of building frontage and building use. There is a decrease in convenient access for the aged, and for the physically disadvantaged, but there is a compensatory increase in the numbers of other people, and other types of visitor using the space, at all seasons,

Fig. 33.1. Images of the city centre of Munich after pedestrianization, showing the vitality of its use for both summer outdoor activities and the Christmas Fair in winter (photographs courtesy of Munich City Council).

Fig. 33.1. Continued.

at all times, and in nearly all weathers! The open-air precinct is least successful in rainy conditions. There are zonal variations within the Munich central pedestrian area, achieved by differences in use, and in landscape treatment. In spring and summer, spatial enclosures are created by trees, by the placing of flowerpots and seating. The edge areas created for seating follow the principle of backing where people sit with a containing wall of planting and flowers, so that they look out from contained and identifiable, non-transit spaces. The richness of monuments, fountains, statuary and signs create both visual vitality and interest to the pedestrian users of the spaces.

Tourism

The historic pull of Munich to tourists is associated with its rich mix of attractions and events ranging from arts, culture and sports, to the Oktoberfest – the great beer-garden festival that celebrated its 200th birthday in 2010, and annually draws six million visitors to the fair. This event made Munich a famous destination long before the Olympic Games came to the city in 1972. The quality of the 100 plus museums and the three great art galleries are added pulls to the Christmas Fair, where nearly €23 million are spent annually. These were all add-on attractions for the holiday tourists, the business tourists and conference and meeting goers who are vital to Munich's commercial, industrial and business life. Holiday tourism and cultural tourism have grown in importance, and the quality of the upgraded pedestrianized centre has strengthened the appeal, and increased the length of stay by visitor and resident, in the centre.

By 2007, some 9.5 million nights were being spent by tourists in Munich – 5 million of which were by German domestic visitors, and 4.5 million by foreign visitors. In that year, some 4.7 million total arrivals were recorded at tourist accommodation in Munich. However, with a generous 36,937 tourist bed spaces in the city, a buoyant mix of tourisms has to be retained to support the strong service economy.

Evaluation of the Pedestrian Zone

From the desk research, the site visits to German schemes, plus the interviews with providers and users, a number of findings or conclusions may be made about the approach to design and management in such schemes:

1. Pedestrian-zone planning is more than simply a process of vehicular traffic removal. It is sustainable spatial planning integrated into comprehensive planning for an historic central area, linked to and served by transportation planning.
2. The simplicity or complexity of legal procedures for achieving traffic removal, street

closure and planned reuse for new purposes is a critical factor.
3. Wholehearted political commitment is necessary to get adequate budgeting for comprehensive street planning, paving, containment and street furnishing that is required for success. Activity or event programmes, required at the later stage, also need pre-budgeting. You need to plan an environment which is right for pedestrians, and respond to external voluntary-sector group initiatives for on-street animation!
4. Temporal segregation of traffic and pedestrians works well (i.e. set times are needed for service vehicles to come, and other times for sole pedestrian use). Rear-servicing is not necessary.
5. Comfort and safety criteria of pedestrian users of such spaces, mean that there is a need to adjust designs to have safer surfaces to walk on, shelter from rain, ice and wind, vertical baffles to modify the effects of wind and cold, and provision of cross-canopies – so that walkers can cross spaces safely and comfortably in bad as well as in good weather.
6. The pedestrian areas need to be clearly and distinctly designed, so they are places of interest with their own identity and distinct boundaries. If underground light rail systems or tram routes are below them, this is ideal in terms of easy access. This provides a sustainable environment for people on foot, with ease of access to and from sustainable public transport below, or via separate cycle routes from and to home, or work.

Evaluation of Pedestrian Cores and Tourism

The Munich model (and that of Birmingham, see Chapter 34) shows how historic city cores can be made more sustainable and appealing, than out-of-town motorized shopping centres, which are designed for private car access, and are less sustainable. Fully designed pedestrian cores are good and lively places both for local residents to use, and a magnet for visitors – whether they be domestic or foreign tourists, or day trippers. This is because such places have vitality, identity, safety and manifold attractions that make them long-stay locations.

34 Post-industrial Urban Centre Landscape Transformation: Central Birmingham (UK) as a Test Case 1960–2010

Introduction

The case study of central Birmingham's transformation over a 30-year period, from the 1970s to the first decade of the 2000s, is an extraordinary one, relating to the death of a great industrial city, and its reinvention, or recycling into a post-industrial city of great quality.

This chapter describes the various strategies that were employed as part of a complex process of transformation of the physical infrastructure and associated building superstructure of central Birmingham to create an urban environment of great quality, in which inherited resources – both natural and man-made – have been enhanced, and activity levels in the transformed spaces vastly increased.

Early 20th-century Birmingham was 'the workshop of the world' – a city with traditions of religious non-conformity, trade, manufacture and innovation. It had been a 'city of a thousand little meisters'. By the 1960s, however, Birmingham was a tired and drab city, slowly recovering from the Second World War, reconstructing its war-damaged and blighted environments, and needing massive industrial reinvestment. The launch of the Mini car's production here in 1960, and the growth in car ownership, came with the building of the inner ring road and the start of the motorway building phase. Birmingham's central location

nationally, and its entrepreneurial traditions augured well for the future, but many of its small old metal and jewellery industries were in decline. The opening of the Bullring shopping centre in 1964, with its siting on the inner ring road, hailed the 'Motorway City' as devised by the City Engineer Manzoni. However, 1960's central Birmingham was a down-to-earth 9.00 to 5.00 o'clock city, with dirty inaccessible canals, a colourless centre that lacked trees and was noisy from excessive vehicular traffic, with a need for its residents to go out to the countryside to find decent eating places and escape from the limited range of cultural activities in the city centre. It was a city lacking quality, losing its identity and in danger of losing its great civic pride.

Though the 1970s started encouragingly, with the opening of the new Repertory Theatre in 1971 and of a grand new Central Library in 1973, the Middle East 'Oil Crisis' soon led to industrial collapse in manufacturing. Two hundred thousand industrial jobs were lost in the 1970s in the West Midlands, and it seemed as though a great industrial city was about to die. However, it is characteristic of this confident city that collapse led to positive and creative responses. By 1976 the National Exhibition Centre (NEC) was opened at the Solihull rail-entry point to Birmingham. Also in the late 1970s, Project Aquarius brought the Department of the

Environment, British Waterways and the Birmingham Inner City Partnership together to start improving the system of canals in the city. This involved: (i) cleaning the canals; (ii) repaving the towpaths; (iii) opening up access to the canals; (iv) creating new bridges; and (v) interpreting and presenting the canals as a fine new resource for the city. These economic and environmental changes were the start of an economic and environmental quality renewal process that over time was to transform the central city totally.

The key is that reinvestment had to go with a reorientation of the economy, life and values of the city, whereby existing natural resources had to be regained and enhanced, and a city had to find vital new functions for its survival and well-being. It is significant, that in the 1970s too, the first conservation battle was won in Birmingham, when the fine Victorian Head Post Office building was saved, and the principle of conservation of selected built heritage, together with new buildings, was established. The small city centre was choked by a tight inner ring road of concrete, the car was king, and pedestrians were made into troglodytes scurrying through nasty underpasses.

The Use of Responsive Instruments

The 30-year production or transformation process carried out in central Birmingham, has involved the use of some six distinct instruments. These are:

- economic developments;
- planning of infrastructural systems;
- building or superstructural creation, and reuse;
- arts development strategies;
- event strategies; and
- landscape treatment.

Economic developments

Economic developments have laid the foundation for changes, with a shift from a primary focus on manufacturing, to a multi-pronged economy, with a growth of the services sector –

particularly relating to the exhibition, conference and congress sector, retailing, catering and hotels, plus banking, insurance, accounting, education, research and development. This economic diversification has aided the greater diversification of the labour force, and has also been the basis of a multi-pronged urban tourism strategy that was to emerge later.

By 1984, the new International Airport was open in the city, and in the same year a design evaluation was done for an International Convention Centre (ICC) to be built in the city centre. By the late 1980s an economic development strategy was using booster grants from the European Commission (worth £143 million) to: (i) complete the NEC and develop the NEC Arena (1980); (ii) fund part of the development of the ICC; (iii) develop the Aston Science Park; and (iv) help fund pedestrianization of the central area. In the late 1980s the use of urban design consultants led to the possibility of a pedestrian and open-space system in the city centre, linking activity centres. The 1990s were to see key work done by the Birmingham Heartlands Development Corporation, training and business development by the Birmingham Training and Enterprise Council (£39 million), promotion of the finance sector by City 2000, and capital assembly for the development of four major building complexes: (i) the ICC; (ii) the Brindleyplace development (Fig. 34.1); (iii) the Mailbox; and (iv) by the early 2000s creation of the second Bullring (shopping) Centre, which opened in 2003.

Planning of infrastructural systems

Infrastructural systems planning saw the work on the canals that had started in the 1970s leading on to extensive waterfront developments by and during the 1990s, and the development of the pedestrian system across the city centre in 1992, using the former trafficked streets, and linking to a growing number of all-weather, under-cover pedestrian shopping malls in the city centre (Fig. 34.2). By 2004, Birmingham had already achieved the UK's largest continuous pedestrianized system across the whole of its central area. Furthermore, this was a landscaped and varied system with indoor

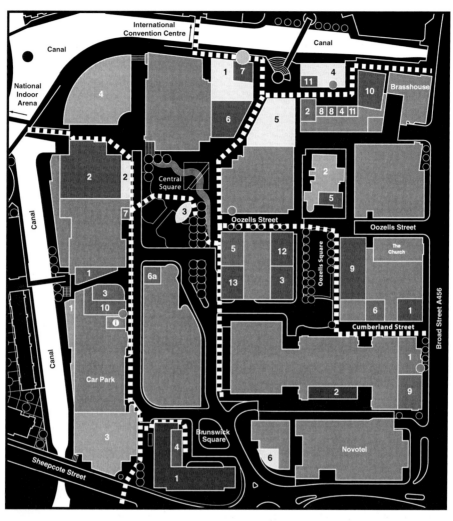

LEISURE PLAN.

Restaurants
1 Around the World in 80 Dishes
2 Bank Restaurant
3 Cielo
4 City Café
5 Café Ikon
6 Café Rouge
7 Handmade Burger Co.
8 Mash House Café Bar
9 Piccolino
10 Pizza Express
11 Shogun Teppan-yaki
12 Thai Edge
13 Edmunds

Cafés & Bars
1 All Bar One
2 Bank Bar
3 Costa Coffee
4 Pitcher & Piano
5 The Slug and Lettuce
6 Nuvo

Leisure
1 Bannatyne's Health Club
2 Ikon Gallery
3 The Crescent Theatre
4 The National SEA LIFE Centre

Retail
1 Baguette du Monde
2 Boots
3 Ethos
4 Eye Q Opticians
5 EAT
6 Number Nine the Gallery
6a The Buttermarket
7 PLACES
8 Umberto Giannini
9 Sainsbury's
10 Spar in the City
11 Zen

Accommodation
1 City Inn
2 SACO @Livingbase

Banking
1 NatWest

□□□□□□□□□□□□ Disabled Access Route ◉ Cash Points
□□□□□◉□□□□□ Disabled Lift

Fig. 34.1. Central Birmingham renewal: the Brindleyplace development (courtesy of www.brindleyplace.com).

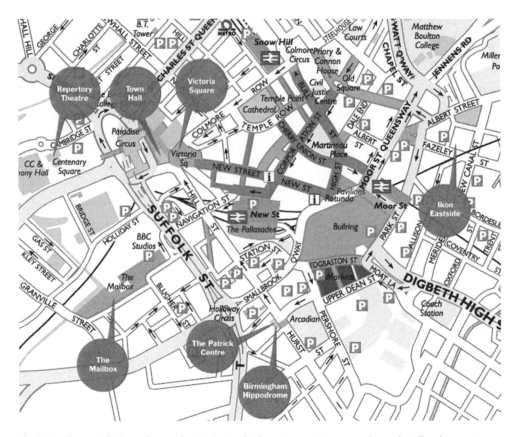

Fig. 34.2. The central Birmingham pedestrian network (shown in grey) (courtesy of www.brindleyplace.com).

and outdoor elements, waterfronts, attractions, shopping, rest and recreational elements making it a mature system in its own right. The variety in the use of spaces was also critical – some as shopping spaces, some civic, some recreational and so on.

Building or superstructure realization

Building or superstructure realization had highlights in the opening of the NEC in 1976, the NEC Arena added in 1980, the new International Airport in 1984, and then the triple achievement in 1991 of the ICC, Symphony Hall and the National Indoor Arena (NIA). The ICC, in turn, generated the speeded up development of the new Brindleyplace district, plus the opening of the Mailbox complex in 2000, construction of new hotels and restau-

rants, and in 2003 the completion of the huge new Bullring Centre, which alone cost £500 million to create. Finally in 2007, the historic 1830's concert hall – named 'The Town Hall' – opened after total renovation. The expansion of the city's three universities over this period, to cater for more than 30,000 students, reinforced all these other major changes.

Arts development strategies and events strategies

Perhaps, most interesting of all, was the evolution of arts and events strategies in Birmingham in the 1980s and 1990s, as these were vital in changing the image of the city, or its 'rebranding' or 'repositioning' as marketeers would call it. In 1980 Sir Simon Rattle was appointed conductor of the City of

Birmingham Symphony Orchestra (CBSO), and set about improving it so it became a world-class orchestra. Part of his strategy was the battle to get a new Symphony Hall, with over 2000 seats, and superb acoustics – this was finally realized in 1991, as part of the ICC complex.

In 1986, Birmingham mounted a major bid to bring the 1992 Olympics to Birmingham. It lost out to Barcelona, but so raised the profile of the city, that huge inward investments followed. A feasibility study was done to see if a 'World Expo' could be brought to the city. This all boosted economic development strategies, and led on to arts strategies. The city's bid was to become a major cultural centre, and this led to housing the CBSO in the new Symphony Hall and bringing the Sadler's Wells Ballet from London in order to create the Birmingham Royal Ballet (BRB) in 1990. During the 1990s the BRB's new home in the Hippodrome Theatre, was to be totally rebuilt and reopened in 2001. The opera component of the strategy was less successful.

By 1992, Birmingham had three venues for exhibitions, conferences, trade shows and indoor sports events: (i) the NEC; (ii) the ICC; and (iii) the NIA. It developed a unified management to market and manage all three great venues. The marketing was focused on Birmingham as 'Europe's Meeting Place', and the Birmingham Marketing Partnership working jointly with the Birmingham Chamber of Commerce and Industry (BCCI) became a major player in the marketing and promotion field. Physical changes were reinforcing the strong identity and vitality of the place.

In the 1990s an events strategy, 'Towards the Millennium', changed the image of the city, catching up with the changing reality on the ground. In 1992 Birmingham was the UK's 'City of Music'. In 1993 it had an 'Early Music Festival', also by 1993 Birmingham City Pride was underway, and efforts were being made to get integrated urban strategies. In 1995 the city was voted 'UK's Cleanest City' and in 1996 it won the 'Britain in Bloom' competition. Finally, in 1998 three major events took place in the city: (i) the Eurovision Song Contest; (ii) the 24,000-delegate World Lions Congress; and (iii) the World's 'G8' Meeting – getting the world's media to focus positively upon

Birmingham as an event venue, for the first time! Manzoni's 'Motown' was re-emerging as a civilized city of quality and activity.

There was great expansion of the hotel sector, an explosion of the catering sector (Birmingham now has over 200 restaurants, some Michelin starred), and the number of events of national significance held in the city continued to grow (e.g. by 2002 Crufts International Dog Show and the British Motor Show were at the NEC, and Davis Cup tennis was at the NIA), while four major new tourist attractions were created in the city centre. These attractions were: (i) the National Sea Life Centre; (ii) the Ikon (Art) Gallery in Brindleyplace, (iii) the 1992 Jewellery Quarter Museum; and (iv) the National Trust 'Back to Backs' Museum that opened in 2004. All this, plus first-class shopping, meant Birmingham had become a major city-break tourist destination, in world terms, with impressive responses to its tourist marketing.

Landscape treatment

The landscape treatment of the resulting pedestrian realm of central Birmingham reflects and reinforces its transformation into a post-industrial city, where quality of surroundings provide a safe, attractive and varied pedestrian environment, with choices of places to walk, sit, eat, drink, relax, be entertained, educated, watch people or see events. Many resources have had to be transformed, to achieve this possibility. Former industry-serving canals have had to be cleaned, stocked with fish, their towpaths repaved and new access points and interpretation boards created. 'Pedestrian zones' have been created by removing vehicular traffic from streets and introducing mature trees, seats, quality paving and lights and a range of excellent sculpture, fountains and cascades. The ideas of a vibrant modern 'townscape', as first set out to the architectural and planning professions in the 1960s by Gordon Cullen, became the model for Birmingham. The high calibre of officers and staff members in the local authority meant that standards and costs were not compromised in this process.

Evaluation – the Effects of Change

The cleaning of the urban air is another posi-tive resource change: since the Clean Air Act became law, only smokeless fuels have been permitted in Birmingham and it now has very good air quality. Traffic removal has dimin-ished urban noise, dirt and vibration, making the city centre not only visually improved, but also quieter and more peaceful.

The pedestrian system is over 3 km in extent, and gives a choice of busy places and quiet places, with variations in mood and activity level at different times of day, week and year. Saturdays are very busy, and farm-ers' markets, German Christmas markets and street festivals provide highlights of atmos-phere and character. Creating civic squares such as Centenary Square, Chamberlain Square and Victoria Square, with their foun-tains, sculptures and large spaces, allow for the city to have major street exhibitions and events such as New Year's Eve celebrations, concerts and dances in the heart of the city. Even an urban beach has been introduced at the height of summer, and a temporary out-door ice rink in winter.

The canal sides have become lively places for cafés and nightlife, promenading and clubbing, while longboats on the canals offer trips and music events, and water-taxis are also on offer. Thus a city without a major river now uses its many miles of canals as a great recreational and amenity asset. Birmingham, as 'Europe's Meeting Place' is not only a great exhibition, conference and convention centre, but is a place where you now see the famous and the great from the worlds of politics, music and theatre, in its restaurants, shops, promenades and squares. The production of a post-industrial city, with a vibrant urban landscape, has been realized.

35 Sustainable Transport in and at Tourist Destination Areas (TDAs)

_____

Introduction

Tourist Destination Areas (TDAs) are described in detail by the author in his chapter 'Tourism destination area development (from theory into practice)' in Witt and Moutinho's _Tourism Marketing and Management Handbook_ (Travis, 1994a). In essence, TDAs are the areas within which the tourist finds all the components he or she requires for their holiday experience (i.e. the accommodation, the attractions, and all the support services that meet their require- ments during this leisure time). Just as the TDA should be made up of sustainable development elements, so also should the tourist transport be sustainable.

Three levels of tourist transport may be differentiated, in relation to TDAs:

- international and national travel _to_ the TDAs;
- transfers _within_ the TDAs themselves; and
- circulation _at_ the attraction, or in the city core, at the TDA.

Travel to the TDAs

Travel by tourists to the TDAs has already been addressed, earlier in the book in Chapter 9. There it was concluded that because of their much lower carbon footprint, the preferred travel mode (i.e. the more sustainable one) was the train or the coach, which were far less harmful than the use of travel modes such as the aeroplane, the sea ferry, ocean liner or petrol-driven car.

Transfers Within the TDAs

Transfers are characteristically the elements of the transport system that the tourist uses to travel from the transport arrival hub (be it rail- way station, coach station, sea port or airport) to the sleeping accommodation, or the transfer may be required from the hotel, pension, camp site or other accommodation, to the attractions, city centre or other required locations.

The preferred or more sustainable forms of transport, for such journeys include:

- Local trains, S-Bahns, light rail systems, U-Bahns, undergrounds or 'tubes', as found in for example Mumbai, Madrid, London, Moscow, Paris, Munich and New York.
- Cable cars are an attraction in them- selves, for example as in San Francisco, or Wellington, New Zealand.
- Urban funicular railways are sustainable and have special appeal, as seen in Naples, Italy or Haifa, Israel.
- Traditional and new 'super-trams' are available in a range of countries around the globe, from the UK and Austria, to Hong Kong, Melbourne, Australia and Christchurch in New Zealand (Fig. 35.1).

Fig. 35.1. Traditional trams are one of the forms of sustainable transport within cities (photograph by A.S. Travis).

- Rickshaws and cycle rickshaws are familiar eco-transport forms from the Far East and Pacific nations.
- Travel by bicycle grows increasingly easy in many places, not only in the Netherlands where cycle hire and use is readily available and there are plenty of bike stores and hire centres, and attractions like the Hoge Veluwe National Park, offers 400 white bikes, free to visitors. Some French cities make bike stocks available for ease of local city centre movement.
- Last, but most important, is movement on foot – especially with the growth of paved areas only for pedestrians, as seen in the range of examples given in the chapters here in Part IV.

Less sustainable, but very rich in identity and experience are the urban sea ferries of Istanbul, Hong Kong, Sydney and the smelly 'Vaporettos' of Venice!

Circulation at the Attractions, and in the Historic Cores

The sustainable transport priorities at tourist attractions, and within heritage or historic city centres, include:

- Travel on foot provides the greatest gains in terms of appreciation of the detailed environment, with chances to linger, sit, chat or window shop.
- Local travel by bike, preferably where there are cycle paths, cycle parking provision and lack of on-site conflict with pedestrians!
- At a water attraction, or waterside locale, then site travel by punt, gondola or canoe enriches the site experience (e.g. punting on the river in Oxford or Cambridge, UK, or Christchurch, New Zealand; gondola hire in Venice; or the electro-boats in Plitvice Lakes in Croatia).
- At large resorts or extensive city centres, the tram car is an acceptable transport form, especially where its design is traditional and characterful (as in Blackpool, UK, Lisbon, Portugal, or Melbourne, Australia).
- Local travel by mechanical 'Travelator', if powered by an alternative energy, can aid the movement of people over some distance, and if they are aged, physically disadvantaged or parents with small babies, then such aids may be very helpful, or even essential.

Part V

Local and Site Scale of Tourism and Leisure Services Planning

———————————

36 Heritage Conservation Planning, at the Site Scale: Management and Interpretation

Introduction

In this book, case studies have followed a descending spatial scale – from the national and supra-national scales, via the regional and subregional, down to the local, and finally the site or heritage attraction level. Many of the case studies throughout this book have emphasized a twin-planning focus – equally upon conservation and upon balanced development – so as to strive for sustainable development.

Heritage conservation action has been evident in regional plans in Poland, the Netherlands and Denmark, as in subregional work in the Tatras, or National Park planning and management at Plitvice in Croatia, or the Peak District National Park in the UK. Work done on the Heritage Trails in Slovenia, the Mid-Wales Festival of the Countryside and the UNEP's TCCA projects in the Mediterranean exemplify progressive examples. In an urban context, conservation work in the Old and New Towns of Edinburgh, Salzburg and Colonial Wiliamsburg provide models of good practice that could be templates for others across the world.

Here in Part V we turn now to the site level, or attraction scale of action, and examine a range of case studies which show the 'state of the art' in progressive modern practice – whether in the treatment of heritage sites or of attractions.

These range from sites of key historic events such as battlefields to regional parks, where large-scale tree-planting programmes start to help on a small scale towards combating global warming. No attempt is made to try to cover all categories of site attractions in this chapter, but a range of types are examined from theme parks with their heavy energy dependence, to converted landed estates (e.g. Beaulieu), the new 'museumology', and Dutch integrated leisure centres.

Heritage site conservation and interpretation can relate to buildings, historic ships, industrial architecture, gardens, birthplaces, sites associated with famous persons and historic events – the list is almost endless. In the late 20th century increasing attention was given to topics or categories which had been relatively neglected earlier, such as slavery, industrial archaeology, industrial working-class life and labour, immigration and emigration.

The challenges in the 21st century are:

- how we can help interpret new phenomena such as the megalopolises, to the poor millions who inhabit them in the developing world; and
- how we can sustain cultures and habitats that are at risk, whether they be of tribes like the Yamomani in the shrinking Amazon rainforest, nomadic desert peoples such as the Bedouin, the Tuaregs,

the Kalahari Bushmen or the Australian Aborigines, or of wetland cultures like those of the Marsh Arabs, and of their war-damaged marsh habitat, in Iraq.

Management challenges will increase, as the inadequacy of resource allocations, and shortage of skilled personnel in ecosystem management and maintenance, become evident at a time when environmental change will grow and Man may face unprecedented scales of challenge on this fragile and much-abused planet. The process of re-humanizing old cities, and especially former industrial cities in the Western world, has been an encouraging one, but the new one will be to ameliorate the unhealthy and dirty industrial agglomerations that are still growing in China, India and Third World countries. These include the megalopolises referred to earlier.

Heritage Interpretation

A vital educational and cultural activity which evolved in the 20th century is the interpretation of our heritage, or telling the stories of our natural and human history, at the locations where events and phenomena happened, or happen. The now classical work *Interpreting our Heritage* by Freeman Tilden (1978) in the USA defines this field as: 'An educational activity which aims to reveal meanings and relationships through the use of original objects, by first-hand experience, and by illustrative media, rather than simply to communicate factual information.'

This approach was first extensively developed under the auspices of the US National Park Service, but then taken and further developed widely, especially in Europe, North America and Australasia.

Some six general principles were developed by Tilden and the US National Park Service:

- Any interpretation that does not somehow relate to what is being displayed or described to something within the personality or experience of the visitor will be sterile.

- Information, as such, is not interpretation. Interpretation is revelation based upon information. But they are entirely different things. However, all interpretation needs information.
- Interpretation is an art, which combines many arts, whether the materials presented are scientific, historical or architectural. Any art is in some degree teachable.
- The chief aim of interpretation is not instruction, but provocation.
- Interpretation should aim to present a whole rather than a part.
- Interpretation addressed to children (say, up to the age of 12) should not be a dilution of the presentation to adults, but should follow a fundamentally different approach. To be at its best it will require a separate programme.

In applying Tilden's principles to site attractions, or heritage sites, it is useful to note that there are at least five alternative ways of providing heritage interpretation:

1. *In situ* (i.e. on site) – At the original location of the artefact, relic or event (e.g. at Culloden on the field where the battle took place, or in Plitvice Lakes National Park where you can see the karst limestone caves, lakes and waterfalls).
2. With original artefacts or exhibits – These may be grouped or presented not *in situ*, but in a visitor centre or museum on the heritage site (e.g. Gettysburg).
3. Away from the original site location – This would involve real artefacts, even whole original buildings, transferred to another site, to tell the story where the visitors live, not where the original buildings or events took place (e.g. Skansen in Stockholm, or Beamish in the north of England, UK).
4. Museum interpretation, distant from the original site – such as the Elgin Marbles from the Athens Parthenon, now in the British Museum in London, or original Pharaonic exhibits at the Egyptian Museum in Cairo. This is off-site, heritage interpretation, and distant from our current intent.

5. Storytelling in a museum context, using non-original artefacts – This is a relatively new type of environmental or social history presentation, which uses photography and inventive displays to tell complex stories (e.g. as in Urbis, an exhibition centre focusing on city life, in Manchester, or the history of the Jewish Diaspora, in a museum of that name, in Tel Aviv).

Our case studies in this chapter mainly focus upon examples of categories 1, 2 and 3, but special attention is also given to the new museumology which draws upon 3, 4 and 5.

37 Historic Sites: Case Studies of Three Battlefields

Introduction

Historic or heritage sites cover a vast array of categories ranging from castles and palaces, to industrial archaeology, archaeological sites, cave paintings and sites associated with the lives of famous people or great events. Few sites have greater emotional and historic weight than battlefields, as there so many died meaningfully or pointlessly. Battles have sometimes shaped nations and the values of peoples.

The great battlefields of the First and Second World Wars often still have meaning to millions. Thousands upon thousands died in the Battles of the Somme in the First World War and on the Normandy Beaches of 'D-Day' in the Second World War. Earlier battles and their sites still have significance for nations around the globe.

Gettysburg was the turning point in shaping the Federal nation of the USA in its Civil War; the Battle of Waterloo in Belgium was also a turning point, and the start of the end of the Napoleonic Wars in Europe, while Culloden Field in Scotland is the site of the last hand-to-hand battle on British soil, between the Scots and the English. The telling of the stories of these battles, their presentation and comparative treatment, now provides a focus for the next three case studies.

Case Study 1: Gettysburg, Virginia, USA

The site of the Battle of Gettysburg is now managed as the Gettysburg National Military Park, by the National Park Service (NPS) of the US Department of the Interior (Fig. 37.1). It is a very large site, where in the summer of 1863 a key 3-day battle of the US Civil War took place. Here, the Union (i.e. the North's) victory ended Confederate General Robert E. Lee's 'second and most ambitious invasion of the North'. Some historians refer to it as 'the high watermark of the Confederacy'. It was a long battle, and the bloodiest in the War, with some 51,000 casualties.

The battlefield is not a single field, but an extensive territory, whose coverage today by the visitor, involves a 17-mile, self-guided, auto-tour. The Military Park lies to the immediate south of the town of Gettysburg. Some elements of the historic site, such as the David Wills House, are located in the town itself.

A new US$135 million Gettysburg Museum and Visitor Center was opened in 2008. It was largely funded by donations to the Gettysburg Foundation. The scale of its backing reflects its high emotional appeal. The large building complex, with its surrounding car parks, can also be accessed from the railway station in Gettysburg. The new Center features a museum gallery on the Civil War, with detailed displays about a

©T. Travis 2011. *Planning for Tourism, Leisure and Sustainability* (T. Travis)

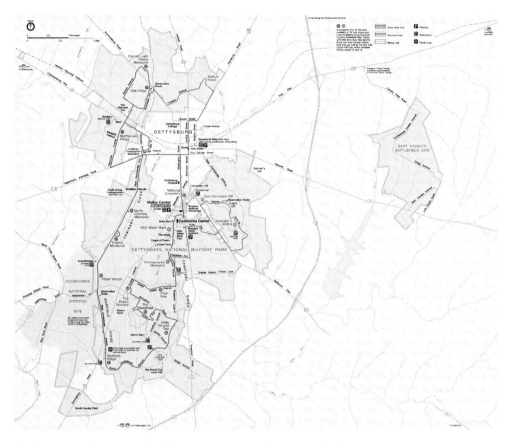

Fig. 37.1. Gettysburg National Military Park (courtesy of US National Park Service).

soldier's daily life in war. Every half-hour a film on the battle *A New Birth of Freedom* is shown, and this alternates with a 'Cyclorama' – a monumental painting in the round, of Pickett's Charge in the battle. A book store, library, research facilities, refreshments and toilets are all included in the generously large, if undistinguished building.

Evaluation

A summer ranger programme of excellent guided battlefield walks, 'Anniversary Battle Walks', and evening campfire events is offered. Maps for self-guided driving tours over the wider battlefield area are available. In the town, visitors can go to the David Wills House, now a museum, where President Abraham Lincoln

stayed and prepared his famous 'Gettysburg Address'. The large extent of the Military Park, and the rather non-descript external design of the new Visitor Center, detract somewhat from the skilled storytelling by the NPS of the battle and the war, but the site remains a popular and important cultural tourist destination for Americans, and is seen as part of their identity formation, and not just a remote event in time.

Case Study 2: Culloden, Scotland, UK

The Culloden Battlefield, in the north of Scotland, near Inverness, relates to the last land battle to take place on British soil, in 1746. It is where an English army of King George III fought and defeated the Scots Jacobite army of the 'Young Pretender', Bonnie Prince Charlie.

The redesign and treatment of the single site, which is a definable stretch of moorland, was the subject of an international architectural competition, held by the National Trust for Scotland (NTS) in 2003. The competition was won by Gareth Hoskins Architects, an impressive Glasgow firm, which was then commissioned to build and furnish their designed building and its site treatment. The site is a remarkably complete one in archaeological terms, and 2000 dead soldiers' bodies still lie beneath this bleak moor.

The architects have carefully sited a sensitively handled and beautiful building in a corner of the site, strategically located relative to the battle lines, as well as carefully screening the visitor parking from the moor which was the battlefield site. It remains an atmospheric place. A 150-m long wall, rising out of the landscape, gives access to the green roof, which is also a viewing point over the battlefield. The layout of the building is logical and clear, and the design and materials used are both sympathetic and honestly modern (Fig. 37.2), unlike the Gettysburg Center. The building contains reception, shop, exhibition, audio-visual displays, education suite, staff areas, restaurant and toilets. It tells the story of the battle in a lively and clear way. Maps and audio-visual displays explain the battle, and the views from the rooftop and the walks around the open and undisturbed site give a full and rewarding experience to the visitor (Fig. 37.3).

Evaluation

The battleground on the open moor is undisturbed, the few paths are un-intrusive, and the one original feature of the Leonach Cottage, with its three surrounding trees, act as a statuesque monumental group on the bleak and moody, open moor. The building design and its treatment both of the battle story and of the visitor are exemplary in modern, unpretentious design terms.

Culloden is a model of how such historic sites should be handled today.

Fig. 37.2. The visitor centre at Culloden: the scalloped roofs are over the public spaces in the building (photograph by Andrew Lee).

Fig. 37.3. View from the battlefield of the new visitor centre at Culloden (photograph by Andrew Lee).

Case Study 3: Waterloo, Belgium

Introduction

The Waterloo Battlefield site of 1815 is located close to Brussels in Belgium, and is one of the most significant historic sites in Europe. Here was fought Napoleon's last great battle of the Napoleonic Wars, one that involved no less than 350,000 soldiers, not only from France and the UK, but also from Germany, Holland and other countries. The site covers a rural plain of about 500 ha, divided between several private farms and crossed by a major regional road. The site is protected under a 1914 law, but because there was nearly a 100-year wait to get such action, there is a plurality of land ownership and interests which made the possibility of achieving a global management plan seem like a pipe dream, as late as the 1990s. Then some 15 historical associations were competing to put forward their own ideas of how to treat this important site. Farming was still taking place on the site, and the visit to Waterloo was a confusing one for visitors. Some 300,000 visitors come to the battlefield annually, almost as many in number as the soldiers who fought here in 1815.

Coordinated action

In the last 15 years it has been possible to get public and private interests together, and a project has achieved federating these initiatives, through a single development plan focused on the cluster of attractions around the Visitor Centre, next to 'La Butte du Lion' or the Lion's Mound – an artificial tumulus, created between 1823 and 1826, on the site where the Prince of Orange was wounded.

The implemented project offers the visitor a single ticket, which enables entry or visits to a whole range of attractions/points of historical interest on the site. A common marketing policy has been adopted, buildings adapted for larger scale visiting, signs coordinated, organized battlefield tours offered and a regular programme of animation and events achieved. Unlike the US situation where the Gettysburg National Military Park is owned and operated by the Federal State, or the Scottish situation where NTS, a major voluntary-sector agency, manages the heritage site, the Belgians have used a public–private sector mix to achieve a compromise arrangement that employs a commercial agency to act on behalf of a federation of interests. The online web site now tries to give a coordinated package of offers to the interested visitor.

A planned cultural trail, now called 'The Battlefield Tour', takes visitors on a 45–50-minute ride in a specially adapted vehicle to the positions of the English batteries, the French cavalry charges and to strategic points on the battlefield, such as the Hougoumont and Mont St Jean farms. Official registered guides provide the commentaries.

The central cluster of attractions is located next to the Lion's Mound and comprises:

- The Visitor Centre, with all catering, interpretation and sales services, and adjacent car parking. A Russian film of the 1815 Battle is shown here. A library, bookshop and battle display model are also provided.
- The Wax Museum situated in an old hotel of 1818, founded by a British sergeant major.
- The Panorama – a huge circular gallery containing a 1912 canvas painting of the battle.
- The Lion's Mound itself – whose 226 steps may be climbed to view the battlefield (if you are fit, and not physically disabled).

Across the battlefield there are no less than 40 interactive kiosks, with information in four languages, explaining what happened at these key historical points on the field of battle. The kiosks deal not only with phases of the battle, but also museums and headquarters, commemorative buildings, historic sites and other attractions. On the site is the Hougoumont Farm where one of the deadliest periods of the battle occurred.

Off-site, in the heart of the town of Waterloo, is the Wellington Museum, where the Duke of Wellington lodged. Napoleon had his last headquarters at 'Le Caillou' Farm located on-site some 5 km from the central cluster of attractions.

Animation and events

The Waterloo site now offers events and animation of three sorts:

- daily happenings such as 'firing the cannon', 'infantry parades' and 'cavalry exercises' carried out by actors in costume (i.e. 'animations by animateurs');
- son et lumière and firework displays; and
- less frequent events which include a large event held every year on the 18 June to commemorate the battle and a full re-enactment of the battle held every 5 years that can attract up to 100,000 visitors.

Evaluation

As late as 1992 when plans for changes to the then anarchic arrangements at the site were announced, it seemed that the proposed changes were unlikely, and the prospects sadly disappointing. Now all the planned changes have occurred, and a coordinated offer is given by the 'Culture Spaces' Company, which is coherent, if at times a little confusing, as there are 135 commemorative monuments on the site created by different interest groups in the past, so the site has a rather 'busy' feel to it, compared with the bleak, open and moody moor of the Culloden field in Scotland. It is to be welcomed that the initiative has succeeded though, but it is sad that successive Belgian governments did not intervene earlier to protect and control the site, and prevent the 'rag bag of elements' that interested parties feel they had the right to put here. There are some memorable-experience elements at Waterloo, but as an overall product, it is not in the same league of heritage site interpretation, as Gettysburg and Culloden.

38   Tivoli: a Unique Danish 'Pleasure Ground' and Theme Park

Introduction

Tivoli in Copenhagen is the most important urban leisure resource or facility in Denmark (Fig. 38.1). At least three other attractions of a similar type are found in the same country: (i) 'Tivoli Friheden' in Århus; (ii) Karoline-Lund in Aalborg; and (iii) 'Dyrehaven' in a forest area to the north of Copenhagen. In the context of international comparisons, the inclusion of Copenhagen's Tivoli is essential. It provides an historic yardstick against which to measure American theme parks, and special British attractions, such as the Beaulieu Estate.

The first question which must be asked is: 'What is Tivoli?' Originally, it comprised a 20-acre green segment next to Copenhagen's classic system of defence ramparts and was made up of networks of water areas, geometrically laid out dykes, ditches and bastions. The landscape base gave rise to its modern 'fairy-tale urban garden quality'. It still has a garden gate for entry. It is a place for a choice of activities: one in which to wander and relax, to eat, to play, to drink, to watch or to participate actively or where to be passive. The Tivoli Company sets out to cater for the needs of: (i) old and young alike; (ii) residents and tourists for recreation; (iii) those with low and high income; and (iv) users who range from the sophisticated to those whose requirements are basic. It is an attraction that is open for three seasons, and closed annually from January to March.

Tivioli's resources include:

- natural resources – such as lakes, gardens, trees and walks;
- built resources – including open-air theatres, funfairs, playgrounds, many restaurants, cafés, bars, a pantomime theatre (Fig. 38.2), a major concert hall, conference centre, amusement arcades, park benches and follies; and
- activities – linked to the use of these resources which are cultural, commercial, recreational and educational – spanning longstanding live traditions of pantomimes, firework displays, orchestral concerts and marching bands.

The long life of this set of offers, rely on activities that go back to the time of Copenhagen's Tivoli and Vauxhall's opening celebrations in 1843. At that time, London's equivalent pleasure grounds were at Vauxhall and Ranelagh Gardens, while Paris had its Jardin du Tivoli, all of which were enjoying their social and economic heyday. The English attractions died before the end of the 19th century. Tivoli, however, thrives until now, dealing with over four million visitors p.a. in 2007! Its central location at the heart of Copenhagen, immediately adjacent to the city's shopping core and surrounded by central transport termini and

Fig. 38.1. 2009 plan of Tivoli Gardens, Copenhagen (photograph courtesy of Tivoli Gardens).

interchanges, give it peak accessibility by train, bus and car, but also by air (via nearby urban air terminals), and it is within easy distance of both sea ferries and the rail-and-road bridge to Sweden. It is a 'central place' in its own right.

Tivoli Management Criteria

Tivoli management criteria may be considered under three subheadings, namely:

(i) economic; (ii) social; and (iii) skills bases and labour force.

Economic

Tivoli is run by a highly competitive commercial company, dealing with a large turnover or throughput and is based on: (i) strict product quality control; (ii) high repeat trade;

Fig. 38.2. Tivoli's Pantomime Theatre is sometimes called the 'Peacock Theatre' and is created and decorated in Chinese style (photograph by A.S. Travis).

and (iii) low per capita turnover, yet long-life profitability. Entry charges are variable in order to boost use at quieter times, and to dampen down periods of high demand. A range of 'free activities', such as concerts, firework displays and acrobatics, are included in the entry charge.

The Tivoli also has a rental income from many concessionary lettings, including restaurants, retail shops and some forms of entertainment. The concessionaires pay the company a rent equal to 10–35% of their total income, less tax. The company's total turnover was equal to £14.5 million in 1974/5 and by 2007/8 this had increased to DKr1031 million, or equal to approximately £120 million by 2007.

Social appeal and economic viability reinforce the Tivoli 'product'. By 1975 over 200 million visitors had already passed through its turnstiles, since it was first opened. With annual visitor throughput of about four million, daily visitor levels can be as high as 60,000. The record number of visits in 1 day was in 1943, during the Nazi occupation, when in a protest 'show of faith' occasion, 112,000 people crammed into Tivoli!

The theme park's economy needs a mix of tourist support and resident recreation, but generates pressures upon the quality of the environment, which the Tivoli Company have to work hard to maintain. Some 40,000 local people buy season tickets, which cover a season from 1 May to 30 September.

Social

In essence Tivoli is not just amusement gardens and a park, but a social institution, steeped in tradition. It is at the core of the city's way of life, part of its external self-image, as well as reflecting Copenhagen's spirit. The core of its support comes from those who are season ticket holders, who live in Copenhagen itself. Its pattern of activities gives it a wide social base, fulfilling its set objective to provide a variety of activities for everyone – aged from one to 90, regardless of their income level. The high quality of product maintenance means that not only are design and management standards high, but the landscapes are designed to deal with variable set capacities in different parts of Tivoli. Marketing and promotion, combined with social response to name, reputation and experienced reality, lead to the management's achieving its social goal of continuing to attract simultaneously both young and old. A stock of familiar facilities and activities is balanced by a number of new features added annually to give variety, interest and change, without disturbing the provided sense of continuity.

Skills bases and labour force

The Tivoli Company has built up and maintained a skills base in planning, marketing, site management and visitor management. The Tivoli Company employs a total labour force of 1200 people which includes a permanent core staff of 500 people who cover planning, administration, management, marketing and waiting staff. Tivoli has its own architects, engineers and skilled tradespeople. There is a 'house style' at Tivoli, and this is reflected in site design work, marketing and management.

Evaluation: Goals versus Realization

Tivoli's objective is 'to provide something for everyone from the age of one to the age of 90'. The range of age groups using Tivoli, the dedication of its 'regulars', and the continuing appeal of this attraction to tourists, both domestic and international, are the base of Tivoli's economic success. Its location, spirit, character and management advantages, suggest a sustainable future, as well as a long history. Quality maintenance of visitor experience, the fit of product reality to the marketed image and expectation – whether at its exquisite restaurants, such as the Michelin-starred Paul, and the Herman, its many popular cafés, bars and beer haunts, or in its sophisticated flower gardens. Tivoli only has 20 acres of land, yet it achieves great variety for four million visitors p.a.

Tivoli management is not complacent. While recognizing their historical leadership role internationally, they constantly innovate in their offers and monitor performance, and that of their competitors. They are aware of environmental issues and monitor: (i) electricity consumption; (ii) impacts of traffic generation; and (iii) its production of wastes.

Tivoli successfully appeals to the whole family by introducing its pubs, cafés, orchestras, concerts, bands and firework displays in an integrated layout, without subdivision for age or market segments. It is a mini-city along whose pedestrian boulevards and walks you can constantly make choices: to opt in or to opt out; to pay or to go to 'free activities'; be gregarious or isolated; or be crude or sophisticated in your choices. This is the nature of the varied appeal Tivoli constantly offers its loyal clientele.

39 US Heritage Parks and High-capacity Theme Parks in Virginia

Introduction

The US State of Virginia has a tripartite heritage park called the Colonial National Historical Park (CNHP), and it has attracted 'theme parks' to be sited nearby. First, it is necessary to define the term 'theme parks'. A theme park is an amusement park, which has one overall design theme, or is divided into several themed areas. For example, such themes can be a 'Wild West' area or an 'African Safari Park'. Theme parks are generally developed by commercial developers as profitable businesses. They provide for big throughput of visitors, at high-density use of site, with a large choice of leisure and amusement attractions. It is the quality of their presentation, providing opportunities for entertainment, recreation, and sometimes education, which enables them to attract thousands, or even millions of visitors annually.

Theme parks, particularly in the USA, have increasingly become a significant focus of tourism and recreation provision since the 1960s. Because of their wide appeal, their professional development and management, they have been able to deal with mass visitation, yet still maintain high quality of provision, and achieve high levels of safety. The theme parks effectively market their offers. They can serve a strategic role in environmental conservation, as they can act as 'honey pots', which can deflect and draw off mass visitor pressures from more sensitive sites. Thus they can aid and complement sensitive natural resource sites, and built or cultural heritage attractions of limited capacity. Theme parks are designed to handle very high capacities. Disney World, opened in Florida in the 1970s, had 11 million visitors in its first year, equal to the number of foreign tourists visiting London annually in that period!

Visitor numbers to theme parks, that were first developed in the USA and later spread to Europe, Asia and Australasia, reflect the scale of their mass market appeal. This magnetic draw has to be analysed, and compared to more traditional amusement parks and pleasure grounds, such as Tivoli. It is also necessary to explain the totally different approach taken at the CNHP in Virginia to that in the theme parks.

Heritage Park and Theme Parks

The CNHP of Virginia (shown on Fig. 39.1) is an important national outdoor museum, comprising three key sites from the original Elizabethan settlement period in the 1600s. Its central focus is Colonial Williamsburg, which is described in detail in Chapter 32. That original capital is linked by a Colonial

Fig. 39.1. The Colonial National Historical Park (CNHP) of Virginia (courtesy of US Travel Service).

Parkway to the sites of the two original riverside settlements: (i) Jamestown on the James River; and (ii) Yorktown on the York River. In Jamestown research-based reconstructions of first settlers' homes have been built on the original foundations. At the port of Jamestown, a festival park, with exact replicas of the three original ships that brought the 140 settlers here, has been created. As at Williamsburg, high quality restoration, animation by costumed staff and on-site interpretation, provide a live museum attraction of great integrity.

By comparison, one finds Busch Gardens – 'The Old Country' theme park – on the James River, near Williamsburg. It is basically a large amusement park, with themes relating to the 'Old countries from which migrants came to America'. Thus Germany and Oktoberfest are next to France/Aquitaine, and England. Rides and water splashes supposedly represent the iconic features of Paris, Munich and so on. All is crude pastiche, with opportunities for sale of junk foods and crude souvenirs. There is no integrity in the offer, and no attempt is made to educate, or have any cultural or artistic

function. Its quality is far below that of the Walt Disney World Resort in Florida. In the Disney case a huge tourist resort is made up of five huge theme parks, a beach resort, and an inland resort of hotels, shopping and catering outlets. Disney is pastiche, but has integrity in its quality of management, presentation, hygiene and interpretation. It is an unreal escapist dream world in the sun, which can 'pack in' the millions of clients, but in no way is it 'heritage', and with its dependence on air and car access, it is not environmentally sustainable.

Virginia Attractions – Accessibility and Catchment

The CNHP has attracted two theme parks to be developed in its vicinity – Busch Gardens and Kings Dominion – both belonging to commercial chains. The whole area is approximately 3 hours' drive by car from Washington, DC, or 2.2 hours' drive from the edge of the USA's east coast megalopolis. The megalopolis that stretches from Washington to Boston contains a resident population of over 36 million.

This catchment area generates great demand for entertainment and heritage attractions. With freeway systems, a major airport at Richmond, Virginia, and effective marketing, demand and supply are easily linked. With very high levels of private mobility, the population of the 'North-East' look south to better weather and quality attractions.

The roles and use of the theme parks is relevant to planning for tourism and conservation in Virginia. As a result of market responses rather than planning, a deflection of large-scale visitation partly to the theme parks enables the more limited capacity of the heritage park to function satisfactorily. The high capacity theme parks are the 'honey pots' which draw off the surplus visitors. As was shown in the Clyde model in Chapter 13, and in the capacity planning used in the Danish Silkeborg National Park, a theory of balance can be used to handle visitor levels at inter-related provisions. In Virginia, this has evolved as a market response; elsewhere it can be achieved by tourist destination area strategies for development and conservation.

What has evolved in Virginia reflects such an approach. The CNHP, with its built heritage and natural heritage sites, has limited absorption capacities, and variable sensitivity levels to visitor pressures. The high-capacity nearby theme parks absorb surplus pressures, and enable the managed visitor capacity in the heritage park to function, and achieve quality maintenance and sustainability.

Recognition of the different cultural, educational and entertainment roles of these very different tourist attractions is critical. The heritage sites are a quality museum based on research, renovation, reconstruction, integrity and interpretation. The theme parks are elaborate commercial entertainment complexes, with profitable attractions and rides; they are hard selling and fun offering, but make no attempt to provide any integrity in the cultural or historical realms. Thus the roles and character of theme parks and of heritage attractions may differ fundamentally, but their uses and targeted markets may complement each other.

Evaluation

It is interesting to evaluate the location, and the 'story base' used by each of the Virginia theme parks. Generally their displays or stories do not relate to their location or to their principal themes. As indicated, Busch Gardens sells itself as 'the Old Country', but the architectural examples used are crudely from the UK, France and Germany. The Kings Dominion does have its 'Old Virginia Area', plus its 'International Street', and a supposedly scaled-down model of the Eiffel Tower in Paris next to a 'safari country'. The geographical combination is confused and disorientating! The choice of siting in relation to markets is good, and makes the parks viable for their financial backers. However, American user-transport still primarily relates to the love of the private automobile. Kings Dominion is sited adjacent to Inter State 95, and has its own slip road into the site. Busch Gardens' siting is related to its proximity to Colonial Williamsburg, and has a high carbon footprint, with 92% of its clients coming to it by car.

In terms of site capacity, theme parks as major attractions have a visitor capacity which is perceived in perceptual rather than absolute physical terms. Busch Gardens often experiences visitor numbers of 25,000–30,000 per day, while the Disney theme parks in Florida deal with massively greater daily numbers. The management approach to capacity handling in such places is focused on avoiding 'too much congestion', to prevent visitors having to wait too long for rides, by heightening the feeling of personal involvement and enjoyment, and using on-site, mass-transit means of increasing traffic flow, without diminishing the visitor experience. To demonstrate this, Busch Gardens use a fleet of London buses to transfer visitors from peripheral car parks to the main entrance. As in Williamsburg, extravagant, edge-of-site, space consumption for car parking is vital, but visitors accept mass transit transfers to the site proper, so as to have on-site freedom as a pedestrian, when finally there.

In summary, what may be said then on the general value of theme parks? They have been commercially successful and profitable for their promoters and investors. Socially they have proved useful as places of mass recreation and escapist fun for their users, even though their evident lack of integrity is noted. In Virginia, their deflection role has aided protection of the sensitive natural resources of the Shenandoah Valley, and the built and cultural heritage resources of the CNHP of Virginia. The sustainability of theme parks is both connected with addressing their very high-energy use on site, and the huge carbon footprint of their primarily car-based clientele. While attractions in Europe are starting to address their high energy use problem, this happens more slowly in the USA. The changeover from the petrol-driven car to vehicles that are relatively carbon neutral is slower than is needed, but as and when it comes it could advantageously change the carbon impact of theme parks.

40 The New Museumology – Site Interpretation and Animation

Introduction

Children's fairy tales start with the line of 'once upon a time', so in a storytelling mode, let us review the history of the new museumology! Once upon a time there was a building called a 'museum', it was a big, dark, musty place, where they preserved and maintained a set, or many sets of original artefacts. They were put in secure showcases, in which they put pins through 50 types of butterfly, or 25 types of ship model, or 250 types of drab ancient pots. They were all real objects, and locked up, and looked after by curators and conservators, who conserved them. Your school teacher, or your parents on a wet day, would force you to go to such places, to stop you getting bored, keep you out of the puddles, and expect you to study and learn, so that you improved your mind in that way. It was a quiet and serious place, not fun, as it was for your 'improvement'.

It was all the opposite of 'fun places' like fairs! As in ancient times, the medieval world developed its commercial and recreational meeting places, and these were rural markets or 'fairs'. They were linked to the religious and natural cycle of the year. The fair became a bawdy place, for fun, games, entertainment, dance and music, as well as trade. These rustic traditions have continued through to the modern American State Fair, in the UK to the Nottingham Goose Fair, and in Germany to the Christmas Fairs.

Over time rural traditions at fairs and circuses were linked to the skills of new showmen, like the Barnums in the USA and the Chipperfields in the UK, and equipment evolved from coconut shies and roundabouts to elaborate swings, carousels and paid entertainers. A commercial rationale and hedonistic working-class traditions became married to those of the theatre and of side shows. Separate buildings for fairs became permanent fairgrounds and urban amusement parks.

The pleasure garden evolved: first in France, and then via 18th-century UK places like Vauxhall and Ranelagh Gardens in London, on to great continuing amusement places such as Tivoli Gardens in Copenhagen. Tivoli is a total contrast to the 19th-century museum. Elements in modern Toronto's Ontario Place have their roots in Tivoli. Commerce and shopping are part of this new type of experience, which draws upon folk traditions – both urban and rural. The 19th-century museums were all unconnected to this story, until the end of the 19th century.

Urban museums, like libraries, baths and gymnasia, were all essentially part of the Victorian belief in social improvement and learning. Encyclopedic information collection, classification and storage were remote from storytelling and the fun of the fair;

remote too from the idea of heritage interpretation. The idea of having fun was remote from the notion of the Victorian library.

How then did it change, and why did some developments in remote Sweden, lead towards a coming together of so many things that had been opposites?

The Skansen Story

Throughout Europe in the 19th century, industrialization led to urbanization: people left the countryside for work in the towns. In Sweden it was feared that the migration would lead to a loss of rural customs, occupations and architecture. Arthur Hazelius, a man who had already founded the Nordic Museum, came to create 'Skansen' in Stockholm (Fig. 40.1). This was an open-air museum, where over time, he brought 150 original houses from all over Sweden, and one from Norway, to reconstruct them on site, interpret them with costumed craftsmen and women, demonstrate crafts, dance, music and give chances to dine, have snacks and enjoy rural fun. Thus the bridge was made between the museum story and that of the rural fun-fair story.

By 2009 the Skansen Open Air Museum was attracting over 1.3 million visitors p.a. It is a museum, a zoo with a wide range of Scandinavian animals, a fun fair, a social meeting place, a place to eat, to drink and to have fun. It also embodies the finest rural live architecture collection anywhere – so it is a place of learning, where the interpretation is done lightly and effectively. 'Craftsmen in traditional dress such as tanners, shoemakers, silversmiths, bakers and glass blowers demonstrate their skills in period surroundings' to quote the Skansen web site (www.skansen.se accessed 1 October 2010).

The Skansen model was an innovative lead that was the forerunner for Denmark's 'Frilandsmuseet', and Wales' National Folk Museum at St Fagans. Furthermore, the idea of the outdoor museum also came to be applied to the industrial folk museum, now found in diverse places such as: (i) Lowell in the USA; (ii) Beamish, Ironbridge Gorge and the Black Country in England; and (iii) Roros in Norway. In France and French Canada/Quebec the Écomusée movement has extended the idea of costumed animation out into widespread community participation, identification and social ownership of such industrial and rural community 'Skansens'. The creative fun elements of the fun fair and the pleasure garden have become absorbed into the reinvigorated 'museums', and step by step more traditional museums have modified and modernized their interpretation methods, and some can beat commercial theme parks at their own game of lively presentation, without any loss of curatorial integrity.

Innovation in Mainstream Museums

The revolution in museum presentation techniques and design of interactive exhibits are evident in selected places across the globe today. They include:

- the Astronaut Training Experience at the Kennedy Space Center in Florida, USA;
- the almost totally reconstructed Vasa, the Swedish 17th-century wooden royal warship in Stockholm, with its films and displays;
- the voluntary-sector run MOTAT, Auckland's Museum of Transport and Technology in New Zealand;
- the interactive science exhibits at the London Science Museum;
- the anthropological collections and displays at the musée du quai Branly, Paris;
- the interactive family search opportunities at the Museum of the Jewish Diaspora in Tel Aviv; and
- the extraordinarily inventive new Darwin Centre, at the Natural History Museum, London.

Site innovations

On-site, progressive, environmental interpretation has often become light in touch and low cost compared with these multi-million museum developments. Length of walks on mountain trails in the Polish Tatra National

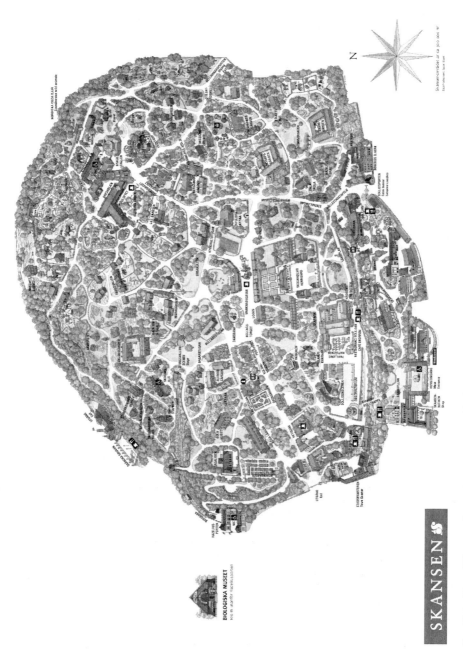

Fig. 40.1. Plan of Skansen Open Air Museum, Stockholm (courtesy of Skansen, Sweden).

Park are identified by colour spots on the trees – one colour indicates a walk of an hour, another colour a walk of 2 or 3 hours. Similarly in Norway branches laid on the snow in winter, by volunteers, indicate the trail for cross-country skiers.

The animation developed by use of costumed craftsmen and guides at Skansen, and at Colonial Williamsburg, has been taken much further in some of the industrial folk museums. At Wigan Pier, in Lancashire, England, sadly no longer open, the use of a team of specially trained actors, each for a period of up to 6 months, took animation to a new level. Here, not only were visitors taken into a classroom, and subjected to a fairly accurate Edwardian school lesson, complete with finger-nail inspections and hair inspections for lice, but visitors would also experience a 'wake'. In a room, by the coffin of a deceased coal miner, the grieving son would welcome visitors to the tribute occasion, give an oration of his dad's life, and accept condolences from the visitors as if consoling friends and relatives. One could see tourists so engaged by the performance that some would cry, and others would seriously try to comfort the grieving son. As a way of involving visitors in the past life of a mining community it was a brilliant re-enactment that must have been exhausting for the performers.

Theme parks started with Disneyland in 1955, and by 1983 had a Disneyland Tokyo, with Euro-Disney then at the planning stage. By the year 2000, individual theme park developments in Asia, Europe and the Americas were involving investments of from £20 million to £600 million, but again, as at Wigan Pier, it is the lessons of interpretation and animation, which are their most interesting innovations. Already by the time that 'EPCOT' ('Experimental Prototype Community of Tomorrow') was developed by Disney in Florida, the divide between interactive exhibits, computer games, fun-fair elements and the related roles of playing animators had vanished. There is now a fund of techniques shared by theatre, museums, theme parks and écomusées, so the definitional problem of what an attraction is categorized as, is a growing one!

Evaluation: Convergence

In summary, arising from this review, the reality is becoming one of integration and convergence of many ideas and applications, whereby:

1. Tourist, recreational, entertainment, shopping mall, theme park and museum site designers are now increasingly drawing upon a shared new set of elements that include interpretation, animation, trading components, catering and refreshment facilities, and services. What were distinctly museums, or leisure complexes, or shopping malls in the past, now become confusing mixes of each other.

2. Separate buildings for separate uses are increasingly giving way to an integrated range of uses. This will be seen further in Chapter 43, where Dutch developments may end the old idea of a town centre, or neighbourhood centre made up of different building uses.

3. What were separate outdoor and indoor activities on separate sites increasingly combine in the same complex with shared management and/or shared ownership.

4. Urban central destination space, which in some cities – in terms of their use – was split into areas used by separate classes or different religious groups (e.g. in Belfast), will increasingly be shared, but its components will attract different sub-markets.

5. Hosts (i.e. residents) and guests (i.e. tourists/visitors) can share facilities or attractions that were previously designed for either tourists or hosts, but the interests and well-being of the host group must be put before that of the visitors, if this relationship is to be sustainable socially and economically.

Site users at tourist destinations may want variety and change – they want stimulus but risk limitation, interest but not real challenge. Containable risks mean eliminating mugging in Barcelona, preventing hijacking in Rome, and not being bombed in a Mumbai hotel, nor irradiated in Chernobyl or Kiev. Interpretation and animation can upgrade the quality of experience at sites, but the associated order of risks needs to be controlled if a destination's offers are to be sustainable.

41 Regional Park Systems, Identity and Outdoor Recreation in Metropolitan Areas

Introduction

The parks, 'piazzas', 'bois' and woods within the world's great cities are vital to their identity, appeal and quality of life – both for residents and for tourists. Paris is unthinkable without the Bois de Boulogne, the Parc des Buttes Chaumont, the Jardin des Tuileries and its urban 'places' or squares. Similarly, London's appeal would be diminished without Hampstead Heath, Hyde Park, Trafalgar Square and St James's Park. However, our parks and green squares are a relatively new heritage resource in our cities.

England was the first country to go through the processes of industrialization, and the consequent uncontrolled urbanization, with its attendant urban chaos, dangers and risks. Urban park development was largely a product of municipal enterprise, within the context of necessary public health administration. Cholera and tuberculosis in the 19th-century towns threatened life and economic production. Public health legislation was reluctantly introduced for economic survival. Housing standards, sanitation and parks were all by-products of this survival response. The first UK ameliorative Health Act was in 1848, and the first municipally provided urban park was in the year 1847 at Birkenhead, in the new port-city cluster on Merseyside.

Across the Atlantic, from the UK, New York's Central Park was the first of a new wave of provisions in the Americas. In the burgeoning cities of 19th-century America, it was a struggle to save blocks of land for outdoor recreation in urban areas, from the relentless building developer. New York, America's largest metropolis in the 19th century, had an urban population of 700,000 by 1850. Population in the city had trebled in half a century. Cities were becoming synonymous with crime, overcrowding, immigrant poverty and lack of green space.

It took 10 years of discussion, pressure, bargaining and friction, before New York could agree to put aside a land block of 629 acres to create a central 'greensward', to become the city's Central Park. An independent Park Commission was appointed, which sponsored a design competition that was won by Olmsted and Vaux. These landscape architects created the imaginatively designed great urban park, after looking at progressive European experience. New York's Central Park was opened in 1862/3 and revolutionized concepts of urban park design, not only in America but worldwide. One large park offered an inventive range of outdoor recreational opportunities for a metropolis. Fabos, Milde and Weinmayr tell the full story in *Frederick Law Olmsted Senior – Founder of Landscape Architecture in America* (Fabos *et al.*, 1968).

Olmsted went on from this project to revolutionize concepts of metro park provision across the North American continent. Central Park became not only New York's identifying park but one beloved by residents, and a magnet for tourists. Influenced by what he saw in Baron Haussmann's Paris, about urban park networks, Olmsted's ideas shaped park developments in Montreal, New York, Buffalo, Rochester and the metro project for parks in Boston, Massachusetts after 1875.

Parks and Urban Leisure Systems – 1860s

By 1869 urban commentators, such as William Robinson in his seminal work *The Parks, Promenades and Gardens of Paris*, was already evaluating the complex leisure provisions of Haussmann's Paris, and showing London that urban leisure provision involved not just providing urban parks and informal outdoor recreation, but also sports and recreation grounds, walks, playgrounds, lakeside and riverside promenades, woods, plant nurseries, sitting areas, cafés, toilets and the gamut of publically provided entertainment in the parks. From such roots, and from the development of public wash houses and pools, a vast range of elements were to develop by the 20th century. Reactions to water-based urban diseases are at the root of our later leisure provisions.

Anticipating 1980s' Integrated Leisure Services

From the remote roots in American and French park initiatives can be seen the eventual growth of Integrated Leisure Services departments in the UK, so that by the 1980s one could find examples of progressive British practice in places as varied as urban Greenwich Leisure Services, as developed under C. Field, or Torfaen District's Leisure Services, in the valleys of industrial South Wales, by J. Munn.

Integrated Leisure Services is the ultimate stage in such developments, beyond separate functional departments, and providing:

- parks, woodlands, heaths, walks, playgrounds for different age groups, walks and the full range of opportunities for active and passive outdoor recreation;
- sports and playing fields provision (including maintenance systems), within and separate from parks, including changing rooms and showers in pavilions;
- swimming and leisure pools;
- libraries and information services; and
- cultural and arts provisions, that may include theatres, art galleries, museums, exhibition facilities and related public events and animation.

Mass spectator sports, such as football, were to remain the realm of the voluntary sector and then the commercial sectors.

Nineteenth-century innovations were at the root of our later Western world models of provision. For example Boston's Metropolitan Park System was developed by Olmsted and Vaux for the new Park Commission that was set up in 1875 to develop a general park system. Olmsted and Vaux's genius converted local problems of drainage, flooding and nuisance from smells into opportunities to create parks and lake systems, that solved the past problems and created new links to commons, waterways and existing spaces, thereby creating an edging 'emerald necklace' or park system around Metro Boston. Because of high inner urban land values, most big cities try to create a few compensatory parks out on the urban fringe where land is cheaper. Boston showed how to evolve systemic answers to public open space needs.

Even by the 21st century, many major post-industrial cities, such as Birmingham in the UK, provided over time some compensatory urban-fringe park provisions, but as shown in *Recreation and the Urban Fringe* by Travis and Veal (1976) they were using a 'rag bag of ad hoc agencies' to plan and manage them. The great historic city of Amsterdam, even by the late 20th century, was also demonstrating 'the mockery of ad-hockery' in the range of national, regional and joint-local agencies upon which it had to rely to plan and to manage its major parks, on the outer urban periphery. To see good models of metro park systems, we can look back to Boston in the 1890s, or to another remarkable model that was to emerge in the USA around 1940, in the Detroit Metropolitan Region, with the creation of the Huron–Clinton Metropolitan Authority (HCMA). It is paradoxical that in the 'land of free enterprise' we find two of the most interesting regional park-system templates of public sector joint planning.

'Green Infrastructure' in 2010

By the 21st century progressive practice in planning, landscape design and ecology have all come to embrace a concept more wide ranging that that of Olmsted's regional parks and networks, namely that of 'green infrastructure'. This can be found in Greater Detroit's Huron–Clinton metro parks system, the green ways of the German Ruhrgebiet, or in the Greater Stockholm 'green and blue infrastructure', and the current 6Cs Green Infrastructure strategy for the English East Midlands, which sets out:

> to provide high quality green spaces near to where people live, enhancing people's physical and mental health wellbeing … creating space for wildlife, and linked-up habitats, relates to climate change and mitigation, improves access to heritage, landscape and townscape, and reduces flood risk.
>
> (6Cs Green Infrastructure, 2010)

Networks of green trails for sustainable recreational land transport that can be used by cyclists and walkers, and blue trails for canoeists, swimmers and dinghy sailors, also become realizable, where the green infrastructure links to and integrates with river and canal networks.

Case Study: The Huron–Clinton Metropolitan Authority (HCMA), Detroit

The growth of the Detroit metropolis in the later 19th century, and the first half of the 20th century, across the road-grid landscape of South East Michigan, was concomitant with the emergence of the automobile industry. The burgeoning city, with its radical traditions, was poor at providing itself with adequate public open space, and only slowly created its motorway system to enable the free movement of its 'blue-collar work force' to the plants of Ford, General Motors and Chrysler that were all developing in the metro region, and a road network adequate to serving the needs of industry, for production and sales.

By the late 1930s the need for radical responsive action was recognized, and in the Michigan Public Act 147 of 1939, the HCMA was established. It allowed the four counties of Oakland, Wayne, Washtenaw and Macomb (later to be joined by Livingston) to come together to form a metropolitan district, for purposes of parks and highway provisions. The wording was important, as their purposes were deemed to be for those of: 'planning, promoting, developing, owning, maintaining and operating parks, connecting drives, and/or limited access highways'. By self-taxation and democratic representation on a Board of Commissioners, the region had the powers, means and mechanisms to provide adequate parks to meet the region's recreational needs, and a system of freeways/motorways to aid industry, journeys to work, and to leisure, as well as easier road access to industrial markets.

What was particularly interesting about the work of the HCMA was that it did not proceed to stitch together a random scatter of new open spaces, but set out to develop a coherent and logical ring of large-scale provisions, which residents could drive out to, from 'Motown'. The range of provisions extended from lakeside resorts and riverside parks, to walking, cycling, riding and canoeing opportunities along lineal resource systems of river valleys and waterways. The Huron and Clinton rivers, lakesides on Lake St Clair and on Lake Erie were venues for new leisure provisions, as well as sites involving the creation of new, or adjustment of existing lakes.

Since the HCMA started its work, it has completed a system of no less than 13 metro parks, at sites in five counties and covering a total area of nearly 24,000 acres. The two largest parks (Stony Creek and Kensington) are each well over 4000 acres in extent (Table 41.1), and offer an incredible range of all-season facilities and opportunities for outdoor active recreation. The plans shown of four of the parks in Figs 41.1 and 41.2 demonstrate the range of provisions made, whereby the equivalent of seaside resorts, lake resorts and forest parks are all publically provided, and on offer at a small charge to metro users. Table 41.1 lists the 13 metro parks, with their sizes, and their locations are given in Fig. 41.3.

Evaluation

In terms of the completion of its set tasks, and the quality, extent and range of leisure provisions created, the HCMA's story is one of extraordinary success. At first, its newly opened provisions were used essentially by the region's white residents, but with time and conscious effort by the ground staff and publicity by the HCMA, many in the Black community joined in use of the facilities on an equal basis. The quality of design and landscape, and range of leisure choices in the metro parks is extremely impressive.

Due to the collapse of the car industries in Greater Detroit in the period after 2007, the economic well-being of the urban region has been severely affected, at least in the short term. Inner-city housing and economic conditions are extremely bad (in 2009), and the reduced income base of the city has made it impossible to provide new leisure and tourism improvements in the inner city equal to those already existing in the HCMA parks on the urban fringe. Birmingham is the UK's 'Motown' or car-producing centre, but fortunately its central area had been renovated before the collapse of the car industry hit its urban finances. Despite all these externalities, the lesson of the HCMA story is a positive one, of direct relevance to the expanding megalopolises across the world, whose quality of life for their residents, as well as tourists, is diminished by the lack of park systems, and of identifying urban open spaces, within their ever-growing, built-up tracts.

Table 41.1. The HCMA park system (courtesy of HCMA).

Metro park name	Location	Area (acres)
Delhi	On Huron River, in Washtenaw County	53
Dexter-Huron	On Huron River, near Ann Arbor in Washtenaw County	122
Hudson Mills	On Huron River, more distant from Ann Arbor in Washtenaw County	1,549
Huron Meadows	South of Brighton, contains Maltby Lake in Livingston County	1,540
Indian Springs	At headwaters of Pontiac River, in Oakland County	2,215
Kensington	Near Milford, Brighton, and contains Kent Lake in Oakland County	4,357
Lake Erie	On Lake Erie, and in Wayne County	1,607
Lower Huron	On Huron River, near Belville, in Wayne County	1,258
Metro Beach	On Lake St Clair, in Macomb County	770
Oakwoods	On Huron River, in Wayne County	1,756
Stony Creek	Near Rochester/Utica, and contains Stony Creek Lake, in Macomb County	4,461
Willow	South-east of New Boston on Huron River in Wayne County	1,531
Wolcott Mill	Near Romeo, in Macomb County	2,625
Total area		23,844

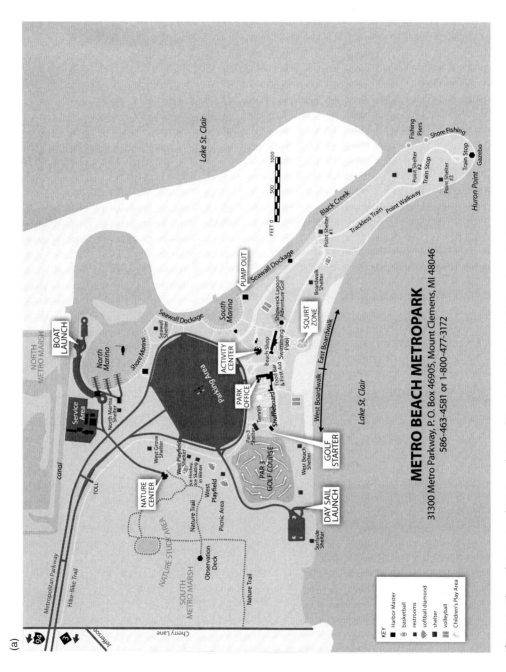

Fig. 41.1. Plans of Metro Beach Metropark (a) and Kensington Metropark (b) (courtesy of HCMA).

(b)

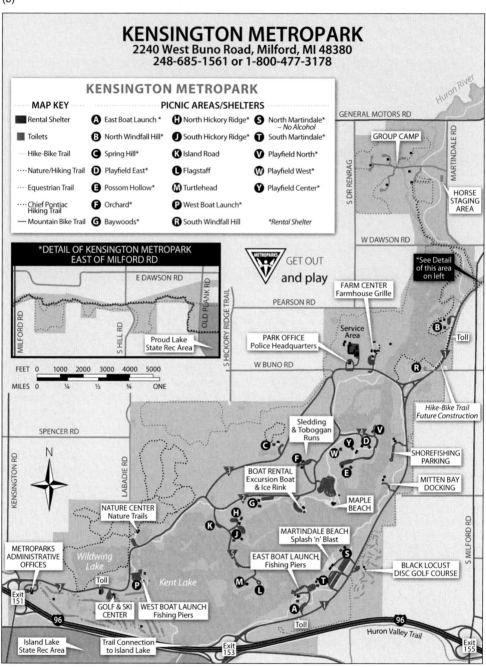

Fig. 41.1. Continued.

(a)

LAKE ERIE METROPARK

32481 West Jefferson, P.O. Box 120, Brownstown, MI 48173
734-379-5020 or 1-800-477-3189

PICNIC SHELTERS /AREAS
- **a** American Lotus Shelter (RS)
- **b** Blue Heron Shelter (RS)
- **c** Shoreline Picnic Area
- **d** Muskrat Shelter (RS)
- **e** Wood Duck Shelter (RS)

KEY
- toilet
- softball diamond
- shelter
- basketball
- Children's Play Area
- tennis / volleyball

(RS) = Rental Shelter

S. Gibraltar

Woodruff

Hike-Bike Trail

NATURE STUDY AREA

Nature
Trails

Cherry Island Trail

BOAT, CANOE
& KAYAK LAUNCH

OUTER BUOYS
Latitude: 4204.72
Longitude: 8311.44

MARSHLANDS
MUSEUM
& NATURE CENTER

West Jefferson Avenue

PARK
ENTRANCE

PARK OFFICE
& TOLL

Service Area

Huron River Drive

Sledding
Hill

Play
Area

a

b

c

Hike-Bike Trail

GREAT WAVE
AREA
- Wave Pool
- Children's Play Area
- Basketball /Softball
- Volleyball
- Sledding
- First Aid
- Food

Detroit River

McCann

Pleasant

Streicher

Shore Fishing

CANOE & KAYAK
LAUNCH

d

e

COVE POINT
PICNIC

GOLF
COURSE

Driving
Range

W. Jefferson Avenue

GOLF COURSE
ENTRANCE

Lee

Heide

GOLF STARTER
BUILDING

Hike-Bike Trail

Marina Point
Observation Deck
Fishing Site

Marley

MARINA

OUTER BUOYS
Latitude: 4203.20
Longitude: 8310.85

Erie Drive

Milleville

Ice Fishing
in Winter

Lake Erie

Campau

Milliman

Pointe Mouillee

Wassanova

South Huron

Sigler

Pointe Mouillee
State Game Area

FEET 0   500   1000   1500   2000   2500

MILES 0   1/8   1/4   3/8   1/2

Fig. 41.2. Plans of Lake Erie Metropark (a) and Lower Huron Metropark (b) (courtesy of HCMA).

(b)

LOWER HURON METROPARK

17845 Savage Road, Belleville, MI 48111
734-697-9181 or 1-800-477-3182

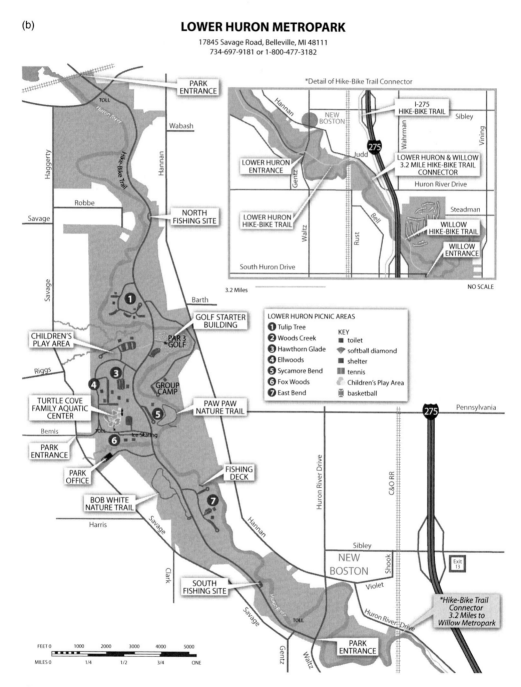

Fig. 41.2. Continued.

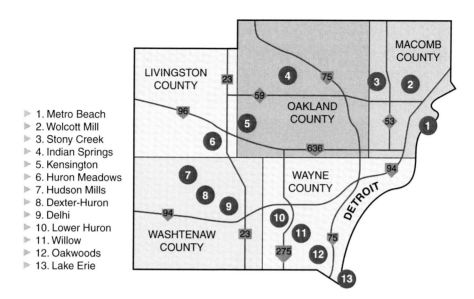

1. Metro Beach
2. Wolcott Mill
3. Stony Creek
4. Indian Springs
5. Kensington
6. Huron Meadows
7. Hudson Mills
8. Dexter-Huron
9. Delhi
10. Lower Huron
11. Willow
12. Oakwoods
13. Lake Erie

Fig. 41.3. HCMA park locations in five counties (courtesy of HCMA).

42 Beaulieu, UK: Recycling an Historic Private Estate as a Major Tourist Attraction

Introduction

In 1952, a year after inheriting the estate and against a background of rapidly growing interest in veteran and vintage motor vehicles, Edward, the present Lord Montagu of Beaulieu, opened his stately home and estate to the public, and placed a few quality old cars in front of the Palace House, at Beaulieu, Hampshire, in the south of England. This was done in memory of his father, a famed motoring pioneer, who was the first to drive a car into the yard of the House of Commons. From this very modest beginning in 1952, a major motor collection grew at Beaulieu, first as the Montagu Museum and later becoming the National Motor Museum of Great Britain.

Resources for Development

The strategic location in Hampshire of this museum development was important, as the site had six definable sets of tourist-resource assets, on the 7500-acre Beaulieu Estate, namely:

- the built heritage resource of a stately home (dating in part to 1538), a ruined Cistercian abbey and outbuildings (dating to 1204), and two separate villages – Beaulieu, and two miles from it Bucklers Hard, an 18th-century riverside ship-building centre;

- associated heritage resources of a landscape park, six farms on 3700 acres, vineyards, plus 2000 acres of woodlands;
- the linked natural heritage resources of the whole of the Beaulieu River on the estate, a stretch of Solent shoreline, with access to Southampton Water and the south coast;
- an existing and improving infrastructure of local and regional roads, railways, piped and wired services, and services in the two villages;
- a location adjacent to the high quality scenic resources of the New Forest (later to become a National Park) and closeness to major seaside resorts such as Bournemouth, and ports such as Southampton;
- high accessibility regionally and nationally to large population catchments as potential markets.

The museum development process was a steady one, with the increasing number of exhibits acquired gradually, but continuously. Old buildings were converted into museum space. In 1956 the world's first motorcycle museum was added. By 1957, over 100,000 visitors were attracted to Beaulieu annually, and the museum was gaining a worldwide reputation. However, from 1957 to 1959 queuing, overcrowding and congestion became

 ©T. Travis 2011. *Planning for Tourism, Leisure and Sustainability* (T. Travis)

the norm, with debasement of the resource and of the visitor experience.

In 1957, Lord Montagu decided to spend a large budget on new premises. A modest new prefabricated museum building was constructed in 1959, next to Palace House. Positive public response led to a decade of further growth in visitor numbers, beyond those forecasted. Increasing demand from across the world for information on car history led to the setting up of a national road transport library in 1961. From its complex collections, it was able to offer a unique service and facility.

Accessibility and Markets

The development of the specialist motor museum and the potential of the site's countryside, water-related and built heritage needs to be related to the area's high accessibility, already mentioned. From the late 1960s, Hampshire was starting to develop as a national growth centre. Beaulieu is 2 hours' drive from London or Bristol, and about 3 hours' drive from the populous West Midlands and South Wales. With rail, coach and evolving motorway systems, Beaulieu thus had growing access to very large markets. Limitations of local road capacity, was more of a constraint than wider market accessibility.

By the early 1960s visitor numbers at Beaulieu had reached over 500,000 p.a. and the motor museum was firmly established as a very popular national tourist attraction. It became clear by then that even the new museum building was inadequate to meet market demands, in terms of space for visitors and for growing exhibit numbers. Capacity and management problems thus led to a review of overall estate management, and the role of the museum.

Development of a Museum Complex

Lord Montagu decided to create a comprehensive museum complex, which could best display the car collection, and consequently a Beaulieu Museum Trust was set up, with industry support, aiming to create a quality building to house a permanent national motor museum.

As Beaulieu is a farmed and wooded estate in an 'Area of Outstanding Natural Beauty' (AONB), careful consideration had to be given to the contextual planning of the museum/estate, and its setting involving planning at three spatial scales. In 1970 planning approval was given for the layout of: (i) the building complex; (ii) the estate plan; and (iii) the traffic plan. Construction started the same year. The new building complex, designed by Leonard Manasseh and partners, combined a magnificent new museum building, with separate library accommodation, and a special hard-standing exhibition arena for rallies. A charitable trust was set up related to the museum.

A contextual Management Plan for the use of the 7500 acres of estate lands, transport services and recreation provisions was prepared by three distinguished designers. The estate plan set out to preserve the character of the inherited estate by maintaining a prosperous agricultural sector and conserving most of the woodlands. To maintain the physical and economic character of the conserved 7350 acres of the rural estate, changes were planned for the other 150 acres.

The two managed core areas, of about 150 acres, were to act as visitor magnets, drawing off pressures, and enabling sensitive conservation elsewhere. This development zone was to give the profitable tourism base, that could cross-subsidize conservation of heritage fabric (Fig. 42.1).

Removal of traffic through roads from the villages of Beaulieu and Bucklers Hard, and from the heart area of the estate, was achieved by the construction of by-pass roads and new traffic points. Thus nearly all vehicular traffic was removed from the villages and core areas, and a system of controlled visitor-management access, entry and egress achieved. Outside the core areas or development zones, the estate was to permit only limited educational use of its countryside areas, and controlled public access on selected and managed walks in woodlands and along the river.

The two core development zones comprise:

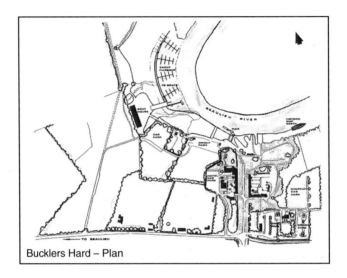

Bucklers Hard – Plan

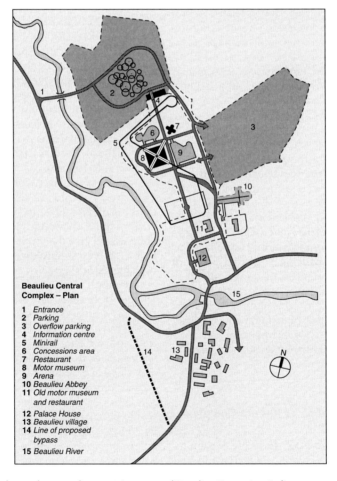

**Beaulieu Central
Complex – Plan**

1 Entrance
2 Parking
3 Overflow parking
4 Information centre
5 Minirail
6 Concessions area
7 Restaurant
8 Motor museum
9 Arena
10 Beaulieu Abbey
11 Old motor museum
   and restaurant
12 Palace House
13 Beaulieu village
14 Line of proposed
   bypass
15 Beaulieu River

Fig. 42.1. Central complexes on the estate (courtesy of Beaulieu Enterprises Ltd).

- the National Motor Museum area including Beaulieu Abbey and Palace House, all associated with (but separated from) Beaulieu village; and
- Bucklers Hard village.

Thus, many separate components came to comprise the comprehensive Beaulieu Scheme of Development and Management, which was implemented and provides a coordinated set of choices and services for the visitor. Re-adjustment of the road system and creation of a central 'pedestrian super-block realm' is linked to a separate planned parking zone for 1250 cars and 55 coaches. There are site-transfers of visitors by mini-train bus, monorail and on foot from car parks to the

destination attractions in the pedestrian core zone. Thus activity pressures are spread and site magnets identified. Environmental capacity can be maintained, as can the character of sub-areas of the estate.

Away from the central core zone, there is a set of retained managed countryside resources, including a National Nature Reserve, low-density woodlands, park and picnic areas, and 'closed' farmland. The transport plans and parking provisions are integrated within the general estate and management plan.

The set objectives of the Beaulieu Museum Trust were the conservation and enhancement of the Beaulieu Manor Estate, and the creation of the National Motor Museum (Fig. 42.2). The objectives have been realized. At each of the

(a)

Fig. 42.2. Aspects of the Beaulieu Estate: (a) the National Motor Museum; and (b) location in relation to major roads (courtesy of 'Design' and Beaulieu Enterprises Ltd).

(b)

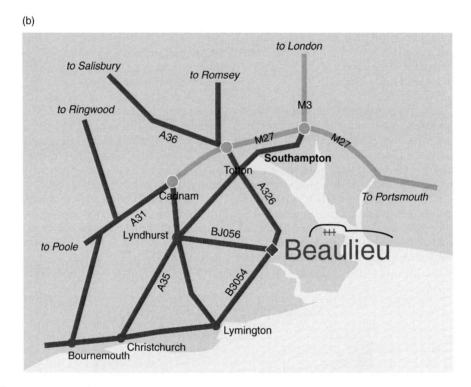

Fig. 42.2. Continued.

locations within the Estate Plan, tourist attractions, services and facilities are provided. A series of stories are told, interpreted and presented with adequate related catering, sales services, toilets and rest points for visitors. Bucklers Hard provides a different and distinct offer – a pedestrianized village street, maritime museum, hotel and café, marina, boatyard and maritime spirit and character.

Thus, the combined offer at Beaulieu has grown into a resort complex in its own right. While it includes little provision for sleeping accommodation, visitors do stay an average of 4.5 hours, easily achieved when many are tourists from Bournemouth and the New Forest, or day visitors from a wider catchment area.

Staffing, Management and Visitors

The Beaulieu Estate facilities generate 150 full-time job equivalents, and in the peak tourist season staff increase to 350, showing its major employment role in the local tourist economy. In the key development period

between 1959 and 1973, over six million visitors came to Beaulieu. By 1978, up to 650,000 visitors p.a. were visiting Beaulieu (of whom 300,000 were visiting Bucklers Hard), all travelling on average 26.3 miles to get there. Some 31% of visitors were day tourists travelling on average 60 miles from their homes.

Management strategy and marketing strategies evolved in this key development period. Trusts were established for: (i) the motor museum; (ii) Beaulieu; and (iii) countryside education. These trusts were to sit alongside the trading company of Beaulieu Enterprises Ltd. Marketing developed annual programmes, with TV, press, radio and hard copy, plus later on-line marketing and sales. The pricing policy is to have high entry pricing to give an all inclusive offer for the motor museum and main estate, whereas at Bucklers Hard differential charging is used to control capacity, and generate sufficient income for local improvements. Beaulieu is part of a joint marketing group with six other leading historic attractions (the 'Campaign of the Magnificent Seven').

By 2007 and 2008 annual visitor numbers were steady at about 325,000, but in 2009 they were expected to rise to about 350,000, due to the draw of the 'World of Top Gear' exhibition, held in June.

Evaluation

The Beaulieu story is one of innovation, market response and then of a series of responsive strategies, until an imaginative, expensive, long-term plan, combining a skilful combination of development and conservation elements was devised and totally implemented. The results have been long-term visitor repeat trade, and satisfaction at a unique tourist attraction group, without major overnight accommodation elements.

All the planning and management objectives at Beaulieu have been achieved. The central historic cores or 'development zones' have provided a useful base for large-scale tourism to develop. However, it is the management, marketing and conservation skills, which have converted the raw materials into a large-scale profitable enterprise and major tourist attraction, which is a world leader in its field.

In the key period of development, much of the tourist traffic coming to Beaulieu was car based. Perhaps that was seen as appropriate for a national car museum, but it was not sustainable in carbon footprint terms. It is perhaps paradoxical that Beaulieu is now part of the Green Leaf Tourism Scheme. This is a national pilot scheme for sustainable tourism in the UK, and its members are committed to supporting six targets:

- car-free tourism;
- New Forest Marque produce;
- energy waste and recycling initiatives;
- landscape conservation;
- Forest Friends Visitor Stewardship; and
- community tourism.

Effort is made to increase the proportion of non-car-based visits to Beaulieu, where its great exhibited car collection will take on an ever-increasing historical interest.

43 Integrated Community Building Complexes: Experimental Provisions in the Netherlands and the UK

Introduction

Experiments of great significance in the realm of integrated community building design and concept have taken place at two different points in time, and in two European countries. The first spanning the 1930s and 1940s took place in London, and the second in the 1960s and 1970s at three different locations in the Netherlands. The concepts, in social, economic, energy and design terms, were radical and important, but these case studies remain relatively unknown in both countries. In the context of sustainable development, and of potentially sustainable communities, these experiments are seen as sufficiently important, as to have a chapter devoted to them.

Case Study 1: The Pioneer Health Centre, Peckham, London (1935)

In the midst of the Great Depression, in a modest inner suburb of London, the Halley Stewart Trust backed an experiment in 'the living structure of society', which was focused on the development of a unique community health centre, which was designed for nurturing community well-being, based on the family, with a system of monitoring and nurturing health and leisure, rather than dealing with remedial treatment of illness. The whole story is meticulously told in Pearse and Crocker's (1943) book *The Peckham Experiment*.

The Trust commissioned Sir Owen Williams, one of the outstanding modern architects of that time, to build the Peckham Health Centre, at a cost of £38,000 in 1934/5. It was to be a health centre, leisure centre and family club, for 2000 families. 'The scale of the experiment was determined by the needs of health – health can only come forth from the mutuality of action within society – provide for needs of mind and spirit, as well as of body' (Pearse and Crocker, 1943). It assumed that the future 'unit of living' was not the individual but the family, and that modern community provision should be for integrated leisure and well-being, where the health of all could be monitored and aided. For biologists and doctors it was to be a place to study 'normal families and individuals in their leisure and daily lives' (see Fig. 43.1).

Families paid weekly subscriptions to become members of the centre, which offered an incredible range of leisure, study, social opportunities and health monitoring facilities. The centre was a club for families, who had to pay modest sums, and meet two conditions: (i) 'that they would accept getting health reviews for every individual in the family'; and (ii) 'that they make full use of the Club, and of all its facilities, at all times'.

In return for their weekly 'subs' families could use the centre's swimming pools,

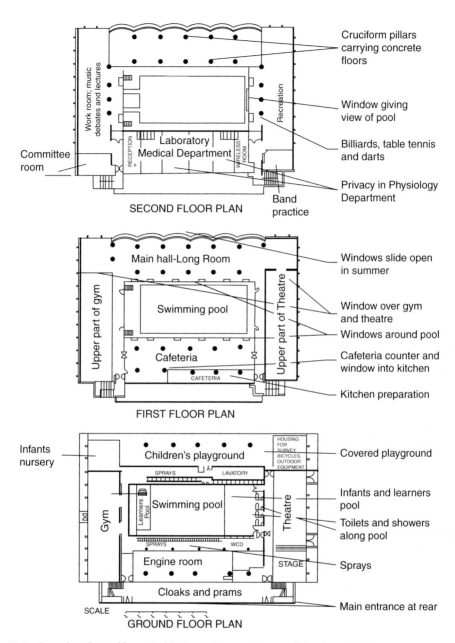

Fig. 43.1. Floor plans for Peckham Health Centre (Source: Pearse and Crocker, 1943).

self-service cafés, gymnasia, halls and play spaces; they could go to dances, play darts and billiards, learn skills, go to exercise classes and have their health monitored. There were also mother-and-baby classes and sex education for youngsters. Occasionally families could go to the two associated facilities: (i) a 'home farm'

in Kent for country stays; and (ii) a 'holiday camp' in Kent for holidays.

Evaluation

The design of the building itself was revolutionary: 'the whole building is...characterized by a design which invites social contact, allow-ing equally for the chance meeting, for formal and festive occasions, as well as for quiet fam-ily grouping' (Pearse and Crocker, 1943). As can be seen in Fig. 43.1, the plans and layout are for an essentially social and leisure build-ing with smaller space allocations for the mon-itoring of health and well-being. The aims of the Trust were fully met in this experimental provision, and the four resultant books, and published data, which resulted from the moni-toring was unique in the UK, prior to some work in the 1970s. The centre could, in physi-cal and positive social response terms, have remained as a long-life facility, and become the model for other developments, but it was, paradoxically, killed by the coming of the state's National Health Service, which in its first phase, was essentially having to deal with remedial health care, in a country where health neglect was the norm. The stock of ideas in the Peckham experiment have, by 2009, great social relevance for developed countries, where obesity, family disintegration and 'junk-food' cultures, present great social challenges.

Case Study 2: The 'Meerpaal', Dronten in Flevoland (1967)

On the Flevoland Polder of the Netherlands, experimental work on new settlements and their centres was ongoing by 1960, and an early example from this period was work at the town of Dronten. There, a settlement of about 10,000 was planned, with a further local catchment of 10,000 in its rural surroundings. First thoughts of the architect-planner Van Klingeren were of a building which housed all the central func-tions, but this was soon compromised, by limit-ing the roles of a multipurpose hall, to serve commercial, religious and recreational func-tions. The new facility was planned in 1960 and was opened and operational by 1967.

The facility, named the 'Meerpaal' (or 'mooring post for a boat'), comprises a total floor space of 3700 m^2, with a central multipur-pose hall or hangar of 1600 m^2 (Fig. 43.2). The Meerpaal's central hall was to serve a range of uses: (i) as a market hall serving the commu-nity; (ii) as an exhibition venue for livestock sales; (iii) as a purpose-designed theatre and

congress hall; and (iv) as a locale for commer-cial shows and for the annual carnival in February. Cinema, church and political meet-ings could be accommodated, and a television studio was also provided. A restaurant and toi-lets were included in the complex.

Detached from the complex were school-ing facilities, a health centre and a major competitive sports space. Despite this, the facil-ity was a unique, prototype in that country, at that time. It cost 3.2 million guilders to build, and in its first 10 years was running at a trading deficit of 450,000 guilders p.a. It was a public-sector provision, with a total of eight staff, including the Director, with a general manager in charge of the whole complex, and responsi-ble to a managing Recreation Foundation. The restaurant was independently managed. No user organization was created, and publicity was handled on the local TV station (in the building), and via a monthly paper.

Evaluation

While the design basically worked, and the Meerpaal was intensively used, the use pres-sures were so great that the original floor had to be replaced after 15 years with an asphalt one. Acoustic problems occurred when cin-ema or theatre use of the inner theatre coin-cided with sports events in the surrounding hall. The lack of a swimming pool led to one being built elsewhere. Popularity of the centre led to the restaurant and bar being open 13 hours daily for a 7 day week! The centre has been popular and effective, but even in a small community it could not satisfy all local needs.

In extent of use, the Meerpaal was a great success. Some 450,000 visits were made by users p.a. including: (i) 200,000 visits were in the outer hall; (ii) 25,000 in the inner hall; (iii) 25,000 in the foyer; (iv) 10,000 in the café/restaurant; (v) 10,000 in sports activities; and (vi) 6000 in other activities. The monitoring of use has provided this detailed evidence. Entry to the complex was free, but payment was made for theatre, cinema and entry to pop concerts. By 1980, social and cultural use made up 90% of centre use, but it was hoped to raise commercial use from 8 to 30%. Facilities for the disabled were included in the design, and the facility

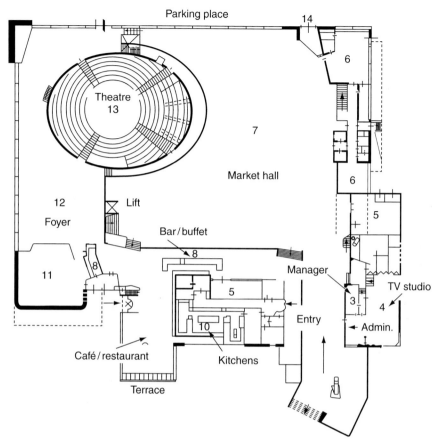

Fig. 43.2. Plan of the Meerpaal in Dronten in Flevoland (courtesy of Meerpaal).

remained popular and effective in meeting its goals. The success of this experiment led to at least two follow-up provisions elsewhere in the Netherlands. Later plans to build a new complex to replace the Meerpaal met with fierce local opposition, so eventually a compromise was agreed, whereby the new centre that was built was an expansion of the retained and popular Meerpaal.

Case Study 3: 't Karregat in Eindhoven (1973)

The Karregat centre in the suburb of Herzenbroeken is located about 10 minutes' cycle ride from Eindhoven city centre. Here, once again, the architect Van Klingeren was asked to design an integrated centre building, but with an even more ambitious brief than in Dronten for a mixed public/private-sector funded project. Educational, commercial, social, cultural and recreational services were all to be provided under a shared roof. Proposals were drawn up in 1970, and the building opened in 1973. Two-thirds of the funding was provided by the local municipality, and one-third by the Amrobank Group. Ownership on completion remained proportional to the investments.

The brief required the building to accommodate under one roof: (i) a municipal nursery school and primary school; (ii) a Roman Catholic nursery and primary school; (iii) a gymnasium; (iv) a youth and hobby centre; (v) a toddlers' play centre; (vi) a general meeting place (called the 'Pit'); (vii) a community centre; (viii) premises for the managing care-takers; (ix) a supermarket, four shops and a café; (x) a medical and social centre; and (xi) a branch library. In its provisions it was more demanding than either the Peckham Health Centre or the Meerpaal, but there was no underlying deep philosophy as in the London instance. The architect employed an open-plan layout, with only bookcases separating different use areas, and all was placed under a single management. Within 7 years, this was found unworkable, and integrated management gave way to separate management units, and walls were built to separate uses, because of acoustic (i.e. sound intrusion) problems. The large floor area was some 6750 m² in extent.

While most facilities were to serve the local neighbourhood of 5000 residents, the 'Pit' was to be a venue for pop concerts and folk festivals drawing people from all over the city and further afield.

The development cost was of 6 million guilders (or about £1.5 million). As a proto-type, all agreed that this was a unique venture, in world terms. After its design modifications, its management was divided into three separate structures:

- for commercial-sector elements;
- for community-sector elements; and
- for the schools managed by school staff.

High durability flooring materials and very light and airy structures characterize the development, which has a 'young' and 'infor-mal' feel to it all. No formal monitoring of use occurred as at Dronten, where numbers of users are recorded.

Evaluation

The Karregat was, and is, popular with its users, especially for events such as its 'Country and Western Nights'. School staff and medical staff find the layout and sound insulation inadequate, and noise intrusion affects their activities. Those who work in the building find it 'has too dry a work climate, and it is too dusty and noisy as a workplace'. No one disagrees with its approach, but find fault with its detailed design. It is used by families, and is a truly community-based centre, but its ambitious

aims perhaps required extra research on sound insulation, and heavier materials, plus subtler air control systems, to aid user comfort and roles. Had the Karregat been given a research trust as at Peckham, we would have had the best urban social laboratory in Europe.

Nevertheless, by 2009 the continuing management problems and inadequate sound insulation between component parts of the centre were leading to proposals either to re-design, or totally rebuild the Karregat.

Case Study 4: The 'Agora', Lelystad in Flevoland (1977)

Conceived in 1967 and opened in 1977, the Agora was a multipurpose leisure centre serving a new city, which had a population of 40,000 by 1980, and later grew to 100,000. It was also designed by the architectural firm of Van Klingeren, at a budget of 14.5 million guilders (approx. £3.6 million), funded partly by the municipality, and partly by the Dutch central government.

The building integrated provision under one roof for: (i) a swimming pool; (ii) a mul-tipurpose hall; (iii) a theatre; (iv) a chapel; (v) conference rooms; (vi) a library; (vii) a central forum; (viii) a café-restaurant and bars; (ix) an art gallery and exhibition space; (x) a youth centre; and (xi) offices. The lesson fed back from Eindhoven was to exclude the school uses and the shopping facilities.

Furthermore, as this was a large complex, a better management structure was created from scratch. A general manager who was res-ponsible to the Executive, and the Board of Directors, had three divisions under him:

- an events department;
- a maintenance department; and
- an administrative department and book-ing centre.

User management was done via the clubs and interest groups, who applied to the Central Booking Register of the Agora. A Council of user groups met once every 6 weeks, and had representation on the Board of Directors. The use of the Agora was for non-school groups, as all schools in the new city have their own social and sporting facilities (see Fig. 43.3).

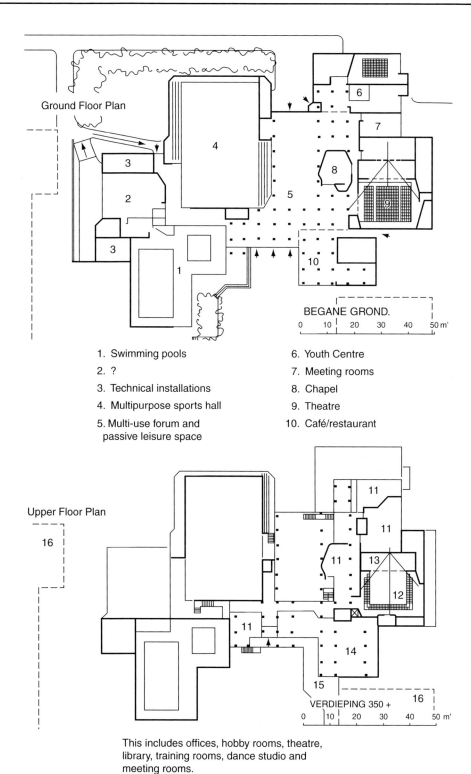

Ground Floor Plan

BEGANE GROND.

0   10   20   30   40   50 m'

1. Swimming pools
2. ?
3. Technical installations
4. Multipurpose sports hall
5. Multi-use forum and
   passive leisure space

6. Youth Centre
7. Meeting rooms
8. Chapel
9. Theatre
10. Café/restaurant

Upper Floor Plan

VERDIEPING 350 +

0   10   20   30   40   50 m'

This includes offices, hobby rooms, theatre,
library, training rooms, dance studio and
meeting rooms.

Fig. 43.3. Floor plans of the Agora, Lelystad (1977) (courtesy of Agora's Management).

Evaluation

The Agora had limited flexibility and open-ness, but it was a great improvement over the Karregat, and in design terms used robust materials, but a little too much wood, which affected the acoustics. The lack of a back-stage tower prevented theatre productions from having drop sets. However, Lelystad, which feels relatively remote in Dutch terms, tried to give its residents a good quality of life through a lively choice of cultural, social and sporting events in the Agora, copies of whose annual programme were sent to all residents of the city. It is estimated that about 500,000 p.a. visits were made by users to the Agora, and this included some 120,000 users of the swimming pool. The young used the swimming pool, the theatre's use was skewed to higher-income groups, but a wide cross-section of the town's population used the centre for a range of purposes. It was a popular, dynamic and successful provision, very broadly based socially in its use, and was a responsively managed, urban leisure-provision, prototype.

By 2000, the rapid expansion of Lelystad, and excessive demands and pressures upon the Agora, led to its being replaced by a far more expensive, larger, very progressive arts complex, which is now a notable feature of this major city on the polders.

Part VI

'Slicing the Cake Differently' – Resorts, Spas, Pilgrimages and City Tourism

44 Introduction

One may ask: why has the book been structured the way it has? Or: why now introduce topics like spas, resorts, shrines and the nature of cities? The reason is simple and clear: it is because 18th-century rationalist philosophers in France and Scotland gave us a philosophical foundation which is accepted by the author. That philosophy was then coloured by 19th-century beliefs in the nation state, the regional philosophy of French geographers, which led to Patrick Geddes' approach to planning, giving a spatial hierarchy that has been used in this book. Geddes, in his writing and practice, innovatively linked geographical approaches with biological and sociological analyses, so that both he and the author agree to view planning, or tourism planning, as a type of applied dynamic ecology. From the national, via the regional, down to the local and the site scales, the Man/place/work/life/leisure-dynamic environment interactions, account for the identity, vitality and distinctiveness of places, which are the destinations of tourism.

In the final three chapters, Chapters 45–47, some alternative ways are taken of reviewing tourism, namely by focusing upon three recurrent themes that occur in the history of tourism, namely:

- resorts and spas;
- the pilgrimage; and
- the city.

Resorts and Spas

For thousands of years there have been resorts, places set apart, to which Man has gone in his non-work time. However, they do not last forever: resorts have life cycles and sometimes individual resorts have several life cycles. Resorts and spas (as places apart for health, refreshment, leisure and retirement) have for 3000 years needed travel to get to them, whether by donkey, camel, chariot, horse, boat, ship, train or plane. Sometimes resorts were seasonal, for courts or elites to escape the heat or the cold, to escape the plague, or the stressful pressures of the overcrowded city. Resorts and spas are linked to the restorative or renewal function of Man, over time, and in a place and space set apart from the pressurized world.

The Pilgrimage

'Man does not live by bread alone' – he is a cognate being, who queries his existence and looks for understanding and meaning in the natural phenomena that he meets, and queries the nature of life and being. Since he was a hunter and a gatherer, Man has recorded – in the cave paintings of Altamira and Lascaux, in the rock pictures made in the ice deserts of Northern Scandinavia, or in the sand deserts of Australia and Africa – images and implicit questions about life and death, about sun, heat, fire and flame, sea and waves.

The cycles of life and death, fear, hunger and plenty have led to ideas and to beliefs. Belief systems or religions have identified places and events linked to personalities, to concepts, values, happenings and miracles, which were central to their beliefs. These are the events and holy places, shrines, or special places to which believers in a religion, are required to go. It may be to a holy river like the Ganges for Hindu pilgrims, or on the once-in-a-lifetime pilgrimage called the Hajj to Mecca, for Moslems, or the visits by Christians or Jews to their holy places such as those in the 'Holy Land'. Many religions have pilgrimages. Pilgrimages may have been with us from 1400 to 4000 years – they are a long-lasting form of tourism and generate purpose-related travel, or sustainable forms of tourism, and so we need to understand them.

The City

The city is a key phenomenon for Man, and has been for several thousand years since Man started to settle in specific localities, which was first made possible by agriculture. Since then settlement growth has occurred through migration, transport, trade, exchange of materials, goods, people and ideas. Civilizations have essentially developed within cities. Man's development, his creativity, variety of expression and activity are all reflected in the history and nature of the city.

As many as 200 types of tourism are associated with the city as a destination based on a manifold range of activities. Thus in a city if any one sort of tourism has a limited life, other sorts of tourism can replace it. So the city is perhaps the destination for sustainable tourism, based on orchestrating these many tourisms over time and space. The focus of tourism planners is to consider:

• Which sorts of cities?
• What size of cities?
• What relationships does the city have to resorts, spas and belief systems?

These are questions which will be summarily addressed.

45 Resorts Are Not Forever

Introduction

The dictionary definition of a 'resort' is 'a place to which many people go for recreation'. However, there are various sorts of resort ranging from holiday resorts to winter resorts, hill stations to summer resorts, and this notion of such places has been with mankind for several thousand years. In the ancient kingdoms of the Middle East, Babylonia and the Nile Valley, there were seasonal resorts to which kings and pharaohs went either to escape the great heat of summer, or the severe cold of winter. Such places were created to meet a need or a demand, and existed until they no longer met such a need, and then went through a process of decline. Some 30 years ago, Butler writing about the 'resort cycle', introduced the notion of the phases of life of a resort from its concept, initiation, growth and development, on to its decline processes (Butler, 1980). It is only in recent times that we have become concerned with the question of the long life of resorts, or their sustainability. This is because in developed countries, such as those in Western Europe and North America, resorts that were developed extensively in the 19th and 20th centuries, then became significant settlements in their own right, and so the question of the economic and social survival of their populations became tied up with the life and renewal of such resorts.

Historical Perspective

There is no standard classification of resorts, though such places have been with us for over 2000 years. Today one can visit the heritage sites of Pompeii or Taormina in Italy and get a clear idea of what the resort was like in Roman times. In fact, cities like Bath in England, which have had a life cycle of over 2500 years, inherited Roman baths, which were restored nearly 2000 years after they were created. The 'Raj' or the British in India created hill resorts such as Simla and Poona to escape the intense heat of a lowland summer in India, just as those working in interwar British Mandatory Palestine would escape the summer heat by going to a cooler hill town such as Safed, to survive and escape a difficult season's weather.

Resorts have been places to which to go to on holy days relating to religious belief and practice, and later for holidays for rest and recreation. Similar to the journeys to resorts, have been visits to places for other reasons, such as going to a destination for educational tourism purposes. On the Grand Tour the English nobleman made his tour of months through exotic locations to get to Rome or to Athens, in order to study the classical world. In communist or socialist societies tours were made as political pilgrimages to places which were not recreational or educational, such as the tomb of Lenin in Moscow, Mao's birthplace in China, or Tito's birthplace in Federal Yugoslavia.

While Butler's 'resort cycle' evolved in 1980, when there was concern about understanding the process of decline, and choice at the apparent end of the life cycle of many seaside resorts in developed countries, the concern increasingly became focused not upon the process of decline, but with active renewal. It was a case of finding ways of extending an existing life cycle for the resorts, be they seaside or other, and even contemplating a series of further life cycles for them, by renewing either their tourism base, or finding other economic activities to keep the settlements alive and thriving.

Phases of Resort and Spa Development

While there is evidence from ancient Egypt and Greece of forms of resort development taking place there, the most detailed evidence is from the Roman Empire, which provided a complete civilization of the Mediterranean world, extending from the Near East to the cooler climes of Scotland and North-West Europe. The range of seaside resorts, retirement and holiday cities, as well as hill resorts, already existed, so that from Herculaneum and Capri on the one hand, to Roman Tivoli on the other, one had a spectrum of offers that would seem to meet almost modern criteria. In Roman times, the baths within cities were social, health and recreational meeting points, and in addition to the urban baths there were spa baths to which people went for recreational and rest reasons. The provision of baths in the Roman Empire extended from Timgad in North Africa, via Caesarea in the Holy Land, through to Bath and Buxton in the UK.

After the Roman Empire, and the long period of the Dark Ages, we have little evidence about the use and nature of the vestige of Roman spas, baths and resorts, but we do have evidence that in the medieval period, people in Central and North-West Europe were again using the inherited Roman baths as places of health and recreation. In medieval times, when travel had become much more hazardous, the characteristic journeys were to places set apart as holy places or shrines, as the notion of religious pilgrimage was deeply engrained in European societies in this period. Writings such as Chaucer's *Canterbury Tales* give us a detailed picture of the lively social life associated with the travels of pilgrims on such holy pilgrimages.

Things were changing by the 16th century, after the impacts of the plagues and the decimation of the population in Europe. It is interesting to note that G.M. Trevelyan (1964) writes that:

> The medieval custom of pilgrimage had helped to give people a taste for travel and sightseeing, which survived the religious custom of visiting shrines (in Shakespeare's England). The medicinal spa in the late 1500s was taking the place of the holy well.

A 400-page book could easily be given over to the extraordinary evolution of spas in Europe in the period from 1575 to 1675, for in this time increasing attention was given to the medicinal value of mineral waters at springs, as a foundation for small medicinal spas in several European countries. Though much historical writing focuses on the development of the Great Spas of the 19th century throughout Europe, there was this earlier phase of the development of small spas in the period from 1575 to 1675, by which time the medical profession was encouraging those who had the means to travel 'to take the waters' as a way of improving their health and dealing with their illnesses. Of particular interest is the fact that some of these spas and mineral waters were near the sea, and by the 1660s doctors were recommending the use not only of mineral waters and inland spas, but also of sea bathing for medicinal reasons, at the settlement of Scarborough on the east coast of England.

This phase of travel to watering places, developing for medicinal reasons started in the 1660s, and was to move into a key phase of development by the mid-18th century, when the settlement of Brightholmstone on the south coast of England started attracting such health tourists. By 1790 this settlement had become Brighton, which became a fashionable resort, when it came to be patronized by the Prince Regent, at the end of the 18th and the beginning of the 19th century.

The evolution of the seaside resort is a fascinating story, taking us from Scarborough in the 1660s, via Brighton's phases of development from 1753 to 1815, by which time seaside resorts were starting to develop elsewhere, and could be found not only in England, but emerging in Holland, Belgium and North Germany too. A process which was speeding up in these countries between 1790 and 1830, was to be fundamentally changed in the period beyond 1840 because from 1840 to 1880 was the 'railway age' in Europe. This totally changed the accessibility of the seaside to the rapidly urbanizing countries of North-West Europe, as the process of industrialization spread the process of urbanization in the north-west of that continent. Thus at the beginning of the 19th century, it was small elites who could afford the expensive and relatively difficult forms of travel through to the emergent small seaside resorts, whereas by the end of the 19th century the whole scatter of seaside resorts not only around the coasts of Britain and of the North Sea, but around the Baltic and elsewhere, were being linked by the growing network of European national and imperial rail systems, to inland centres of population.

Even in 1851, the development of the commercial sector in tourism was such that, according to Swinglehurst (1982), Cooks were taking 120,000 trippers by rail to see the Great Exhibition. By the end of the 19th century it was possible not only for elites to travel by rail from Vienna to Adriatic watering places, or from Warsaw to the resort of Zopot on the Baltic, but equally, for the first time, for industrial populations from the North of England to go by rail to seaside resorts such as Blackpool on the west coast and Scarborough on the east coast of England. Similarly, the Grand Tour for landed gentry in Britain and North-West Europe that evolved in the 1600s continued, grew and developed through to a peak in the 18th century, and, paradoxically declined by the 1840s when travel accessibility made destinations more open first to the emerging mercantile and middle classes, and eventually to the working classes of Europe.

Historic Markers

Throughout the world, one can find 'historic markers of resort development', or key early resort hotels. These were resorts which marked the evolution of tourism in different countries, and at different phases across the globe. Thus in the UK, one can find markers such as 17th-century Scarborough and early 19th-century Tenby in Wales as watering places, or spas such as Buxton, Cheltenham and Brighton. Similarly in the mid- to late 19th century, the evolution of winter resorts (for sunshine) on the south coast of France became the French Riviera. In the early 20th century one can find the first resort hotels in Las Palmas de Gran Canaria, and in Madeira, for seaborne tourists who came by passenger liners. An early Adriatic resort of the Austro-Hungarian Empire, such as Opatije, was an historic marker, as were early Norwegian Fjord hotels, like the 19th-century Hotel Dalen.

The purpose here is not one of detailed historical analysis, but to note that there have been phases of spa resort development, from ancient through to modern times, as well as phases in seaside- and mountain-resort development, first in the European world, then in the Americas and the Far East, and latterly in younger European-settled continents such as Australasia. Our interest is in the fact that as a result of worldwide resort development during the 19th and first half of the 20th century, by the latter part of the 20th century and now in the early 21st century we have large numbers of seaside resorts, mountain resorts and spas coming to the end of their physical lives, or the end of significant economic or social life cycles. This issue has become the dramatic one of the death of old resorts, or the possibility of renewal through new cycles of development and reinvestment.

Butler's Resort Cycle

Butler's revised resort cycle published in 1980 in the *Canadian Geographer* and shown in Fig. 45.1, suggested a process over time of exploration, involvement, development, consolidation, stagnation and then likely

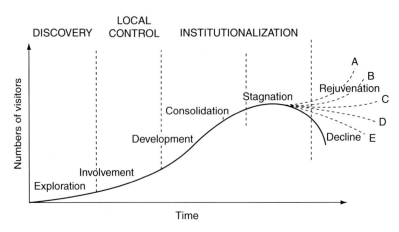

Fig. 45.1. Butler's tourist resort cycle (Source: Butler, 1980).

decline of resorts. Butler had modified his theory to suggest there were possibilities of rejuvenation, and therefore continuing or extending that life cycle further by renewing the physical stock of the building, and finding new reasons for the resort to continue its life.

Much evidence since then has suggested that an individual resort may in fact have not just one or two life cycles, but several life cycles – thus enabling it to have a very long life. Thus when we talk about sustainability, there is the implication of long life, but not necessarily of permanency in the specific function of a destination, or its economic activities. Examination of the 2500 year history of Bath in England must give us food for thought. There, at Bath, in 500 BC a pagan prince had found a cure to his illness in the medicinal waters of that location, and created a settlement at that point. The Romans, aware of such medicinal waters, created baths and a spa 500 years later, as well as a permanent settlement at this point, and though there are limits of information as to Bath's history during the Dark Ages, there is evidence of the Roman baths being reused in the late medieval period, when the town once more took on a spa or health-resort function. This continued through further cycles in the 1600s and 1700s, before a new fashionable phase of Bath as a resort was heralded in the 18th century. The renewal of the Roman baths in the late 19th century, and the creation at the end of the 20th century of a new bath and new types of 'wellness-tourism' was restoring Bath as a

resort yet again. Thus a 2500-year cycle of activities at Bath means that the settlement has been physically renewed several times; several different cycles of social fashion, as well as economic use, have taken place at that destination, and we can thus refer to 'the multiple cycles of the life of a destination or resort', such as Bath.

Later in this chapter, this issue of different life cycles will be further addressed. As shown in Fig. 45.2 in the late 20th century one could see market forces funding a further cycle of change at a major European seaside resort, Scheveningen in the Netherlands. This also occurred in the post-communist period when the seaside resort of Sopot on the Baltic coast of Poland went through a new phase of renewal. Late 20th-century sun-based, winter tourism by North-West Europeans was leading to the large-scale development of seaside resorts for airborne tourists on Red Sea coasts in Egypt, Jordan and Israel.

Resort Development/Resort Renewal

By the 1970s, the whole issue of resort renewal was giving rise to a phase of seaside resort changes in North-West Europe. This was because many resorts here were declining as North-West Europeans were increasingly moving to the Mediterranean and further afield for their summer holidays as a result of the development of aircraft-based,

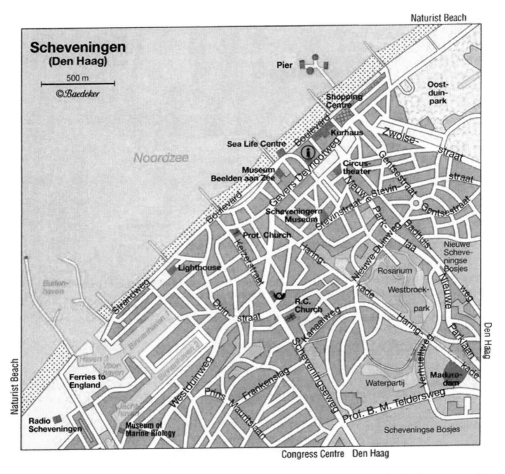

Fig. 45.2. Scheveningen Resort Plan and its contextual setting in The Hague, the Netherlands (courtesy of www.scheveningenbad.nl).

mass-tourism holidays. Dropping market demand at home led to responses which can be seen in the stories of major private-sector renewal of a North Sea resort such as Scheveningen in the Netherlands on one hand, the renewal by market forces at Blackpool in England on the other, and a general review which was taking place in 1975 via European Architectural Heritage Year (EAHY). In that year the British Tourist Boards produced a major report on the evaluation of British resorts and spas, and conducted case studies of three of the declining heritage resorts: (i) Llandudno in Wales; (ii) Buxton in England; and (iii) Rothesay in Scotland.

In the 1980s one can find examples of resort development and renewal such as the development of Whistler in British Columbia, Canada, as a major new ski resort and the 1984 review by the Wales Tourist Board entitled *The Opportunities for the Conservation and Enhancement of our Historic Resorts* (Lingard and Partners, 1984). In a review of all of the Welsh resorts, particular attention was given to two heritage resorts, Llandudno and Tenby. The problem of the decline of the large number of British seaside resorts in the late 20th and early 21st century has been a constant subject of discussion, but one of inadequate action. In 2008 the Department for Culture, Media and Sport (DCMS) in the UK government was responsible for a new 'Sea-Change Programme', which was launched to deal with ageing and declining seaside resorts. It is now important to look more closely at these examples, first that of Scheveningen in the Netherlands, secondly the 'Sea-Change Programme' in England, and thirdly the case study which was done in 2003 of Bournemouth, in England, and its potential as a sustainable seaside resort.

Case Study 1: The Scheveningen Story

As indicated by Hans van de Weg in 1982, the Scheveningen story is a fascinating and fruitful one. It is the instance of the leading seaside resort of the Netherlands, and its renewal over a 20–25 year period. Scheveningen had first developed at the beginning of the 19th century and developed continuously up until the time of the Second World War. After the Second World War it was increasingly in decline, and by the end of the 1960s there were public discussions as to how to introduce 'New vitality and sort out some planned rehabilitation and re-orientation of the resort'. Finally by 1973:

> the initiatives of local government found a response in private enterprise/industry.... A consortium of investment companies acquired all the land not already owned by the city; thus consolidating a site of some 12 hectares (a 30 acre site) with a beach front of 500 metres at the heart of the seaside resort.
> (van de Weg, 1982)

The consortium carrying out the development was the Bredero Real Estate linked in the Netherlands to Nationale Nederlanden – a major Dutch insurance company. Redevelopment was possible as a joint venture between the city of The Hague and a consortium of private enterprises. The aim, via their Basic Plan, was to: (i) conserve the vital natural resources of the area; (ii) enhance the developed resources through all-weather developments; (iii) carry out comprehensive planning of the resort area of the sea front and its adjacent urban facilities, in concert with the local community; (iv) maintain the

high accessibility; and (v) retain the image and reality of the Kurhaus, which was the focal building of the resort, linked to the pier and the circus theatre. The Master Plan was for 760,000 m² of development, and the redevelopment started in 1974, with the former Grand Hotel area having some 270 new housing units with 480 parking places on its former site. Approximately 750 m² of shopping and 2,400 m² of offices were to be built, and the national monument and the seafront area of the Kurhaus kept, but completely rebuilding it as a major hotel, casino and shopping centre with a series of restaurants and bars. This was linked to a new entertainment square and restaurant complex, again next to high quality seafront housing. A new facility was to be a surf pool, including saunas, solaria and water sports accommodation, plus a covered development called the 'Palace Promenade' for entertainment, shopping, restaurants, fast foods and tourist attractions. In all a development worth £130 million was proposed. The development was not only carried through, but careful attention was given to the mechanisms of management and marketing, and these are of particular interest.

The great advantage of Scheveningen resort is that it forms part of the city of The Hague, which is a city with a population of 0.5 million, and contains the seaside resort, a fishing harbour, a marina, sports-fishing enterprises and a number of restaurants. The city also has major museums, a circus theatre, and, as a capital city has developed a conference and tourist industry, with its own hotels, plus the separate cluster of 50 hotels and boarding houses contained within Scheveningen itself.

The management was to be vested in the Scheveningen Resort Board, which would bring together all the partners in the seaside resort including the Chamber of Commerce and the local tourist board, and have an operating company Scheveningen. This company would operate certain of the key properties, except for the Kauhaus hotel and casino which are organized by the consortium in a single company. In the 1980s a marketing budget of £500,000 p.a. was given for Scheveningen; this was in addition to the marketing budgets of the city of The Hague itself. Marketing by the resort authority was to develop a four-season programme of events annually, so that the all-round attractions of the resort and its backing capital city could be maximized. In addition The Hague has its own major tourist organization, the Hague Visitor and Convention Bureau, to promote the city as a conference, meeting and congress centre. Tourism and the appeal of the city's attractions outside of Scheveningen, therefore complement the work and activities of the revamped resort. Further development work was done in the 1990s, so in the 2000s the fully renewed resort was again enjoying its place among the premier European seaside resorts. The great advantage of Scheveningen is that as this resort forms part of a capital city of half a million residents, all the mutually reinforcing activities of resort and capital city maximize opportunities for both tourism and the sustainability of activities in this destination.

Case Study 2: The UK 'Sea-Change Programme 2008'

In 2008 the UK national government, through its DCMS, funded a major capital grants programme to aid the renewal of seaside resorts in England. This was a combined effort by a government ministry, led by the Commission for Architecture and the Built Environment (CABE), linked to Regional Development Agencies, English Heritage, the Arts Council and the Heritage Lottery Fund. The notion of this programme was to allocate £45 million over a 3-year period to local authorities that was to be match funded locally (i.e. a minimum of 50% of grants up to £1 million, and match funded for 100% of grants for projects over £2 million). The aim was to fund a range of cultural heritage, public-space projects (including theatres, museums, libraries, galleries, archives, outdoor performance spaces, landscapes) and projects that would promote new forms of cultural engagement. Launched in 2008, the first seaside resort towns to benefit from this in 2008 were Blackpool, Dover and Torbay, each of which was to receive up to £4 million, and

this was to be match funded from local sources. In certain cases, such as that of Folkestone, major private-sector funding started off comparable initiatives, and this was likely to lead on to attract 'Sea-Change' funding at a later stage. This programme was, and is, a major initiative to try and generate a new range of activities and initiatives, which may themselves spark off the recycling and renewal process in a range of the livelier resorts in the country. It is perhaps paradoxical that the first of the resorts to gain from it was Blackpool, which has traditionally been renewed by major private-sector initiatives, throughout its life history. It is to be hoped that the unfortunate timing of this programme, starting off just before the international banking collapse and resultant economic recession, will not stop it having the desired effect of recycling this set of national resorts.

Case Study 3: Bournemouth – a Sustainable Resort?

Bournemouth Borough Council is a unitary local authority which has overall responsibility for planning, environmental and tourism-related matters. It is a resort city with a population of about 150,000. Since its 18th-century foundation, Bournemouth has grown to be a leading British seaside tourist resort, which has supplemented its general appeal with language courses, congresses and conferences, having created a Bournemouth International Centre for conference use. Bournemouth's prosperity is due to tourism, which generates more than 15,000 jobs locally. It has over 500 tourist accommodation establishments, providing almost 22,000 tourist beds. About 1.5 million holidaymakers a year come to Bournemouth, in addition to 4.5 million day trippers.

Bournemouth decided to become a 'Local Agenda 21' authority in the UNEP context, not because it was a failing resort, but because it had concerns about sustainability, and wanted to minimize the impact of global environmental problems upon it. The 'Local Agenda 21' aims at allowing Bournemouth to be globally promoted on the European market as a green resort, in recognition of its environmentally friendly activities such as Blue Flag, Green Flag and Green Globe Tourism Awards (awards for water quality, beach cleanliness and overall quality of a destination, respectively).

The 1995 Environmental Charter for Bournemouth, and an annual 'corporate environmental programme' and a 'community plan' bring together all the measures carried out by the different arms of the local authority, towards its environmental sustainability.

In order to sustain itself as a tourist destination, Bournemouth undertakes many measures aimed to: (i) deal with the seasonality of tourism; (ii) promote the Bournemouth Conference Centre; (iii) encourage longer stays; (iv) promote alternatives to car use by encouraging use of cycle-ways, footpaths and public transport; and (v) encourage the development of 'green tourism', and through providing management plans carry out related action.

Bournemouth tries to integrate sustainable tourism via its local management tools. These include:

- its environmental management system;
- the use of a corporate environmental strategy working group;
- the approval and use of a corporate environmental programme; and
- the fact that these strategies and quantified objectives towards sustainability are signed by more than 100 partners of the local authority.

The Bournemouth Environmental Forum has been in existence for several years and the Bournemouth Partnership looks closely at its plans to see how far active implementation can be achieved of all these desirable environmental intentions. Bournemouth embarked upon 'Local Agenda 21' essentially on a preventative basis, in order to try and manage tourism growth in the directions to which it aspires, and as indicated it is trying to integrate a strategy of sustainable development in its local management, through the Environmental Forum and Bournemouth Partnership arrangements.

Evaluation

Progressive examples, first that of Scheveningen in the Netherlands, where the resort is part of a capital and congress city, and secondly through the work done by a range of management agencies in a resort like Bournemouth, under 'Local Agenda 21' schemes, show progressive ways forward, in terms of seaside resorts. The reviews of spas and resorts done in the 1970s and 1980s in England, Scotland and Wales showed the need particularly for heritage resorts to find new bases for life, interest, activity and renewal. Thus governmental collaborative programmes, such as the 2008 Sea-Change Programme in Britain, and a further UK government initiative in 2010, create incentives and critical initiating finance for this desirable process of change, to be built into this phase of recycling old seaside resorts.

Spas, which led to the development of resorts, have themselves seen further phases of evolution from the late 19th century to the 21st century. They have evolved from remedial and curative spas, involved in 'water cures' using mineral and/or sea water, through to diet control, fitness and beauty treatments, and on to 1980s' 'mother and baby' programmes at Evian les Bains, to aroma therapy, yoga, pilates, meditation, and new sports and exercise regimes, throughout the five-star spa hotels across the globe. Since the 1980s, these facilities have been the attractions which have drawn new 'health tourists' to 'wellness' programmes, internationally, and given rise to 'wellness tourism', something that the philosophy of the pioneering Peckham Health Centre, in London anticipated in its 1930s' programmes!

46 Long-life Pilgrimage Tourism and its Destinations

Introduction

The term 'pilgrim' is defined by dictionaries as 'a person who undertakes a journey to a sacred place as an act of religious devotion'. Similarly the word 'pilgrimage' is defined as 'a journey to a shrine or other sacred place', or alternatively 'a journey or long search for exulted or sentimental reasons' – 'to make a pilgrimage'. It is noteworthy that the tourist industry and tourism schools tend to treat pilgrimage tourism as yet another miscellaneous tourism market segment, among others. However, as today the tourist industry seeks to find 'sustainable tourisms', and 'sustainable destinations', as 'resorts are not forever', and the forms of holiday and conference tourism may have limited lives, we need to look more closely at pilgrimage tourism. The reason for this is that pilgrimage tourism has been the most sustainable form of tourism in human history. It has been there in Zoroastrianism for about 4000 years, Judaism for 3000 years, Hinduism for over 2000 years, Christianity for nearly 2000 years and Islam for nearly 1400 years.

The Size and Ranking of Religions

As there is a pilgrimage element in most religions, it is important first to look at the scale and importance of religions across the world. The largest religion in terms of numbers of its adherents in the world is Christianity, variously estimated to have from 2 to 2.1 billion followers, or 33% of the world's population; the second largest is Islam, which is variously attributed to have from 1.2 to 1.5 billion believers, or some 21% of the world's population; and the third largest religion is sometimes given to Hinduism which has 800–900 million followers, or 14% of the world's population (Noss, 1974; Winston and Wilson, 2004). However, some reviewers rank the third largest as being the secular, non-religious, agnostic and atheist population of the world, which they – by unknown means – assume to equal about 1.1 billion or 16% of the world's population. Ranked at fifth are Chinese traditional religions (Confucianism and Taoism), which are estimated to have 394 million adherents or 6% of the world's population, compared with Buddhism at sixth, having from 360 to 376 million followers, according to different estimates. While next in ranking some analysts place Shintoism with 110 million Japanese followers, others claim that that is the nominal religion of Japan, but that the realistic following is only 4 million. Some rank primal or indigenous beliefs including some of the animist beliefs at 300 million, and then African traditional and diasporic beliefs relating to about 100 million people. Below these come Sikhism with about 23 million, Juche with 19 million, Spiritism with 15 million, Judaism with 14 million, Bahai with 7 million, Jainism 4.2 million, Cao Dai 4 million, Zoroastrianism 2.6 million, Tenrikyo 2 million, Neo-Paganism 1 million, Unitarism and Universalism at 1 million, Rastafarism 0.6 million and finally Scientology at 0.5 million followers.

What finally is without doubt is that the two largest religions on earth in terms of the numbers of their followers, are Christianity and Islam, and the element of pilgrimage has been important in one, and is a vital element in the other. In Christianity there are the set of original sites within the Holy Land associated with the life and work of Christ, and then later sites associated with the institution of the Church, and with sites of miracles and associations with saints in the history of the Church. In Islam one needs to examine two sites in particular, namely Mecca and Medina, associated with the Hajj because one of the tenets of Islam is that every believer is expected to make the Hajj at least once in a lifetime.

When one considers the relatively small religions such as Sikhism, Shintoism or Bahai, one again finds the significance of pilgrimage to believers or followers of these religions. In the case of Sikhism, visits to the Golden Temple at Amritsar in the Punjab in India is the most revered of pilgrimage sites, while for followers of the relatively young Bahai faith, which is of 19th-century origin, the Shrine of the Bab in Haifa, Israel, is one of the religion's most holy sites.

Rather than trying to review all religions and their pilgrimage places, we will now look briefly at Far Eastern religions, religions that originated in the Middle East, Islam's pilgrimage destinations and finally consider the Holy Land, where no less than six of the world religions have key pilgrimage sites.

Far Eastern Religions

According to Noss (1974) the Mother Ganga or the River Ganges is the focus of visits to holy places of pilgrimage to receive a special blessing for Hindus. There is a multiplication of sacred places along the Ganges, and perhaps the best known of these is Varanasi (previously known as Benares), but other major pilgrim centres for Hindus include Haridwar and Allahabad on the Holy Saraswati. On 15 January, 2010 *The Times* stated that: 'More than 50 million pilgrims are expected to attend the Kumbh Mela ceremony – regarded as by far the biggest religious festival in the World.' The event is also known as the Pitcher Festival, taking place in the northern city of Haridwar, and aiming to cleanse the sins of the pilgrims and break the cycle of life and death, via their bathing in the River Ganges.

It is understood that the Temples of Angkor Wat are devoted mainly to Hindu Gods Shiva and Vishnu and have always been the destination for pious pilgrims, both Hindu and Buddhist, since the late 12th century AD.

Religions that Originated in the Middle East

Turning to the great monotheistic or Abrahamic faiths, we may first note a quotation by M. Goodman (cited by Norwich, 2009) that:

> 2000 years ago, Jerusalem, in the time of Herod and Jesus…the daily rhythm of worship was disrupted three times a year when the Temple and the City were invaded by huge crowds of pilgrims at the festivals of Passover, Pentecost and Tabernacles…by devout Jews from every nation.

It is the Western Wall of the Temple Mount in Jerusalem that has remained a key site of Jewish pilgrimage since late antiquity (Fig. 46.1). Considering Christian pilgrimages to the Holy Land, according to Noss (1974) these historically have focused on: (i) baptism in the River Jordan; (ii) Jerusalem itself, with the opportunity for pilgrims to follow the Stations of the Cross on the Via Dolorosa in addition to worshipping at the Church of the Holy Sepulchre; and (iii) praying in the churches of Bethlehem and Nazareth. Later with the evolution of the Roman Catholic Church, pilgrimage to Rome and to the Piazza De San Pietro (i.e. to the square in front of

Fig. 46.1. The Western Wall of the Temple Mount in Jerusalem a key site of Jewish pilgrimage (photograph courtesy of www.goisrael.com).

St Peters) for pilgrims to receive the Pope's blessing has become important. Across the Christian world, sites of miracles and their associations with saints have all become pilgrimage destinations, whether to Lourdes in France, Czestochowa in Poland, Assisi in Italy, or Santiago de Compostela in Spain.

Islam

Turning to Islam, according to D. Behrens-Abouseif (cited by Norwich, 2009):

> Muhammed was born in Mecca about AD 570…According to Islamic tradition around 610 the Koran was revealed to him…The new religion was not well received by all…In 622 Muhammed fled…to Medina…This 'Hijra' or migration marks the beginning of the Islamic calendar…Medina remained the capital of the new Muslim community, while Mecca and more specifically its Ka'ba, became the Qibla or the direction towards which Muslims pray. The pilgrimage to Mecca, the Hajj, at least once in a lifetime is one of the five tenets of Islam.

The Ka'ba, the holiest shrine in Mecca, is visited in the holy month of Dhu al Hijju and some four months are reserved each

year for pilgrimages and trade. Muslims are expected to be in Mecca during the sacred month of Dhu al Hijju and it is then that the annual observance of the circumambulation of the Ka'ba – the lesser and greater pilgrimages take place. What is of extraordinary interest about the Hajj is that this is possibly the second largest regular pilgrimage which takes place on earth and it takes place to a country, namely Saudi Arabia, which does not have a tourist board, and does not officially recognize tourism. It is estimated that up to three million people annually go on the Hajj pilgrimage to Mecca (Fig. 46.2).

This mass movement of people from around the Islamic world is now largely conducted by tour operators and travel agents, who offer commercial packages enabling people to fly and/or travel by sea, as well as overland, to get to Saudi Arabia and to Mecca. However, for a thousand years Islamic pilgrims made the pilgrimage across the deserts of the Middle East by caravanserai (i.e. camel trains) and B. Rogerson (cited by Norwich, 2009) writing about Damascus, states that:

> For over a thousand years the vast crowds associated with the Hajj pilgrimage would

Fig. 46.2. The Great Mosque, Mecca.

annually assemble outside the walls of Damascus for the desert crossing to Mecca (the last such caravan departed in 1864, after which the sea journey down the Red Sea to Jeddah took over).

Pilgrimages to the Holy Land

Of all the locations on earth, what is quite extraordinary is that a concentration of key holy sites to some six religions, are found in the relatively small Holy Land – now contained partly in Israel, and partly in the Palestinian territories. This Holy Land has the biggest range of Christian sites on earth – all related to the life of Christ. Jerusalem has the second most important site of Islam within it, because the Mosque of Omar, according to Islamic belief, is where Muhammed ascended from earth to Heaven. The rock on which he ascended is also believed to be the rock on

which Abraham was about to sacrifice Isaac, a fact of great significance to both the Jewish and the Christian religions. Also virtually all the key sites associated with Judaism and its pilgrimages are located here, plus two of the key sites of the Bahai religion, the central holy site of the Samaritan religion, and one of the key sites of the Druse religion.

A Modern Itinerary for Christian Pilgrimage to the Holy Land

By the 1860s Thomas Cook, the first tour operator, was offering Holy Land pilgrimages and holidays (Swinglehurst, 1982), when tourists and pilgrims had no choice other than to sleep in tents in the desert and wild habitats that then existed there.

To give an indication of the adjustment in modern times of religious pilgrimages to the development of tourist industries and destinations we can look at a 4-day Christian pilgrimage tour to the Holy Land offered online in 2009 (visitisrael.com accessed 5 May 2009), and which indicates the range of pilgrimage sites that can be covered in a relatively short time by the modern international pilgrim.

- Day 1 – to Jerusalem, the Mount of Olives, the Garden of Gethsemane, Temple Mount, Dome of the Rock, on to the Pool of Bethesda, then to Via Delarosa to follow the Stations of the Cross, and a visit to the Church of the Holy Sepulchre, Mount Zion and the Church of St Peter, King David's Tomb and the room of the Last Supper in the Church of the Dormition and finally the Garden Tomb.
- Day 2 – travel by coach through the Judean Desert to the Inn of the Good Samaritan, on to Qumran, Ein Gedi and to Massada, returning to Jerusalem.
- Day 3 – to Jaffa, St Peter's Church and Tel Aviv, then up to Caesaria National Park and through the Mountains of the Galilee.
- Day 4 – visit the Christian sites around the Sea of Galilee, including the Mount of the Beatitudes, Capernaum, Tabgha, Bethsaida and the Galilee boat. Finally visits to Cana, Nazareth and the Basilica of the Annunciation, the Church of St Joseph, and the end of the pilgrimage.

What is interesting about this programme, or whether one considers similar programmes for Jewish pilgrimages in the Holy Land, or for Moslem pilgrimages to Mecca, is that the modern religious pilgrimage involves all of the classical elements of tourism. These include: (i) the characteristics of the journeys, whether these are by land, sea or air; (ii) the advantages of sustainable forms of transport to get to these destinations; (iii) the increasing interest in sustainable transport forms at the destinations, as the destinations themselves are fixed because of their religious significance; and (iv) the opportunity for pilgrims to choose, according to their means and wishes, from a range of accommodation. The accommodation on offer extends from the great tent cities associated with the Hajj for Islam, or the use of traditional church hospices in the history of Christian pilgrimages, to modern offers to followers of all religions, in hotels, camping sites, caravan sites and the full spectrum of visitor accommodation, catering and other services.

Evaluation

On the basis of the historic evidence we have, although the forms of pilgrimages today have changed, what is clear is that because of the importance of religion to much of humanity, pilgrimages which were such a feature in the past, would appear to have a continuing importance to followers of many of the world's religions. Further, with regards to looking at forms of sustainable tourism, to date pilgrimage tourism has represented the most sustainable form of tourism in human history, and on the basis of current evidence, there is a likelihood of it remaining an important form of tourism in the future.

47 Cities as Sustainable Tourism Destinations

Introduction: the Changing Nature of the City

Past dictionary definitions of a 'city' simply referred to it as being 'any large town or populous space' or 'urban' being defined as 'of, relating to, or constituting a city or a town' or 'living in a city or a town'. Cities or major settlements had occurred historically because of their grouped human needs for food, water, raw materials and labour. They were located on rivers (e.g. the Nile, the rivers of Mesopotamia, the Indus, the Rhine, the Rhone, the Ganges, the Yangtze, the Thames, or the Danube), by the sea (as at Ostia and Rome, or Alexandria), by major lakes (such as Geneva), or at points that had access to water and food supply, but were in defendable positions (for instance the hill towns of Italy, or high up for defence and sun worship such as the mountain towns of the Aztecs and the Incas).

The changed phenomenon which Man has to face in the 21st century is that of mega cities because, as indicated in the UN (2009) *Global Report on Human Settlements*, by 2008 half of the world's population lived in towns and cities. Not only was world population becoming urbanized, but as referred to earlier, some 40 mega cities were developing. These are urban agglomerations with a population of ten million or more each, and it has been noted that eight of the ten most populous cities in the world now stand on earthquake fault lines.

Problems

The new urban agglomeration issue can be seen particularly in great cities like Sao Paulo in Brazil, where the greater city is fast approaching 20 million in size, and includes over two million people living in 'favelas' or shanty towns. Even in the developed world, great cities, such as Toronto in Canada, now sprawl over vast areas, but they do not have the problems of the Third World megalopolis. The urban sprawl problems can be seen in the vast Mexico City, which has encroached on two adjacent states, or in Egypt where Cairo and Alexandria, located some 200 km apart, may merge in the foreseeable future. Major cities like Buenos Aires already cover 30 different municipalities. Worst of all in this context though, is the fact that the slums of these mega cities are mushrooming, and it is now estimated that 1.6 billion people are urban slum dwellers (i.e. living in shanty towns). As pointed out in the report of the Brundtland Commission (1987), the urban challenge is one not only of half of humanity living in urban centres, but we are living in an increasingly urban world and it is the urban component which has exponential growth. Furthermore, the governments responsible for these mega cities lack and need to have settlement strategies to guide these processes of growth and change for the sake of human habitability.

Opportunities

The biggest hope for the world's urban population is that at the moment half of that population is located in towns and cities under 500,000 in population, and if this smaller scale of settlement can be maintained for a large number of settlements, there are then hopes for both sustainability and opportunities for creating more habitable long-life settlements, with tourism possibilities. Other sources of hope for mankind are in our concern for heritage, whether this relates to work in the last 100 years in protecting the natural wonders of the world (e.g. waterfalls, National Parks, selective mountains and deserts), or the built and cultural heritage (e.g. in the maintenance of cathedrals, temples, mosques and places which are the embodiments of belief and faith and which have been guiding influences for 4000 years or more).

Already we have seen that there are magnets which draw people over time to certain destinations, whether for a religious reason such as the pull of Mecca to Moslems, or for rest and relaxation which has drawn people to the successive rivieras of the Mediterranean. Beliefs, and the pull of meaning and beauty, have drawn generations of visitors to cities – for example to the Imperial Palace of Kyoto, to the skyscrapers of New York, to the beauty and vitality of a Paris or a Rio de Janeiro, or the pull of exotic locations such as Lhasa, Petra or Madeira. Opportunities are presented by cities because cities generate so many forms of attraction to so many different types of visitor. As indicated earlier, there may be 200 types of tourism that draw visitors to a city, whether for business or pleasure, health treatment or study, worship or escape, sport or employment.

The Nature of Sustainable Urban Tourism

Already it has been seen that there are some forms of tourism which are very long life, and these grow out of functions of destinations, for example:

- capital cities, which draw on official or governmental tourism;
- religious centres such as Kandy, Rome, Beijing, Mecca or Jerusalem;
- industrial cities, which draw business tourists;
- conference cities, festival cities or resort cities; and
- cities that draw tourists for educational reasons (educational tourism or edutourism).

Educational tourism has many forms, and has been a draw to cities for hundreds of years starting with the landed gentry who would go on their 'Grand Tours' to Rome, as part of the preparation for life. In modern societies students travel the globe to study, or take 'gap years' between study, or to be volunteers in totally different societies to their home society.

The variation in climate, location, altitude and culture give rise to an enormous variety of cities across the world in terms of their character, architecture, feeling, food and dress. By the 20th century the 'imageability' of cities, and the distinctiveness of different urban destinations, and their 21st-century marketing, has become an art and a highly competitive game. The need to renew old resort cities and the need to find new economic bases for post-industrial cities that have past their manufacturing stage have become opportunities that have been taken up for the development of new forms of tourism.

The type of changes conducted in the cities of Boston and Baltimore, referred to as the 'Boston/Baltimore effect', have already had applications in cities elsewhere, such as Rotterdam, Sydney, Glasgow and Birmingham. The constraint on these opportunities has been the changing need for safety (safety from war, disease and illness, terrorism, personal attack such as mugging and robbery, or food poisoning where quality control has been inadequate). Urban economic diversification and the recycling of so many cities, because of change, has created enormous new opportunities, as has the use of mega events such as World Congresses and Expos, and the use of the Olympic Games, to change fundamentally the character and quality of resource offers in major cities around the world.

City size and quality

Throughout history, there have been writers, theorists and innovators who have postulated about the ideal size for a city and the ideal nature of a city. These range from ancient times with Plato's writings on *The Republic*, to the age of rationality, reflected in the theories and work of Robert Owen, through to a series of thinkers in the 19th century who were concerned with the need to humanize the new industrial cities and evolve paternalistic answers to the need for humane smaller societies, for those in working communities. Thus one finds for example in the UK Titus Salt's Saltaire settlement in Yorkshire, Cadbury's Bourneville in Birmingham and utopian developments by Lever and Fry. Ebenezer Howard and the Garden City movement laid down the notion of ideal cities having a population of from 40,000 to 60,000, and this gave rise to the development of such ventures as Welwyn Garden City and Letchworth Garden City, which led on to creating the new towns of the UK. Many of these questions of size were based on assumptions about social contact, and the human scale of the settlement, but became challengeable, because they often lacked economic criteria of viability in their functioning for residents on the one hand, and the variety of activities in them to appeal to visitors on the other hand.

Quality of urban life and of destination

In a major exercise (as yet unpublished), the author examined a range of cities whose population ranges from 300,000 to over a million to test them out against 20 criteria that define urban quality of a place both for residents, for economic viability and appeal, and also

appeal to visitors. The weights for these 20 factors were applied to this range of cities. What is interesting arising from the exercise, is that of the ten cities which came out top in this process, many were of the half million size, as far as their greater urban areas were concerned. However, more indicators backed the cities of the 350–500,000 population level, than others. The ranking of the top ten cities were as follows:

1. Edinburgh, Scotland, UK.
2. Prague, Czech Republic.
3. Wellington, New Zealand.
4. Cardiff, Wales, UK.
5. San Francisco, USA.
6. Haifa, Israel.
7. Florence in Italy and Quebec City in Canada.
8. Vancouver, Canada.
9. Auckland, New Zealand.
10. Krakow, Poland.

It is noteworthy that Nice, and large seaside resorts in the list, were ranked below this level. Three of the top four were not only cities in the 350,000–500,000 population level, but were also: (i) small capital cities which were also ports; (ii) places whose scale enabled one to see the landscape beyond the city; and (iii) tourist destinations for conference tourism, governmental tourism, festival tourism, cultural tourism and sports tourism.

Sustainability and life cycles

As already discussed in Chapter 45, Butler's (1980) 'resort cycle' basically considered the phases in the life of a resort, and at the point of its stagnation and decline, the possibilities of its either continuing decline, or its rejuvenation through activities to create a second cycle of life. However, as already indicated, this theory is inadequate to explain the many life cycles that for instance a spa town such as Bath has gone through, which include not only several physical life cycles, but also several economic and social life cycles as well. As a result it is necessary to disaggregate these life cycles, and look carefully at a series of different life cycles with which one is concerned in cities and resorts in order then to see if they can be correlated, to give us new theoretical bases for action in the realm of sustainability.

We therefore need to look at the physical life cycle of resorts (i.e. the life of buildings, plants and people) as compared with the economic and social life cycle of different activities and fashions that make use of our physical environments over time. The physical life cycle itself is a big variable, because though financial and legal organizations may use 60 years as the amortization period for the legal life of a building, its physical life may vary from 10 to 20 years if it is some sort of rough shack, to at least 60 or 80 years if it is a poor quality brick building. If it is a high quality brick building, as we see with the Georgian developments in England, its life could be well over 200 years, and if the buildings are made of stone, 200 years could – with adequate maintenance – extend to 400 or more years. Individual great monuments of stone, for instance cathedrals, may well last a 1000 years or longer.

However, if one compares the economic or social life of different types of resort, or a watering place based on the notions of healthy sea bathing, it may perhaps last from 50 to a 100 years, whereas to date our experience of so-called seaside or holiday resorts, may have a basic life of something like 100 or 200 years. After life as a holiday resort, such a centre may then become either fundamentally a conference and research centre, or largely a retirement settlement that almost ceases to have a holiday function because its population is a sequence of retirement groups, who are self-replacing, for as one cohort dies they are replaced by another retirement cohort.

Thus the first correlation one needs to make is between the physical resource life cycles, for instance of an urban resort, compared with the life cycles of the different tourist activities that take place within that physical shell. This allows for natural decay or entropy processes over time, and processes of maintenance, cleaning, clearing, demolition, renewal and replacement. Similarly, it allows for fashions of summer tourism, winter tourism, new types of tourism over time, and the peak in the life of one form of tourism, as opposed to the decline of that form and its replacement

by another. These cycles are shown in Fig. 47.1, devised by the author in the 1980s. If numbers or weights are given to these physical resource life cycles, and the tourism product life cycles, then one can correlate them, and obtain a correlated life cycle's theory of sustainability, which for the sake of simplicity, could be called a 'COLIFET' theory of sustainability.

Sustainable Urban Tourism Destinations

From the foregoing comments it can be seen that there are strong advantages in certain types of medium-sized capital cities, which are also ports, and are well sited in relation to the landscape. Four or five immediate examples become evident in this context, namely: (i) Edinburgh, Scotland; (ii) Greater Wellington, New Zealand; (iii) Scheveningen in The Hague in the Netherlands; and (iv) Cape Town in South Africa. A city or urban area with a population of 350,000–500,000 has enormous advantages in the scale of services it can offer, not only to its resident population, but also the range of activities growing out of its inherent functions, which give rise to its long-life appeal as a destination for a range of tourisms.

Already in case studies of Edinburgh (Chapter 29) and Scheveningen/The Hague (Chapter 45), one can see how the resort function of a capital city, the conference function and the seaport function, all reinforce each other. Further, capitals tend to be relatively white-collar cities with a high level of maintenance because of the issue of imageability of capitals and of nations, and this further reinforces the appeal of Edinburgh and The Hague, or for that matter of Cardiff and Wellington. One may well question the long-term viability of the megalopolises, particularly those in the Third World, which have such a large scale of slum or shanty town associated with them. This is because in such megalopolises there is an inherent danger to the visitor because of poverty and the pool of unemployed/under-employed people, who for survival will be drawn into various forms of crime,

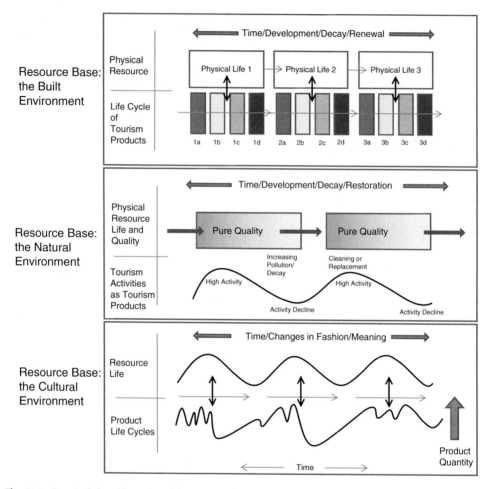

Fig. 47.1. Sustainability: life cycles of the resource base and of the sequence of related tourism products.

affecting the safety of visitors and residents alike. To date mega cities in the developed world, for example Greater London and Greater New York, have seemingly managed to control their domestic crime situations. However, in the late 20th century the phenomenon of international terrorism on the one hand, and growing problems of inter-personal crime in these large cities on the other, has raised questions of their long-term viability as appealing sustainable tourism destinations as the risk levels to the visitor increase over time. As yet, smaller cities have greater advantages, even over their counterparts with populations of one million, because it is notable that cities

with populations of one million to two or three million include for example the Birminghams, the Detroits and the Beiruts, which have been described as crime capitals in the last 25 years.

There are some shared principles one can find in a number of the tourist destinations looked at in this book, and if we take the case studies of Munich in Germany (Chapter 33), Beaulieu in the UK (Chapter 42) and Colonial Williamsburg in the USA (Chapter 32), some common characteristics are noteworthy. These are: (i) that the core destination for the tourists (whether it is the city centre cluster of Munich, the central cluster of attractions in Beaulieu, or the central cluster of high density attractions in Colonial Williamsburg) is a safe, clean, pedestrian environment; and (ii) access is provided to the core attraction. In the German case this is by underground and over-ground trains, while in the British and American cases it is by having surrounding edge car parks, bus parks or railway stations, from which some form of mass transit transfer (usually by bus) is provided to the core attraction. This is equally true of Tivoli (Chapter 38) or Skansen (Chapter 40), as it is of the pedestrian zone of central Birmingham (Chapter 34) or the core area around the Kurhaus in Scheveningen resort in the Netherlands (Chapter 45).

It is not one form of tourism which is the magical answer to providing any destination with long-life or sustainable tourism, but a number of tourisms at one point, or at different points in time, may make a destination sustainable. This may be the case whether it is a form of holiday tourism, conference tourism, religious tourism, heritage-based tourism, youth tourism, or a combination of new forms of market segments or niche market tourisms. Such niche market tourism can be seen, for instance, in Jenkins's (2007) work on literary festivals, or the emergence of forms of youth tourism associated with pop festivals, facebook, Spice UK (an adventure sports and social group that organizes leisure events and holidays), online explorations leading to meetings, or the manifold new forms of association which become central in the developed world.

There are manifold reasons for people in cities to come together, such as associations between people who are garden lovers, line dancers, trade unionists, members of a particular profession or occupation, or members of cross-professional organizations such as Rotary, Lions, Probus and the Freemasons. These give reasons for meetings, associations and coming together for holiday and social group meetings, work contact, or competitive forms of meetings, all giving rise to the so-called '200 tourisms', which can aid the process of making cities more sustainable, and which in turn helps them to become sustainable tourist destinations.

Appendix Sources and Acknowledgements

What is unusual about the sources of this book is the large amount of primary data it includes, based upon the main author's and contributing authors' roles and interviews in the range of countries involved. Sincere thanks are given to all who have helped.

Eve Randall is thanked for all her help in word processing and editing drafts of much of this book.

Professors M. Pryer and M. Dower, Doctors R.M. Denman, T. van Egmond (the Netherlands) and I. Jenkins (Switzerland) are all warmly thanked for their thoughtful comments, time and support.

Below is a list of specific acknowledgements, however, in a major enterprise such as the writing of this book, many people have given their help and have not been specifically acknowledged. Thanks are given to them all.

Poland

This relates to about ten visits to Poland, from 1962 to 2009, the longest of which was for 15 months – working full time as Programme Director of the EU PHARE Tourism Development Programme in Poland. There were special interviews with the late Professor B. Malisz, of the Polish Academy of Sciences, and Dr J. Kozlowski, and working contact with Professors K. Przeclawski and G. Golembski and Mr R. Dylewski, plus with the Polish specialist, Professor J. Fisher of the Johns Hopkins University in Baltimore, USA. Staff were interviewed in Polish central government, the Voivodic government, cities and rural bodies.

Netherlands

Travis has made over a dozen working visits to the Netherlands between 1958 and 2009, and spent 2.5 months sabbatical, based at the Planologisch Studiecentrum, TNO, Delft – from where he visited and interviewed over 40 staff in Dutch central government, provincial and local government agencies, tourism, recreation, conservation and voluntary-sector agencies. Travis has worked as a consultant with the RBOI Dutch consultancy, and for the NBT as a consultant. He wrote an Organisation for Economic Co-operation and Development (OECD) report on Dutch tourism. Dr D. Opt Veld, Mr C. Verwijs, Mr H.P. Krolis, Mr F. Vonk and Mr C. Paans are thanked for their help, and for accessing a range of recent documentation. Mr O. Ponti of the Amsterdam Toerisme en Congres Bureau is thanked for his help.

Scheveningen

Travis worked as an RBOI Consultant to Nationale Nederlanden, when it was engaged in one of the phases of planning and renewal of Den Scheveningse Bad.

Building complexes

Travis as Director of the Centre for Urban and Regional Studies (CURS), University of Birmingham, led a study team of three, visiting and assessing three Dutch complexes and interviewing their staff and users. Online updated information was used for temporal comparisons.

Israel

Travis has made five working visits to Israel, in tourism and conservation contexts. He has worked in an Israeli New Town, and interviewed all the past key players in the local tourist industry. He prepared a report to the OECD on Israeli tourism. He was involved in a key peace conference on tourism, together with Jordanian, Israeli and Egyptian delegates.

Denmark

At least four evaluative working visits were made for UK sponsors to Jutland, the islands and the Copenhagen region, with extensive interviewing of planning, conservation, recreation and tourism agencies, at the local, regional and national levels. Special thanks are given to Mr B.J. Christianson, former City Architect of Århus, for help with access to a range of past documentation.

Tivoli

Some three visits have been made to Tivoli, and thanks are given for extensive documentation, use of illustrations and answers to queries by Ms Ellen Dahl (PR) of the Tivoli Company.

The Maldives

Early in the tourist life of this island nation, Travis led a tourism training course there for the Pacific Area Tourism Association (PATA), serving staff from the Maldives and four other South-east Asian nations. This involved close working with the national government and commercial operators. Online data has provided updated comparisons.

Slovakia

Two official visits were made to the Urbion Consultancy Office, where long interviews were conducted with the late Mr R. Aroch and his colleagues, plus the staff of the Tatra National Park Office. Stays in the National Park, allowed for on-site evaluation.

Croatia

Plitvice Lakes

Working visits both to the Institute of Tourism in Zagreb, and three visits to the Plitvice Lakes National Park included interviews with the late Professor S. Markovic (consultant to the National Park), and *in situ* interviews with Mr Z. Kramaric and Mr J. Movcan – immediately before the park's capture and damage by the Serbian Army. My thanks to Professor Z. Klaric for getting me away from there in time!

Adriatic Coastal Planning

Working visits to Federal Yugoslavia, and to independent Croatia and Slovenia, permitted interviews with teams of planners responsible for Jadran I, II and III. Special thanks to Professors Tomasevic, Markovic, Dragicevic and staff of the UK Consultancy of Shankland Cox.

Algeria

Travis led the World Tourism Organization (WTO) mission to southern Algeria, where he organized the United Nations (UN)/ WTO's International Seminar on Alternative Tourism. The close involvement with Tuareg cameleers and Algerian government staff, plus long on-site discussions, were of great value.

USA

Williamsburg

This was visited during a US study visit to Virginia, organized by Travis for staff from British Tourist Boards. The informative help of the Foundation staff and of the US Travel Service for photos is much appreciated.

Virginia

Federal, state and local government, as well as commercial agencies in Virginia were all visited in the study tour referred to above, organized by Travis.

Huron Clinton

In a sabbatical semester spent at Wayne State University in Detroit, Travis conducted extensive interviewing at the Huron–Clinton Metropolitan Authority (HCMA), with its headquarters staff, field staff and site users. Online data updates from the HCMA were obtained for temporal comparisons. Thanks are also given to Mr M. Rohwer (Frey Foundation, Grand Rapids) for help in access to recent materials.

Belgium (Waterloo)

Thanks are given to Mr E. Ricci of Geneva, for his helpful summary translation of very verbose Belgian documentation in French.

Germany (Munich)

Thanks are given both to Mr G. Meighoerner and to a range of staff of the Municipality of Munich for their help with data and use of photos.

England

Peak District

Work visits to the Peak District National Park have been regularly made from the time of Mr J. Foster, as Park Director, to Professor M. Dower's time as Park Planner and Director. Interviews regarding the Derwent Valley were done for PIEDA Consulting, as part of the work of the UK National Task Force's research work on tourism and the environment.

Tarka Project

The Devon Tarka Project and its staff were visited and interviewed, under the auspices of PIEDA for the Task Force. Travis was the Research Director of the PIEDA team on the Task Force.

Birmingham

Thanks are given to all the key role players (too many to list) who have been interviewed over the years in Birmingham. Special thanks are given to Brindleyplace. com for their help and permission to use their photos in this text.

London

Thanks are given to Mr N. Hockley and Miss K. Clark of London Organizing Committee of the Olympic Games and Paralympic Games (LOCOG), London, for their time, trouble and help with documentation on the London 2012 Olympics.

Beaulieu

Mr P. Collier and Ms N. Appleton of Beaulieu Enterprises Ltd are thanked for their help with data.

Wales (South Wales Valleys)

Travis directed the ten-member consultancy team, which did this major study for the Wales Tourist Board in the 1980s.

UK (Coastline England and Wales)

Thanks are given to Mr J. Davidson (Cheltenham) for help in borrowing copies of key official documentation on this work, which was no longer readily available elsewhere.

Scotland

Edinburgh

Warm thanks are given to Mr C. Macleod for his specially taken excellent photos of Edinburgh, to Professor R. Carter for helpful telephone discussions, and to staff of the Edinburgh Fringe office (and especially Mr J. Olea) for their help with information and photos.

Culloden

Thanks are given to the staff of the Gareth Hoskins Architectural firm in Glasgow (and especially Mr N. Domini) for their help, permission to reproduce plans, and details of commercial photographers employed.

Thanks are given to three commercial photographers in Scotland for permission to reproduce their photos, namely Messrs A. Lee, E. Weatherspoon and N. Rigden.

Figures

Thanks are given to the following named sources for their permission to reproduce the following illustrations.

A.S. Travis for Figs I.1, I.2, I.3, I.4, I.5, 6.1, 10.1, 11.1, 12.1, 12.2, 13.1, 13.2, 13.3, 15.1, 16.2, 18.1, 28.1, 35.1, 38.2 and 47.1; International Union for Conservation of Nature (IUCN) Fig. I.6; India Tourism Fig. 1.1; Greater London Council (GLC) Fig. 2.1; Olympic Delivery Authority (ODA) and Ordnance Survey Fig. 2.2; LOCOG Fig. 2.3; The English Tourist Board (ETB) Fig. 2.4; R. Dylewski Fig. 3.1; R. Dylewski and A.S. Travis Fig. 3.2; Z. Karpowicz Fig. 3.4; Government of Western Australia Figs 4.1, 4.3 and 4.5; Gordon Bluk Fig. 4.4; W. and J. Kaucz Fig. 4.2; Rijks Plasing Dienst (RPD; the Netherlands) Figs 5.1 and 5.2; Delta Commissie (Netherlands) Figs 5.3 and 5.5; Veluwe Authority (Netherlands) Fig. 5.4; Israel National Park Authority Fig. 6.2 and Fig. 6.3b, c; Company for the reconstruction of the Jewish Quarter Fig. 6.3a; Århus Regional Authority Fig. 7.1; visitmaldives.com Fig. 8.1; Polish Tatra National Park Fig. 12.3; Scottish Tourist Board/Visit Scotland Figs 13.5, 13.6, 13.7 and 13.8; Roly Smith and the AA for the map from National Parks in Britain used in Fig.16.1; visitwales.co.uk Figs 17.1 and 17.2; J. Jafari (Wisconsin) Fig. 19.1; Valene Smith (USA) Fig. 19.2; Mid-Wales Festival of the Countryside Fig. 20.1; Countryside Commission Fig. 24.1; Mediterranean Action Plan (MAP) and Blue Plan Figs 25.1 and 25.2; Priority Actions Programme Regional Activity Centre (PAP/RAC) Fig. 26.1 and also Cyprus Tourism Fig. 26.2; Delta Commissie (2008) *Working Together with the Sea* Figs 27.1 and 27.2; Colin MacLeod Figs 29.1, 29.2 and 30.1; Youngson (1966) *The Making of Classical Edinburgh 1750–1840* Fig. 29.3; Edinburgh Fringe (www.edfringe.com) Fig. 30.2; Peter Watt (www.peterwatt.co.uk) Fig. 31.1(a) and www.insidersguide-online.com Fig. 31.1b; Colonial Williamsburg Foundation Figs 32.2 and 32.3; US Travel Service Figs 32.1, 32.4 and 39.1; Munich City Council Fig. 33.3 (comprising: Christmas market, Marienplatz, Munich – photograph by Fritz Witzig; Karlsplatz genannt Stachus (city hall) and Munich's main shopping street – photographs by Christl Reiter; Munich's pedestrian zone – photograph by B. Roemmelt); www.brindley-place.com (Birmingham) Figs 34.1 and 34.2; US National Park Service Figs. 37.1

and 37.3; Andrew Lee (Scotland) Fig. 37.2; Tivoli Gardens (Denmark) Fig. 38.1; Skansen (Sweden) Fig. 40.1; Huron–Clinton Metropolitan Authority (HCMA; Michigan) Figs 41.1, 41.2 and 41.3 and Table 41.1; Beaulieu Enterprises Ltd Fig. 42.1 and plan in Fig. 42.2; 'Design' for photo in Fig. 42.2; Pearse and Crocker (1943) Fig. 43.1; Meerpaal Fig. 43.2; Agora's Management, Lelystad Fig. 43.3; *Canadian Geographer* Fig. 45.1; www.scheveningenbad.nl Fig. 45.2; www.goisrael.com Fig. 46.1; Chapter 13 illustrations are by R.D. Cameron, M.E.S. Paynter, F. Perry, I. Samuels and A.S. Travis. Apologies are given to any whose photos were excluded after this was written; this was due to the excessive costs of too many illustrations.

Disclaimer: Every effort has been made to contact all known holders of copyrights of all illustrations used in this book. Apologies are given to any who could not be traced, and are therefore not acknowledged.

A.S. Travis
2010

Bibliography

Aas, Ø. (2008) *Global Challenges in Recreational Fisheries*. Blackwell Publishing, Oxford, UK.

Abercrombie, P. and Plumstead, D. (1949) *A Civic Survey and Plan for the City and Royal Burgh of Edinburgh*. Oliver and Boyd, Edinburgh, Scotland, UK.

Adler, C. (1981) *Tourists: Cannibals of Culture*. Ethno-Verlag, Argelsried, Germany.

Alejziak, W. (2008) *Globalization and Decentralization as Directions for the Development of Tourism Policy in the 21st Century* in *New Problems of Tourism 1/2008*. K. Przeclawski, College of Tourism and Hospitality Management in Warsaw, Warsaw, Poland.

Alexander, C. (1966) A city is not a tree. *Design* 206, 46–55.

Alexander, C. (1967) The city as a mechanism for sustaining human contact. In: Ewald, W.R. (ed.) *Environment for Man: the Next 50 Years*. Indiana University Press, Bloomington, Indiana, USA, pp. 406–434.

Alkjaer, E. (1978) *Research on Trade Fairs and Conventions*. Volumes I–VI. Institute of Transportation, Tourism and Regional Science, Copenhagen School of Business Administration, Copenhagen, Denmark.

Allemand, S. (2006/7) *Quels Transports pour un Tourisme Durable? Carnet d'initiatives 8es Sommets du Tourisme de Chamonix Mont-Blanc* 2006. Sommets du Tourisme, Editions le Cavalier Bleu, Chamonix, France.

An Foras Forbatha (1966) *Planning for Amenity and Tourism*. National Institute for Physical Planning and Construction, Dublin, Eire.

Armstrong, J.L. (1984) Contemporary prestige centres for art and culture, exhibitions, sports, and conferences: an international survey. PhD thesis, University of Birmingham, Birmingham, UK.

Aronsson, L. (2000) *The Development of Sustainable Tourism*. Continuum Press, London, UK.

Australian Bureau of Statistics (1966) Available at: assda.anu.edu.au/census/c66/rtf/c66cdmf.rtf (accessed 1 October 2010).

Australian Bureau of Statistics (2006) Available at: www.abs.gov.au/census (accessed 1 October 2010).

Automobile Association (AA) (1979) *AA Book of British Towns*. Drive for the AA, London.

Bakken, T. (1993) Alternative and Sustainable Tourism in North Norway: How to Promote Sustainability. MSc. thesis, University of Ghent, Belgium and University of Surrey, Guildford, UK.

Bartkowski, T. (1977) Recreationally attractive regions and zones in Poland, and their function in satisfying the recreational needs of urban industrial agglomerations. Paper presented to the British Association Conference, Birmingham, UK.

BBC (September 2009) *The Frankincense Trail*. Programme with Kate Humble.

Beaudouin, E., Baud-Bovy, M. and Tzanos, A. (1962) *Cyprus Tourism Development Plan*. SCET Co-operation, Nicosia, Cyprus.

Beaulieu (1972a) *Design 286*. October 1972. National Motor Museum of Beaulieu, Brockenhurst, Hants, UK.

Beaulieu (1972b) *Beaulieu Palace House and Abbey Guide*. Beaulieu Enterprises, Brockenhurst, Hants, UK.

Beaulieu (1973a) Architectural Awards 1973. *RIBA Journal* (Special Issue).

Beaulieu (1973b) www.beaulieu.co.uk (accessed 1 October 2010).

Benedict, M.A. and McMahon, E.T. (2006) *Green Infrastructure: Linking Landscapes and Communities.* Island Press, Washington, DC.

Benoit, G. and Comeau, A. (2006) *A Sustainable Future for the Mediterranean: the Blue Plan's Environment and Development Outlook.* Earthscan, London, UK.

Berg, J. (1997) *Positively Birmingham.* Birmingham Picture Library, Birmingham, UK.

Berndsen, J., Saal, P. and Spangenberg, F. (1985) *Met Zicht op Zee (Tweehonderd jaar bouwen aan badplaatsen in Nederland, Belgie en Duitsland).* Staatsuitgeverij's Gravenhage, The Netherlands.

Binney, M. and Hanna, M. (1978) *Preservation Pays: Tourism and the Economic Benefits of Conserving Historic Buildings.* SAVE Britain's Heritage, London, UK.

Bisgrove, R. (2008) *William Robinson: the Wild Gardener.* Francis Lincoln Publishers, London, UK.

Bisio, A. and Boots, S. (eds) (1997) *The Wiley Encyclopaedia of Energy and the Environment,* Vol. 1. John Wiley & Sons, Hoboken, New Jersey, USA.

Boccaccio, G. (1995) *The Decameron.* (Translated by G.H. McWilliam). Penguin Books, London, UK.

Bolli, J. (1986) *The 10 Guiding Principles of Kuoni's Corporate Policy.* Kuoni, Zurich, Switzerland.

Boo, E. (1991) *Ecotourism: the Potential and Pitfalls,* Vols 1 and 2. WWF, Washington, DC, USA.

Bord Failte (1990) *Developing Heritage Attractions: a Conference to plan the development of culture and heritage-based tourism attractions in Ireland.* Hillview Securities, Galway, and the European Regional Development Fund (ERDF).

Borja, E. (1999) *Zen Gardens,* Ward Lock, London, UK.

Bosselman, F.P. (1979) *In the Wake of the Tourist: Managing Special Places in Eight Countries.* The Conservation Foundation, Washington, DC, USA.

British Tourist Authority (BTA) (1972) *Tourism and the Environment.* BTA, London, UK.

British Tourist Board (1975) *Resorts and Spas in Britain. A Study Commissioned by the British Tourist Boards for Europe's Architectural Heritage Year (EAHY) 1975.* British Tourist Authority, London, UK.

Britton, S. (1987) *Tourism in Small Developing Countries. Development Issues and Research Needs.* University of South Pacific, Commonwealth Foundation, Suva, Fiji.

Brook, F. (1977) *The Industrial Archaeology of the British Isles. The West Midlands* (Vol. 1). B.T. Batsford Books Ltd, London, UK.

Brundtland, G.H. (1987) *Our Common Future: Report of the World Commission on Environment and Development.* Oxford University Press, Oxford, UK.

Buchanan, R.A. (1974) *Industrial Archaeology in Britain.* Penguin Books, London, UK.

Burchell, R.W. and Listokin, D. (1975) *The Environmental Impact Handbook.* The Centre for Urban Policy Research, The Urban Land Institute, Rutgers University, New Jersey, USA.

Butler, R.W. (1980) The concept of tourism area cycle of evolution. Implications for the management of resources. *Canadian Geographer* 24(1), 5–12.

Bystrzanowski, J. (ed.) (1989a) *Tourism as a Factor of Change: a Socio-Cultural Study.* The Vienna Social Science Centre, Vienna, Austria.

Bystrzanowski, J. (ed.) (1989b) *Tourism as a Factor of Change: National Case Studies.* The Vienna Social Science Centre, Vienna, Austria.

Ceballos Lascurain, H. (1996) *Tourism, Ecotourism and Protected Areas.* International Union for Conservation of Nature (IUCN), Gland, Switzerland.

Chapman, J.M. and Chapman, B. (1957) *The Life and Times of Baron Haussman. Paris in the Second Empire.* Weidenfeld and Nicolson, London, UK.

Chaucer, G. (1976 reprint) *The Canterbury Tales.* (Translated into Modern English by N. Coghill). Penguin Books, London, UK.

Chinn, C. (1994) *Birmingham: the Great Working City.* Birmingham City Council, Birmingham, UK.

Ciborowski, A. (1956) *Tourism-planning in Poland, 1945–59.* Polonia Press, Warsaw, Poland.

Clivaz, C., Hausser, Y. and Michelet, J. (2003) Tourism monitoring systems based on the concept of carrying capacity: the case of the regional Natural Park Pfyn-Finges (Switzerland). In: *Proceedings of the 2nd International Conference on Monitoring and Management of Visitor Flows in Recreational and Protected Areas,* Rovaniemi, Finland. PAN Parks Foundation, Gyor, Hungary.

Coccossis, H. and Mexa, A. (2004) *The Challenge of Tourism Carrying Capacity Assessment: Theory and Practice.* Ashgate Publishing Ltd, Aldershot, UK.

Cohen, E. (1972) Towards a sociology of international tourism. *Sociological Review* 39(1), 164–182.

Cohen, E. (ed.) (1979) *Annals of Tourism Research: a Special issue on 'The Sociology of Tourism'.* University of Wisconsin, Stout, Wisconsin, USA.

Commission for Architecture and the Built Environment (CABE) (2009) *Planning for Places: Delivering Good Design through Core Strategies*. Available at: www.cabe.org.uk (accessed 1 April 2011).

Commission for Building, Town Planning and Architecture (CBTPA) (1962) *Town Development and Planning Problems in People's Poland*. CBTPA, Warsaw, Poland.

Cottrell, S., Van den Berg, C. and Van Bree, F. (2003) PAN parks principles: a cross-cultural comparison – Bieszczady and Slovenski Raj National Parks. In: *Proceedings of the 2nd International Conference on Monitoring and Management of Visitor Flows in Recreational and Protected areas*, Rovaniemi, Finland. PAN Parks Foundation, Gyor, Hungary.

Council of Europe (1978) *Pressures and Regional Planning Problems in Mountain Areas*. Report of the Seminar held at Grindelwald, Switzerland. Council of Europe, Brussels, Belgium.

Countryside Commission (1970) *Planning of the Coastline: a Report on a Study of Coastal Preservation and Development in England and Wales*. HMSO, London, UK.

Countryside Commission (1991a) *Heritage Coasts: Policies and Priorities*. Countryside Commission Publication No. 305. Countryside Commission, Cheltenham, UK.

Countryside Commission (1991b) *Visitors to the Countryside*. Countryside Commission, Cheltenham, UK.

Countryside Commission for Scotland (1989/90) *The Mountain Areas of Scotland: Conservation and Management*. Countryside Commission for Scotland, Perth, Scotland, UK.

Crowe, S. (1958) *Landscape Masterplan for Basildon New Town*. S. Crowe and Partners, London, UK.

Crowe, S. (2003) *Garden Design*. Packard Publishing's 2003 Paperback edition of Crowe's 1994 Work. Antique Collectors Club Ltd, London, UK.

Dahle, B. (1993) *Nature: the True Home of Culture*. Norges Idretts Hogskole (NIH), Oslo, Norway.

Dann, G.M.S. (ed.) (2002) *The Tourist as a Metaphor of the Social World*. CABI, Wallingford, Oxon, UK.

Dash, J. and Efrat, E. (1964) *The Israel Physical Master Plan (no.2)*. Ministry of Interior Planning Department, Jerusalem, Israel.

Dasmann, R.F., Milton, J.P. and Freeman, P.H. (1973) *Ecological Principles for Economic Development*. John Wiley & Sons, Hoboken, New Jersey, USA.

De Bruin, T. (1988) *De Recreatieve Betekenis van het Nationale Park de Hoge Veluwe (1) Recreatie in de Natuur: Literatuur Studie. (2) Empirische Studie*. Papers of the Working-group on Recreation 14. Landbouw Universitet, Wageningen, The Netherlands.

Delta Commissie (2008) *Working Together with the Sea: 2008 Dutch Response to Global Warming*. Available at: www.deltacommissie.com (accessed 1 October 2010).

Demers, V. (1987) *Le Developpement Touristique/Notions et Principes*. Les Publications du Quebec, Quebec Provincial Ministry, Quebec, Canada.

Denman, R. (The Tourism Company) (2001) *Guidelines for Community-based Ecotourism Development*. World Wide Fund for Nature (WWF) International, Gland, Switzerland.

Denman, R. and Denman, J. (1990) *A Study of Farm Tourism in the West Country (of England)*. Tourism RMD, Ledbury, Herefordshire, UK.

Den Norske Turistforening (DNT) (1989) *Mountain Hiking in Norway*. DNT, Oslo, Norway.

Department for Culture, Media and Sport (DCMS) (2003) *Strategic Plan 2003–2006*. DCMS, London, UK.

Department for International Development (DFID) (1999) *Changing the Nature of Tourism: Developing an Agenda for Action*. DFID, London, UK.

Department of the Environment (DOE) (1990) *This Common Inheritance: Britain's Environmental Strategy*. HMSO, London, UK.

Department of the Environment (DOE) (1994) *Sustainable Development: the UK Strategy – an Outline*. HMSO, London, UK.

Department of Regional Economic Expansion (1970) *The Canada Land Inventory: Report No. 1 – Objectives, Scope and Organisation*. Department of Regional Economic Expansion, Ottawa, Canada.

Deshmukh, I. (1996) *Bulgaria Global Environmental Facility BioDiversity Report. 1st Annual Report*. US Aid and the Government of Bulgaria, Sofia, Bulgaria.

Deuel, L. (1973) *Flights into Yesterday: the Story of Aerial Archaeology*. Penguin Books, London, UK.

Devon County Council (1986) *Project for Integrated Rural Development in Devon*. Devon County Council, Devon County Hall, Exeter, UK.

Dower, M. (1974) Tourism and conservation working together: recommendations and the governments and people of Europe. *Architects' Journal* 166, 941–963.

Doxey, G.V. (1975) A causation theory of visitor-resident irritants: methodology and research inferences. In: *Proceedings of Travel and Tourism Research Association 6th Annual Conference*, San Diego, USA.

Doxey, G.V. (1976) When enough's enough: the natives are restless in old Niagara. *Heritage Canada* 2(2), 26–27.

Doxey, G.W. (1985) A causation theory of visitor-resident irritants: methodology and research inference. In: Murphy, P.E. (ed.) *Tourism: a Community Approach*. Routledge, London, UK.

Dragicevic, M. (1978) *Ekoloski Problem i Usmjeravanje Privrednog Razvoja*. University Faculty of Economics, Zagreb, Croatia.

Dragicevic, M. and Kusen, E. (1990) *Methodological Framework for Assessing Tourism Carrying Capacity in Mediterranean Coastal Areas*. Mediterranean Action Plan, and Priority Actions Programme, Regional Activity Centres/UN Environment Programme, Zagreb, Croatia.

Dresner, S. (2002) *The Principles of Sustainability*. Earthscan, London, UK.

Dumazedier, J., Riesman, D. and McLure, S. (1967) *Towards the Society of Leisure*. Free Press of New York and Collier MacMillan, London, UK.

Dutch Ministry of Agriculture, Nature and Food Quality (2008) *National Parks in the Netherlands*. Dutch Ministry of Agriculture, Nature and Food Quality, The Hague, The Netherlands.

Dutch Ministry of Housing, Spatial Planning and Environment/Ministry of Agriculture, Nature and Food Quality/Ministry of Transport, Public Works and Water Management/Ministry of Economic Affairs (2006) *National Spatial Strategy: Creating Space for Development*. The Hague, The Netherlands.

Duuyst, D. (with Hens, L. and De Lanney, W.) (2001) *How Green is the City? Sustainability Assessment and the Management of Urban Environments*. Columbia University Press, New York, USA.

Ebers, S. (1992) *Beyond the Green Horizon: Principles for Sustainable Tourism*. Tourism Concern and WWF, London, UK.

Edinburgh Convention Bureau (1998) *Edinburgh: Guide to Meeting Space and Services 1996–1998*. Edinburgh Convention Bureau, Edinburgh, Scotland, UK.

Efrat, E. and Gavriely, E. (1969) *Settlement Sites in Israel (from pre1881 to 1947)*. Israel Ministry of Interior Planning Department, Jerusalem, Israel.

English Tourist Board (ETB) (1978) *London Tourism Regional Fact Sheets: 1977*. ETB, London, UK.

English Tourist Board (ETB) (1988) *Visitors in the Countryside: Rural Tourism, a Development Strategy*. ETB, London, UK.

English Tourist Board (ETB) (1989) *Visitors in the Countryside*. Proceedings of a Rural Tourism Conference held 17 November 1988. ETB, London, UK.

English Tourist Board (ETB)/Countryside Commission (CC)/Rural Development Commission (RDC) (1992) *The Green Light: a Guide to Sustainable Tourism*. Glasgow Associates, London, UK.

English Tourist Board (ETB) and Employment Dept Group (1991) *Tourism and the Environment: Maintaining the Balance. Report of the Task Force*. Glasgow Associates, London, UK.

English Tourist Board (ETB) in association with Welsh Tourist Board, Rural Development Commission, Countryside Commission and Countryside Commission for Scotland (1992) *Tourism in National Parks: a Guide to Good Practice*. ETB, London, UK.

Euracademy (2003) *Thematic Guide One: Developing Sustainable Rural Tourism*. Prisma Centre for Development Studies, Athens, Greece.

European Commission (1999) *Towards Quality Rural Tourism, Integrated Quality Management (IQM) of Rural Tourist Destinations*. European Commission, Enterprise Directorate General, Tourism Unit, Brussels, Belgium.

European Travels and Action Group (ETAG) and European Travel Commission (2006) *Tourism Trends for Europe*. European Travel Commission (ETC), Brussels, Belgium.

Evenari, M., Shanan, L. and Tadmor. N. (1971) *The Negev: the Challenge of a Desert*. Harvard University Press, Cambridge, Massachusetts, USA.

Fabos, J.G., Milde, G.T. and Weinmayr, V.M. (1968) *Frederick Law Olmsted Senior: Founder of Landscape Architecture in America*. University of Massachusetts Press, Amherst, Massachusetts, USA.

Farb, P. (1969) *Man's Rise to Civilisation*. Secker and Warburg, London, UK.

Federation of Nature and National Parks of Europe (FNNPE) (1993) *Loving Them to Death (on Sustainable National Park Planning)*. FNNPE, Regensburg, Germany.

Festival of the Countryside Office (1990s) *Annual Reports of the 'Festival of the Countryside for Rural Wales'*. Festival of the Countryside Office, Newtown, Wales, UK.

Fisher, J. (1966) *City and Regional Planning in Poland*. Cornell University Press, Ithaca, New York, USA.

Fleischer, A. and Pizam, A. (1997) Rural tourism in Israel. *Tourism Management* 18(6), 367–372.

Foster, A. (2005) *Birmingham: Pevsner Architectural Guide*. Yale University Press, London, UK.

Furnham, A. (1984) Tourism and culture shock. *Annals of Tourism Research* 11, 41–57.

Gareth Hoskins Architects (2008) *Gareth Hoskins Architects 0–10 Years. The Lighthouse Architecture Series*. The Lighthouse, Glasgow, Scotland, UK.

Geddes, P. (1925) *Tel Aviv Development*. Published by Geddes for the World Zionist Organization (WZO), Montpellier, France.

Geddes, P. (1949) *Cities in Evolution*. Edited by the Outlook Tower Association, Edinburgh. Williams & Norgate Ltd, London, UK.

Geddes, P. *Manuscript Collection: Patrick Geddes Correspondence*. National Library of Scotland, Edinburgh, Scotland, UK.

Getz, D. (1989) Special events, defining the product. *Tourism Management* 10(2), 125–137.

Getz, D. (1991) *Festivals, Special Events and Tourism*. Van Nostrand Reinhold, New York, USA.

Goethe, J.W. (1786–1788) *Italian Journey*. (Translated by W.H. Auden and E. Mayer, 1970 for Penguin Books, London, UK).

Gonsalves, D. (1985) *Alternative Tourism: a Resource Book*. Gonsalves Publications, Bangalore, India.

Gössling, S. and Peeters, P. (2007) 'It does not harm the environment!' An analysis of industry discourses on tourism, air travel, and the environment. *Journal of Sustainable Tourism* 15(4), 402–417.

Graburn, N. (1983) Anthropology of tourism. *Annals of Tourism Research* 10(1), 9–33.

Grant, M. (1976) *Cities of Vesuvius: Pompeii and Herculaneum*. Penguin Books, in association with Weidenfeld and Nicolson, London, UK.

Granville, A.B. (1841, republished 1971) *Spas of England, and Principal Sea-bathing Places: the North* (Vol. 1). Adams & Dart, Bath, UK.

Greater London Council (GLC) (1971) *Tourism and Hotels in London: a Paper for Discussion*. GLC, London, UK.

Greater London Council (GLC) (1978) *Tourism: a Paper for Discussion*. GLC, London, UK.

Greater London Council (GLC) (1980) *Tourism: a Statement of Policies*. GLC, London, UK.

Greenwood, D. (1972) Tourism: an agent of change: a Spanish Basque case. *Ethnology* 11(1), 80–91.

GTZ (1999) *Sustainable Tourism as a Development Option: Practical Guide for Local Planners, Developers and Decision Makers*. German Federal Ministry for Economic Cooperation and Development. GTZ-Eschborn, Germany.

Gunn, C.A. (1988) *Tourism Planning (Revised and Expanded)*, 2nd edn. Taylor & Francis, London, UK.

Halhead, V. (2005) *The Rural Movements of Europe*. Published on behalf of Prepare-Partnerships for Rural Europe, by Forum Synergies, Brussels, Belgium.

Hall, C.M. (1992) *Hallmark Tourist Events* Belhaven Press, London, UK.

Hamele, H. (1988) *Wie Wild auf den Sanften Tourismus*. Studienkreis for Tourismus e.v. Starnberg, Germany.

Hanbury-Tenison, R. (1984) *Worlds Apart: an Explorer's Life*. Granada Publishing Ltd, London, UK.

Harrison, D. and Hitchcock, M. (2004) *The Politics of World Heritage: Negotiating Tourism and Conservation*. Channel View Publications, Clevedon, Somerset, UK.

Hatton Associates (Undated) *Brindley Place, Birmingham*. Hatton Associates in Association with Core Marketing, Syon Print, Birmingham.

Heart of England Tourist Board (HETB) (1998) *Case Study: Birmingham Waterfront*. HETB, Worcester, UK.

Henderson, B. and Vikander, N. (2007) *Nature First: Outdoor Life the Friluftsliv Way*. Natural Heritage Books, Toronto, Canada.

Henderson, S. (2009) *What Killed Detroit?* Detroit Free Press, Detroit, Michigan, USA.

Heytze, J.C. (1972) Experiences with open-air recreation in Dutch forests. In: *Tourism and the Environment in Scotland, Conference Report*. Published in Report of Town Planning Summer School held in St Andrews. St Andrews, Fife, Scotland, UK.

Hudson, K. (1988) *Museums of Influence*, 2nd edn. Cambridge University Press, Cambridge, UK.

Hughes, J.T. and Kozlowski, J. (1968) Threshold analysis: an economic tool for town and regional planning. *Urban Studies* 5(2), 133–143.

Hughes, P. (1994) *Planning for Sustainable Tourism: the ECOMOST Project*. International Federation of Tour Operators (IFTO), Lewes, Sussex, UK.

Institute of Ecology (1972) *Man in the Living Environment: Report of the Workshop on Global Ecological Problems*. Institute of Ecology, University of Georgia, Athens, GA, USA.

International Atomic Energy Agency (IAEA)/United Nations Department of Economic and Social Affairs/International Energy Agency (IEA)/EUROSTAT and European Environment Agency (EEA) (2005) *Energy Indicators for Sustainable Development: Guidelines and Methodology*. IAEA,Vienna, Austria.

International Council for Local Environmental Initiatives (ICLEI) (1996) *The Local Agenda 21: Planning Guide, an Introduction to Sustainable Development Planning*. UN Environment Programme and ICLEI Freiburg and United Nations Environment Programme (UNEP). ICLEI, Bonn, Germany.

International Council for Local Environmental Initiatives (ICLEI) (1999) *Tourism and Sustainable Development, Sustainable Tourism: a Local Authority Perspective*. ICLEI, Bonn, Germany.

International Council on Monuments and Sites (ICOMOS) (1990) *Heritage and Tourism: Proceedings of the ICOMOS European Conference at Canterbury, UK*. ICOMOS, Paris, France.

International Institute for Sustainable Development (IISD) (1993) *Indicators for the Sustainable Management of Tourism*. IISD, Winnipeg, Canada.

International Union for Conservation of Nature (IUCN) (1978) *Categories, Objectives, and Criteria for Protected Areas*. IUCN, Gland, Switzerland.

International Union for Conservation of Nature (IUCN) (1980a) Protect the Mediterranean: a special bulletin report on IUCN's contribution to the inter-governmental meeting on the Mediterranean Specially Protected Area. *IUCN Bulletin*, New series Vol. II Nos 9/10. IUCN, Athens, Greece.

International Union for Conservation of Nature (IUCN) (1980b) *World Conservation Strategy: Living Resource Conservation for Sustainable Development*. IUCN/United Nations Environment Programme (UNEP)/ World Wide Fund for Nature (WWF), Gland, Switzerland.

Iso-Ahola, S.E. (1980) *The Social Psychology of Leisure and Recreation*. Brown-Dubuque, Indiana, USA.

Israel Department of Antiquities (date unknown) *The Antiquities Law: of the State of Israel*. National Government of Israel Publications, Jerusalem, Israel.

Israel Environmental Protection Service (1972) *Environmental Protection*. Israel Environmental Protection Service, Jerusalem, Israel.

Israel Knesset (1978) *Action Control of Roadside Advertisements*. Israel Knesset, Jerusalem, Israel.

Israel Ministry of Interior Planning Department (1961) *Kanowitz Environmental Protection Law*. National Government of Israel Publications, Jerusalem, Israel.

Israel Ministry of Interior Planning Department (1964) *Israel Physical Masterplan*. National Government of Israel Publications, Jerusalem, Israel.

Israel Ministry of Interior Planning Department (1972) *The National Masterplan for Israel Tourism*. National Government of Israel Publications, Jerusalem, Israel.

ITB Switzerland (1988) *Tourismus mit Einsicht* [*Tourism with Insight and Understanding*]. ITB for a Consortium of Swiss and German Agencies, Starnberg, Bavaria, Germany.

Jafari, J. (1982) Understanding the structure of tourism: an avant propos to studying its costs and benefits. Paper presented to Association Internationale d'Experts Scientifiques du Tourisme Annual Conference.

Jafari, J. (1987) Tourism models: 'the socio-cultural aspects'. *Tourism Management* 8(2), 151–159.

Jenkins, I. (2007) Post-modern tourism niches: UK literary festivals and their importance for tourism destination development. PhD thesis, University of Wales, Swansea, Wales, UK.

Joint Tourism Steering Group, Dept of Planning and Transportation, Greater London Council (GLC) (1974) *Tourism in London: a Plan for Management*. GLC, London Boroughs Association, English Tourist Board and London Tourist Board, London, UK.

Jones, A. and Travis, A.S. (1983) *Cultural Tourism: Towards a European Charter*. A Report to the Wales Tourist Board. East West Tourism Consultancy, Birmingham, UK.

Kaplan, M. (1975) *Leisure: Theory and Policy*. John Wiley & Sons, Hoboken, New Jersey, USA.

Karpowicz, Z. (1977) *The Organization of Tourism in Poland and Some Aspects of Its Development*. Centre for Russian and East European Studies (CREES), University of Birmingham/Centre for Urban and Regional Studies (CURS) paper. CURS, University of Birmingham, Birmingham, UK.

Karpowicz, Z.J. (1987) The Polish park systems. PhD thesis, University of Birmingham, Birmingham, UK.

Katz, E. and Gurevitch, M. (1975) *The Secularization of Leisure: Culture and Communication in Israel*. Farber, London, UK.

Keeley, G. (2009) Trains in Spain, race across the plain and could come to a station near you. *The Times* 29 June, p. 45.

Kelly, J.R. (1989) *Leisure*, 2nd edn. Prentice Hall International, Hemel Hempstead, Herts, UK.

Klaric, Z. (2007) *Final Report to the Cyprus Coastal Area Management Programme (CAMP) on Tourism Carrying Capacity Assessment (TCCA), Including the Larnaca Study*. United Nations Environment Programme/ Mediterranean Action Plan (MAP), Split, Croatia.

Knowles, T., Diamantis, D. and El Mourhabi, J.B. (2004) *The Globalization of Tourism and Hospitality: a Strategic Approach*, 2nd edn. Thomson, London, UK.

Koscak, M. (1992) Rural development in Trebnje Municipality. MSc. thesis, University of Ljubljana, Ljubljana, Slovenia.

Koscak, M. (1993) *CRPOV for CATEZ Commune Development Strategy and Action Plan*. Trebnje Municipality, Trebnje, Slovenia.

Koscak, M. (1998) Integral development of rural areas, tourism and village renovation. *Tourism Management* 19(1), 81–86.

Koscak, M. (1999) Transformation of rural areas along the Slovene-Croatian border. PhD thesis, University of Ljubljana, Ljubljana, Slovenia.

Kozlowski, J. (1968) Threshold theory and the sub-regional plan. *Town Planning Review* 39(2), 99–116.

KPMG (1993) *A Comparative Analysis of Tourism in 34 European Cities*. KPMG, Amsterdam, The Netherlands.

Krippendorf, J. (1977) *Les Devoreurs des Paysages*. Editions 24 heures, Lausanne, Switzerland.

Krippendorf, J. (1987) *The Holiday Makers: Understanding the Impact of Leisure and Travel*. Heinemann, London, UK.

Krolis, H.P., Opt Veld, A.G.G., Travis, A.S. and de Groot, E. (1999) *De Ontwiikkerling van het Vacantie-Bezoek van Senioren in Nederland 1996–2005*. TNO (Dutch National Organization for Scientific Research on the Environment)/Inro (Planning Research Institute at TNO), Delft, The Netherlands.

Labov, W. (1963) The social motivation for a sound change. *Word* 19, 273–309.

Labov, W. (1966) The effect of social mobility on linguistic behaviour. *Sociology Inquiry* 36, 186–203.

Laurie, I.C. and Travis, A.S. (1965) *Tyne Landscape*. I.C. Laurie & Partners, Newcastle Upon Tyne, UK.

Lazarek, R. (1972) *Ekonomika organi zacja turystyki*. PWE, Warsaw, Poland.

Leitersdorf and Goldenburg (1976) *National Master Plan for Tourism and Recreation*. Report to National Government by consultants. Tel Aviv, Israel (published in Hebrew).

Lingard, B.E. and Partners Ltd (1984) *The Opportunities for the Conservation and Enhancement of our Historic Resorts*. Wales Tourist Board, Cardiff, Wales, UK.

London Organising Committee of the Olympic Games and Paralympic Games (LOCOG) (2007) *Towards a One Planet 2012: London 2012 Sustainability Plan*. LOCOG, London, UK.

London Tourist Board (1978) *Towards a Strategy for the London Tourist Board*. London Tourist Board, London, UK.

London Tourist Board (1982) *An Assessment of Current Needs*. London Tourist Board, London, UK.

London Tourist Board (1988) *Annual Report of the London Tourist Board for year ended March 31st, 1988*. London Tourist Board, London, UK.

Lord Holford (1968) *Report to the London County Council on High Building Policy for London*. Holford & Associates, London.

Lord Sandford (1974) *Report of the National Parks Policy Review Committee*. (Sandford Report). Department of the Environment, London, UK.

Lublin Town Council (1955) *Lublin Town General Development Plan*. Lublin Town Council, Lublin, Poland.

MacCannell, D. (1976) *The Tourist: a New Theory of the Leisure Class*. MacMillan Press, London, UK.

Mairet, P. (1957) *Pioneer of Sociology: the Life and Letters of Patrick Geddes*. Lund Humphries, London, UK.

Majewski, J. (2008) *Product Approach in Polish Rural Tourism* in *New Problems of Tourism 1/2008*. College of Tourism and Hospitality Management in Warsaw, Warsaw, Poland.

Maldives Tourism Promotion Board (2008a) *Destination Maldives: Resort/Hotel Guide*. Maldives Tourism Promotion Board, Malé, Maldives.

Maldives Tourism Promotion Board (2008b) *Maldives: Visitors Guide 2008*. Available at: www.visitmaldives. com (accessed 1 October 2010).

Malinowski, B. (1931) Culture. In: *Encyclopaedia of the Social Sciences*, Volume 4. Macmillan, New York.

Malisz, B. (1972) *La Formation des Systemes d'Habitat: Esquisse de la Theorie des Seuils*. Dunod, Paris, France.

Malisz, B. (date unknown) Some theoretical problems of national planning in Poland. *URBANISTICA* 34. (published in Italy).

Malisz, G. (undated) *The Analysis of Urban Development Possibilities*. Warsaw, Poland.

Mann, M. (2000) *The Community Tourism Guide*. Tourism Concern, Earthscan, London, UK.

Mann, R. (1973) *Rivers in the City*. David & Charles, Newton Abbot, Devon, UK.

Margetson, S. (1971) *Leisure and Pleasure in the Nineteenth Century*. The Victorian (and Modern History) Book Club, Newton Abbot, Devon, UK.

Markovic, S. (1972) *Evolution of Tourism in Yugoslavia*. Institute of Tourism Economics, Zagreb, Croatia.

Maslow, A.H. (1954) *Motivation and Personality*. Harper, New York, USA.

Mathieson, A. and Wall, G. (1982) *Tourism: Economic, Physical and Social Impacts*. Longman, London, UK.

Mazanec, J.A. (1997) *International City Tourism: Analysis and Strategy*. Pinter, London, UK.

McCaskey, T.G. (1970) *Researching Your Public: Turning Travelers into Visitors*. Technical Leaflet 29. Association for State and Local History, Nashville, Tennessee.

McHarg, I.L. (1971) *Design with Nature*. Doubleday/Natural History Press, New York, USA.

McIntyre, G. (1993) *Sustainable Tourist Development: Guide for Local Planners*. United Nations/World Tourism Organization (WTO), Madrid, Spain.

MEDEAS-France (1979) *The Blue Plan for the Mediterranean*. MEDEAS-France, Toulouse, France.

Meier, R.L. (1962) *A Communications Theory of Urban Growth*. MIT Press, Massachusetts Institute of Technology, Cambridge, Massachusetts, USA.

Meleghy, T., Preglau, M. and Tafertshofer, A. (1985) Tourism development and value change. *Annals of Tourism Research* 12(2), 181–199.

Miller, D.L. (1989) *Lewis Mumford: a Life*. Weidenfeld and Nicolson, New York.

Ministry of Tourism and Civil Aviation, Republic of Madives (2006) *Maldives Third Tourism Master Plan 2007–2011*. Maldives Government, Malé, Republic of Maldives.

Ministry of Tourism and Civil Aviation, Republic of Madives (2007) *Tourism Yearbook 2007*. Statistics and Research Section, Maldives Government, Malé, Republic of Madives.

Mishan, E.J. (1967) *The Costs of Economic Growth*. Pelican, London, UK.

Mory, E., Keller, H. and Jaeger, M.D. (1920s) *Health Resorts of Switzerland: Spas, Mineral Waters, Climactic Resorts and Sanatoria*, 3rd edn. Julius Wagner, Zurich, Switzerland.

Müller, D.K. and Jansson, B. (2007) *Tourism in Peripheries: Perspectives from the Far North and South*. CABI, Wallingford, Oxon, UK.

Mumford, L. (1938) *The Culture of Cities*. Harcourt, Brace and Co., New York.

Mumford, L. (1961) *The City in History: Its Origins, Its Transformations, and Its Prospects*. Harcourt, Brace and World, New York.

Murphy, P.E. (ed.) (1985) *Tourism: a Community Approach*. Routledge, London, UK.

Nacionalni Park Plitvice (1989) *Plitvice Lakes National Park: the World National Heritage*, 2nd edn. UNESCO and Nacionalni Park Plitvice Turistkomerc, Zagreb, Croatia.

National Commission for Building, Town Planning and Architecture (1962) *Tourism Development and Planning Problems in People's Poland*. Warsaw, Poland.

National Parks Commission (1968a) *The Coasts of Yorkshire and Lincolnshire: Report of the Regional Coastal Conference in York, 1967*. HMSO, London, UK.

National Parks Commission (1968b) *Coastal Preservation and Development*. HMSO, London, UK.

NEC Group (1996) *Celebrating 20 years of the National Exhibition Centre*. NEC Group, Birmingham, UK.

Nicholson, M. (1970) *The Environmental Revolution*. Hodder & Stoughton, London, UK.

Noronha, R. (1979) *Social and Cultural Dimensions of Tourism*. World Bank Staff Working Paper No. 326. The World Bank, Washington, DC, USA.

Norwich, J.J. (2009) *The Great Cities in History*. Thames and Hudson Ltd, London, UK.

Noss, J.B. (1974) *Man's Religions*, 5th edn. MacMillan, London, UK.

O'Grady, R. (1981) *Third World Stopover: the Tourism Debate*. World Council of Churches, Geneva, Switzerland.

O'Grady, R. (1988) *Visions for the Future in Tourism: an Ecumenical Concern*. Ecumenical Coalition on Third World Tourism (ECTWT), Bangkok, Thailand.

Olympic Delivery Authority (ODA) (2007a) *Demolish, Dig, Design: Update on the Milestones of the Beijing 2008 Games*. ODA, London, UK.

Olympic Delivery Authority (ODA) (2007b) *Move: Transport Plan for the London 2012 Olympic and Paralympic Games, Consultation Report*. ODA, London, UK.

Olympic Delivery Authority (ODA) (2009) *The Big Build Structures Milestones to 27.7.2010*. ODA, London, UK.

Outdoor Recreation Resources Review Commission (ORRRC) (1962) *Outdoor Recreation for America* (18 Volumes). Rockefeller Commission Reports. Department of the Interior, Washington, DC, USA.

Pachulia, V. (1985) *The Black Sea Coast of the Caucasus*. Planeta Publications, Moscow, Russia.

Pearce, D. (1992) *Tourist Organizations*. Longman Scientific & Technical, London, UK.

Pearse, I.H. and Crocker, L.H. (1943) *The Peckham Experiment: a Study in the Living Structure of Society*. George Allen & Unwin, London, UK.

Peeters, P. and Schouten, F. (2006) Reducing the ecological footprint of inbound tourism and transport to Amsterdam. *Journal of Sustainable Tourism* 14(2), 157–171.

Peeters, P.M., van Egmond, T. and Visser, N. (2004) *European Tourism, Transport and Environment*. The Netherlands School of Tourism, Hotels and Transport (NHTV), CSTT, University of Breda, Breda, The Netherlands.

Pickford, A. (2009) Historical parallels in Pilbara City debate. *Business News* [Perth, Western Australia], 17 December, p. 36.

Pizam, A. and Milman, A. (1984) The social impacts of tourism. *UNEP Industry and Environment* 7(1), 11–14.

Planning [editorial] (2009) High speed veers west: quoting the case for new (high speed rail) lines. *Planning* Issue 1839 (4 September), 8.

Planning Institute of Croatia (1969) *Jadran I: Physical Development Plan for the South Adriatic Region.* Govt. of Croatia, Zagreb, Croatia.

Planning Institute of Croatia (1972) *Jadran II: Physical Development Plan for the Upper Adriatic Region: Tourism Sectoral Study.* Govt. of Croatia, Zagreb, Croatia.

Planning Institute of Croatia (1974) *Jadran III: Project for the Protection of the Human Environment in the Yugoslav Adriatic Region: an Interim Report.* Govt. of Croatia, Zagreb, Croatia.

Plato (2003) *The Republic*, 2nd edn of reissue (Desmond Lee translation). Penguin Classics, London, UK.

Plog, S.C. (1974) Why destination areas rise and fall in popularity. *Cornell Hotel and Restaurant Administration Quarterly* 15, 13–16.

Plog, S.C. (1998) Why destination preservation makes economic sense. In: Theobald, W.F. (ed.) *Global Tourism.* Butterworth-Heinemann, Oxford, UK, pp. 251–266.

Priority Actions Programme Regional Activity Centre (PAP/RAC) (1997) *Guidelines for Carrying Capacity Assessment for Tourism in Mediterranean Coastal Areas.* PAP/RAC, Split, Croatia.

Priority Actions Programme Regional Activity Centre (PAP/RAC) (2003) *Guide to Good Practice in Tourism Carrying Capacity Assessment.* PAP/RAC, Split, Croatia.

Prisma Centre for Development Studies, Athens (2005) *Eco-Route: a Route to Sustainable Rural Development through Eco-Tourism Labelling. Good Practice Guide.* Eco-Route Project Partnership, Athens, Greece.

Przeclawski, K. and Travis, A.S. (1985) *Socio-cultural Impacts of Tourism: a Six Country Study.* The Vienna Social Science Research Centre, Vienna, Austria.

Rijks Planning Dienst (RPD) (1976) *1976 Year Book on Dutch National Planning.* RPD (National Planning Service), The Hague, The Netherlands.

Robinson, W. (1869) *The Parks, Promenades and Gardens of Paris: Described and Considered in Relation to the Wants of Our Own Cities.* John Murray, London, UK.

Roxburgh, I. (1979) Theories of Underdevelopment. Macmillan, London, UK.

Royal Town Planning Institute (RTPI) and Institute of Landscape Architects (ILA) (1974) *The Future Shape of British Landscape: Report of Seminar held in West Bridgeford, 21 November 1973.* Eyre & Spottiswoode Ltd at Grosvenor Press, London, UK.

Russell, B. (1959) *Wisdom of the West.* Rathbone Books Ltd & MacDonald, London, UK.

Satterthwaite, D. (2004) *The Earthscan Reader in Sustainable Cities*, 3rd edn. Earthscan, London, UK.

Schmoll, G.A. (1977) *Tourism Promotion.* Tourism International Press, London, UK.

Schumacher, E.F. (1973) *Small is Beautiful: a Study of Economics as if People Mattered.* Abacus edition of Sphere Books, London, UK.

Searle, M.V. (1977) *Spas and Watering Places.* Midas Books, Tunbridge Wells, Kent, UK.

Sharon, A. (1951) *Physical Planning in Israel: the First National Physical Plan for Israel.* The Government Publisher, Jerusalem, Israel.

Sigaux, G. (1966) *History of Tourism.* Leisure Arts Ltd, Vevey, Switzerland.

6Cs Green Infrastructure (2010) Green Infrastructure Strategy for the 6Cs Growth Point in the East Midlands. Available at: www.emgin.co.uk (accessed 26 November 2010).

Skansen (2009) Skansen (Swedish Folk Museum), Stockholm, Sweden. Available at: www.en.wikipedia.org/wiki/skansen (accessed 1 October 2009).

Škaričic', T. (2009) *Sustainable Coastal Tourism: an Integrated Planning and Management Approach.* Commissioned by United Nations Environment Programme (UNEP) Division of Technology, Industry and Economics (DTIE) and prepared by Priority Actions Programme Regional Activity Centre (PAP/RAC). UNEP, Paris, France.

Smith, R. (2008) *National Parks of Britain.* AA Publishing, Basingstoke, Hants, UK.

Smith, V.L. (1978) *Hosts and Guests: the Anthropology of Tourism.* Blackwell Publishing, Oxford, UK.

Smith, V.L. (2008) Tourism: the five research thresholds. *New Problems of Tourism* 1, 7–14.

Spencer, R. and Spencer, J. (1983) *The Spencers on Spas.* Weidenfeld & Nicolson, London, UK.

Stanley, G.H. and Lime, D.W. (1973) *Recreational Carrying Capacity: an Annotated Bibliography. USDA Forest Service General Technical Report.* United States Department of Agriculture (USDA) Forest Service, Washington, DC, USA.

State Sport and Tourism Administration (SSTA) Programme Management Unit (1993a) *PHARE Activities: Programme for the Development of Tourism in Poland: Project No. PL9201.* Government of Poland SSTA Programme Management Unit/Commission of the European Communities, Institute of Tourism, Warsaw, Poland.

State Sport and Tourism Administration (SSTA) Programme Management Unit (1993b) *Progress Report 1 on the First 6 Months' Programme 1 Jan to 30 June 1993*. Government of Poland SSTA Programme Management Unit, Institute of Tourism, Warsaw, Poland.

State Sport and Tourism Administration (SSTA) Programme Management Unit (1993c) *Lower Siberia and Opole Region: Regional Tourism Product*. Government of Poland SSTA Programme Management Unit, Institute of Tourism, Warsaw, Poland.

Stern, N.H. (2006) *The Stern Review of Economics of Climate Change*. HMSO, London, UK.

Stichting Het Nationale Park de Hoge Veluwe (1990) *Ons Nationale Park: De Hoge Veluwe, and Rijksmuseum Kröller-Müller*. Koninklijke drukkerij, G.J. Thieme bv, Nijmegen, The Netherlands.

Stone, M.K. (1989) *Mid-Wales Companion*. A. Nelson Ltd, Oswestry, Shropshire, UK.

Study of Critical Environmental Problems (SCEP) (1970) *Man's Impact on the Global Environment: Assessment and Recommendations for Action*. Report of the Study of Critical Environmental Problems (SCEP). MIT Press, Massachusetts Institute of Technology, Cambridge, Massachusetts, USA.

Sunday Times (2009) *Travel Section. Sunday Times* 18 October.

Svalastog, S. (1998) *The Nature of Resources for Tourism and Recreation*. Working Paper No. 68/1998. Hogskolen Lillehammer, Norway.

Swarbrooke, J. (1999a) *Sustainable Tourism Management*. CABI, Wallingford, Oxon, UK.

Swarbrooke, J. (1999b) *The Development and Management of Visitor Attractions*, 2nd edn. Butterworth-Heinemann, Oxford, UK.

Swinglehurst, E. (1982) *Cook's Tours: the Story of Popular Travel*. Blandford Press, Poole, Dorset, UK.

Switch Design Consultancy (1998) *A Tourism Strategy for the City: Birmingham*. For Birmingham City Council, by Switch Design Consultancy, Birmingham, UK.

Taylor, D. (1977) *Fortune, Fame and Folly: British Hotels and Catering from 1878 to 1978*. The Caterer and Hotelkeeper, IPC Business Press Ltd, London, UK.

Think Green (1987) *Three Year Report of a National Campaign for Greener Towns and Cities*. Think Green, Birmingham, UK.

Tilden, F. (1978) *Interpreting our Heritage*. University of North Carolina Press, Chapel Hill, North Carolina, USA.

Tivy, J. (1972) *The Concept and Determination of Carrying Capacity of Recreational Land in the USA*. Countryside Commission for Scotland (CCS) Occasional Paper No. 3. CCS, Perth, Scotland, UK.

Towner, J. (1984) The European Grand Tour, around 1550–1840: a study of its role in the history of tourism. PhD thesis, University of Birmingham, Birmingham, UK.

Travis, A.S. (1966) *The Challenge of Change in Edinburgh*. The Saltire Society, Edinburgh, Scotland, UK.

Travis, A.S. (1969/70) *Ends and Means: Planning for a Changing Society*. Heriot-Watt University, Edinburgh, Scotland, UK.

Travis, A.S. (1974) *The Nature of Urban and Regional Studies*. Occasional Paper No. 32. Centre for Urban and Regional Studies (CURS), University of Birmingham, Birmingham, UK.

Travis, A.S. (1975) *The Urban Environment: a Current Appraisal*. Centre for Urban and Regional Studies (CURS), University of Birmingham, Birmingham, UK.

Travis, A.S. (1977) Planning as applied ecology: the management of alternative futures. *Town Planning Review* 48(1), 5–16.

Travis, A.S. (1978a) The need for tourism policy definition and action. Paper presented to the Organisation for Economic Co-operation and Development (OECD) Salzburg Conference 'Tourism and the Environment'. OECD, Paris, France.

Travis, A.S. (1978b) The recreation planning and management process. In: *Papers of the Yates Committee's Weekend Seminar at Stratford on Avon*. UK Government Yates Committee on Recreation Management, Birmingham, UK.

Travis, A.S. (1979a) A British perspective of Dutch planning and management for recreation. *Recreatievoorzieningen* 6.

Travis, A.S. (1979b) Tourism development and regional planning in the East Mediterranean countries. In: *Report of the International Technical Cooperation Conference and Association of Engineers and Architects of Israel (AEAI) Conference*. Tel Aviv, Israel.

Travis, A.S. (1983) Measuring the physical environmental impacts of tourism. Three papers presented to the International Workshop for Pacific Nations, Hong Kong. The Pacific Area Travel Association (PATA), San Francisco, USA.

Travis, A.S. (1984) The social and cultural aspects of tourism. *UNEP Industry and Environment* 7(1), 22–24.

Travis, A.S. (1989a) *Definition and Scope of Alternative Tourism*. United Nations/World Tourism Organization (WTO), Madrid, Spain.

Travis, A.S. (1989b) *A French Canadian Perspective on Cultural Animation and Tourism Development*. Northern Ireland Tourist Board, Mid-Wales Development and West Midlands Arts. Centre for Urban and Regional Studies (CURS), University of Birmingham, Birmingham, UK.

Travis, A.S. (1990a) *Stage 1 Draft Report on Tourism and the Environment for the UK National Task Force*. Pieda Consulting, Reading, Berkshire, UK.

Travis, A.S. (1990b) *Eastern Europe: Sustainable Tourism and Eco-Tourism Practice*. Lillehammer Tourism High School, Lillehammer, Norway.

Travis, A.S. (1991a) *Tourism and the Environment UK Government Task Force: Case Studies on Visitor Management*. Pieda Consulting, Reading, Berkshire, UK.

Travis, A.S. (1991b) *New Tourism Trends, and New Tourism Products: Report of 26 Nation European Seminar in Nicosia, Cyprus*. World Tourism Organization (WTO), Madrid, Spain.

Travis, A.S. (1992a) *Tourism, Cultural Heritage Sites, and the Challenge of Environmental Planning and Management for Sustainability*. Report of International Union of Architects Conference, Cairo, Egypt.

Travis, A.S. (1992b) Adapting UK experience to Bulgarian National Park needs. Paper presented to Bulgarian Conference at Bansko, Bulgaria. UK Know How Fund (KHF), UK Government, London, UK.

Travis, A.S. (1992c) *Report to the Bulgarian Ministry of the Environment on Developing Eco-Tourism in the Rila Pirin National Parks, Bulgaria*. UK Know How Fund, UK Government, London, UK.

Travis, A.S. (1993a) *The PHARE Tourism Programme and the Role of Tourism in Lower Silesian Economic Development: Feedback from West European Experience*. Government of Poland State Sport and Tourism Administration (SSTA), Institute of Tourism, Warsaw, Poland.

Travis, A.S. (1993b) The PHARE Tourism Project: constraints upon sustainability. Paper presented to the Royal Geographical Society's Conference on 'Sustainable Tourism', London, 6 October 1993.

Travis, A.S. (1993c) *The Planning and Marketing of Major Tourist Events for Big Polish Cities*. THR Consultancy Team for the European Union, Warsaw, Poland.

Travis, A.S. (1994a) Tourism destination area development (from theory into practice). In: Witt, S.F. and Moutinho, L. (eds) *Tourism Marketing and Management Handbook*, 2nd edn. Prentice Hall International, Hemel Hempstead, UK, pp. 29–40.

Travis, A.S. (1994b) *Sustainable Concepts and Innovations in Coastal City Tourism*. Paper presented to the International Union of Local Authorities Conference, Skiathos, Greece.

Travis, A.S. (1995) Tourism-led events and urban development strategies for Glasgow and Birmingham. Inaugural Lecture for the Department of Tourism Management, Glasgow Caledonian University, Glasgow, Scotland, UK.

Travis, A.S. (1996) *Report to the IUCN on Environment and Natural Resources Management and Conservation at the Local Scale, in Poland, Hungary, the Czech and Slovak Republics*. International Union for Conservation of Nature (IUCN), Gland, Switzerland.

Travis, A.S. (1997) *Strategy for Bulgarian Eco-Tourism, for the Bulgarian GEF Project*. ARD Associates/US Aid for the Government of Bulgaria. ARD, Burlington, Vermont, USA.

Travis, A.S. (1998) *Report to Duchas and Wicklow County Council, Eire, on Glendalough National Park Visitor Management Study, Eire*. Travis/East West Consultancy, Colin Buchanan & Partners and J. Meldon, Birmingham, UK.

Travis, A.S. (1999) *Assessment of the PHARE Tourism Development Programme in Romania*. OMAS Consortium, Brussels, Belgium.

Travis, A.S. (2003) *Adriatic Tourism Planning, Yesterday, Today and Tomorrow*. Johns Hopkins University Urban Fellows Congress Report on Split, Croatia. John Hopkins University, Baltimore, Maryland, USA.

Travis, A.S. (2005) Sustainable rural tourism: opportunity and challenge for the 10 new member countries of the EU. Paper presented to the ITB Annual Tourism Trade Fair and Congress, Berlin, Germany.

Travis, A.S. (2006) *Itineraire du Patrimoine de la Region Dolenjska Bela Krajina en Slovenie*. University of West Switzerland, Lullier, Switzerland.

Travis, A.S. (2007a) *South West Serbia: Sustainable Rural Tourism Development Strategy*. Rockefeller-Brothers Fund, New York, USA.

Travis, A.S. (2007b) *First Report to the Cyprus Coastal Area Management Programme (CAMP) on Tourism Carrying Capacity Assessment*. United Nations Environment Programme/Mediterranean Action Plan (MAP), Split, Croatia.

Travis, A.S. and Hamblin, J. (1977) *Report of a Study Visit to Denmark on Tourism Development, Conservation and the Environment.* Centre for Urban and Regional Studies (CURS), University of Birmingham, Birmingham, UK.

Travis, A.S. and Klaric, Z. (1996) *Report to the Priority Actions Programme Regional Activity Centre (PAP/RAC) on Tourism Carrying Capacity Assessment (TCCA) for Lalzit Bay, Albania.* East West Tourism Consultancy (EWTC), Birmingham, UK.

Travis, A.S. and Veal, A.J. (eds) (1976) *Recreation and the Urban Fringe.* Conference Proceedings. Centre for Urban and Regional Studies (CURS), University of Birmingham, Birmingham, UK.

Travis, A.S. and Veal, A.J. (1978) *The Role of Central Government in Relation to the Provision of Leisure Services in England and Wales.* Centre for Urban and Regional Studies (CURS) Report to the UK Department of the Environment. CURS, University of Birmingham, Birmingham, UK.

Travis, A.S. and Vonk, F. (1978) The Netherlands: an alternative image of planned urbanization. In: *Planning in the Netherlands Conference Handbook.* Royal Town Planning Institute (RTPI), London, UK.

Travis, A.S and White, J. (1983) *North European Seaside Resorts: a Report to the English Tourist Board.* Centre for Urban and Regional Studies (CURS), University of Birmingham, Birmingham, UK.

Travis, A.S. and Consulting Team (1970) *Recreation Planning for the Clyde, Firth of Clyde, Scotland, Phase 2. Proposal for the Development and Conservation of the Region's Recreation Resources.* Scottish Tourist Board, Edinburgh, Scotland, UK.

Travis, A.S. and Consulting Team (1983) *Realising the Tourism Potential of the South Wales Valleys.* Wales Tourist Board, Cardiff, Wales, UK.

Travis, A.S. and Team (1988) *Study of the Social, Cultural and Linguistic Impacts of Tourism in and upon Wales.* European Centre for Tourism and Regional Cooperation (ECTARC), Llangollen for the Wales Tourist Board, Cardiff, Wales, UK.

Trevelyan, G.M. (1964) *English Social History: a Survey of Six Centuries: Chaucer to Queen Victoria.* Penguin Books, London, UK.

Tunnard, C. (1948) *Gardens in the Modern Landscape,* 2nd edn. The Architectural Press, London, UK.

Turner, L. and Ash, J. (1975) *The GoldenHordes.* Constable, London, UK.

Tylor, E.B. (1871) *Primitive Culture: Researches into the Development Mythology, Philosophy, Religion, Art, and Custom.* Gloucester, Massachusetts (1958 reprint).

Tyrrwhit, J. (1947) *Patrick Geddes in India.* Lund Humphries, London, UK.

UK Govt. Task Force on Tourism and the Environment (1991) *Tourism and the Environment: Maintaining the Balance: Report of the UK Task Force.* English Tourist Board (ETB), London, UK.

UK Govt. Task Force on Tourism and the Environment (1992) *Tourism and the Environment: Challenges and Choices for the '90s.* English Tourist Board (ETB), London, UK.

United Nations (UN) (1992) *Conference on Environment and Development,* Rio de Janeiro, Brazil. UN, New York, USA.

United Nations (UN) (2002) *World Summit on Sustainable Development: Rio +10,* Johannesburg, South Africa. UN, New York, USA.

United Nations (UN) (2009) *Global Report on Human Settlements.* UN, New York, USA.

United Nations Environment Programme (UNEP) (1975) *Mediterranean Action Plan (MAP).* UNEP, Paris, France.

United Nations Environment Programme (UNEP) (1999) *Contribution of UNEP for the Secretary General's Report on 'Industry and Sustainable Tourism for the 7th Session of the CSD: Tourism and Environment Protection.* UNEP, Paris, France.

United Nations Environment Programme (UNEP)/International Council for Local Environmental Initiatives (ICLEI) (2003) *Tourism and Local Agenda 21: the Role of Local Authorities in Sustainable Tourism.* UNEP, Paris, France and ICLEI, Freiburg, Germany.

United Nations Environment Programme (UNEP) and World Tourism Organization (WTO) (2005) *Making Tourism More Sustainable: a Guide for Policy Makers.* UNEP, Paris, France and WTO, Madrid, Spain.

United Nations Organization (UNO) (1962) *Report of the European Seminar on Urban Development Policy and Planning.* UNO, Warsaw, Poland.

United Nations World Tourism Organization (UNWTO) (1983) *The Risks of Saturation in Tourist Carrying Capacity Over-use in Holiday Destinations.* Report of UNWTO Conference in Athens. UNWTO, Madrid, Spain.

United Nations World Tourism Organization (UNWTO) (2002) *Sustainable Development of Eco-Tourism: a Compilation of Good Practice.* UNWTO, Madrid, Spain.

United Nations World Tourism Organization (UNWTO) (2004a) *Indicators of Sustainable Development for Tourism Destinations: a Guidebook*. UNWTO, Madrid, Spain.

United Nations World Tourism Organization (UNWTO) (2004b) *Tourism and Poverty*. WTO, Madrid, Spain.

Urry, J. (2002) *The Tourist Gaze*. Sage, London, UK.

Van de Weg, H. (1982) Revitalization of traditional resorts (case study of Scheveningen). *Tourism Management* 3(4), 303–307.

Van den Berg, L., Van der Borg, J. and van der Meer, J. (1995) *Urban Tourism: Performance and Strategies in Eight European Cities*. Avebury Publishers, Aldershot, Hants, UK.

Van der Berg, A.J. and Vink, B.L. (2008) Randstad Holland towards 2040: perspectives from national Government. Paper presented to the 44th International Society of City and Regional Planners (ISOCARP) Congress, Dalian, China 19–23 September 2008.

Van Egmond, T. (2007) *Understanding Western Tourists in Developing Countries*. CABI, Wallingford, Oxon, UK.

Van Egmond, T. (2008) *The Tourism Phenomenon Past, Present and Future*, 3rd edn. Uitgeverij Toerboek, Leiden, The Netherlands.

VROM [Dutch Planning Ministry in National Govt.] (2008) *Spatial Planning and Development*. Available at: www.vrom.nl (accessed 1 October 2010).

Wahab, S., Crampon, L.J. and Rothfield, L.M. (1976) *Tourism Marketing: a destination-oriented programme for the marketing of international tourism*. Tourism International Press, London, UK.

Wang, N. (2000) *Tourism and Modernity: a Sociological Analysis*. Pergamon, Oxford, UK.

Warszynsk, J. and Jackowski, A. (1977) Tourist accommodation of territories within the conurbation of the Upper Silesian Industrial District. Paper presented to the British Association Conference, Birmingham, UK.

Webber, M. (1976) *The Protestant Ethic and the Spirit of Capitalism*. George Allen & Unwin, London, UK.

Wechsberg, J. (1979) *The Lost World of the Great Spas*. Weidenfeld & Nicolson, London, UK.

Weiler, B. and Hall, M. (1992) *Special Interest Tourism*. Belhaven Press, London, UK.

Welsh Country Holidays (1987, 1988 and 1989) *Festival of the Countryside Holidays in Wales*. Welsh Country Holidays, Machynllech, Wales, UK.

West Australian Tourism Commission and Environmental Protection Authority (1989a) *Eco Ethics of Tourism Development*. West Australian Government, Perth, Australia.

West Australian Tourism Commission and Environmental Protection Authority (1989b) *An Administrative Guide to Environmental Requirements for Tourism Developments in Western Australia*. West Australian Government, Perth, Australia.

Western Australian Planning Commission (2009) *Pilbara Framework: Regional Profile*. Government of Western Australia, Perth, Western Australia.

Wheatley (1969) *Royal Commission on Local Government in Scotland 1966–1969*. HMSO, Edinburgh, Scotland, UK.

White, P.E. (1974) *The Social Impact of Tourism upon Host Communities: a Study of Language Change in Switzerland*. Research Paper, No. 9. School of Geography, University of Oxford, Oxford, UK.

Wilkinson, P.F. (1989) Strategies for tourism in island microstates. *Annals of Tourism Research* 16(2), 153–177.

Williamson, H. (1971) *Tarka the Otter*. Puffin Paperbacks, London.

Wilson, J. (1989) *The History and Traditions of Friluftsliv*, 2nd edn. Friluftsliv Research Trust, Norges Hogfjellsskole, Hemsedal, Norway.

Winston, R. and Wilson, D.E. (2004) Belief. In: Winston, R. and Wilson, D.E. *Human*. Dorling-Kindersley, London, pp. 287–299.

Wober, K. (1998) *City Tourism in Europe: Annual Statistical Report of the Federation of European Cities Tourist Offices*. Institute for Tourism and Leisure Services, Vienna University of Economics of Business Administration.

World Tourism Organization (WTO) (1990) *Final Report of the Seminar on 'Alternative Tourism' held in Algeria, 1989*. WTO, Madrid, Spain.

World Tourism Organization (WTO) (1993) *Sustainable Tourist Development: Guide for Local Planners*. WTO, Madrid, Spain.

World Tourism Organization (WTO) (1998) *Guide for Local Authorities on Developing Sustainable Tourism*. WTO, Madrid, Spain.

World Tourism Organization (WTO) (1999) *Guide for Local Authorities on Developing Sustainable Tourism*. WTO, Madrid, Spain.

World Tourism Organization (WTO) (2000) *Sustainable Development of Tourism: a Compilation of Good Practices*. WTO, Madrid, Spain.

World Tourism Organization (WTO) and World Travel and Tourism Council (WTTC) (1995) *Agenda 21 for the Travel and Tourism Industry: Towards Environmentally Sustainable Development*. WTO, Madrid, Spain.

WWF International (2001) *Guidelines for Community-based Eco-tourism Development*. WWF International, Gland, Switzerland.

Young, G. (1973) *Tourism: Blessing or Blight?* Pelican, London, UK.

Youngson, A.J. (1966) *The Making of Classical Edinburgh 1750–1840*. Edinburgh University Press, Edinburgh, Scotland, UK.

Websites

www.algeria-tourism.org
www.amsterdampromotion.nl
www.beaulieu.co.uk
www.brindleyplace.com
www.beaulieu.co.uk
www.colonialwilliamsburg.com/visit/
www.deltacommissie.com
www.dnt.org
www.e-architect.co.uk/convention_centres_htm
www.edfringe.com
www.edinburghfestivals.co.uk
www.egypt.travel
www.en.wikipedia.org/wiki/skansen
www.farmholidays.com
www.foc.org.uk
www.forum.turystyke-goroka.pl
www.garethhoskinsarchitects.co.uk
www.goisrael.com
www.haj.co.uk
www.hajjinfo.org
www.holland.com
www.2holland.com/uk
www.iguide.travel.Negev
www.jordanholidays.co.uk
www.london2012.com
www.metroparks.com
www.muenchen.de
www.muenchen.de/rathaus/tourist_office
www.nbt.nl
www.np-plitvice.tel.nr
www.nps.gov/gett
www.olympiclegacycompany.co.uk
www.peakdistrict.gov.uk
www.planbleu.org
www.planning.wa.gov.au
www.poland.travel
www.salzburg.info
www.salzburgfestival.at
www.scheveningenbad.nl
www.skansen.se
www.slovakia.travel
www.slovenia-heritage.net
www.slovenia.info

www.sustainabletourism.co
www.tanap.sk
www.tarka-country.co.uk
www.thenewforest.co.uk/greenleafscheme.html
www.tivoli.dk
www.tourism.gov.mv
www.travelmaldives.com
www.turistforeningen.no
www.unwto.org
www.ustravelservices.com
www.visitamsterdam.nl
www.visitbritain.co.uk
www.visit.egypt.travel
www.visitisrael.com
www.visitjordan.com/en
www.visitlondon.co.uk
www.visitscotland.co.uk
www.visitwales.co.uk
www.vrom.nl
www.waterloo1815.be
www.wikipedia.org/wiki/sahara
www.world-tourism.org

Index

_____

Note: page numbers in *italics* refer to figures and tables